Good-bye, America?

by
Jonathan West

PRESCOTT PRESS, INC.

Copyright © 1999 Jonathan West
All rights reserved. No part of this book may be reproduced
without permission from the publisher, except by a reviewer who
may quote brief passages in a review; nor may any part of this
book be reproduced, stored in a retrieval system or copied by
mechanical photocopying, recording or other means, without
permission from the publisher.

Prescott Press, Inc.
P.O. Box 53788
Lafayette, Louisiana 70505
or
www.huntingtonhousebooks.com

PRINTED IN THE UNITED STATES OF AMERICA

FIRST EDITION

Library of Congress Card Catalog Number 99-61668
ISBN 0-933451-46-6

Dedication

Dedicated to my wife Ester, who helped with the
research files, and to Lowell Ponte, a former
Roving Editor of the Reader's Digest, for
his advice and encouragement and to
the precious few I have known who
fight for others with a
courageous heart.

Contents

"Prologue"		vii
Introduction		9

Part One
The Breakdown of the American Legal System

Chapter One	"An Overview—Before It's Over"	14
Chapter Two	"Once upon a Time"	19
Chapter Three	"What about Our Constitution?"	22
Chapter Four	"Uncivil Law in America"	32
Chapter Five	"Law and Disorder"	45

Part Two
The Responsible Elements

Chapter Six	"The Lawyers"	102
Chapter Seven	"Law Enforcement—The Good and the Bad"	112
Chapter Eight	"Self-protection and the Return of the Vigilante"	126
Chapter Nine	"Looking at the Courts"	137
Chapter Ten	"Crime and Consequences"	154

Part Three

The Legal System: A Search for Solutions

Chapter Eleven	"Changing the Legal System"	164
Chapter Twelve	"Changing the Enforcement"	208
Chapter Thirteen	"Changing the Incarceration"	216
Chapter Fourteen	"Your Role in American Law"	221

Part Four

So Many Problems—So Little Time

Chapter Fifteen	"The Drug War That Never Was"	230
Chapter Sixteen	"Drugs: A Search for Solutions"	243
Chapter Seventeen	"Politics"	257
Chapter Eighteen	"Politics: A Search for Solutions"	287
Chapter Nineteen	"Other Problems to Consider"	304
"Epilogue"		325
Appendix A	Organizations of Interest	328
Appendix B	Federal Contact Information	339

Prologue

Good-bye, America. No, I'm not leaving, but it would seem that you are. Little by little you have been going away. Soon you will be only a shadow of what you once were. In your place we are becoming a violent, debt-ridden and sometimes very oppressive nation of sad and lonely consequences. It would seem that your time is over—your day is done.

Good-bye, America. I grieve for all the pain and misfortune you leave behind. Good-bye. I will miss you.

Introduction

It was the best of times, it was the worst of times, it was the age of wisdom, it was the age of foolishness, it was the epoch of belief, it was the epoch of incredulity, it was the season of Light, it was the season of Darkness, it was the spring of hope, it was the winter of despair . . .

—Charles Dickens'
"Tale of Two Cities"

Never was a time so well described for us as with that famous quotation. Never before was there so great a need for us to rise to the occasion with a courageous heart, a strong resolve, and a great measure of genuine wisdom. With all the good things we have—in our economy and with our possessions—we also have a full measure of the foreboding harbingers of our decline and fall as a great nation.

We have it all. We have the best and the worst of it. And little by little, we are losing it. We are losing the best and starting that long and tortuous decline. And that is the why and wherefore of this book.

In blunt truth, you're not going to like it, but you must read it. This book will make you mad, maybe at the author, most likely at the politicians, lawyers, judges, educators, bureaucrats, and so many of the others who are definitely going to do things their way, no matter what all-too-obvious disasters result.

You're also going to discover whose fault it is. You won't like that either. You see, basically it's *your* fault. I'm going to show you how it has come to be *your* fault and what *you* can do about it. (Of course, I'm not sure there are nearly enough folks out there who are actually willing to take on the daunting responsibility to really make a difference—to reverse the ominous trend—but then, maybe you and a number of others will prove me wrong. We'll see.)

Meanwhile, what have I got in store for you here? You will discover far more than you ever wanted to know about the breakdown of our legal system, the drug war that never was, today's politicians, your loss of rights and the growth of an ever-increasingly oppressive government. And there's more.

There's lots more, and it's well documented. There's no doubt about any of it. It's very real. What's more important, this book will not just leave you there to wallow and whimper in the deepening shadow of it all. If that was the limit of what this book could do, it would be another waste of time, like so much else that's out there.

You will find many of our major problems thrust right in your face, all right, but you will find them accompanied by genuine searches for real solutions. Now that's what can make the difference. That's what can be *really* important. That's why you have got to read this book and take it all very seriously. It is *your* responsibility to help make that important difference that can be made. Enough of you must be willing to make the appropriate and sustained efforts to make it so.

Part one deals with the breakdown of our legal system. It's a mess that's so bad it's almost beyond belief. It is one of the crucial systems and a major pillar of support for any true civilization. Major changes must be made, and they must be made right now!

Part two covers who and what is responsible and what must be done if we are ever going to have a nation we can be proud of again. Major changes must be made, and they must be made right now!

Part three addresses possible solutions concerning our legal system, our enforcement, and our prisons. It's a matter of what must be done by each and every one of us. Major changes must be made, and they must be made right now!

Part four gives you an overview of everything from the drug war that never was to American politics as it never should have become. Other nightmares are also addressed. Major changes must be made, and they must be made right now!

You are clearly and most definitely shown how *you* can become a part of the solution—how you *must* become a part of the solution.

So, that's what you're in for. It isn't pretty, but I guess it's as Kingsley Amis said, "If you can't annoy somebody, there's little point in writing." I also like what Winston Churchill said about this approach:

> If you have an important point to make, don't try to be subtle or clever. Use a pile driver. Hit the point once. Then come back and hit it again. Then hit it a third time—a tremendous whack.

We have *all* got to roll up our sleeves and make one hell of an effort. If not, if it really can't be done, you might as well say goodbye to America because it will be long gone.

Just remember that solutions are seldom really difficult to find. Successful implementation is the *really* big problem. That's where *you* come in. This may be the age of perpetual whining, but I won't accept that. I'm waiting for you to prove to me that being human is not a birth defect.

Is this going to be the beginning of the end or the end of the beginning for America? Will we make it possible to actually have a true American Renaissance? Don't tell me. Show me.

Part One

The Breakdown
of the
American Legal System

Chapter One

An Overview—Before It's Over
A Hard Look at the Mess We're In

> *Every government degenerates when trusted to the rulers of the people alone. The people themselves therefore are its only safe depositories.*
> —Thomas Jefferson

Unless you've been spending your life in a cardboard box under some interstate overpass, or perhaps fell asleep several years ago in front of your TV set, unless you've really been out of it, you're more than slightly aware that something is wrong, *really* wrong with the way things are going. It's not as though it's some kind of secret.

The way it is. When crime, in general, is down a bit, and the more immediate economic picture seems not to be so bad, we tend to forget what is *really* going on. Are you aware of the government misconduct and mismanagement on all levels, and of the crime, the drugs, and the tax burden?

Are you not aware of the tendency of government on all levels to drift into the growing oppression of more and more of the people, of the massive national debt (which has not been dealt with properly), the educational crisis, the breakdown of the American legal system, and all the many other problems that are very clearly pulling us down? Has it occurred to you that the linchpin that is supposed to hold it all together in a positive and effective way is the basic legal system of the country?

Many philosophers and historians will argue that a lot of the dysfunction in many parts of a national system will often be a reflection of the disintegration of the legal system in that nation. This is because the legal system is one of the most vital elements, if not *the* most important element. It's the foundation from which all else proceeds. It's the outline for the interactive dynamics of the people, their institutions, and practically everything that's done in any civilization.

We have entrusted it all to the lawmakers, the lawyers, and the judges. We have believed their claim of superiority in such matters and have taken on the mantle of ignorant subservience. We have let them run the government, run the legal system, and regulate our lives to a degree that (a number of thoughtful people suggest) easily steps over the border to genuine oppression.

As if you didn't know. Actually, none of this should be news to you. People have been complaining for a long time now. Back in 1991, *Parade* magazine's Washington bureau did a poll of three important forums in our nation. They examined letters to the editor, radio talk shows, and congressional mail. They found definite dissatisfaction in ten major areas, most of which we will be covering in this book.

In 1994 an ABC News survey was reported to have shown that nearly three-fourths of the American people are dissatisfied with the way the federal government works. There have been many similar polls and surveys before and after these examples, and there are many more to come.

The natives are restless. Could it be that something is wrong? Might Thomas Paine have had the right idea when he wrote that, "Government, even in its best state, is a necessary evil; in its worst state, an intolerable one." Is somebody trying to tell us something?

Where have all the heroes gone? How about our heroes? Can they help? How do we feel about them? Well, even way back in 1975, a Gallup poll showed that when Americans (18 or older) were asked to name a man and a woman they most admired, 47 percent were unable to come up with the name of even one man and 57 percent couldn't name a single woman.

At this time, this author's own informal survey has yielded a hodgepodge of answers, all the way from TV and movie stars to rock stars, shock jocks, public sex objects of one kind or another, and no one at all. Certainly no lawyer, judge, or legislator was ever on their minds.

How did they feel about their choices? Many of them just wanted to be entertained. If they do what they think is a good job of that, they're satisfied, to some extent, for now. Hardly *any* seemed able to think of someone in politics, the literary world, science, industry or any other area of real responsibility.

Michael Maccoby, a psychologist and director of the Project on Technology, Work and Character at Harvard (in 1981) told us some time ago that the leaders needed today are not those who repeat the pattern of the gamesmen of the near past. UPI quoted him as saying "The kids feel we have no leaders they can look to and that depresses them terribly."

Now these "kids" are young adults in our nation. The conclusion was in the headline of that story. It simply said, "EXPERT SAYS U.S. HURTING FOR NATIONAL LEADERS."

The American educator/philosopher Alan Bloom has stated clearly that "we are not sure what leadership is, what the objects of it are, or whether anyone possesses it." (A statement made at an Ethics and Leadership Conference at the University of San Diego.) Possibly we could consider a definition by Ivern Ball who said, "A politician is a person who can make waves and then make you think he's the only one who can save the ship." Have we come down to that?

The headlines have gone over and over this issue. "Another Shortage: Leaders"—*Newsweek*. "Where has all the leadership gone?"—*San Diego Union-Tribune*. "In Quest of Leadership"—*Time* magazine. Some of these quotes are a couple of decades old, some are much more current, but they all have that same basic message: did somebody hold a leadership conference and nobody came? You'd think so.

So, who is really in charge around here? What kind of people do you think most fervently covet the halls of power? Maybe you should consider this somewhat dramatic statement for our time: "Government is not reason, it is not eloquence—it is force! Like fire, it is a dangerous servant and a fearful master; never for a moment should it be left to irresponsible action."

That sort of statement sounds more and more reasonable to an ever-growing number within our population. Of course there are still many who think it is a bit dramatic and, therefore, not a particularly responsible thing to say. I guess some would imagine it to be the work of an extremist or a rabble rouser of some sort. Wouldn't the author, George Washington, have found that interesting?

You've had enough of this stuff? Some of you have. Some of you have already come to the same understanding this author arrived at a long time ago when faced with these same truths. But many of you *still* don't seem to see what's happening.

So, the rest of you, hold tight, be patient. We'll get to the heavy-duty area soon enough. Right now I want to be as sure as I can be that as many of you as possible are finally, at last, willing to accept the breakdown for what it is—a dangerous and oppressive echo from what is left of our crumbling nation and our dysfunctional American legal system!

No leaders—no values. A while back, Walter Cronkite was asked about the moral and ethical dilemma in America, on the "Regis and Kathie Lee" show. His answer was that we're "going to hell in a hand basket." The author, Tom Wolfe, was asked to speak at Brown University in Providence, Rhode Island, and told the audience that all through the twentieth century people have been relaxing their ethics and traditional values and will have to somehow relearn the art of civilization.

The Committee on Developing American Capitalism (one of those "think-tanks") put out a study observing, "Something strange and ominous is happening to the moral values of American society. Widespread corruption, fraud, lying, and deceit have been uncovered among the rich and powerful and at high levels of responsibility in government and business."

Naturally there are critics who like to try and debunk such things with the comment that we've had some bad people in places high and low throughout our history. The committee saw all of this as a much larger and more critical difficulty now than ever before and emphasized this with the further observation that, "Unfortunately, mounting evidence indicates that the erosion of moral values in society, particularly in the last 20 years, is a real and present danger."

Perhaps some of you don't think much of such reports. Perhaps they don't know what they're talking about. Well, it was a fully researched effort and Don Bauder wrote that the effort involved such intellectually renowned individuals as Andrew Brimmer, Benjamin Friedman, Paul McCracken, Allen Sinai, James Tobin, Walter Hoadley, and John Winthrop Wright. If you don't know who they are, please take my word for it; they are knowledgeable and thoughtful people.

In May 1997, astronaut Story Musgrave and former astronauts Buzz Aldrin and Walter Cunningham testified at a congressional hearing on "America's Vision for the Future of Space Exploration." They spoke of how we have lost our inspiration and our fascination with science.

Television producer Norman Lear told the National Press Club some time ago that "at no time in my life has our culture been so estranged from spiritual values." Michael Josephson writes of a "hole in the moral ozone."

The late Daniel Yankelovich, internationally renowned public opinion analyst, in a speech before a National Civic League conference decried the loss of our core values. Mr. Yankelovich offered that "we have always been a hopeful and optimistic people. Europeans have marveled at this characteristic of American life when, time after time, we have plunged ahead to take on problems that other nations have regarded as insoluble. Today, however, the levels of American cynicism and resignation and shoulder shrugging equal or even surpass those of world-weary Europeans."

We certainly see this in the way so many of us now seem to accept the lawbreaking and general inadequacies of so many, if not all of the president's men in the Clinton administration. In some very disturbing ways, it's not so much different from those old Nixon days.

I'll never forget that Louis Harris and Associates poll that showed more than 70 percent of Americans don't seem to care whether President Clinton has been unfaithful in his marriage or not. Well, what do we expect in a society where, not so long ago, it was illegal to make an obscene phone call, and now the phone company charges you for it on a 900 line?

The price we pay. Of course, we all have seen the news and read the papers, haven't we? We all know that even with decreases in many crimes from time to time, many crimes still remain at high levels and some types are even on the increase.

We see how poorly our legal system deals with these things so much of the time. We read about the significant increase in drug use among our youth, even at the lower grade school level. We hear how foul-ups and errors of almost every type imaginable have crippled so many of our courts and bureaucracies.

We see very obvious examples of how constitutional law has changed by interpretation to suit the perceived changing needs, without having to consider that bothersome little annoyance called "the amendment procedure." We see the disintegration of the family unit and its corresponding values. We see communities trying to find new ways to protect themselves. We see justice at a cost that fewer and fewer people can afford.

Chapter Two

Once upon a Time
The Way It Used to Be

Right now, I want you to play an uncomfortable little game with me. What do you think might have happened if, 40 or 50 years ago, the people of that time in America were suddenly to wake up one morning and find themselves living in the nation that we have become today? What do you think they would find? How do you think they would have reacted?

Remember now, we are talking about a sudden change from a reasonably solvent economy that was without an enormous national debt, a place where very few felt they had to lock their doors, where there were solid values and genuine heroes, a time of positive attitudes and honorable commitment.

I know it wasn't perfect. No period is ever perfect (unless you somehow manage to subtract the human factor in the equation). But, it was one devil of a lot safer than now; and there was a willingness to get involved, a can-do attitude. Those of you who lived through that period know *exactly* what I mean.

A new kind of future-shock. We are talking about a sudden change forward to our current society, to all you have just read about and so much more. There are the burdensome taxes for poorly-maintained government services. There is the enormously increased authoritarian nature of the government over the general population. There is the almost unbelievable national debt.

There is the loss of so many of our primary wealth-producing industries. There is the degrading of our environment. There is the rising anger in group polarization (us vs. them). There is the loss of so many rights and protections and so much of our human dignity, mostly through the dysfunction of our legal system.

There are all these problems and so many more. There are an enormous number of other examples that just can't be enumerated here without turning this book into an encyclopedia. And yes, I hear those of you who try to cajole with such comments as, "Well, gee, we do *lots* of nice things and we *have* lots of nice things and *some* people are trying to make it all better, really they are."

I never doubted it for a minute. In fact, I am one of those who has spent a considerable part of his life in all sorts of voluntary efforts to try and make a positive difference. I know where you're coming from, and I know how you feel. The thing you have to learn to understand is that sometimes what is done has little effect other than making the doer feel good. What is left that might be of real help is not enough! Not nearly enough and by the efforts of *far too few!*

You've got the picture, right? All the folks from back then going from then to now, overnight, right? With all that there was, to what there is now. You've got the picture.

Even with all our modern (and sometimes confusing) elements of today's world, there are still the dangers and the enormous dysfunctions. Even if some of these unfortunate time travelers tried to escape to the television set, to the movies or to the popular music industry for solace, what do you think they would find? I don't even have to tell you, do I?

Watch out! So, what do you think they might end up doing? Remember what sort of people we really *were* back then. What do you think would happen? I'll tell you what would happen. We would end up having one hell of a slam-bang revolution! They wouldn't have put up with it in any way, shape or form, and you know it! They probably would have thought some horrendous dictatorship had descended upon the land, along with all sorts of related breakdowns. It would have ended up as one hell of a party, let me tell you.

I've talked with political scientists, behaviorists and ordinary people, and I get the feeling most of them agree with this scenario. So, why are we so wimpy and ineffective now, with what we have to deal with today? What's *wrong* with us?

A new trickle-down theory. Let me suggest what's wrong. We are the very understandable victims of what is sometimes called the "gradual syndrome." It's like that old story about the camel in the tent. You know the one. The camel started out by poking his snout through the entrance of the tent. It was kind of funny at first (have you ever taken a good look at the face of a camel?) and then nobody gave it much attention after a while.

So, the camel, who rather liked the look of things in there, got himself in that tent a little bit more, a little at a time, inch by inch. After a while, you know what happened? The camel ended up wearing the tent and the former occupants were wondering what happened.

That's what's happened to us. What we never would have put up with all at once, we learned to tolerate (becoming desensitized) as so many unfortunate things happened to us *a little bit at a time.* Now things have gotten so bad in so many critical areas that we feel it's beyond our abilities and besides, it's too late anyway.

It's never too late! Unless, of course, you decide to continue as you are. Then you will be right. It *will* be beyond you and very much too late. But remember, the nature of self-fulfilling prophecies like that are such that they can be overturned. It's up to you.

Chapter Three

What about Our Constitution?
The Discarding of America's Heritage

As stated in our Declaration of Independence, "Whenever any form of government becomes destructive . . . it is the right of the people to alter or abolish it." So, we went forward and began the great experiment, the establishment of our Republic, a form of government which paid great attention to the dignity and rights of its citizens, and we were warned by so many of the great men of our past. (They evidently were very good students of human history.) We were warned that the job was never going to be easy and was never going to be over.

> No free government, or the blessings of liberty can be preserved to many people but by a firm adherence to justice, moderation, temperance, frugality, and virtue, and by a frequent recurrence to fundamental principles.
>
> —Patrick Henry

> The essence of Government is power, and power, lodged as it must be, in human hands, will ever be liable to abuse.
>
> —James Madison

> What country can preserve its liberties, if its rulers are not warned from time to time, that this people preserve the spirit of resistance?
>
> —Thomas Jefferson

We were told by these men and by so many others, back then and all the way down to now. But, evidently we have evolved some very thick skulls in the majority of our population. None of this seems to penetrate through to very many people. The way Will Rogers put it, "Liberty doesn't work as well in practice as it does in speeches." I guess not.

The great experiment. And just what did they try to do back then that we seem to have divorced ourselves from? Well, originally, when the delegates to the Constitutional Convention met in Philadelphia in 1787, they only planned to work over the Articles of Confederation a little bit. But, somehow, something very special seemed to have happened, and James Madison and his friends ended up throwing out the original articles altogether and creating the constitutional form that we are supposed to have today.

They initiated the amendment procedure (in 1791), a procedure that would allow for inevitable change, for they realized that times would change as they have all through history. They began those additions with the agreed-to first ten amendments that we refer to as our Bill of Rights. For as Anne Morrow Lindbergh said many years later, "Only in growth, reform and change, paradoxically enough, is true security to be found." (See Article V in our U.S. Constitution for the description of the methods given to us for the adding of amendments to the Constitution. As you can see, three methods were outlined in an effort to make the process more readily available, as it was clearly perceived to be necessary.)

Those first ten amendments are really something. The first eight amendments delineate most of the primary and fundamental rights and freedoms that we are supposed to have. The last two prohibit Congress from passing laws that violate those precious rights. In other words, the Bill of Rights is basically a *prohibition* against the government. It is intended to keep our government from becoming an oppressive force against its citizens as the British government was perceived to have been to the citizens of colonial America.

Of course, today we have a massive government of bumbling bureaucracy that is far, far more oppressive than the old British Empire ever thought of being. How come? Well, it's again that matter of things happening a little bit at a time, now beyond a 200 year span. But, in this writer's opinion, what we had originally tried to do was a good idea, and it *still* is a good idea, even if we don't seem to act as though it is anymore.

So maybe this would be a good time to lay down the first ten amendments. Here they are. They were written in plain English and are really not at all hard to understand.

Your Bill of Rights are as follows:

I. Congress shall make no law respecting an establishment of religion, or prohibiting the free exercise thereof; or abridging the freedom of speech, or of the press, or the right of the people peaceably to assemble, and to petition the Government for a redress of grievances.

II. A well regulated Militia, being necessary to the security of a free State, the right of the people to keep and bear Arms, shall not be infringed.

III. No Soldier shall, in time of peace be quartered in any house, without the consent of the Owner, nor in time of war, but in a manner to be prescribed by law.

IV. The right of the people to be secure in their persons, houses, papers, and effects, against unreasonable searches and seizures, shall not be violated, and no Warrants shall issue, but upon probable cause, supported by Oath or affirmation, and particularly describing the place to be searched, and the persons or things to be seized.

V. No person shall be held to answer for a capital or otherwise infamous crime, unless on a presentment or indictment of a Grand Jury, except in cases arising in the land or naval forces, or in the Militia, when in actual service in time of War or public danger; nor shall any person be subject for the same offence to be twice put in jeopardy of life or limb; nor shall be compelled in any criminal case to be a witness against himself, nor be deprived of life, liberty, or property, without due process of law; nor shall private property be taken for public use without just compensation.

VI. In all criminal prosecutions, the accused shall enjoy the right to a speedy and public trial, by an impartial jury of the State and district wherein the crime shall have been committed; which district shall have been previously ascertained by law, and to be informed of the nature and cause of the accusation; to be confronted with the witnesses against him; to have compulsory process for obtaining witnesses in his favor, and to have the assistance of counsel for his defense.

VII. In Suits at common law, where the value in controversy shall exceed twenty dollars, the right of trial by jury shall be preserved, and no fact tried by a jury, shall be otherwise re-examined in any Court of the United States, than according to the rules of the common law.

VIII. Excessive bail shall not be required, nor excessive fines imposed, nor cruel and unusual punishments inflicted.

IX. The enumeration in the Constitution of certain rights, shall not be construed to deny or disparage others retained by the people.

X. The powers not delegated to the United States by the Constitution, nor prohibited by it to the States, are reserved to the States respectively, or to the people.

Yes, the "Miracle of Philadelphia" gave us the documented foundation for a free people, with a limited government intended for only those tasks that cannot be done at all well or not at all by individuals or by the separate states. The major need, of course, was for a common defense. And, there were other needs, but there were severe limitations. We were to truly be a *free* people (with some glaring exceptions that, fortunately, were later corrected by additional amendments).

The end of the experiment? Now what has happened? What has happened is that, little by little, the judges appointed to lifetime tenures started to legislate, under the guise of "interpreting" constitutional law.

They call it interpreting the constitution in the light of modern times and current needs, as they see it (or words to that effect). What they have actually done is to ignore the amendment procedure, which was specifically designed to allow for this need, and they have moved forward to a new form of legislation that often has no similarity to anything that was ever written or contemplated for our Constitution.

As sometimes-dissenting U.S. Supreme Court Justice Scalia has said of this philosophy of legislative action in the courts, "it equates those many things that are or should be proscribed as a matter of social policy with those few things that we have the power to proscribe under the Constitution." That's right, they know what's being done, and many judges defend the practice. They make no excuses for it.

Someone should remember what George F. Will warned. He said, "Once they have stopped interpreting constitutional language by its traditional usage, and in the context of historic practices traditionally viewed as constitutional, the craft called constitutional law, and indeed the Constitution itself, effectively disappears." That someone who should remember this is *you!*

Why is it not such a good idea for our judges to be legislating new law rather than sticking to strict and proper interpretation of the

Constitution and its amendments? Well, first of all, because their job is really to render decisions according to the *actual* Constitution, as it was written and as it is amended. Additionally, we wanted to be able to have the power to vote out anyone who would have the powers of legislation. Further, our founders went to a lot of trouble to create a definite separation between our major divisions of government and a separation of specific assignments of responsibility. They knew *exactly* what they were doing.

Our executive division is supposed to be primarily administrative in nature. Our two houses of Congress are intended as the legislative division. Our courts are supposed to follow the judicial responsibilities according to the Constitution and its amendments, as they were written! See Article II, Section 1, of our U.S. Constitution for the allocation of the executive powers. See Article I, Section 1, of our Constitution for the duties of the legislative powers. And, see Article III, Section 1 and 2, for the assignment of the judicial power.

As I've said, there's a good reason why the high judges were *never* supposed to legislate. We want to be able to elect our legislators. They make our laws, and we want to have at least some recourse over anyone who has that kind of power in our nation. We don't want to have people making our laws who are appointed judges and have a lifetime tenure. At least we never did before. Now I don't know.

Maybe you just don't care that much anymore? After all, so far it doesn't seem to have interfered with your television reception and you're at least fairly comfortable, right? So what if the constitution is being relegated to the status of a no-account scrap of paper. What do you care? And besides, you aren't about to actually get up and *do* anything, right?

Well, if that's not right, don't tell me about it. *Show* me!

Shameful examples on parade. Let's take a look at some of those ten amendments. Let's see what we're dealing with today. That first amendment is a good start. So, what about Congress not making laws that involve the establishing of a religion or prohibiting the free exercise of a religion? Is that what we have today?

It would seem that today's interpretation means the abolishing of anything that even vaguely suggests a religious feeling in almost any public place. Funny, isn't it? That's definitely not what was originally written. My, how things do change.

What about this business of not abridging the freedom of speech? It is my understanding that even Justice Oliver Wendall Holmes made it very clear that we are not free to cry "fire" in a crowded theater when there is no fire. He made it crystal clear that there most

What about Our Constitution?

certainly do have to be some limits with regard to dangerously irresponsible statements and the need for common decency. Freedom was never intended to be exercised without at least some responsibility. Why has that changed?

Another currently controversial amendment is the second one. It speaks of the need for militias, and makes it very clear that the people have the right to keep and bear arms. In fact, in that time in our history, a rather large percentage of our citizens did just that. Whether they were in a militia or not, they needed guns to hunt game (not so bad), fight Indians (not so good) and to keep a ready arm in case the British ever returned (as they did in 1812).

Of course now we don't really have any such needs, right? We are always absolutely secure and safe in our communities, on our highways and in our homes, right? Sure we are.

We have that sixth amendment wherein we are supposed to be guaranteed a trial, in all criminal prosecutions, by an impartial jury, and there's a whole bunch of other considerations that are supposed to be honored in today's courts. Well, that's no longer true. (We'll have more about that later on.)

More examples. As you may remember, the U.S. Supreme Court decided it's okay if a national magazine depicts a well-known, moral, old-fashioned evangelist as having a sexual encounter with his mother in an outhouse. Is that what our founding fathers had in mind to protect? Of course not!

However, it should also be noted that the U.S. Supreme Court is on record (in 1986) as making the decision that the public schools had the right to discipline a student who had made a speech that was described as, "lewd and indecent speech." In another example brought in from Tacoma, Washington, the U.S. Supreme Court said that double entendres (double meanings) a Bethel High School senior used in a speech in school were disruptive and not entitled to any constitutional protection.

Evidently, they decided that the legal considerations are not the same inside the classroom as they are on the outside. Nor is free speech clearly the same anywhere. It seems to bend with the ever-changing attitudes of the "black robes." This seems to be so, in spite of the simple wording in the first amendment which was clearly intended for the values and constraints of that earlier time, with appropriate provision for amendment at any later time by clearly defined Constitutional procedures.

Not all judges agree with the philosophy of such capricious legislation in the courts. The chief judge of the 9th U.S. Circuit Court of Appeals, J. Clifford Wallace, has gone on record as saying that, "I would disagree with those who believe the court should be a political power and that it should do the social engineering for the country." Too bad that the final judgment in the highest court seems so determined so often to go the other way. It's amazing how such power is taken at almost every opportunity and so cleverly justified at every turn.

In another interesting constitutional controversy, the matter of the relationship of church and state shows us some very interesting non-sequiturs in actions. Hilltop crosses and other similar memorials all over our nation have been coming under attack and are even sometimes being removed.

There is the historical war memorial cross on Mount Soledad in San Diego. There is the giant cross on a military reservation above Pearl Harbor. There is the 103-foot cross atop San Francisco's Mt. Davidson that has been in place since 1934. There is the cross on public property in East Greenwich, Rhode Island.

Many other interesting examples exist where religious expressions have come under similar attack. There was the Christmas carol program for Texas state employees in the rotunda of the state capitol. There were the lights that formed a cross above a fire station in St. Charles, Illinois. There was the nativity scene in the city of Downey in California. There were the Salvation Army's public service ads on the city buses in Fresno, California. There was the cross in the Austin, Texas, city seal.

Institutionalizing God-bashing. Every few years, around Christmas time, we can expect a season of God-bashing. (I wonder how long it will take before they have removed the little prayer at the beginning of legislative sessions and "In God We Trust" from our money.)

It is a war *against* religion. It has absolutely nothing whatsoever to do with the original concept of not establishing a state religion and *not* prohibiting its free exercise And, if there's any doubt of that, just take a good look at the attitudes and practices of our founding fathers at that time and following the passage of the Bill of Rights. It doesn't take a rocket scientist to see what they were talking about and what the vast majority of them definitely *didn't* mean.

Supporters of this form of suppression tend to call attention to what they feel is a constitutional command for the separation of church and state. Most of those with that mind-set with whom I have talked actually believe it is so written in our constitutional document.

Take a good long look at that document, and tell me just where the separation of church and state is mentioned. Go ahead. I dare you to find it! In fact you won't. It's not there (except in the minds of those who would use it as a tool for their own idea of how things ought to be).

Maybe we should remember what Chief Justice William Rehnquist said in a minority opinion (Wallace vs. Jaffree). "The wall of separation between church and state is a metaphor based on bad history, a metaphor which has proved useless as a guide to judging. It should be frankly and explicitly abandoned."

And on and on it goes. In other areas we find the courts often overturning the sincere efforts of the voters to do an end-run around the various state legislatures and the courts with ballot propositions. Yes, sometimes the legal ground is not solid, but at other times it's obvious that it is a clear attempt by the voters to reverse the efforts of court-based legislation that just doesn't have a solid constitutional foundation.

There is also that business of what is often called "taking the fifth." Of course it refers to that part of the Fifth Amendment that tells us no person "shall be compelled in any criminal case to be a witness against himself." It was clear that this was to protect the accused from various intimidating pressures of the powerful state. You see, we hadn't yet reached the sophisticated level where we would be able to have strong oversights and penalties that worked, involving things like cross-examinations in the station house with rubber hoses and such.

Of course now we can apply such sophisticated controls and penalties if we wish to, especially since, in theory, we're supposed to be doing so now; but we still don't yet seem to be able to be sure we have such problems completely under control. So, we take the easy way out. We restrict the search for truth in the court rather than punish those who are responsible for the unacceptable acquisition of such information in the police station. (Except that now we sometimes offer immunity from prosecution and are then able to compel such testimony, which often lets some of the criminals get away with a crime with the blessing of the court.)

Then there is that business about making it unlawful to tape record something without the knowledge of the other party. It's a real mess. Sometimes it seems to be acceptable and at other times it is not. There don't seem to be many clear boundaries with this issue.

We certainly don't want to apply logic to this situation, right? You know what I mean? Shouldn't everyone have the right to make a permanent record (electronic or otherwise) of any conversation he or she has with anyone else, with or without the awareness or special permission of the other party?

That is a very personal thing. If someone chooses to enter your home by phone or to reach into your own personal space to speak to you in person, why wouldn't you have the right to your own private record of this? It's your life, isn't it? Well, as this book will show you, there's little left that's really your life anymore.

In other areas you have such things as court decisions that allow various aspects of free speech (getting signatures, handing out literature, etc.) in private shopping centers, while, at the same time, we have a number of publicly owned facilities and assembly areas (such as convention centers) where the restrictions can be so severe that any real attempts at usually acceptable free speech activities are cut off entirely.

How have we allowed all this to happen? I realize that many of you are well aware of this mess that I've been describing. Your concern is not a new phenomenon. *Time* magazine published a two-page essay way back in 1979 in which Evan Thomas wrote that "Today many Americans do resent an ever-more-activist judiciary. Beware, warns a vocal group of scholars: the Imperial Presidency may have faded, but now an Imperial Judiciary has the Republic in its clutches."

The essay also noted the constitutional scholar Alexander Bickel's observation that "too many federal judges view themselves as holding 'roving commissions as problem solvers, charged with a duty to act when majoritarian institutions do not.'" Mr. Thomas further stated that "Judges do not just judge any more; they legislate, make policy, and even administer."

What is most frightening is Thomas's further statement that "For all their power, judges remain remarkably unaccountable and unknown . . . Federal judges are appointed for life; they can be removed only by a two-thirds vote of the Senate, and so far only four have been so punished (the last in 1936)." There is also a very interesting quote of an Indiana judge who proclaimed that "An aura of deism is essential for the maintenance of respect for the judicial institution."

The criticisms continue. In Walter Bern's book, *Taking the Constitution Seriously*, he correctly observed that "the judges, and more precisely, the Supreme Court Justices, have taken upon themselves the authority to create rights, and with every right created they have narrowed the range of that public or political area."

As Fenton Bresler said in his *Los Angeles Times* review of the book, "Perhaps, in the end, it does boil down to a question of trust. Americans—even their most distinguished scholars such as Berns—do not seem to trust their senior judges to do what they consider right."

And as USD law professor Bernard Siegan put it, "What's the problem with going back to the original intention? I think that the Constitution is so set forth that original intention can be accommodated. The other side of that is to say that the Supreme Court or five members of the Supreme Court can tell us what the existing values are, what the existing concerns are."

Even George Washington got into the act. Our first president said, "If in the opinion of the people, the distribution or modification of the constitutional powers be, in any particular, wrong, let it be corrected by an amendment, in the way the Constitution designates. But let there be no change by usurpation; for though this, in one instance, may be the instrument of good, it is the customary weapon by which free governments are destroyed."

The bottom line. This could go on almost forever. I've got examples, studies, opinions, important quotations, and legal citings that could fill a dozen books. The files are literally bursting with the material. What I've given you should be more than enough to establish the clear and unquestionable fact that the Constitution is only followed when it suits the black robes. The rest of the time, most of them seem perfectly satisfied to go their own way, to legislate, and to, in effect, rewrite the Constitution to their own personal values as they choose to apply them.

When you get right down to it, this all ends up becoming the most unfortunate realization: that *we do not currently have a truly constitutional government!* Not as it was written, we don't. They have three ways to amend, but they have chosen to abandon it whenever they choose to. At this time, we just do *not* have a constitutional government! How many of you realize what this is doing to our country and to you personally?

∽ *Chapter Four* ∽

Uncivil Law in America
The Near Collapse of a Cumbersome System

I'm sure it's not a great stretch to see how the disintegration of original constitutional law can adversely affect all the rest of the legal system. In fact we do find our legal system careening in all directions. It's not hard to see the wheels of justice are in dire need of realignment.

One of the serious problems is a two-edged sword. On the one hand, we have extensive errors and general breakdowns throughout the civil (and criminal) system. On the other hand, we find ourselves in the middle of a massive explosion of lawsuits running every which way.

Some suits are legitimate and truly justified. However, a significant and growing number could only be classified as fodder for the comedy channel. In both categories we find customers suing merchants, clients suing lawyers, readers suing newspapers, stockholders suing corporations, students suing teachers, patients suing doctors, citizens suing the government, neighbors suing neighbors, children suing their parents and even burglars suing their victims.

Everybody's getting into the act. When you put all of that together in a system that seldom works, it becomes a gigantic mess. So, guess what we have?

This didn't happen overnight. It's been building up for years, you know. The annual report of the administrative office of the U.S. Courts reported civil filing in federal district courts alone, way back in 1985, rose to 273,670, an increase of five percent from the previous year. Then it was reported by the Bureau of Justice Statistics (in a 1987 report) that lawsuits filed in federal courts had increased almost three hundred percent since 1970. This, in the face of the fact that the number of U.S. district judges went up only forty-three percent in that same period. Of course, what the lawyers charge keeps going up and up and up and up and up.

In the 90s the situation has gotten so bad that we find prestigious legal publishers like the Nolo Press reporting such things as, "More than 100 million people who have legal problems can't afford to hire lawyers, according to the American Bar Association. Even if people are willing to handle routine legal procedures themselves, often they can't get even the most rudimentary information or advice." The report goes on to say, "Even worse is the larger failure of the legal system. It often hurts those who turn to it for help. No matter where you look—divorce, auto accidents, medical malpractice or probate—the civil legal system, which is supposed to fairly resolve disputes, routinely makes problems worse."

Loony toons time. And what are we talking about here? What kind of lawsuits *do* get filed? Some that are deserving of attention, to be sure, but some that are phenomenally ludicrous. By way of example, there is that listing that was published by *U.S. News & World Report* some time ago, which included the following:

> A former student is seeking $853,000 in damages from the University of Michigan, in part for the mental anguish he says he suffered after being given a "D" grade rather than the "A" he expected in an advanced German course.
>
> A prisoner ordered to serve extra time for escaping from a county jail in Pennsylvania tried without success to collect 1 million dollars from the sheriff and two guards for letting him escape.
>
> A 41-year-old California man, upset at being stood up on a date, unsuccessfully sued his would-be companion for $38 to compensate him for sprucing up and driving 40 miles for nothing.

In December of 1996, Larry Gerber of the Associated Press reported the "Loony Lawsuit" awards given by Citizens Against Lawsuit Abuse. The reluctant recipients included such individuals as a Grateful Dead fan who sued his law partner for making fun of Jerry Garcia's death. Then there was the K-mart shopper who claimed damages because she pulled out the bottom box in a blender display stack and brought it down on her. (Believe it or not, the case took more than three years to resolve.)

Now there are the "Stella" awards for what are considered to be some of the other outlandish lawsuits. The award was named for the woman in Albuquerque, New Mexico, who won a $2.7 million judgment against McDonald's (later reduced to $480,000). She bought a cup of coffee and was driven off with it nestled in her lap. The coffee was hot, of course, and the coffee spilled, of course. So McDonald's gets sued, of course. Joseph Perkins of the *San Diego Union-Tribune* published these awards, which included the following:

> After attending a party, Carol Roland went to visit Karen Shortell, a neighbor in her apartment building. While the two were having cocktails, Shortell's pit bull attacked Roland, biting her 27 times on the arms and legs. An unemployed bartender, Roland faced medical bills of roughly $40,000. But she didn't sue her girlfriend Shortell. She went after the owners of the apartment building.
>
> Thomas Passmore was working on a construction job in Norfolk, Virginia, when he thought he saw the number 666, the mark of the devil, on his hand. Recalling the biblical admonition, "If thy right hand offend thee, cut it off," the construction worker sliced off his hand with a circular saw.
>
> Passmore was rushed to a local hospital where surgeons attempted to reattach his severed hand. But the construction worker refused to consent to the surgery, saying he thought he would go to hell if he was reunited with his offending hand. As time passed, Passmore began to miss his right hand. So he sued the hospital for $3.3 million for failing to reattach it.

Then there's the one about the robot that was supposed to have terrorized a little boy when the promotional robot bumped the child's stroller. A Delaware County jury awarded $250,000 in damages when the defendant firm failed to respond to the suit. Why did they not respond? It seems that they sued the wrong company. Even so, we understand the firm was told it *still* had to go to court and show why it shouldn't have to pay the fine. (And just doing that cost plenty.)

The criminal option in the civil system. There's the one about the burglar who was surprised by tenants of a house in the San Fernando Valley. They shot at the burglar and missed. The burglar then ran into a sliding glass door, which shattered, cutting a major artery. The burglar died and the widow got an attorney to threaten a lawsuit against the owner of the home. The late Dr. Barbour said it reminded him of a case of a burglar who fell through a skylight in a school while trying to break in. Since he was badly injured, he sued, of course, and, "a court awarded him handsome damages. It also ordered the school district to pay his medical expenses for the rest of his life."

That was similar to one I have been hearing about from time to time. It seems a burglar was busting his butt trying to break into a particular warehouse. He was unsuccessful, so he went up on the roof and tried to break in through the skylight. He fell through and was seriously injured. He sued the hell out of the owners of the warehouse. (It is my understanding that this one didn't fly, however. But of course it still cost the warehouse owners a great deal of money just to deal with it.)

No wonder such a huge number of businesses in our nation have liability insurance. You will find most homeowners who have any form of comprehensive insurance on their property have liability coverage in that mix. Without it, you can be destroyed. Never mind that you are innocent—that you never did anything wrong. That's not what this is all about. This is about taking you to the cleaners one way or the other, through high insurance premiums or through expensive lawsuits.

We are always hearing about the mountain of frivolous lawsuits that are filed by inmates, using the law library and other facilities provided by the jailers. You must remember, a failing legal system is the best refuge and greatest asset for the most lawless among us. (And some of them are living better than they ever did on the outside.)

Storming a bachelor's castle. Are you finally getting a little bit mad? I hope so. If you're not, I've got another one for you. Robert Nolin did a great job writing up this nightmare in the *Fort Lauderdale Sun-Sentinel.* He told about a 45-year-old bachelor named Kevin Moore who was slowly being destroyed by a stranger with his same last name.

As Robert Nolin wrote it, "Anne Moore insisted (Kevin) Moore was her husband of six years, and half his house was hers. After spending $996 in attorney's fees, (Kevin) Moore won a judge's order protecting his finances. Palm Beach Circuit Judge Edward Fine also ordered Anne Moore to pay Moore's legal fees. She didn't."

However, she did force the hapless bachelor back in court again and went through a strange tale, backing off her original claim of being his ex-wife but still claiming that his home also belonged to her, at least in part. It was reported that Kevin Moore's attorney made it very clear that "He's never been married. She's been uncooperative and hostile and insisted on going to court no matter what." What I will never understand is how the legal system can go through this sort of charade and keep a straight face. If it wasn't such a terrible thing to do to another human being, it would be hilarious.

As columnist Arianna Huffington wrote, "Since legal resources and public attention are both finite, the more we clamor against made-up abuses, the less we focus on the real ones proliferating around us." She illustrated her point with such ridiculous examples as Girl Scouts who want to be Boy Scouts, a vegetarian bus driver who didn't want to hand out hamburger coupons, and a chain store that got in trouble because it had the audacity to display boys and girls toys on different aisles. Yes, believe it or not, all of these things ended up in court.

The media doesn't get off lightly either. Remember when television producer Aaron Spelling was nailed for almost five million dollars by a disgruntled actress because she was fired for not fulfilling her contract correctly? (She was not willing to accept another important role in the same show.) She was not supposed to change her appearance significantly. It was extremely important for her role. Let's face it, characters are developed with very specific visual presentations in mind. It is often critical for proper dramatic presentation.

She got pregnant. The jury considered it as an enormously expensive discrimination against a pregnant woman. I guess you could say that "Melrose Place" vixen did all right for herself. We probably haven't heard the end of this one.

Other shameful examples. There is so much more that goes on in our civil courts. The ancient sage Cicero is reputed to have said that "when you have no basis for an argument, abuse the plaintiff." This advice seems to have been followed by lawyers practically from the beginning. (When you have an antiquated adversarial system that goes back to medieval times, such a "contest" between opposing sides in bound to produce a myriad of abuses.)

I've heard of many attorneys who brag about how they can wipe out the opposition in most cases through brutal depositions, even before it gets to court. I also know of many cases that have gone to small claims courts and the winners ended up finding that it would cost almost as much and sometimes more to collect than the award was for in the first place.

This writer appeared as a witness for a friend in a civil court just a few years ago in San Diego, California, and, right there in the court room, in front of many witnesses, the protagonist on the other side came up to me, asked who I was and what I was doing there. When I told him I was a witness for my friend, he actually threatened my life, right there in front of everybody! That was bad enough. What was much worse is that the court and the marshals were unwilling to do anything about it other than to send us out of the court room. (Yes, some of the witnesses protested. You can imagine how much good that did.)

Then there's the bankruptcy court. This has proven to be such a marvelous shelter for everyone from the totally inept to the professional con. Under "Chapter 7," one is able to eliminate all debts and lawsuits and keep the car, home, and personal property. It's a great haven for those who would live high on other people's money and not have to pay it back. It's a perfect arrangement for those who have grievously wronged others and want to get away with it, without having any lawsuits bringing them to their day of reckoning.

Other things to consider. Then there are the debtor's prisons. You say we don't have debtor's prisons in this country? Where have you been? Where do you think you're living, in the land of the free and the home of the brave? Think again. There are ways, in the United States of America, through which certain debtors, under certain conditions, may be jailed after due process of law is supposed to have taken place.

Citizens have been thrown in jail by judges when being held in contempt of court for refusing to pay what the judge or a previous court decision may have demanded. Many times it was never really a case of refusal. Many times the poor soul just didn't have enough money and sometimes no money at all. Never you mind. The American Legal System will never let that stand in the way, right?

We also find ourselves in a land where a jury's award can be changed or simply set aside by judges who don't happen to like the decision that was made. Why do we even bother with the window-dressing of a jury trial in the first place if their determinations can be wiped out that way?

Maybe they just keep it going because sometimes the jury can be as idiotic as so many of the judges can be, which therefore maintains the norm. Of course maybe it's also because they really don't want you to get any ideas about what kind of a sham it can sometimes be. They want you to think the juries are always the decision makers.

Of course you must understand that a good number of suits are brought to trial for good and just reasons. Sometimes these trials are resolved in a good and just manner. The problem is that there is a growing mass of humanity that has been made the unjust victim of the many growing dysfunctions of that fool's gamble we dare to call our civil courts. Yes, it works, when it works, and when it often doesn't work as it should, that's what we're talking about. That's our problem.

It's complicated. It's involved with rigid procedures that have blinders built in. It's involved with rules of evidence that can take away any semblance of truthful revelation. It's often a matter of looking the other way while the adversary game is played, for the "game" is what is *really* important. It may have been instituted as a method of bringing out the truth but now it has become the best of all possible ways of obscuring it or eliminating it altogether. That's what it has come to.

Divorce, American style. Oh boy! We had to get into that one, didn't we? We seem to be living in an age where all that's needed for a divorce is a wedding. The attitude of many couples seems to be to have and to hold, until the going gets a little tough. The statistics seem to run in many directions (all bad). One of the worst I've seen was the determination by the University of Wisconsin's Center for Demography which suggested that only one in three marriages could be expected to last.

I suppose you could say it's all part of the disintegration of the conventional family. A Menninger Foundation psychiatrist and psychoanalyst (and chief officer in those capacities in 1979), Dr. Harold M. Voth, made it clear quite some time ago that the collapse of the family unit is creating a society of immature and emotionally unhealthy adults. It's been brought out many times by many other experts since then. It shouldn't be a secret to anyone.

This enormous divorce rate plunks down a big fat number of people right in the middle of that muddle we have come to know of as our civil courts—in this case, our divorce courts. You've heard about the problems. I know you have.

There's the sometimes-discovered sexual bias (against either men or women), the scrapping of prenuptial agreements, the custody battles, the uses of debtors prison when somebody can't pay the alimony, the confiscatory legal fees of the lawyers, the "palimony" fiascoes, and so on.

You do recall what "palimony" refers to, don't you? The word entered the public consciousness when Lee Marvin was sued by a showgirl to acquire half of his income for the time they had been living together (*without* benefit of marriage). The judge ordered Mr. Marvin to pay up in the amount of $104,000 for her "rehabilitation." Nice job if you can get it. Even though a higher court reversed the decision, it was kept alive and became a continuing problem that has put the fear of God in quite a number of people who had easy-going, informal "arrangements" without the responsibility of marriage (they had originally thought).

I recall one very different case of a lesbian who gave birth to a child through artificial insemination, and her ex-lover went to court and won the right to sue her estranged partner for joint custody (a decision of California Superior Court Judge Richard Denner). This has got to have been a first.

I'll never forget comments Eddie Murphy once made about the state of matrimony. "Just because you're rich and you married someone, this person doesn't have to be rich for the rest of her life if the marriage doesn't work." Oh yeah? Tell *that* to the judge.

I remember when Lee Iacocca got a divorce from a flight attendant after about one-and-a-half years of marriage. It was reported that he settled with her for an amount somewhere between $2.5 million and $3 million. Hey, that's like winning a lottery!

Then there are the endless jokes. There's the wife who tells the hapless husband that, "I'm getting a divorce. I'm leaving you, and so is the house and so is the car." And there's the one about the guy who is telling his buddy about the equitable nature of his divorce. As he explains it, "Everything is split down the middle. She gets half and the lawyers get the other half."

Sometimes the woman has to pay and pay big-time. There have been a few celebrated cases with actresses and other wealthy women where that can be found. Not only do many men and women get taken to the cleaners, there are quite a number of cases where women have been left with practically nothing. (Often the man just skipped out on his child support payments.)

The Everson case. There have been many interesting divorce cases that I could tell you about, but this is just one book, and I don't want it to end up the size of that Russian novel *War and Peace*. So, I'll give you one interesting example of just a few years back that contains about as much corruption and oppression as anyone could ever want in any Russian novel, only this time it's in the civil court system of Phoenix, Arizona.

There once was a prosperous building and development company in the Phoenix area that was doing its exceptional work all over the country. Some in the area might still remember it—The Visioneering Corporation. I say it *was* a prosperous company because, after a year or so of marriage (without children), the corporate owner had to face a Decree of Dissolution of Marriage and Distribution of Property, which by all accounts we have ever been able to find amounted to more than the sum total of his entire estate! (Everson vs. Everson)

Then, even though a decision was handed down from an appeals court (Judge Jacobson) for the lower court to correct various inequities, the lower court chose to ignore the instructions and proceeded to place an even heavier judgment on Mr. Everson than before (before Judge Broomfield and then Judge Strand).

Needless to say the mess was appealed, but no stay of judgment was allowed to protect his assets until the appeal process would be completed, and the appeal was expected to drag out over a long period of time. As a result of all of this, Mr. Everson found it necessary to tell his people that, due to all that was happening to him, everything that he had would be in jeopardy. Therefore, he felt he was no longer able to continue in business.

If some of his employees wished to continue to do business, they would have to form their *own* corporation. He indicated he would allow them to use his furniture and they had his permission to use the name, "Visioneering," in the title of their new corporation if they wanted to.

Shortly thereafter, Mr. John H. McKeever formed a new corporation in the state of Delaware entitled, Visioneering Corporation, a Delaware Corporation. Former Everson employees thus became employed there. (Frankly, no one really trusted the court system. Even though Mr. Everson was, theoretically, given all stock in the *original* Visioneering Corporation, under the terms of the Everson divorce judgment, it was felt that nothing was truly safe anymore.)

The pressure by the courts, through the efforts of the ex-Mrs. Everson's attorney (Sidney B. Wolfe), were making things very uncomfortable for everybody. As time went on, the ownership of the stock in the new corporation changed hands a couple of times. Everyone wanted very much to distance themselves from that divorce situation—a situation that should actually have had absolutely nothing to do with this new company.

In fact, Mr. Everson had told the leadership of the new corporation that he did not mind giving advice to the management and personnel, as requested, and making an introduction or two, but no more than that. He indicated, very clearly, that he would not invest his money in the new corporation, take a leadership position therein, or have any sort of ownership or control.

The seizures begin. Then court actions were initiated for the seizure of various Visioneering corporations, and, mistakenly, that included the new and *independent* corporation as well. The ex-Mrs. Everson and her attorney and the appointed receiver marched into the Tempe offices of the new and unassociated corporation and announced that they were taking over. They demanded all the keys and told everybody to go home. They were told that this was the wrong corporation, and they most certainly were not going to comply.

Attorneys for Mrs. Everson returned in a few days, with hastily changed court documents and a deputy sheriff and successfully seized the company at that time and sent everyone home. As soon as possible, the new owner tried to obtain some semblance of due process but the court denied his motion to intervene, along with everything else that was tried. The corporation was no longer in business. Due bills, garnishments and other responsibilities that were now supposed to be under the control of the court-appointed receiver (Joseph E. Stern) were not being taken care of.

This was the case, in spite of the fact (as we have been told) that it is the legal responsibility of the receiver to properly answer such items and to try to preserve the corporation and its assets until everything can be properly adjudicated in the courts. Of course, the receiver was instructed to answer the Tender of Issue and other important actions as well. He did not.

The ex-Mrs. Everson's attorney launched countless efforts, even as far away as Pennsylvania and Delaware to try and seize whatever they could that might have any possible connection to Mr. Everson, including his mother's estate.

Then, under immense pressure, one of the previous and brief owners of the corporation was bullied into signing a document claiming transfer of ownership of the stock, which he did not have and did not own. The bogus transfer was to the ex-Mrs. Everson.

Then, Judge Perry entered a Default Judgment against the corporation for slightly over $600,000—a whopping amount—primarily because (as we have been told) his own court appointed receiver, who had all the legal control and responsibility of the corporation, had not answered one of that same court's papers concerning the judgment. (Also, at this point, it is our understanding the ex-Mrs. Everson's attorney was now also acting as the attorney for the receiver as well.)

The making of a fugitive. You think this is about all they would dare do? Not on your life. This was just the beginning. Judge Perry issued a "body attachment" against Mr. Everson. It is our understanding that, considering the unrestrained looting that was going on, Mr. Everson felt that, for his survival, it was then necessary for him to become a *fugitive!*

This respected, responsible businessman, who had earned a fine reputation in national construction ended up becoming a wanted man! It's an unbelievable situation, I know, but that's the sort of thing that can and does happen in this one-time land of the free, home of the brave. It really does.

Had enough? Oh, there's more. A Creditor's Petition for Involuntary Bankruptcy was filed against the Visioneering corporations, including the new and totally independent company which they had seized. This was possible because they had managed to pull together three creditors who were willing to file. It's interesting that none of the three really had a legitimate claim against this one particular independent company (possibly against the receiver but not against the company). In fact, one of the creditors (then known as Mountain States Tel. & Tel.) had a huge unpaid bill that was run up by the *receiver*, who had refused to pay the bills. So, the company was completely destroyed. Evidently, exactly what they wanted to happen.

Court sanctioned oppressions continued. Next, the owner at that time of the seized Visioneering corporation, was ordered to Phoenix for a deposition by the ex-Mrs. Everson's attorney and his associates. The person being deposed was ill at the time. Their response to this was to turn the questioning into an all night marathon. It was an extensive abuse which was called to the attention of the court. As usual, the court just didn't give a damn.

It was all over. There was nothing left. Mr. Everson had become a wanted fugitive. Much, much later he finally won his appeal and became a free man again, but not only had he lost just about everything he had in the Phoenix area, he had to pay even more to finally close it all out. And, of course, the destroyed corporation that was not his in the first place, remained a lasting victim of the American legal system's oppression against the people.

What about the attorneys that should be able to successfully defend against such abuses? And what about the local media in the Phoenix area? Wouldn't this have made an important and rather dramatic story to tell? You'd think so, wouldn't you? Well, think again. The attorneys seldom seemed to know what they were doing and, as one local newspaper reporter had told Mr. Everson, maybe after the court case is all over, it might rate a little story. Of course, after it was over, it was a matter of it being all over now, so it isn't current news anymore.

I have copies of all the court papers, all statements and all other relevant documentation on this matter. (I keep them in a wall of files that I have on the Everson case, along with all the rest of what has gone into this book and much more.) I don't think this example is an exception, as I have seen so many thousands of such cases that I've practically gone cross-eyed.

Some of you may not be too surprised by such examples in the state of Arizona. Some of you know how primitive things are there in the legal system. For instance, did you know it is legal, in that state to sell your child? That's right, it is. Of course you are not supposed to sell the hapless youngster for sex or slavery. Think I'm kidding you? It was reported in the early part of 1998 that a 14-year-old girl was sold in Tucson by her parents. We understand this happened to her twice, once for around $11,000.

Let's just hope the bad examples in this book will enrage Arizona citizens to the point of constructive action. There is much that needs to be changed. There is much that needs to be answered for. Let's hope this and other examples in this book will help to make a difference.

The persecutions go on. There's no end to it. California homeowners and homeowners in a good number of other states can tell you how they can pay a general contractor for work done on their property and, if the contractor doesn't pay his subcontractors, the homeowners can be forced, by the courts, to pay the whole thing a *second* time, even if it completely destroys them financially. No, we don't want to hold the contractor accountable as the single responsible party. We'll lay it on the hapless homeowner. Why not? The courts can do anything!

More businesses in America have become afraid to respond with anything beyond dates of employment and positions held for any released workers. Reference checks have become practically worthless in many areas of employment. Why? Because, more and more, even the worst of all possible employees are suing their former employers whenever they don't like the evaluation that is given. It doesn't matter how honest and correct that evaluation is, and it doesn't matter that the company may win in court. Even if they win, they lose, because it costs so much just to defend yourself in those courts.

As University of Pennsylvania law professor Heidi M. Hurd has commented,

> In communities across the nation, tort liability has milked out of existence softball leagues, evening concerts, petting zoos, ice-skating rinks, horseback riding, swimming pools, amateur hockey, sailboat races and public beaches. Its national sum equals the total profits of our top 200 corporations.

For those who may not be aware, tort liability is what is called the result of successful civil lawsuits for personal injuries. Any business man can tell you how much that costs him in additional insurance premiums, and some can tell you how it put them right out of business.

How does the law get twisted and turned until in becomes this torture chamber of civil persecution? Jonathan Swift put it well in the following explanation:

> It is a maxim among lawyers that whatever hath been done before may legally be done again; and therefore they take special care to record all the decisions formerly made against common justice and the general reason of mankind. These, under the name of "precedents," they produce as authorities to justify the most iniquitous opinions; and the judges never fail of directing accordingly.

Today we refer to that as case law. Actually that's not the only way we screw everything up. We have found an inordinately large number of judges who are quite pleased to operate their little fiefdom with capricious disregard to honorable law, truth, and justice. We all know about juries who buckle to social and ethnic pressures of one kind or another. Let's face it. There are an almost endless number of ways the dilapidated system can go after you. If it hasn't already, chances are it will, sooner or later.

Chapter Five

Law and Disorder
The Criminal Result of Our Criminal Law

I have dragged you through the uncivil side of civil law and now I'm going to expose you to the truly criminal nature of criminal law. You won't like this any better than you liked the last trip, but you need this, and you need it right under your nose. You need to know, without any doubt, what is actually going on. So, fasten your seat belt.

> *Custom reconciles us to everything.*
> —Edmund Burke

A taste of the real world. Dr. Frederick Hacker is the Los Angeles psychiatrist and psychoanalyst who wrote the book on terrorism a few years back entitled *Crusaders, Criminals, Crazies*. He had some choice words on crime in America, which were published in *U.S. News & World Report* several years ago. They are as relevant today as though they had just been written. (Yes, it would seem the message got out but it just never sunk in.)

When asked if the crime wave reflects a decline of respect for human life, he replied, "I certainly think it does, and I think it also reflects a decline of respect for law and order." He also noted that "it strikes one as peculiar that while even Nobel Prize winners have some difficulty getting access to the media, the news organizations give totally free prime time to disorganized criminals or to the crazy ramblings of this, that or the other offender simply because he has a gun in his hand."

As to solutions, he spoke of how, "friends or families can spot early-warning signs when they detect very violent behavior." He said, "They can notify the authorities and get help for the unstable person."

Well that sounds just wonderful, but in the real world, the authorities are often reluctant to act until after a crime has been committed. This is partly due to the way the laws have been written, interpreted, and are applied and partly because police departments are usually swamped with more than they can handle most of the time.

As Jay Alan Samit wrote in *Multimedia Producer* (a high-tech, information/production magazine), "We live in a world of escalating violence." Much of it, he says, is with children, living in a world of video games. Let's face it, everyone, including the kids, are endlessly inundated with senseless violence, from live neighborhood experiences to TV, movies, and video games. There seems to be absolutely no end to it.

So what happens as a result? How about those two teen-agers who were arrested in Tampa, Florida, for allegedly torturing, mutilating, and killing as many as twenty cats. One was a boy of eighteen and the other was a sixteen-year-old girl.

I could fill this book with similar examples of horror committed on animals and on humans by adults *and* by our children in nice neighborhoods and schools. You've read enough about this sort of stuff in the newspapers and heard about it on the radio and on the TV, right? You know about it. But, just to be sure, let me share a little more with you.

A new age of terrorism. A&E (cable TV) "Investigative Reports" gives us some interesting statistics concerning terrorism in America. In a recent sample year, over three thousand bomb calls were made in the U.S., over eight thousand pounds of explosives were stolen in America, and 872 mail bombings occurred. (The numbers vary from year to year but they always represent significant numbers to those who find themselves at ground-zero.)

The report also noted that the most frightening challenge for the twenty first century may end up being the availability of small "atomic" devices for terrorists. The First Amendment is still protecting those who would instruct others in the dubious art of bomb making through mass distribution of books, video tapes, pamphlets, and technical manuals. That is also what the report had to say. I would also add the Internet to that list.

Bill Moyers got into the act, too, with his PBS documentary "So Violent A Nation." If you watched, you would have heard Dr. Bill Nance of Baylor Hospital in Dallas, Texas, warning that "there's a war going on in our streets that's far bigger than anything that happened in Vietnam." Moyers said, "despite all that tough talk by our politicians, the United States still has the highest murder rate in the world."

Terry Fitzpatrick told us that "many people have turned their homes into fortresses." How good are the statistics? As Gloria Burleson (a citizen on patrol) noted, "Half of the crime goes unreported, even in this neighborhood. You get . . . stuff stolen out of the garage and their attitude is, 'Well, why should I call the police? I mean, what are they going to do about it?' "

Letting the statistics fool you. But of course you've seen the headlines. VIOLENT CRIME DOWN ACROSS THE NATION! (Well, that was the latest wrinkle as this book was being written.) According to the Associated Press, this last year, "Violent crime in large U.S. cities dropped eight percent." That was according to an FBI report. Don't let those statistics fool you. The crime rate in just about every area you can imagine has been rising so much for so many years that a piddling eight percent doesn't even make a blip on my meter and shouldn't on yours either.

Don't forget that a number of the crime statistics on certain crimes and in particular areas remain essentially the same or have gone up. The latest figures available to me, as I write these words, tell me that, on a national basis, rapes, assaults and thefts are all up (Source: *Criminal Justice Research Division, Federal Uniform Crime Reports*).

The crime wave is moving out into rural America with a vengeance. You also may have noticed that substance abuse statistics are showing very significant increases in drug use by our young people, even on the grade school level. All of this has been reported. It's only a question of "where have you been?"

A stroll down memory lane. If you don't remember how bad it has been for so long, perhaps a stroll down memory lane will help. So, let's go to some storybook place like Connecticut. Bridgeport, Connecticut, reported the highest homicide rate in the state in 1993 with forty-five people killed per one million residents. That's a very high rate, higher than Los Angeles at that time. So, let's go to the nation's capital. Surely the lawmakers of our country would not be allowing such carnage right under their noses, right? In 1994 Washington D.C. was called the "murder capital" of the nation, and it still deserves a dubious distinction as a place of unspeakable violence. It was also the year that bullet holes were put in the White House dining room window and blood stains on the sidewalk out front.

To top it off, in that year homicide records were set in twenty-two American cities. Did you know that homicide is the third leading cause of death on the job? Well, that's what the National Institute for Occupational Safety and Health reported. In other words, the crime rate in this besieged nation of ours has gradually risen to such an *enormous* height over the years that it will take some really enormous drops over the next several years before we will ever have anything to brag about.

But don't hold your breath waiting. With the new drugged youth movement and other ominous signs, the little drops we have been seeing will soon disappear, and we'll be back to what has become normal for us—rising crime in a nation under constant attack—unless we're willing to make some serious changes.

I realize many of you already know this. None of it is news to you. But there must be an enormous number of people out there that just don't seem to know what's happening. They don't seem to have a clue. Consider these facts as ammunition to use when encountering the countless sleepwalkers of the nation.

And on and on it goes, again. Just a few of the many hundreds of examples I have in my files include such gems as the Girl Scout who was held up in Tampa, Florida. Then there is the 11-year-old girl in Bridgeport, Connecticut, who was shot by a 13-year-old boy because he thought she had shortchanged him in a candy purchase.

There is the report about how the robbers are described in a paper from the Western Behavioral Sciences Institute as being far more violent today in or out of prison. As one of the report's writers, Rosemary Erickson, put it, "The older robbers said they're afraid of the younger ones." She also concluded that "the severity or type of punishment doesn't mean much if these guys don't think they're going to be apprehended. A greater certainty of capture would make more difference than stiffer sentences."

Getting the bad guys. So how are we doing with apprehension and incarceration? We'll get into that in more detail later on in this book. For now you might like to think about just one little example of the problem. Many reward funds have very low collection rates because witnesses are afraid to testify. They're deeply afraid of reprisals if they call the police. (From an Associated Press release.)

Sometimes what law enforcement people and well meaning volunteers try to do creates even more crime than that which they are trying to stop. How is that? Well, one good example is those gun campaigns where people are urged to turn in their hand guns for cash, no questions asked. It is our understanding that a number of these weapons were first stolen and then were turned in, using the community efforts as their "fence" to turn the stolen property into money. How convenient.

And what about the bad girls? That's right. Unless you just fell off the turnip truck, you're aware that women are now as free as men, to be the same damn fools as men are, in many unfortunate instances. As Freda Adler wrote in *Psychology Today* way back in 1975, "we have already become accustomed to the female traffic cop, the female bank executive, the female airline pilot, and the female telephone lineman. But suddenly we are faced with the fact that there are female car thieves, muggers, bank robbers, and embezzlers."

So what have we got? We've got not only men as dangerous criminals, we now have women and children as well.

How to be a successful criminal. You've been following the headlines. You know what's been happening. The O.J. criminal case isn't the only example. You can read. You've seen the stories about the countless cases where somebody forgot to follow a complex little pattern, so critical evidence is thrown out which often means the criminal walks free.

You've seen the stories about law enforcement authorities or even judges who did the wrong thing, but instead of penalizing them for what they did, the criminal walks free. Of course, as one nameless prosecutor is reputed to have said, "All you have to do is look cross-eyed in the wrong direction and everything gets thrown out. Never mind what happens to truth and justice. Everything is out. It's all over."

The Tucker case. San Diego had the dubious distinction of being a great place for con artists and others of similar persuasion, a few years back. (You may have heard of the famous "Dominelli case.") A close examination showed any thorough investigator that, although there were many negative factors at work, an incompetent district attorney (Ed Miller) seems to have been the most obvious cause for such disastrous effects.

One very good example of this developed when a certain David Tucker came to town (apologies to the many wonderful people who just happen to share that common name). He swaggered into San Diego County just a few years ago as some sort of big-time developer and promoter of all sorts of printing and publishing projects and just about anything else that looked good to him at the moment.

He looked good and he made a very convincing presentation of himself. He even managed to get himself set up as a lecturer at a local college and with the famous "Learning Annex." He had everybody fooled, for a while. He was eventually cut off the local lecture circuit when he was finally discovered for what he was.

Yes, after a time, folks began to discover that with all his talk and fancy maneuvering, they were finding themselves on the losing end of things financially, with little or nothing to show for it. They had been taken. Sometimes in amounts of many, many thousands of dollars.

In one example, after Tucker had taken a "client" for thousands of dollars, he refused to tell him who was printing a very time-sensitive manual that was needed right away, nor would he return the camera-ready copy that had been loaned to him, until he was given an additional payoff of a considerable amount.

Even the police seemed unable to help unless the district attorney's office was willing to move on it, which they weren't. Then, when the payoff was made (in desperation), it was found that some old man was printing the job in his garage and it was a mess.

The number who were being conned grew and grew and some of them eventually formed a victims' support group called "Victims of David Tucker." There were over 50 members! And *still* the D.A. was unwilling to move, even though his office received many complaints and reports on what was going on.

In fact, one of his investigators, Larry Buckeye, was inclined to say that Tucker's pattern was not clearly established as yet. This seemed to be his opinion in spite of Tucker's rap sheet, previous felony conviction, and a victims' support group of over 50 members!

When all of this finally began to become painfully obvious to Buckeye, he decided to inform victims that "we don't know what he had in mind when he started out." Eventually Buckeye ended it with just telling everybody that the case load is just too heavy and that there just aren't enough personnel available. (This after about a year of this sort of thing.)

Civil cases were more successful against Tucker, so his next move was to try and declare bankruptcy. You will be pleased to know that a number of the "victims" got together, went to court and were at least successful in stopping him dead in his tracks. (Bankruptcy is a ruse that is used all too often and all too successfully most of the time by all sorts of unsavory individuals who are looking for a sure-fire method of getting away with their various cons and other irresponsibilities.)

He actually laughed at everybody and told some of the victims, in blunt terms, that he could do whatever he wanted to and they couldn't do a thing about it. Eventually he left town, one more con artist who had struck it rich in southern California. (It was found out later that authorities in North Carolina weren't so "understanding" about his cons. He may still be serving a prison term in that state.)

Eventually the D.A., Ed Miller, slipped on just one too many "misjudgments." He decided to prosecute a harmless fellow who was a little short on sophisticated reasoning in a case that ended up blowing up in Mr. Miller's face and ending his career. He was defeated for reelection. Thank God!

What is very disturbing about all of this is that during the flap and after his removal there were so many in the legal profession who were quick to come forward and say what a terrible thing had happened to this wonderful man who had done such a marvelous job for so many years. They seemed unable to face the events that had happened. (Or maybe they just didn't care.)

Somehow, they couldn't see (or just didn't want to see) that, for many cases, his good conviction rate was such because (as it was explained to us) there were so many good cases that might have required a real effort that he just wouldn't deal with. He wanted what he perceived to be the "easy" ones and then a few "high profile" cases. That would do it for him. That wouldn't help the public much, but that would do it for him. He would look good in the statistics.

What is happening is criminal. Remember when the Menendez psychologist lost his license because he had tipped the authorities to Lyle and Erik Menendez's killing of their parents? You see the Board of Psychology in the California Department of Consumer Affairs charged that the psychologist had violated the professional confidence of the brothers.

There is still no consideration of the greater good. If murderers go free, so be it. That's the public's problem. We, in our ivory towers, must maintain the pattern of the game as we have determined it should be played, and we must do so at all costs. Is that the way they see it? It would seem so.

We are all too familiar with the anguished pleading of Nicole Simpson for help on that "911" tape. More and more, we are coming to realize that there are all too many women being battered by their husbands, ex-husbands, boyfriends and ex-boyfriends. (As far as this writer is concerned, even one is too many.)

I'll never forget the story by investigative reporter Joe Cantlupe in San Diego's *Union-Tribune* about what happened to Christine D. Ward. She was raped and beaten repeatedly by her ex-husband, who also waved a loaded rifle at her and threatened to kill her. So, what happened to him? He managed to get a slap-on-the-wrist plea bargain that ended up putting him on a probation that just couldn't seem to be rescinded, no matter how many times he failed drug tests and other requirements.

As Mr. Cantlupe quoted from the court records, "Probation granted. Revoked. Probation reinstated. Revoked. Eight-year prison term ordered. Suspended. Probation reinstated." As the reporter indicated Christine Ward had told him, "The law enforcers were fine; it's the court system that's a sham."

As you might imagine, the perpetrator didn't end up with one day of hard time in a prison. Christine Ward fears for her life. As reported, her letter to a judge made it very clear. "As far as I'm concerned, the fact that he tortured me for four hours, promised to kill me and has violated his probation several times without serious repercussions certainly gives me legitimate reason for concern."

And what happened? Naturally the judge just kept the former husband on probation. She remains afraid for her life. She will never be free. Thanks judge. You're a real gem.

And the beat goes on. Sometimes time limits for the filing of criminal charges are so short that many cases just can't get filed in time. Sometimes the paper work gets so fouled up that the whole thing gets lost in the cracks.

Sometimes the women are so horribly frightened by what is happening to them that the fear of retribution leaves them practically paralyzed and unwilling to file charges. Sometimes it's because they believe the courts will do absolutely nothing to protect them. It's a belief that is often well founded.

There are also horrible cases like that of little five-year-old Julianna Olson. Her mother had evidently said the child was not by her ex-husband but evidently wanted to list a father on the birth certificate, so she listed her former husband. (The ex-husband, Ibrihim Mubarak, vehemently denied being the father.) Next, the mother died and the child went to the care of a loving grandmother.

Then, later on, Mubarak demanded and obtained visitation rights. Then, little Julie comes back from visiting with Mubarak, all black and blue. It got so bad that she would cry when he would come by to pick her up, and she would come back in terrible shape.

The grandmother was a nurse and a neighbor was a nurse. The two of them called the Child Abuse Hotline and, through a social worker, brought the little girl to a children's hospital where she was thoroughly examined. It was found that she was bruised all over and even had a swollen tongue and bruises on her genitals. The child also told them about her beatings at the hands of Mubarak.

For some reason, Larry Capobianco (a county child protective service social worker in southern California) created a very incomplete and misleading report that ended up getting the child taken away from the grandmother and put in a foster home. Next there was a dependency trial in which the grandmother did her best to have little Julie returned to her care. In that trial, psychologist Amy Lamson, who evaluated everyone involved, testified that the little child showed a strong attachment to her grandmother and a strong fear of the man the court was now accepting as her father.

Julie was temporarily returned to the care of her grandmother and another appointed therapist reported to Larry Capobianco that, "I have no doubt that to permit visitation (with Mubarak) at the present time would cause irreparable damage to Julie." Those visitations continued to cause injury to the little girl who continued to recount her abuses at the hands of Mubarak.

Another social worker was assigned to the case and discovered a child deeply traumatized even by the mention of visiting with her "father." It also seems that Mubarak had actually threatened the social worker, Julie's relatives, her therapist, etc. The authorities *still* allowed the "father" to continue to have visiting rights with the terrified child!

As if that isn't enough, that new social worker, Debra Dworaczyk reported that "this worker feels the grandmother has been extremely possessive of Julie and either consciously or unconsciously has attempted to sabotage Julie's relationship with her father." The final blow came from another psychologist's report on Mubarak that, for reasons we will never understand, convinced Judge Napoleon Jones to give custody of Julie to her "father," with very limited visitation rights to the distraught grandmother.

A few months later the judge gave Mubarak permanent custody of the completely terrorized little girl! Of course, Julie continued to show the usual injuries, and then one day her body was discovered in her bed in Mubarak's apartment. It was determined that she had been dead a week and the coroner said there were numerous signs of trauma on her body. In other words, she was apparently beaten to death! Of course, Mubarak had vanished.

The authorities filed murder charges against the man. (They did finally get that much right.) Of course they never caught him. Later it was found that he had fled to Jordan.

Little Julie Olson is dead. Her killer got away with it, and it seems that the heavy hand of criminal law would never come down on those who made it all possible—the social services officials, the judges, and other idiots who were (and most still are) a part of a system that is supposed to protect our little children and *just didn't do it!*

Although child protective services work for a number of endangered children, they definitely do not work for a significant number of others. This is only one example. It will continue, until such a time as our society takes it on as a personal crusade to see to it that those who allow things like this to happen are held *criminally* responsible in a court of law (one that *works*).

I know, I get really mad about things like that, don't I? I'm sure you can see why. I just hope *you* can get really mad about such things, too, and more important, that you are willing to be a part of intense efforts to make extensive changes where they are so sorely needed.

Persecuting the innocent. I could go on forever showing you how the guilty get away with it in our dilapidated system of justice. The numbers seem endless. But now maybe I should take some time to show you how the system does such a beautiful job of fouling itself up in the opposite direction. Let's take a good look at what can happen to *innocent* people who find themselves caught up in this mess.

Remember Donald Connery's book *Guilty Until Proven Innocent* or Joan Barthel's book *A Death in Canaan* or the movie based on this real life drama? It was the true story of Peter Reilly's manslaughter conviction for something he never did. It was also the story of the many officials who acted with total irresponsibility and were too cowardly to ever be willing to admit that an error had been made.

It was also the story of the courageous battle that was fought by ordinary citizens like you and me, in Falls Village, Connecticut, to save this poor young man. What it took was a dedicated bunch of folks who had the courageous hearts to stand up and fight like hell to stop the horrible injustice. (There's been so much written about that case, it would be redundant to go over the whole thing again.)

I imagine you remember that CBS mini-series *Gone in the Night*. It was based on a true story. The promo read, "A terrifying abduction. An unthinkable accusation. The shocking story of a couple arrested for murder . . . of their own child. The police need a suspect. The press needs a story. Now an innocent family is going to need an alibi." And so it goes. The stories are everywhere.

Justice gone crazy. Perhaps you may recall the special report in the *Reader's Digest* about the hapless youngster who was persecuted mercilessly and blindly by the legal system in Florida. His name is Bobby Fijnje, and his story was well reported by Trevor Armbruster.

Law and Disorder

It amply depicts the other side of child abuse prosecution. It also turned out to be one of the longest and one of the most expensive trials in Florida's Dade County records.

It all started with a little girl with an over-active imagination who had the problem that some youngsters sometimes have dealing with the differences between imagination and reality. (Frankly, a lot of adults seem to have that problem as well, in any number of different areas.)

In this case, the little girl was behaving somewhat strangely and was reporting nightmares about a big bad wolf. She decided she didn't want to be touched and started to be somewhat fearful of Bobbie, who was a baby-sitter at the little girl's church. Yes, that does suggest it should be looked into, and it was.

A church member (and state-licensed psychologist) questioned the girl and got no mention of any abuses. Even so, the psychologist, Suzanne Keeley, is reported to have said that she suspected there was abuse. She also then reported her suspicions to Florida state authorities.

A Florida caseworker concluded that there was no evidence of any abuses in this situation, none at all. Also, an interviewer in the then-state-attorney Reno's office came to the same conclusion. However, Suzanne Keeley persisted and proceeded with months of sessions with the little girl, encouraging anything she might be willing to say about any bad things being done to her.

Finally, after a couple of months of that sort of thing, the imaginative little child decided she was willing to say Bobby had touched her. As you might imagine, this sort of thing served to encourage others to try to draw bad stories about Bobby out of their children as well. Eventually, with enough prompting, several of the children were willing to come up with some stories their parents and others seemed to want to hear and also some really bizarre stories that were even further from reality.

A few printable examples of their fertile imaginations were such things as costumed adults chopping up babies, the flying of one of the children to New Zealand and abusing him there, being forced to eat an infant's arm at the church. You can imagine what the unprintable stories were like.

So, with all these unlikely stories, the local police got into the act. They came to search Bobby's room and then to interrogate him endlessly. In his diabetic condition with the stress and the relentless, threatening pressure, he finally said anything they wanted him to say, just so he could go home.

It should also be noted that his so-called confession was not taped. It was not taken down by a stenographer. The principal officer involved, Mark Martinez, claims he destroyed his notes without showing them to anyone, wonderful police work. The officer is also reputed to have told Bobby that he just knew he did it even before he saw him, more wonderful police work.

What happened next? Bobby went to the juvenile detention center to await trial. This, in spite of all the evidence to the contrary, including a court-appointed psychologist's report that claimed the frightened young boy exhibited none of the characteristics usually found in young sex offenders.

So, with the then-Florida State Attorney Reno's approval, it was decided to try Bobby in the adult court system for eight counts of sexually abusing three girls. Bond was then denied and young Bobby was now in the fight of his life.

It might also be noted that there were other inconsistencies found. For instance, an independent insurance investigation concluded that what they had here was an epidemic of false charges, many not credible by any stretch of the imagination.

But, as I said before, adults are also capable of having problems with what is real and what is unreal. It was reported that a Judith Wilson, director of "Justice for Sexually Abused Children," surfaced with the opinion that it was all a part of some sort of Satanic cult and that Bobby's family were most likely involved. There was also talk of some kind of international child pornography ring. Frankly, it just got wilder and wilder. You know, it just sort of built on itself, like negative feedback.

So, as you might expect, television (WCIX-TV) got involved and even the F.B.I. was dragged into it. The home of Bobby's parents was besieged. There were helicopters overhead, strangers out front and bizarre tales on television. There was no escape. It must have been a living hell.

All I can say is, thank God that the defense team of attorneys Mel Black and Peter Miller turned out to be that rare combination of dedication and competence that is so seldom found anywhere, let alone in our decrepit legal system. They were up against a lot. Janet Reno's top aide, John Hogan, was put in charge of the prosecution.

The trial finally started with charges reduced down to six counts of sexual battery against two girls and one count of lewd and lascivious assault and with Judge Norman S. Gerstein presiding. Now, for the first time, a logical presentation was finally possible. In this instance a logical presentation by the defense was being heard by a jury that evidently was not suffering with predetermined zeal.

Why do I say that? Because the verdict came in as a resounding not guilty! But even after that, Judge Gerstein refused to follow Florida law and certify the defense costs so Bobby's family could be reimbursed. He wouldn't do it until an appellate court finally *ordered* him to do it. Nice guy. Just the kind of guy you'd want to have sitting up there as a judge, right?

As a little footnote to this story, you might find it interesting to know that when President Clinton nominated Janet Reno for the job of U.S. Attorney General, and said it was because of her record in going after child abuse and her inclination to put people first, Bobby's father sent a letter to members of the Senate Judiciary Committee. He told it like it was.

What? You don't remember hearing anything about that? You didn't see it on TV or hear it on the radio or read about it in a newspaper? I guess that was because no one did anything about it. It just lay there. (I guess you could say Ms. Reno's story ended up being a case of seeing evil everywhere until she got within spitting distance of the White House. Now it would seem her eyesight has deteriorated considerably.)

What about Bobby and his family? They left the country. (Can you blame them?) You can also see why the excellent report written about this case in the *Reader's Digest* was titled, "Justice Gone Crazy."

The parade of shame goes on. If I don't put at least a fair number of examples in this book, there will always be those who will say I just found a few rare exceptions. So I'm burying you in a good cross-section from a wall of files that covers decades of extensive abuses of the system. Even so, there will still always be those who will discount what we have here, one way or the other. I just trust this effort will make it harder for them to convince you to turn away from the uncomfortable truth.

Another high-profile case you may remember was the so-called "Gentleman Bandit" caper that wrongfully put Catholic priest Bernard T. Pagano in jail and on trial for a series of robberies evidently committed in Delaware and Pennsylvania by another man who looked somewhat like the priest. There was that same investigative incompetence by authorities and that same blind eye to clearly available truths that we have seen so many times before.

As Rev. Pagano said to the *New York Times* News Service after he had been cleared, in the middle of his trial, by the confession of another, "What has happened to me has had application in the lives of many people I have known or counseled—blacks, whites, Hispanics. In their involvement with the police . . . it was all over for them once the police charged them. Now it's happened to me."

He also offered an interesting insight: "the police were being put in a very precarious position by us, the citizenry in general. We were letting go our responsibilities as citizens to see justice done. We were looking for an easy out—'Let the cops do it, they know what they're doing.'"

This had been a really tough one, and the cops were clearly not up to it. To begin with, the priest failed a lie detector (polygraph) test. Since those tests are *not* all that dependable, it should have never been considered in the first place. Then, the man who really did the hold-ups tried, on numerous occasions to convince authorities that they had the wrong man (while also doing his best to not get caught).

So how did they manage to finally bring in the right man? The priest's lawyer had to hire a former FBI agent to track him down. Yes, that's right, the police were not up to it. Somebody else had to do the job.

Next, I'll bet a lot of you remember the Dr. Sam Sheppard case. He's the fellow who was wrongfully convicted of murdering his wife in a sensational trial that grabbed everybody's attention for many years. In fact, his case inspired *The Fugitive* movie and the TV series by the same name.

Not so long ago, new DNA evidence was brought into the picture that seems to vindicate Sheppard and implicate a handyman (in prison for a later murder until he finally died). As you might imagine, Cleveland prosecutors were reported to have refused to reopen the investigation. County prosecutor Stephanie Tubbs Jones made it very clear that she considered such evidence inadmissible even though she had never seen the test results.

Prosecutors seem to be a problem everywhere. In California, the actions of Los Angeles Deputy District Attorney Rosalie Morton were considered so bad that the state Supreme Court overturned the murder conviction and death sentence of Shawn Hill in the early part of 1998, indicating that it was because of Miss Morton's "outrageous and unethical" misconduct.

These are just "high profile" cases. They're the few you may have heard about. This author's files contain seemingly endless numbers of examples of the thousands of unknown nightmare cases that almost nobody has ever heard about.

Yes, it could happen to you. Curtis Hendrix was walking down a street in Ceres, California, when a couple of guys asked him for a cigarette. They also asked him for a light and Hendrix said he asked if either of them might have a quarter so he could make a phone call. It was then reported that they said no and Hendrix went on his way. So that was that, right? Not on your life. You never really know what will ever happen next.

As it turned out, a few minutes later, the police pulled up to where he was walking, got him on the ground and informed him he was under arrest for armed robbery. He was dumbfounded. He couldn't believe what was happening.

As it turned out, those two strangers evidently felt they didn't like him and decided they would claim that Hendrix had brought out a knife and threatened their lives. They claimed he was demanding $1. Then they claimed they escaped by using some heroic karate moves. (Of course no knife was ever recovered and no other witnesses were found.)

Hendrix's attorney for the original trial was evidently the sort of person that is unfortunately obtained all too often in such cases. He was unwilling to do any investigation to determine his client's guilt or innocence. He also told his client not to testify on his own behalf. Sounds like a real winner, right?

Hendrix was summarily convicted in a sham trial lasting less than a day, and *sentenced to eight years in Folsom state prison!* That's right. It's the sort of thing you can't imagine would ever really happen to anybody, or at least not to you, but this sort of thing does happen. It can happen to practically anybody.

Eventually, Hendrix managed to get a court order appointing private detective Alan Peacock to try and find evidence for an appeal and finally Richard Krech was appointed by the court to represent him in the appeal, which was granted.

For the first time, the accusers were checked out and it was found that they were well known as chronic liars and had been under heavy medication for mental illness when the "crime" was supposed to have occurred. It mercifully ended when the two finally admitted, in a superior court hearing, that they had lied about the whole thing.

So, Curtis Hendrix was released, after 22 months in prison, without a home to go to, without a job, and not a penny in his pocket. So much for the American justice system. Just remember, next time it could be *you.*

Get your teeth into this one. I'll never forget the case of the Florida man who lost his faith in the justice system and lost some teeth, both at the same time and in the same place. His name is Derrick Robinson and it all started with a simplistic, unsophisticated decision by the local police that he was probably the man some neighbors were describing as the person who committed a particular recent murder. In fact, one witness decided he was the one because he did seem to look like the murderer.

Then the witness was arrested (for other reasons) and accidently placed in the same cell with Robinson. (That was a bright move by the authorities.) The witness decided to rethink his position on the matter and then, after being placed in another cell, decided to return to his original contention. Robinson, a 32-year-old Jamaican native (the father of two) was thoroughly frightened and demoralized by the oppressive nature of the system and ended up agreeing to a plea of convenience; in other words, innocent but willing to accept a plea to second-degree murder. This gave him a seven-year prison sentence!

How could anyone willingly go along with anything like this when they are innocent? Because he was afraid that if he didn't agree to the plea bargain, if he didn't go along with them, he would be railroaded into the electric chair. That's how a thing like that can happen.

It was during the time he was serving his sentence that he lost three teeth. He also mysteriously had his arms broken from what was said to be falls in the prison shower. Frankly, he didn't do any better in prison than he did in that earlier part of the justice system. He could have done as well, or perhaps even better, in one of those totalitarian countries we hear so many horror stories about. Looks like we don't have to go so far to find our oppressions nowadays.

Turning things around. Thank God his court-appointed attorney, Simon Steckel, was not only convinced his client was innocent, he had the unselfish determination to pay, out of his *own* pocket, to have a private detective investigate the killing his client was sent to prison for. After that, things began to turn around.

And what did the detective find? He dug up two credible witnesses who swore that another man, then awaiting trial for the shooting of a Miami police officer, was the actual murderer. That's what finally got him released. Of course, so far as this writer has been able to discover, Assistant State Attorney Kathleen Hoague was never willing to declare the originally accused as innocent. After all, that would be tantamount to admitting their duplicity in the creation of the living hell that this man was put through.

All I can say is I wish there were far more attorneys like Simon Steckel. Unfortunately, I'm convinced they are few and far between.

Some don't give a damn. Some aren't very good at their job. Some have just lost hope. Some don't seem to know what's happening. Some just want to make money. Some are just too busy constructing intricate justifications for the farce they have the gall to call the American justice system. It takes all kinds and those are the kinds there seems to be the most of.

So, what did this exceptional attorney say about all of this? What seemed to be the most frightening thing to the attorney was the chilling fact that his poor client, "is not the first person I've come in contact with convicted of murder who is innocent." That is one very chilling statement.

And then there's the one about poor Susie Mowbray who was recently acquitted after having to serve nine years in a Texas prison for a murder she clearly did not commit. There are so many others, all over the nation. (You can see why I don't favor the death penalty.)

Deep in the heart of Texas. As with all our states, Texas has had its bad examples, too. One of the many I can't forget is the one that started with a lady and her mother pulling up to their residential garage in Sulphur Springs and ending up being wrestled to the ground by three determined men. The robbers were finally frightened away when someone went from the house to the garage and turned on the light.

No one could identify anyone as a perpetrator of this attempted robbery, but it was felt by the police to be similar to a number of others that had occurred in the area for almost a year to that point. And, only the day before, Dallas police spotted an individual they suspected as the ringleader of this particular pattern of crimes.

Trooper Henry Sibley (of Sulphur Springs) pulled over a car for speeding and found three men that seemed to be worth checking out. They fit the pattern. One of the suspects in the car identified himself as Richard Thomas. Unfortunately for a Rickey Dale Thomas in southern California, a photo of Rickey was included in a photographic lineup and was identified by the trooper as the Richard Thomas in that car of suspects. (Even though he had gone straight and was living and working in southern California for some time, he had, six years before, been involved in a burglary in Hot Springs, Arkansas, with one of the other suspects, so his photo was available to the authorities.)

As you might imagine, having a past record and with this unusual coincidence of association, it was not surprising that this California resident was declared a wanted criminal and was finally pulled in. (There was a lot more going on, with his past catching up to him and all, but he would be fingered for this one and that was that.)

Rickey was tried, and since he couldn't afford a lawyer, the court appointed attorney Ronald Williamson to his case. Williamson ran a little one-man civil practice. He wasn't really equipped for this sort of thing, but he was willing to do whatever he could.

Frontier justice. Unfortunately, a number of critical witnesses were just not available. They couldn't *afford* to go from California to Texas for the trial. Eighth Judicial District Court Judge Lanny Ramsay denied a motion to have the court pay in advance for the travel expenses of Rickey's witnesses.

Still, Rickey's attorney did issue subpoenas for six witnesses in the Chula Vista area (in southern California), but it took too long to get the papers ready. The trial was under way and the judge denied a continuance until the subpoenas could be answered. Also, it was felt that a handwriting expert could have cleared Rickey, but Rickey couldn't *afford* such an expert, and the attorney wasn't about to pay for one out of his own pocket.

In addition, even though computer records were introduced which showed he worked more than six hours on the night of the crime, in Chula Vista, California, the jury seemed unable to read the records correctly or was just unwilling to consider that evidence.

On the positive side, some of Rickey's friends in Chula Vista, California (where Rickey was all that time), did manage to raise enough money to send one of them as a witness. A lot of good *that* did. While the trial was under way, District Attorney Frank Long made a correction of an error in Rickey's indictment, which involved an important change in the date of the crime in question and ended up thoroughly confusing Rickey's one witness who thought they were interested in the entirely different, previously listed date.

You know the drill by now. Rickey Dale Thomas was quickly sentenced to life in prison. This is what happened because the judge and the prosecutor and the police would not consider the *provable* fact that Rickey was over a *thousand* miles away, at work in a restaurant in Chula Vista, California, on the night of the crime he was accused of committing.

Since the trial, ignored evidence continued to rear its ugly head and new evidence was discovered. It eventually made the difference, but only after causing one hell of a nightmare for Rickey. What would you expect? He is a poor black man and he did have a past criminal record. No money and a past record translates into conviction far more often than you would ever believe.

I'm also sure that Judge Ramsay, District Attorney Long, and trooper Sibley don't really feel all that bad about what they did. In fact, Long was quoted after the trial as saying "I'm convinced, based on the evidence the jury heard and what I know about the case, the man committed the offense."

But of course we won't talk about the easily verified facts that were made available to you and you were unwilling to allow to be checked out. As far as I'm concerned, you should be held criminally responsible for such gross mishandling.

'Till death do us part. And then there's the case of Walter McMillian. It involved a store clerk in Monroeville, Alabama, being shot to death. Then another man was arrested for an unrelated murder and ends up fingering Walter for the store clerk's killing. Another man was also inclined to go along with that accusation. (Sometimes, in some areas, those in need of special considerations from law enforcement officials and courts are quick to help the police in any way that they feel the officials want that assistance.)

The fact that Walter was having a fish fry at home with a number of his friends at the time of the killing is just one of those irritants that had to be ignored in that one-and-a-half day trial that ended with his sentence of death. So there he was, six years on death row waiting for his execution. As Richard Cohen of the *Washington Post* put it, this "would have amounted to a kind of judicial murder."

Eventually a kind of miracle happened. Some rarely-shown attention was given to his plight and he actually managed to get his case heard again, this time before the Alabama court of appeals. This was probably mostly because it was a death penalty matter. If he had just been sent to prison, he'd probably still be there today. That's the harsh reality of such things.

Finally, in this case, the court eventually discovered that the witnesses against Walter had little credibility. In fact, they eventually retracted their original testimony altogether. It was also discovered that the prosecution *knew* of the instability of this testimony and even of an earlier denial and purposely withheld this information from the defense lawyer. (Isn't that against the law? But of course we're not going to hold anyone responsible for what happened, are we?)

So, now he is out and free again—as free as anybody can be in a country that can so easily do such inexcusable things to its citizens. Remember, you heard about this one because he was an innocent person who managed to eventually escape being murdered by the legal system.

How many do you think we are not hearing about who were equally innocent and are now dead and buried? As Richard Cohen put it, "The law of averages insists that innocent people are bound to be executed and, indeed, scholarly studies indicate that sort of thing has happened." Now you *really* know why the writer of this book does not favor the death penalty.

A little sidelight that might be of interest—the place where all this happened was the home town of the author of the novel and famous movie, "To Kill A Mockingbird," another trial by fury in an old southern town.

DNA to the rescue. Case after case is now being re-examined, thanks to a very special advance in forensic science, DNA testing. Kirk Bloodsworth is one of the many fortunate recipients of this important new advance. He was convicted of raping, beating and strangling to death a little girl in the greater Baltimore area. Even though the unreliability of well meaning witnesses is well known, the authorities were quick to accept the identifications made by three witnesses who seemed to feel that Kirk was the man they saw in the company of the little girl shortly before she disappeared. Kirk had no idea who the child was and swore he had never met her.

No matter. He was convicted regardless and sentenced to death. Then the Maryland court of appeals allowed Kirk a new trial because it was discovered that the prosecution had *withheld* evidence from the defense lawyer about another suspect for that murder. (Here we go again.)

He was *again* convicted! Altogether, he went through two trials and about nine years in prison, waiting to be executed. Then attorney Robert Morin took on the case, after Kirk's appeal of the second conviction was denied. And he asked that important evidence be re-examined using new, advanced DNA testing procedures. That's what finally did it.

It became clear that he was truly innocent, and he was eventually released from prison. County State's Attorney Sandra O'Connor was not about to apologize to Kirk and, in fact, insisted that "everything that was done was done correctly. I am not prepared to say that he is innocent . . . but we do not have enough evidence to convict him beyond a reasonable doubt" (as reported by the Associated Press).

Thank God for DNA. Thomas Webb III became a free man in Norman, Oklahoma, after thirteen years in prison, thanks to DNA tests on old evidence that now finally ruled him out as a suspect in a rape. Kevin Lee Green walked free in southern California after almost seventeen years in prison for a murder he didn't commit, thanks to DNA evidence that linked another man to the crime. I could fill a whole series of books with these examples.

It may be wonderful that this miracle of science makes justice finally possible, but what is of great concern to me is the fact that this also shows how terribly flawed the justice system really is. How many other cases still have not had the opportunity for DNA testing and how many cases really don't have any biological evidence to test in this way?

And what about those who are actually guilty and the DNA tests that prove it are ignored by the jury? (Remember the O.J. trial?) The main thing that the DNA tests have shown us is how undependable our legal system is. You could very easily be the next victim.

Had enough? I've got some more unpleasant stories to tell you, such as what happened to Johnny Lee Wilson. He was a young retarded man who was manipulated into confessing to the beating death of an old woman and torching her house. Naturally he was convicted. Then after over eight years in prison, and a year's investigation by the governor of Missouri, it was realized that a retracted witness statement, the confession letter by another person and other information had relevant meaning in this case. However, the governor's pardon was not at all appreciated by the authorities.

And the battle goes on and on. Then there's the story about Terence McCracken, Jr., who spent four years in prison for a murder he didn't commit. He was accused and convicted of killing a customer at a delicatessen in the greater Philadelphia area during a robbery. The prosecutor hammered home with circumstantial evidence and a mistaken witness who identified him as the killer.

Terence's attorney, John G. McDougall, filed an appeal. He argued that there was compelling evidence that identified a Florida man, who was found with the murder weapon. Also, the witness against Terence was now disavowing his previous testimony. He finally got a new trial and he finally won.

And what about the prosecutors? District Attorney William H. Ryan, Jr., was not going to reopen the investigation even though there was substantial evidence pointing to that Florida man. It's amazing how entrenched those prosecutors can get. It would seem that some of them will never learn (at least not until they are held truly accountable).

Do we really see what we think we see? A young woman hitchhiker was picked up a few miles south of Seattle, Washington, by a bearded man and then taken to an isolated area and raped. The next day the victim was shown a photographic lineup and identified Steven Titus as the perpetrator. Needless to say, he was convicted.

Thank God, a few months later new information came up that suggested an entirely different suspect, one who might be responsible for a number of rapes. When this particular rape victim was shown his photograph she suddenly realized that this man was the *actual* rapist, not poor Steven who was convicted and was in prison.

So, what happened to Steven? He was released from prison, wasn't he? Yes he was. He faced a thoroughly ruined life. He had spent all his money defending himself, had been abandoned by his girl friend, and had lost his job. Then he fought for four long years to try and sue the responsible authorities for what they had done to him. Then, less than two weeks before the civil case was to go to trial, Steven died of a heart attack. Many months later, his estate got a settlement of over 2.5 million dollars. That did him a lot of good, didn't it?

Fixing the flaw. Daniel Goleman made reference to this case in his *New York Times* News Service report on the unreliability of witnesses. He pointed to a, "review of 1,000 convictions of people who were later found to be innocent." He noted that it "revealed that eyewitness errors were the single largest factor, accounting for about half the cases."

He also wrote of new scientific research that was showing notable flaws in the regular methods used by the authorities when witnesses are brought in to identify suspects. He also stated that, "researchers have come up with recommendations for the police and prosecutors that they say should minimize false identifications without reducing accurate ones." So what has happened? Is there a rush to greater accuracy? Don't you bet on it. As Goleman noted, the researchers, "have found it difficult to get a hearing."

Not everybody doesn't care. There are evidently a few who are or were involved in the system and actually do give a damn. It might not seem so very often, but there are actually a few who are deeply concerned with the way things are going. You've read here about some lawyers and even some judges who went to great lengths to get things straightened out.

Not unlike retired San Bernardino, California, municipal Judge James J. McCartney who has finally admitted he wrongly convicted a man (now long since out and gone) and ended up putting an ad in the newspaper in an attempt to locate him and help him to clear his record.

But the process itself (the way things are done) still commands an enormous amount of mindless allegiance. It's an all too human failing that can be seen in many places and in many different endeavors. It seems to permeate both the civil and the criminal system to an appalling degree.

These are only examples of individuals who have finally been cleared. Do you have any idea how many thousands of innocent people are out there in prison or living with a criminal record they never deserved and no one is listening to them? As might be expected, the dysfunction of the system just about guarantees notable numbers of criminals who will go free and notable numbers of innocent people who will be convicted. It is truly one of the great shames in America.

Now have you had enough? I still don't think so. Now I have a very special case to show you. Up to now you have been mostly reading about fairly serious cases involving murder, rape, and other things like that. Now I want to show you how it really is just the tip of the iceberg. As I've noted, there is an enormous number of lesser cases that just evidently aren't important enough to rate media attention but end up railroading innocent people just as effectively as with these other higher profile cases.

This example I am about to share with you is not only a good sampling of the dysfunction of the system in many different areas of a less important case, it also should be particularly interesting to you readers for two very special reasons. One of the reasons is because it is so well documented with very revealing communications. I'm going to keep the other reason a secret until the end of this particular example.

AN IMPORTANT NOTATION: The following example has had to be very carefully disguised. This is not what we wanted. I know, it should be a matter of truth. But, as you know, it's all about how we are forced to play the "game." That's why this has had to happen.

Thus, in the final cut, in order to protect myself and my wife from being stripped clean of just about everything we have, I have had to make extraordinary efforts to hide the identity of the judges, lawyers, and all others responsible for what was done. Therefore, I have changed individuals' names, locations, and just about everything else except of course the relevant events, which are so important in showing you how the breakdown of the legal system manifests itself.

As you might imagine, I would much prefer a fully exposed presentation. That way, any possible reform effort is much more easily facili-

tated. *In a truly responsible society that's the way it would happen. But this is how we are forced to do it, so here we go.*

The "Sometown," Arizona story. So, what is this all about? Well, it's about paradise lost in beautiful Sometown in southern Arizona. It's what can happen when a community loses much of its ability to maintain a reasonable system of law and justice. It's also a shameful situation that shouldn't have been allowed to happen and could have been corrected (and I don't mean through an expensive appeals system).

Many years ago, the victim in this story (whom we shall call "John Doe" for now) was sent, as a child, from Illinois to Arizona to continue his education in that state (as was his brother a few years later). He ended up falling in love with Arizona, as did his parents who came to visit from time to time and later on to see his younger brother as well, when he attended the school.

Eventually the father, who was an executive in a large eastern company, decided to move there permanently and to bring important research and manufacturing elements of the corporation to Arizona. In a way, one could say that little John Doe was indirectly responsible, in part, for the big company coming to Arizona, an event that represented a notable positive impact on the entire state's economy.

As the years went by, John Doe went to California to make his own future. But he always had a special place in his heart for the Grand Canyon state. In April 1995 he returned with his wife, with a little money to invest, and with enthusiasm and great hopes for once again becoming a part of a state he had always loved so much.

He established a little retail store in a shopping center in Sometown, Arizona, and he purchased some acreage in a magnificent, scenic area nearby. He was planning to build a house there. He was planning to come home.

For much of that initial period he still had to remain in California, taking care of things there. He left the store in the hands of a manager. John Doe's wife also went there for a few days every month or so to help out. John and his wife met many wonderful people who live and work in the area. They made many friends.

They also were becoming aware of one couple who ran a concession in that same shopping center. It was quickly learned that the decidedly unfriendly reputation they had was not exaggerated. It was felt that staying out of their way would be enough. It wasn't.

On 9 December 1995, the manager of John Doe's little store's participation in a special little promotion. It involved a live local radio promotion from the shopping center and giving away tiny little samples of genuine Buffalo Burgers. (The folks in the center were inclined to like this sort of thing because it brings in lots of potential customers for everybody—customers who would not otherwise drop by.)

The original confrontation. Needless to say, John Doe's store manager cleared it with the center's Merchants' Association people and even tried to get the unfriendly concession owner to participate in a way that would lead to extra business for them as well. They weren't interested. In fact, they got mad as hell because they thought it might take AWAY some of their ice cream and snack business.

Since they had the reputation of being mad about just about everything and since the landlord had also approved of the event and indicated that he would handle any problems with them, it was felt the promotion should go on as planned. A restaurant in the center didn't feel it would be a problem for them either and, in fact, offered to cook the little burgers for the promotion (which they did). And, yes, it was a very successful event in many ways but definitely not in one very important way. You see, the angry concession owner and his wife went absolutely nuts over this promotion.

He and his wife came into the store and had a fit, disrupting the business and shouting obscenities in front of customers. And, on 15 December 1995, that concession owner even tried to get John Doe's store manager to step outside and fight him during a merchants' association meeting. (He was demanding that the store or the association or SOMEBODY pay him off for what he claimed were his losses during the promotional event.)

On 19 December 1995, John Doe came over from California and was invited to an unauthorized meeting with the angry concession owner, one of his lackeys, and John Doe's store manager. It was a meeting that a fellow we shall call Larry Moe (the lackey in question) was specifically instructed by the Merchants' Association *not* to conduct (as John Doe discovered later).

Since this fellow was inclined to do whatever the angry concession owner told him to do, he put it on anyway (The landlord was nowhere to be found.). Well, it was a disaster. The angry owner slowly raised his temper until he was ranting at the manager. Somebody was going to pay him off. He was determined.

Finally John Doe had enough. He got up, told the consession owner that it was obvious nothing was ever going to be resolved here and that, if he wanted to, he could see him in court if that's what he would choose to do. He turned to leave.

What happened next was like something out of one of those daytime dramas. John Doe ended up briefly near the front of the angry concession owner as he spoke to him for the last time. The concession owner raised his hands rapidly toward Mr. Doe's face. Mr. Doe's instinctive, protective response was to raise his own hands to protect his face.

Then, as John Doe reported his observation of the event, it ended with the angry owner getting up out of his chair (without having been struck, strangled or pushed), and sitting himself on the floor and saying, in a conversational tone, "Oh my back. Call the police."

One time, not so long after the "incident," when both John Doe and the landlord were in the Plaza, Mr. Doe sent word that he really needed to talk with him and that he would be waiting in his little store. He wanted the landlord to defuse this situation, since, after all, he had indicated that he would take any heat generated by that "difficult" couple.

He waited. The landlord never came. He was also unable, later on, to reach him by phone. He also sent him a FAX. Still no response. Everyone could only conclude that he wanted to distance himself from those threatening characters involved in the mess.

After a considerable time, the angry concession owner decided to charge John Doe with assault. The accused managed to hire an attorney we will call Fred Fine. One of his letters to his new client included a correspondence of 26 February 1996 in which he wrote, "Let me assure you, that there is no way that this matter will 'drag out for a year or more.' No court will allow that to happen. Also, you are not entitled to a jury trial in this type of a case."

How interesting. Of course you recall the crystal clear Sixth Amendment to our Constitution, which states that "in all criminal prosecutions, the accused shall enjoy the right to a speedy and public trial, by an impartial jury of the State and district wherein the crime shall have been committed . . ." and so on. In addition, the authorities' actions guaranteed that the case would drag on and on (as it most certainly did, for YEARS) and no jury was allowed. So much for the Constitution.

What happened next was an aborted trial, the unavailability of a tape, a transcript or ANY written record of the proceedings of that first trial and John Doe's lawyer on vacation and unavailable right after the prosecutor decided to try the case yet a second time.

That's when John Doe committed the unforgivable sin of stepping outside of "the way the game is played" to write the following letter (It had become painfully obvious to John that the "game" was deeply flawed and had absolutely nothing whatsoever to do with finding out the truth or allowing justice to occur. It just wasn't working.).

The letter went as follows:

"To the Chief of the Sometown, Arizona, Police Department
and
The Prosecutor, City of Sometown

Gentlemen: July 13, 1996

"This is not only a totally unconventional action on my part, you can be sure that it is also without the approval of my attorneys, for the criminal case (original case #XXXX) and for the additional civil and possible criminal cases involved or soon to be involved. I am convinced that the enormity of the persecutory travesty involved must be once more addressed outside of the adversary 'game.'

"As you may recall (the Chief's name), I spoke with you on Jan. 9 1996. I had talked with your secretary and, later in the day, you called me in San Diego, through my 800 number, which I had left for you to use.

"At that time, I informed you about the long-standing confrontational pattern of behavior of the so-called 'victim' and his truly psychotic determination for a vendetta that had prompted him to set up the staged assault charge (an admitted minor action, even if it had actually occurred).

"I also made it very clear that there were many witnesses to verify all of this, in many stages, from before his current attacks, to the beginning of the current episodes with his attacks on my now-ex-manager, the store, and finally upon me personally. You had only to see to it that the right in-depth investigation be made. You only had to do your job. That was all I was asking for.

"Most unfortunately, your (on-the-scene officer) chose to take a *strongly* prejudicial position against the reality of what actually had happened, even *before* he spoke to either me or my primary witness. (This he even *admitted* on the stand, in the aborted mistrial.)

"As you might imagine, his very limited 'investigation' reflected this predisposition, in spite of the documentation supplied and the urgings that he conduct a thorough and complete investigation. (I know that you are aware that any officer who knowingly and willingly limits himself in such a manner can very easily become a genuine danger to law abiding citizens wherever they may come in contact with him. This has most clearly been demonstrated here.)

"And, as you may recall, (the Prosecutor's name), documentation was made available to you, and my then-manager of our little store, (store manager's name), even stopped by to talk with you personally. (This was also within the general time frame of my conversation with the Chief.) Unfortunately, you were unwilling to consider what was actually happening here, with this so-called 'victim.' For whatever reason, you were rejecting or ignoring what was right under your nose. And what did I want? I just wanted you to do your job, as you were supposed to do it. That's all I was asking for.

"You two gentlemen might also find it of interest to look more closely at other factors other than the 'scam' that the 'victim' has got you wrapped up in. Among the other factors, there was the *arrest warrant* issued against me, because no one seemed to be able to get the addressing correct on the original summons of Jan. 31, 1996. (You *both* had the correct address, as did the Officer.)

"There is also the *erasing* of important *evidence* (from the police dispatcher's tape), and the reported 'victim's' attempts to influence my defense witnesses. And there is the intolerable and totally inexcusable all-day holding of defense witnesses outdoors during that aborted trial. (Can you imagine what that will be like for this summer's *second* attempt at a trial?)

"It should also be noted that I was informed that the vehicle of my primary witness' girl friend (parked in the court area parking lot) had her rear window completely broken out at that time and at that location. And then, of course there was the bungling that almost ended in a mistrial at one point and that finally succeeded at another point. *And now everybody is going to do it all over again?*

"This unbelievable travesty is costing me many thousands of dollars in legal costs, my little store has almost gone into bankruptcy, my wife is deeply upset and my health has been going steadily down hill. (Unlike the 'victim,' who is a body builder and ex-boxer in his 40s, I am 64 years of age and not in all that good a shape.) It is a very simple thing, gentlemen. I have done *nothing* wrong and yet you are blindly cooperating in a process that is *destroying my life*. It is that simple.

"Once before—before that first trial—I had attempted to get you people to do your job and to do it *thoroughly* and *correctly*. Now, hopefully, with unconventionality not withstanding, I make this unique and final request that you both do that in-depth investigation (with an investigator that is free of predispositions) and that *every* aspect of this mess be reviewed with a fine-tooth comb.

"I am sure that the quick and pat answer to this is just to say that you have already done so and have done it correctly. A genuine reality-check shows, very clearly, that you have *not* found out *why* the 'victim's' one fearful and worried witness is saying what he's saying (even with all his vacillations) and you have not spoken with the many other witnesses that can *clearly* show you the actual motive and related incriminating actions and statements of the so-called 'victim,' etc., etc.

"You just simply have chosen not to do an in-depth investigation and you have simply chosen not to put the pieces together and see what's actually there. Remember this, you don't have to believe me. What you do have to do is to do your job—really do it. That's all I'm asking. If you will do this, the truth will come out.

"As a professional writer, I am one who fervently believes in open and honest communication. That's what this letter is all about. I want you to have this final opportunity to clean this mess up yourselves, right now.

"There is probably nobody left in this nation who is not aware of the sorry condition of our American legal system. This is an opportunity for you to really do something right. That's all I ask.

Most sincerely,

The fat hits the fire. When John Doe's attorney finally returned and read the letter, he evidently became quite embarrassed. (As well he and everyone else in that farce should be.) So, what happened next? As John wrote in his continuing journal of the events, "By the time I was surprised with a copy of my attorney's motion to withdraw from the case, he had (unknown to me) supplied it to the judge three days before and the judge had signed it that very day.

"I had no idea this happened. I assumed, evidently wrongly, that both sides of this issue would be allowed an appropriate voice. (I was sick and stuck in San Diego and the case in (Sometown) was expected to possibly go before the court again, in a very short while. His withdrawal created an extreme hardship.)

"I immediately FAXed my side of this problem to the court without knowing it had been already decided. It should also be noted that *the court held up* sending the signed order to my (withdrawing) attorney (and through my attorney to me) *for almost a month*, shortening the time before trial most drastically. This is just one more thing I cannot understand.

It should also be noted that in his last letter to his client, the withdrawing attorney pointed out that, "This will also confirm that at various times the prosecutor has offered a plea agreement to deferred prosecution with restitution and a dismissal after six months. More recently, at the time of trial, he offered a plea of no contest and restitution as well as a release from (the angry concession owner)."

In other words, John Doe will be let off if he pays off. Of course it's not hard to see this as a form of "legal(?)" extortion. And, of course, John Doe wasn't about to cave in. He's just an average guy in many ways but he's absolutely adamant about his innocence and he will never, NEVER pay off just to get out of the mess.

(I understand they were surprised. This sort of thing works on most people. They buckle under and go off with their tail between their legs. Innocence has nothing to do with it. But not this time.)

No one was willing. Next came the eye-opening hunt for a new attorney. I say "eye-opening" because what happened at this point is very hard to believe, and yet it happened. You see, John Doe phoned, wrote and FAXed an enormous number of attorneys, first in that area of Arizona and then in the Phoenix area and finally everywhere in the state of Arizona, trying to find just ONE attorney who would be willing to take the case. (And yes, he was willing to PAY for such services.)

Finally he managed to find an attorney in Phoenix, Arizona, to take the case. We will call him Hadley Bean. He assured John Doe that he had nothing to worry about. He was in charge now, and he wasn't afraid to take on anyone or anything. Great!

Well, not quite. It wasn't long before he began to realize his new attorney was planning NOT to call the vast majority of practically a dozen available witnesses. John was flabbergasted. He tried to reason with him and noted that his other attorney had quite a credible list of witnesses he had planned to call for that aborted trial.

And, while this was going on, the angry concession owner (let's call him Mad Max) was at it again. He was going after the first and only defense witness who had a chance to testify in that first aborted trial (before it was declared a mistrial). It's my understanding he tried to get the witness fired from his job, he tried to get him into a fight and he started claiming that his car was probably vandalized by this witness. He was doing everything he could (short of killing the witness) and, of course, HE WAS GETTING AWAY WITH IT!

The fateful day is set. Finally the new attorney contacted John Doe (on January 8, 1997) to say the court had set January 22nd as the date for the trial, just two short weeks away. So, the attorney asked the court for a later date because of the time it would take to prepare and also because the attorney was required, by a Phoenix area court,

Law and Disorder 75

to be in that Phoenix court on that same day (Phoenix and Sometown are a considerable distance apart. It just wouldn't work on the same day.).

It was one tremendous shock to everyone when on January 17th that new Phoenix attorney had to inform his client that the request for a continuance to a later date had just been flatly DENIED! Now the attorney felt there probably wouldn't even be enough time for the issuance of ANY subpoenas.

As the date approached, John Doe was once again becoming ill (He had been sick quite often over the last few years.). This time it was a matter of not being able to get more than a few feet from the porcelain throne. The situation was not under adequate control when he was due in court so a signed statement of his condition was made available to the judge from the doctor, and the court was asked for a brief continuance. DENIED!

The judge was also informed that the timing and the court denials were such that no subpoenas had been able to be issued. Now, not only would the accused be absent, none of the key witnesses would be available as well. An extension was desperately needed. DENIED!

The unbelievable happens. So the judge and the prosecutor held their OWN little trial, ostensibly by themselves. You see, John Doe's attorney was observed conducting himself in a most limited sort of way, punctuated by observed tomato juice refreshment (during recess) with a strong alcoholic odor. There evidently was next to no representation for the accused in any true sense(The judge was even heard to make a snide remark about the attorney's performance immediately following the trial.).

Of course you'll never guess what the judge's decision was for that short little farce of a trial. GUILTY! (Gee, how did you ever figure that out?) And now there would be the sentencing on February 18, 1997. It was little different from one of those "trials" in Communist China or in Cuba. Only this was right here in America! And it was just the beginning.

You see, John Doe had always done his best to be a very responsible citizen in California. He had gotten involved in many community projects. In fact, he was one of the founding directors of the Pacific Beach Citizens' Patrol, a representative on the formation group for the San Diego County Citizens' Patrol organization, a participant in citizens advisory meetings with the police department and was in all sorts of other activities.

He was no big deal, just concerned and willing to be involved. That was part of his philosophy of life. Good things don't just happen. You have to get involved (And yes, it was pretty lonely out there for him much of the time. Only a few ever seem to want to get involved.).

Now he was A CONVICTED CRIMINAL, and in deference to the various by-laws he himself had helped create, he felt he had to resign from these activities and did so with great sadness. Believe me, this was the beginning of a very dark time for him. Nothing like this had ever happened to him before. He was definitely not the criminal type.

Trying to get help. And now he had to try to find another attorney, and quickly (in order to get an appeal). And he went like hell in every possible direction, as usual, with totally negative results. NO one wanted to deal with the case. NO ONE!

After a while he began to keep a detailed list of who he contacted, what the results were and when. The list alone contained 48 attorneys! And, yes, *ALL* OF THEM TURNED IT DOWN. Except, of course, for the final one whom he managed to get to take it on.

Sound impossible? Well, I've got a copy of that list right in front of me. I also know what a very few of them were candid enough to say with regard to this case. "You want me to bring them to task for what happened. Just you remember we have to go back into that courtroom again long after you're gone." And, "I want complete control of my cases to make sure everything is always played by the rules, no matter what a client may think of those rules" (Even if they BREAK the rules?).

And, "It looks like a complete mess. I don't like having to deal with cases of this nature." And, "You're a thorn in everybody's side right now. That's not acceptable" (John Doe was inclined to think of himself as more of a bur under the saddle. Evidently that wasn't the case.).

Of course those were just a few isolated comments. Most of the attorneys had nothing to say at all, except that they weren't going to take the case. Since there were suddenly so MANY of them taking that position, it would suggest that something is very wrong somewhere, wouldn't you say?

He really had done everything you could think of, before and after the sentencing, to get a new attorney (for his appeal). He got lists from the proper legal associations. He went through every friend he knew in Arizona. He even put a display ad in a Sunday regional newspaper (And yes, I've got a copy of that ad, too. It's real, believe

Law and Disorder

me.).

He also appealed to the political leadership in Arizona and in his southern California area. He wrote to the then Arizona Governor Fife Symington (and never received an answer or an acknowledgment of any kind). He called, FAXed, and wrote to Arizona Senator John McCain's office (to put pressure on the Arizona State Attorney General's office to open an investigation, which the Senator's office attempted to do). He contacted the offices of Congressman Brian Bilbray, Congressman Duncan Hunter, Congressman Randy "Duke" Cunningham and others.

He also wrote to the Executive Director and the President of the Sometown Chamber of Commerce (of which he was a member). And he sent lead stories and executive summations to local and regional Arizona media.

This included the local newspaper (in Sometown), KNXV-TV (in Phoenix), KTAR (in Phoenix), local radio stations in Sometown, Mark Shaffer, *Arizona Republic* (Phoenix), the "Sam Steiger Show" (Phoenix TV show), *The Arizona Daily Sun* (in Flagstaff), and an endless number of others.

Trying for national media coverage. A considerable number of shocked friends told John Doe that he should let the NATIONAL news media know about this. I mean, it isn't every day that an American court decides to try and convict someone without the accused or his witnesses. It's like a story from old Nazi Germany. It would certainly be news worthy, right?

So, phone numbers, FAX numbers, and names and addresses were researched and assembled, and catchy story lines (with good "hooks") were composed, accompanied by checkable summations. These short, to-the-point communication packets were sent to a good number of newspapers and other national news makers such as:

"60 Minutes"-CBS	"Inside Edition"	*Washington Post*
"ABC News"	"CBS News"	*Parade*
"Dateline"-NBC	"Rivera Live"	"20/20"-ABC News
"NBC News"	"Paul Harvey"	Randy Lee-"Stringer"
"Hard Copy "	*U.S.A. Today*	*American Journal*

How many decided it rated some sort of investigation and possibly some sort of coverage? Well, since you've never heard of this case before you started reading this book, you might have guessed. That's right. ZERO! Nobody was even vaguely interested. Not one soul (except for a couple of exceptions that were cut off at the pass).

The only two exceptions. John Doe had the opportunity of talking with Mark Shaffer of the *Arizona Republic*, a daily newspaper in Phoenix, Arizona. Mark was genuinely interested in the story and, in fact, had a run-in of his own a couple of years before with that same individual (Mad Max, the angry concession owner) who had initiated this current trouble. Unfortunately his editor said no. It was not to be covered.

The other exception was Randy Lee. Randy is what is known as a "stringer." That's someone who films, photographs and/or tapes events and such for stations, programs and networks as an independent contractor. He was willing to go to Sometown, to try to cover the sentencing, but neither before or afterward was anyone willing to pick up the story (And, of course, the judge wouldn't allow cameras in his courtroom for the sentencing.). It was not to be covered.

A final desperate news release, sent to the media, made note of the fact that, "During this same time, a dog is given a reprieve from destruction for killing a chicken, mainly because animal rights protests got national and even international print and TV coverage, but almost no one seems to give a damn about a human being in America condemned by a court that functions in the style of Mainland China or Havana, Cuba." That pretty much sums it up.

And why was no one interested? A few were willing to be frank about it. They said, "It's not a high-profile case." and "Many people all over the nation are routinely shafted by minor cases like that. If we tried to cover them, we'd be inundated. We couldn't handle it." Funny how that is. You'd think with it happening to so many everywhere, that fact alone would make one hell of a big story. After all, we are talking about the breakdown of our legal system.

So, what happened? He was just damn lucky to have a number of friends accompany him to the sentencing, including the "stringer" (willing to sit in on his own—without his camera). Since the accused was planning to make a clear stand against what had happened, he knew he might be running the risk of being thrown in jail.

The suggestion of possible media coverage might give the judge pause for thought on this matter. It was his only hope. Maybe the judge wouldn't know that the media actually really didn't give a damn. In any case, John Doe was prepared to face his persecutors with all the courage he could muster.

Then came the fateful day. The journal of the sentencing ran as follows:

Preface

"This is an accounting of comments made and positions taken at the sentencing procedure following the conviction (for assault) in the quick trial that was conducted without the accused (under doctor's care & unable to travel), without the key witnesses (not enough time to get them) and without adequate counsel on January 22, 1997, in the Magistrate Court of Sometown, Arizona, as conducted by Judge (Jim Shaft—as renamed here).

The Major Comments Made by the Accused at the Sentencing

"Mr. (Doe) gave a little personal background and handed the judge a packet containing a number of samples of his awards, commendations, police participations and other responsible community activities (in his home area of San Diego, California). The judge could also see that Mr. (Doe) is a 65-year-old man who has somewhat limited mobility and that the accuser, (Mad Max), a body builder, weight lifter and ex-boxer in his 40s, is a man in excellent health and vigor.

"The judge was also told about (Mad Max's) very well known reputation as a bully who was trying to extort money from the merchants' association, Mr. (Doe's) store or his manager (with his challenge to fight the manager, disruption in the store, etc.), and how he had bragged, according to witnesses, that he would get Mr. (Doe's) manager, his store and/or Mr. (Doe) in any way he could. And, after he managed to get criminal charges accepted against Mr. (Doe), he was heard to brag that now he had them.

"The judge was also informed about how (Mad Max) was going after defense witnesses. It was particularly noted how he attacked (Mark Vital, as we will call him), the only defense witness called in the first trial, before the mistrial was declared. (Mad Max) tried to get (Mark Vital) fired. (Mad Max) tried to get him into a fight. And, he started claiming that this witness had somehow vandalized his car. The judge was told that no one can understand how he can get away with doing this sort of thing and can operate in any way he likes with complete immunity.

"The judge was also reminded that the prosecutor and the judge used, as their principal excuse for conducting that one-way trial, the fact that the case had been dragging on far too long. The judge was then made aware of the four primary reasons for the delays. They were as follows:

1. The case was originally extended for a notable period beyond the alleged incident because (Mad Max) and the Prosecutor waited quite a while before deciding to prosecute.

2. The mistrial, brought about by the abuses of the Prosecutor, added a great deal of additional time to this mess because it brought

the whole thing right back to square-one again.

3. The court's dismissal of Mr. (Doe's) original attorney [very much against Mr. (Doe's) wishes] put the defense in total disarray, since it took so long finding another lawyer, and a bad one at that.

4. Judge (Jim Shaft) was ill (even as the defendant was for a few critical days) and the case was put off for an even longer period of time.

"It was then stated to the judge that it was very unfair to make the defendant pay the penalty of a quick trial, which they conducted almost entirely by themselves, when the big delays were brought about by (Mad Max), the Prosecutor, and the Judge's illness.

"Mr. (Doe) also indicated that legal authorities in California had informed him that the Prosecutor is supposed to be an officer of the court and is not allowed, by law, to suppress evidence favorable to the defense. He then asked what the judge really thought the Prosecutor was actually working so very hard, and successfully, to do.

"It was also noted that, during the trial, the Prosecutor's own medical witness testified that what he felt could be considered as marks on the 'victim's' neck indicated an approach from the rear, not from the front (It is my understanding that this point was made twice.). Since they claim Mr. (Doe) was in front of him, how does this work out?

"And then there was the medical letter (with appropriate test results) showing that Mr. (Doe) had a major cancer operation about 12 years ago (80 lymph nodes and one salivary gland were removed), and he has had notable handicaps ever since, including a left-hand grip that is severely limited (as the documented test results showed). The doctor made it very clear in that document that Mr. (Doe) was definitely not able to do what was claimed.

"It was suggested that the judge would not have to believe either (Mad Max) or Mr. (Doe). All he would have to do is to believe in the laws of nature. He couldn't choke him from the back when he was supposed to be in the front and his medically established handicaps make any sort of choking action absolutely impossible. Just believe in the laws of physics.

"Mr. (Doe) also told the judge that he has had to resign from board positions and police advisory roles and many other community activities in the San Diego area. Mr. (Doe) is one of the founders of the very successful Citizens' Patrols of Southern California, which work closely with law enforcement authorities everywhere.) Being a convicted criminal has done great damage to his reputation and to his life. And it has become an almost intolerable burden on his wife

(Documents were given to the judge which detail these facts.).

"The judge was then told that he now had the opportunity to correct a grievous wrong and that he should make the move to do so because all of this has happened on his watch and, supposedly, under his control. He was asked to dismiss this case, without prejudice and to demand that a professional investigation be opened to determine what actually happened and who is really responsible.

"He was told that it could hardly be possible for much of any kind of truth to ever emerge from any trial that was held by the Prosecutor and the judge and little else. All Mr. (Doe) ever wanted was to have his due process—to have his day in court—to be able to have a genuine case presented for the defense. That's all he was asking for all along.

The Judge's Reaction

"The judge was very angry. This sort of thing was definitely not what he wanted to hear. And he certainly did take exception to the observation that they held the session essentially by themselves. He pointedly omitted saying anything about the defendant not being there or the key witnesses not being there, but he did get all upset over the matter and finally decided to say that he was represented very well and fairly by a competent attorney.

"He made his big point on that issue of the quality of the attorney and must have not taken notice of the fact that there were people in the audience who were present during the actual 'trial' and remember very clearly that, right after the case was concluded [and he had declared Mr. (Doe) to be 'guilty'], the judge said, to the defense attorney, that if you will appeal, do it fast, for God's sake. He also asked the attorney, in front of witnesses, if he'd only been practicing law for a couple of weeks.

"Then, with a degree of notable anger, the judge sentenced Mr. (Doe) to a fine, restitution and a one year probation. GUILTY AND SENTENCED!"

An additional observation. That was the journal of the sentencing. It should also be noted that the judge showed obvious hostility toward the defendant, when looking at the accused and then showing some trepidation when looking at the news "stringer" (whom he would not allow to film the sentencing procedure) and when looking at the others in the courtroom.

It seemed as though the sentencing might well have been quite different if the courtroom was not so well occupied. It seemed the accused may have been very lucky.

And what about the judge? Because John Doe just doesn't play the "game" the way he's supposed to (a game of broken rules, it would seem), about a month later he sent that judge a very special letter. Some of the interesting paragraphs are as follows:

To: Judge (Jim Shaft)
(Sometown) Magistrate Court

Dear Judge (Shaft),   February 20, 1997

I realize this letter will be considered as most unusual. After all, you've done all the damage you can to me and you will, I am sure, be able to do me no good whatsoever from now on. So why am I writing this to you? You could say it's consistent with my communicative nature but, in reality, it has much more to do with my lifetime reverence for and devotion to truth.

"It is something that has always had an enormous significance to me, whether in the quest of science for an understanding of the real nature of the universe we live in or in the search for reality and meaning in our personal lives. It has been my guiding light.

"There is also another reason for sending you this communication. It is my sincere hope that it can somehow help to make a difference for those who follow me in your court. It may be like trying to whistle in a strong wind. It may be a total waste of time, but I must at least make the effort."

Then he wrote of the importance of the material which he had given the judge and he hoped he would actually read it. In other words he was asking the judge to, "... give this man you have condemned, the small courtesy of that much consideration." He also detailed how so much very real damage had been done in the personal lives of those he has negatively impacted with his decision. He also noted that:

"Something that's even more revealing and quite disturbing, is your comments following my statement at the time of sentencing. As you may recall, you took very strong exception to the information I gave that suggested the trial was little more than your own private trial between you and the prosecution.

"That I couldn't be there and that there was not enough time to get the subpoenas to our key witnesses—these facts seemed irrelevant to you, as was the fact that I had the closest thing to no real professional representation at all at that 'trial.'

"And, as you may recall, part of your statement was that I had a fine lawyer and excellent representation. (And I'll bet you didn't even notice the alcohol on his breath when he fawned over you immediately after the trial.)"

Then he was told of the observers who were at the trial as well as at the sentencing, and heard his comments about the incompetence of the defense attorney, immediately following the trial. He was also told about someone who contacted the defendant after the trial who said he too was a similar victim of the man who started all of this. John Doe then declared his innocence in clear and unequivocal terms, and he further wrote:

"I want you to know that, without a doubt, you have done great damage to a completely innocent individual because you were totally unwilling to allow this to be fully disclosed in a proper court procedure. I know. I know. You will cling to what you have done no matter what. But that doesn't change what was done and what was not able to be done and the travesty that resulted. That is a clear slice of reality and it will live on no matter what you say.

"I can only hope that, somehow, you will be able to show the level of maturity and judgement that is necessary to allow you to step back from your own personal ego and to step back from the procedures and technical escapes and other justifications, and will take a long, hard look at what *really* happened here.

"I know it's hard to do this. We get up in years (and I'm no spring chicken either) and we tend to get into practically immutable patterns. It can be very difficult to step back from it all and *really* see what we have been deeply buried in all these years. Believe me, I too, have had to learn to do this and it isn't easy. But it is worth the effort. Trust me on this. As difficult as it is, it is really worth the effort.

"And, as I've said, I can't see how such a revelation in your life can help me at this point but it can definitely have an important impact on all those who follow me in your courtroom. (What happens to other people is something else that is very important to me.)"

Welcome to reality. If this were one of those fictional stories we read once in a while, we probably would be able to finish with the judge finally seeing the errors of his ways, apologizing, somehow reversing his decision, going after the real culprit in this set-up and everybody living happily ever after. Sure. Needless to say, that's not the real world and that judge has never been heard from since, on this issue. And everything else goes on as always, only now even more so than before.

So, what about some of those other efforts that were made? Let's take a closer look at some of them. To start with, let's look at some of the more important communications between John Doe and the Arizona Attorney General's office in Phoenix.

After many attempts to get that office involved, John Doe wrote to Grant Woods (then the Arizona Attorney General) on 3 January 1997 and, in part, said:

"As you and/or your people are aware, I have been in written and telephonic communication with your offices since 6 September 1996 concerning the specific and checkable breakdown in the criminal legal processes in Sometown, Arizona. You were supplied with exact data that you could quickly verify. You were also told of the interest of many others and that you would receive any and all additional assistance that you might request.

"On good authority, we were told to contact you in this manner because you hold the official position and responsibilities of the Arizona state Attorney General. It is everyone's understanding that this represents the position of the chief legal officer of the state government which includes the primary responsibility of overseeing all legal operations and responding to functional legal problems within this jurisdiction. A breakdown in the operation of the criminal system anywhere within the state would therefore be of major concern to your department."

Here we go, trying to tip windmills again. Communications that were received from the State Attorney General's office were noted with the return comment from Mr. John Doe that, "Two letters, absolutely identical and obviously from your standard 'boiler plate' form, were sent to me. One on 5 December 1996 and the other one on 10 December 1996." It was further noted that:

"We can only assume that whoever chose to respond in this manner did not pay the slightest bit of attention to the content of the complaint. Among other things, the letter stated that, 'Our office represents the State of Arizona and cannot act as a private attorney for individual citizens. This means that we cannot offer private legal advice, opinions, or other legal services.' This, in spite of the fact that the complaint concerned the *breakdown* of the criminal justice *system* in the indicated area, and, as stated on the telephone and in my letter of 11 November 1996, that the example in question, '. . . does not need additional support with regard to the actual merits of the case, but rather, there is a most desperate need to have investigation, prosecution and general court functions operate in a proper and legal manner.'

"In other words, I don't *need* or *want* your help for my *case*. What

I *do* need (and we *all* need) is to be able to function within a working legal system, not the bumbling mess that exists there now. We're talking about the actual *breakdown* in the criminal legal system. Now that's serious. And it is everybody's understanding that it is in your area of responsibility for serious and immediate investigative and corrective response.

"Yes, I know, the legal system all over America is crumbling. A fairly current recognition of this problem could well be the national media quote from New York State Supreme Court Judge, Harold Rothwax (on 28 July 1996). He said, 'Criminal justice in America is in a state of collapse. We have formalism and technicalities but little common sense. It's about time America wakes up to the fact that we are in the fight of our lives.'

"A note on the sorry state of our legal system that is a little closer to home might be the one from Beckie Miller of Glendale, Arizona, who was recently quoted in the *Parade* magazine issue of 15 December 1996. Her comment: 'We, all Americans who are truly outraged and sickened by what we have learned of our system, must speak up now and vote to change things.' "

After that, a Mr. MacDonald called John Doe from the Attorney General's office. Following their conversation, Mr. Doe sent a short letter to him which included the following:

"I realize you feel that restrictions on some states' attorney general offices, including yours in Arizona, do not allow for any formal processes to deal with any regional breakdown in the criminal justice system within the state. This is certainly most unfortunate since Mr. Grant Woods holds the title of the chief legal officer for the State of Arizona.

"However, as I suggested to you on the phone, there is an issue of moral leadership here which can be quite effectively addressed by a public request, most likely to an appropriate panel or committee of the state legislature, for an investigation and/or hearing on such matters. Here is where true leadership can show its courage and great strength. Here is where a difference can be made in a legal system that is coming closer and closer to total collapse."

Do we finally end up having a happy ending to this story? Does the attorney general rise to the occasion and help to expedite the changes that are so desperately needed to return law and order to his state? Don't you bet on it. That was the last word heard from THAT office.

You might also be reminded that Arizona Senator John McCain's Phoenix office had really made an effort to get the state's attorney general to move on this problem, to no avail. In other words, they were fully entrenched and unmovable. They were evidently not about to do a damn thing—ever!

And yet another windmill. And then John Doe started hearing how the chief justice of the Arizona Supreme Court was not unwilling to be an activist from time to time, going out and checking on problems within the system.

So, he wrote to Chief Justice Thomas A. Zlaket and received a reply that stated, "Neither the chief justice, any other justice, nor any member of the court's staff can become involved in any case unless that case is before the court in the proper exercise of its constitutional or statutory jurisdiction." Well, I guess all that social activism in the courts is only with the judges that have their own ax to grind. Evidently some will cling tenaciously to what they perceive as constitutional law while others seem more than happy to leave such restrictions behind as they blithely press forward with "interpretations in the light of modern times."

And the "proper exercise" of the "constitutional or statutory jurisdiction" (as they currently interpret it) guarantees the endless continuation of an extremely flawed system and an extremely expensive process as the "game" goes forward. After all, it's the process of the "game" that is of paramount importance, even at the cost of truth and justice. It never seems to change, does it?

How much justice can you afford? Of course if you are rich, you can afford to tough it out in the courts and if you are poor, you might or might not get a reasonable attorney appointed to represent you. If you are a part of the most unfortunate middle class, you will REALLY pay the price.

You will either have to simply give up or you might have to spend yourself into bankruptcy trying to get even a modicum of justice (Let's face it, when a lawyer first sees his client, the very first thing he SHOULD really say is, "How much justice can you afford?" That's right. And as long as that's the question, THERE REALLY IS *NO* TRUE JUSTICE AT ALL! It's a matter of economics and playing the "game.").

No one can do anything. So, what does all of this that we have been going through really mean? The one thing that all of these efforts shows us, in clear and unmistakable form, is that there doesn't seem to be ANY procedure that can be engaged or ANY office that can be utilized to deal with general breakdowns in the overall system of law and order in Arizona (And, from what I understand, in quite a number of other states as well.).

As stated in a final letter to the chief justice and his chief of staff, "My question to you, Chief Justice Zlaket, to the State Attorney General, to the Governor, and to other various elected officials (all who have been asked) is, who can the citizens turn to when the entire system of law and order has broken down in an area and there is a definite and clearly provable current threat to . . . the citizens of that area? . . . Who do we turn to for protection? Do we have to start some sort of vigilante committee? How do we regain law and order?" Good question, wouldn't you say?

Everyone looks the other way. John Doe's letters to the Chamber of Commerce of the area did no good either. The first letter to the Chamber made a request. "My suggestion is that, after verifying the facts presented in the summation, you might care to take community action to expose what has been going on here (and I'm certainly not the only one this has ever happened to), hold those responsible to a full accounting and see to it that mechanisms are in place to make it very difficult for anything like this to *ever* happen again.

In his second letter to the Chamber, he wrote of why he was asking for involvement by the Chamber, and in fact, by citizens of Sometown in general. He wrote, ". . . when there is such a serious, basic breakdown of such a nature right in your own town, who do you think really does have the first responsibility? When there is any important, basic breakdown in *any* local system within *any* community, who do you think should be the first to investigate and take a public position? Each and every community in America is *always* the very *first* line of defense in breakdowns within their communities."

They seemed sympathetic but they very definitely wanted to distance themselves from the whole thing. You know how most people are. If they ignore it, maybe it will go away. Well, it's NOT going away. And John Doe has vowed to not go away either.

A further appeal to the Chamber of Commerce added, "You know, it's not a chance thing that the phrase, 'Land of the free—home of the brave,' always has those two parts closely associated with one another. It's no coincidence. It's that way on purpose. Freedom is lost, little by little, when most of the people no longer have a brave heart.

"I'm asking your Chamber of Commerce, and you personally, to show the kind of courage and sense of community responsibility that built this great nation. It is really not beyond your responsibility. It is truly something you can do. It is something you can end up being very proud of."

A final letter to the Chamber stated that "Yes, you may think that you folks are in some sort of reasonable control, but, as you can see, someone else thinks he has taken over and is proving it by his actions. . . . I ask that the Chamber take immediate steps to regain control and to pursue a full and effective investigation." In other words, John Doe was asking them to show the courage to TAKE BACK THEIR TOWN!

An exercise in futility. Of course none of this has done any good whatsoever. Of course it was a completely useless gesture of a rather naive individual who thought people might want to try to make a difference.

You see, this John Doe is one of those dreamers who was always quick to get involved helping other people. He seems to have forgotten that, most of the time, he was out there all alone (Most people want help when needed but most people will think twice before sticking their necks out for others. Of course there are exceptions to this fact. But, unfortunately, they are truly exceptions.).

Now he really understood, for the first time, why so many he had helped were so surprised and so very grateful for his assistance, as though it was a truly unexpected and a very rare occasion. Rare, indeed. Now he was finding out what it's like to be out there fighting his OWN battle, all by himself, with precious little help from others. Now he knows what it's REALLY like on the other end of such terrible difficulties.

He has now sold his Arizona land. He is closing his store. He will be out of Arizona for good. He will never again try to make it his home. Never again.

He also decided to spend every last penny he has, if necessary, to successfully appeal his conviction and reverse the injustice. And so he did. And the appeal was successful. But what did the higher court do? "It is ordered judgment is reversed and this matter is remanded to the Sometown Magistrate Court for trial." Back to trial AGAIN, for the THIRD time? My God!

And so it goes—on and on. First, the Sometown prosecutor tried to get the next trial held as soon as possible (without adequate time to locate witnesses, now two years after the event in question). It is my understanding that, much to the chagrin of the prosecutor, more time would be allowed.

So the third trial was set for 30 December 1997 with the following day (the 31st) reserved for the additional time needed for an adequate presentation of the many defense witnesses. Well, the other side never gives up either. Next, John Doe is informed that the 30th has been removed as a court date and only the 31st was to be provided. This, of course, would not allow for any sort of reasonable presentation, and they knew it.

Then, the court date on the 31st was canceled and the prosecutor refused to set a new date until later on, sometime in 1998. In the meanwhile, the new defense attorney asked John Doe, after all this persecution for two years and now up to three trials, "Do you know what you're actually being accused of?"

John Doe wasn't really all that sure. There had been so many ever-changing claims in the overall harangue, he just didn't know the full, terrible nature of the official charges. Then it was that the attorney told him, "You are being accused of TOUCHING him. That's it. Just simply TOUCHING him." Well, it's a good thing he hadn't accidently stepped on the plaintiff's toes. If he had, he'd probably be headed for the gas chamber by now!

In fact, he'd better be careful not to even shake the hands of his friends in Arizona. He could end up being charged with SERIAL TOUCHING! Hey, why not. It's no crazier than what has already happened. And it's not so very different from all sorts of other insanities that seem to be going on, on a regular basis, in so many of the courts from one end of this nation to the other.

So what happened next? They finally set the next, in this series of trials, for 6 February 1998-Judge (we'll call him "Coyote") presiding. And the next attorney that was found kept telling John Doe and his wife that there was nothing to worry about. He had everything under control. "Trust me," he repeated over and over again.

That should have been a tip-off, but what actually began to raise the worry level was this new attorney's insistence that it was unnecessary for him to see or interview any witnesses before the trial. It should also be noted that this attorney was given a long and detailed listing of available witnesses but was not telling his client that he was not actually planning to call most of them.

How did the trial go? As you might imagine. The defense attorney bumbled around as though he really wasn't at all familiar with many of the facts concerning the case. He also displayed an enormous timidity in his presentation that was also reflected in his admonishments to the defendant.

He kept warning the very surprised John Doe not to show any sort of expression on his face at all. He was told that could be very bad. He was also told that he (the defense attorney) must limit his presentation because he didn't want to "aggravate" the judge (in his words and before witnesses at one point).

Now the defendant was REALLY getting worried. It proved to be a fear well founded. The defense attorney let the whole thing slip right through his fingers, and while that was going on, the prosecutor evidently decided a doctor the defendant INSISTED be brought in from California to testify about the defendants handicap (which prevents him from choking or strangling anyone) might be somewhat persuasive.

So what did the prosecutor do? He played down the idea of choking and strangling and decided to go more for the idea that the defendant somehow pushed or otherwise managed to get that poor Mad Max on the floor. Sound like a less than honest thing for a prosecutor to do? Of course it does. But you see, that's what many prosecutors do.

When a truth comes out to show that something claimed could not have happened as charged, they often don't bother to consider what this means, they just go off in another direction. If they can't get 'em one way, they'll get him another. The hell with the truth (That's the way the game is played.).

More of the disgusting details. As the trial zipped along, the lack of appropriate witnesses became more and more apparent. As the prosecutor questioned the defendant, he asked (on page 195 of the court transcript), "So we can anticipate numerous people coming in and explaining that fear that he instills in them?

John Doe had to answer, "It was suggested by counsel that this might not be necessary. I assume that's what was intended. I don't know. I have to go along with what all you people do, because I'm no expert here. I don't know."

Further along, on page 206 of the transcript, the prosecutor was continuing to probe about defense witness supportive testimony that he could see was not going to be there when he asked the defendant, "Are any of those people going to be testifying here today besides Mr. (Mark Vital)?" The answer was, "I was told that it wouldn't be necessary. I don't know. There doesn't seem to be, . . . I'm not in control of that."

And that's the way it went. The witnesses just weren't called. So, what did the judge say, at the end of the trial? On page 260 of the transcript he said, ". . . there was no reason to believe, based on the testimony, that Mr. (Mad Max) would have fallen out of the chair. He has testified himself that he didn't put this thing on and play-act his perception on the other side that he did that. The court is not convinced that he did that."

And on page 262 of the transcript the judge further stated that "... I don't buy the testimony that he staged it and that he very carefully put himself down and did that." That is the end result of not having the several witnesses called who could have very clearly showed his promise and predisposition to do just that.

It should also be pointed out that in his infinite lack of wisdom, Judge Coyote decided that a responsible doctor's live medical testimony and appropriate medical test documentation was somehow completely irrelevant (I would hate to have to come before him with scientific evidence to show that the earth isn't flat. I'd probably lose.).

Oh, and you notice there was an actual court transcript this time. That's because the defendant paid the very high price for a court reporter. It seemed to be the only way such a record could ever be dependably made.

And what about Mr. Mark Vital, the defense witness that Mad Max did his best to intimidate after that first aborted trial? He was put on the stand, and it was very clear that his presentation was now a pale shadow of what he had reported in that first trial. No small wonder.

And the results of that trial? GUILTY! What else would you have expected? And the defendant was also forced to pay $1,516 in restitution to Mad Max for unproven medical claims. And, as the judge said, "... with the understanding that if you appeal you don't get it back."

About the prosecutor. A number of concerned individuals, in Arizona and in California, expressed amazement that such questionable and minimal charges would be retried again and again. We are told, on good authority, that such things are seldom continued on, over and over again, unless, of course, the prosecutor has developed some sort of personal motivation.

Was there anything that could have motivated the prosecutor in this manner? Yes, there was—a number of things. The first could well have been when he mucked up that first trial to the degree that it was declared a mistrial. As you might imagine, the prosecutor was not at all amused with the way things turned out (If looks could kill, Mr. Doe would have been struck dead right then and there.).

The second situation was that rather embarrassing letter that John Doe sent to the Sometown Chief of Police and to the prosecutor. Remember that? It was accurate but it definitely wasn't what the prosecutor wanted to see. It truly exposed him for what he is.

And then, remember the statement that Mr. Doe made before

the judge, during the sentencing of that second trial-the trial they ostensibly conducted among themselves? The judge was told how some of the delay was actually brought about by the prosecutor.

John Doe also informed the court that he was told by legal authorities in California that a prosecutor is supposed to be an officer of the court and is not allowed, by law, to suppress evidence favorable to the defense (Mr. Doe had presented information that suggested this is actually what may have happened.). Then he asked what the judge really thought the prosecutor was actually working so very hard, and successfully, to do.

When it was the prosecutor's turn, he was furious. It's really a shame that the proceedings were not being recorded by the court. It was a real eye-opener, believe me.

During the third trial there were a number of episodes where the prosecutor evidently became further humiliated and, therefore, further angered. One (on page 201 in the transcript), when the prosecutor was cross-examining John Doe. The prosecutor made the mistake of bringing up the defendant's charges of endless foul-ups by the authorities.

Mr. Doe's answer was to reaffirm by saying, "This case is just filled with foul-ups. And I think I mentioned some of them here, including the one where *you* had my address, and the police department and the chief of police talked to me personally, and had my address. But somehow, nobody had the address right. So it (the summons) went somewhere else. And then a warrant was issued for my arrest because it didn't get to the right place!"

Another example was on page 215 in the transcript where the prosecutor was trying to nail down some information as an exact quote where it was clearly not an exact quote. Mr. Doe's answer to the prosecutor was, "Well, I know you're not a writer. So I'll have to explain this to you. You'll notice it's not in quotes. It's not in quotes because it's not a direct quote. Therefore, it's not a direct quote."

Another example was on page 221 in the transcript where the prosecutor was trying to show, by demonstration with the accused, that a claimed reach was not possible. The accused asked the prosecutor to, "Lean forward and put your hands up quickly, and show me what you get."

Evidently without thinking, the prosecutor did this and proved Mr. Doe's point. He immediately saw what he had done and began to do a slow bake.

Another example was on page 222 in the transcript where the

prosecutor asked, "Isn't it true that you have no evidence of Mr. (Mad Max) ever physically assaulting anyone?" Mr. Doe's answer was, "None that can be admitted in court today. It's beyond the ten-year period."

The prosecutor continued to hammer on the issue. "You don't have any arrests or convictions of Mr. (Mad Max) or—" To which John Doe answered, "There are things that are beyond the period where they're allowed in this court. And so we really can't touch on that, or you'll get another mistrial. You had that once before like that."

Now the prosecutor was getting quite upset, as you might imagine. How dare an uppity witness put the prosecutor down in such a manner. He's going to regret that, right? Right!

A final example (page 224 in the transcript) was when the defendant had the opportunity to mention the previous trial, thanks to the prosecutor's wandering questions. Among other things, Mr. Doe noted, ". . . that was the case held this last time, where the judge and you held this without my witnesses and with me home in bed, unable to get here from San Diego. You held it by yourselves."

Well, you can imagine that went over like a lead balloon. And it certainly showed at the end of the trial when the prosecutor did his very best to do just about everything but have the defendant drawn and quartered. So, what does all this mean? It most certainly does bring up the very strong possibility of a genuine vendetta, almost from the beginning of this sad affair. Everything does seem to point directly to that conclusion, like it or not.

The interesting aftermath. So what happened when the latest trial was over? Mad Max wanted the unsubstantiated compensation that he was awarded—a payoff he had been looking forward to—and he wanted it right away. However, something either the clerk told him or the prosecutor told him got him very angry. You'll find that what happened next is hard to believe. But it happened. It really did.

The courtroom was empty, except for the defendant (now a convicted criminal), who was trying to get his papers all back in his rather small briefcase. Mad Max (the accuser) roared past an employee of John Doe's store who was there at the trial. She reported that he went by in a state of extreme agitation, spouting expletives and barged back into the courtroom, heading for the unsuspecting defendant.

When the defendant turned around and spotted Mad Max with his angry face and clenched fists, he had stopped several feet from John Doe. This was because others (the defense lawyer, an investigator, etc.) had noticed what was happening and rushed back into the courtroom to escort the defendant safely out of the area.

What did he have in mind? There was no one else there and there was nothing for him to pick up. What was he thinking of doing? Was he hoping to punch out the defendant and then claim he was defending himself? Who knows?

The incident certainly does show just how totally blind the court system can be. There he was, right there in the courtroom trying to start it all up again! And yes, a letter was sent to the judge about the incident.

Was anything done about it? Was the judge going to check it out and perhaps reconsider his decision? Of course not. That's not the way things work. In fact, the judge was never heard from again.

And what about the lawyer? The defense attorney was no better. He tried to convince the hapless defendant and his wife that he had won and should go home and be happy. In a letter to the attorney (Shifty Sam, as we will call him), of 16 March 1998, John Doe wrote, "I cannot find any way at all to imagine a Reckless Assault conviction, with a court-imposed cost of over $1,000, as equating in any way or by any stretch of the imagination with the winning of that case. I just can't imagine how you could say that I won anything."

And then after going over some of the things that attorney did and didn't do, the convicted man told of others he had shared the letters and documents with who had some very pointed comments to make. "... frankly, you would be amazed at what most of them suggest. They seem to feel that either someone had gotten to you or that you are an incredibly stupid attorney.

"Well, to tell you the truth, I don't like the thought of entertaining either one of those ideas. Possibly you can tell me what *really* happened to you? I think this really needs to be understood, don't you?" And of course, as you would have expected, this question was never answered by that attorney.

The sad search for another lawyer. Finally, after another frustrating search, an attorney was found in the Phoenix area that I will call "Ben Barred." Then, after almost a month (although he certainly must have realized the clock was running for any filing) and at a cost of $900, he sent his evaluation.

John Doe's reply included the following: "The most infuriating comments in your letter include, '... I do not believe there are any errors in the trial worthy of appeal.' You then support this contention with your statement, 'Nor do I have any reason to conclude that your attorney's conduct was not adequate.'

"You've got to be kidding! You mean to sit there and tell me (with a straight face) that my attorney's unwillingness to call the most crucial witnesses, the judge's own comments about the lack of witnesses concerning (Mad Max's) intent, the attorney's unwillingness to confront clear and provable falsehoods when they are presented, his unwillingness to interview or even talk to any of the few witnesses before the trial, that he did finally put on, his unwillingness to present any sort of aggressive defense, his unwillingness to follow almost all of the requests and requirements made by his client, and his filing of a false statement as part of his successful effort to bail out after the trial, . . . you mean to tell me that with all of this, my attorney's conduct was adequate? Is *that* what you are saying?

"If this is what you really mean, I can only conclude that you feel this is an acceptable level of representation in the state of Arizona. If this is so, you have much in your state to be greatly ashamed of, and you know it."

On other matters, John Doe also noted that "All along I have simply needed to know what was required of me and what the time clock setting is, since the filing of that Notice of Appeal. My previous attorney wouldn't tell me, and you seem unable to tell me. Do none of you know? Is there no one who knows what's going on?

"I also found it very interesting when you told me that I do not have the right, through the 6th Amendment of our Constitution, where I am supposed to be allowed, '. . . the right to a speedy and public trial, by an impartial jury of the State and district wherein the crime shall have been committed . . .'.

"I recall you said something about a Supreme Court interpretation of the 14th Amendment somehow eliminating this clearly stated right in the 6th Amendment. Frankly, I have read the 14th Amendment over very carefully and I just can't imagine how that could be possible, except through a repeal of that Amendment (the 6th) by way of 'judicial legislation.' Is that what happened?

"It seems to me that the American justice system has one hell of a lot to answer for. It also seems to me that American attorneys have a great deal to be ashamed of. It's too bad they're not about to disturb the cash-cow and show the courageous heart that is necessary to give our country back to the people. What a shame." And, of course, there was no answer.

You'll never guess what happened next. You'd think that last shot across the bow would be the end, wouldn't you? Well, I doubt if there'll ever be an end, and what happened next is a damn good example of just how sickening this whole thing is getting.

On the evening of 12 May 1998 the Merchants' Association

meeting was held, primarily to try to determine how the mandatory association (reinstated by the landlord) was going to operate. This is the group involved with the center that both John Doe's little store and Mad Max's concession are in.

As usual, Mad Max and his wife were making life difficult for most of those present. Finally a much older man in his 80s who can hardly get around without an electric cart, did his best to stand up and take one or two hesitant steps toward Mad Max, as he argued with him (It was his way of trying to emphasize his point.).

Mad Max's wife then got up and became very upset, saying that the old man was going to attack her husband! It shocked everybody. Were they going to try to do it all over AGAIN? At first, it certainly looked like it.

Mad Max immediately saw the reaction of the group and ordered his wife to sit down. I'm sure he must have realized there were far, far too many witnesses for him to control. It was, most certainly, the wrong place and the wrong time. But it was too late. Just about everybody got the message, not that most of them didn't already know what those two were like.

Actually, it seems just about everybody in that area knows about those two and what they have been up to, and has known it for a long time. And yes, if the police had been willing to investigate, they would have known all about them, too. And yes, the Sometown prosecutor was told about them. He knew the truth, but for reasons we may never know, he just wasn't interested.

A not so surprising revelation. There's also a rather interesting fact about this John Doe that you might already suspect. You see, he writes under the name of "Jonathan West" and, over eight years ago, he began to start to gather material for a book.

About five years ago, he started the most intensive part of the research and writing. And what is this supposed to be about? It's about the breakdown of so many of our nation's most important institutions AND, IN PARTICULAR, WITH OUR LEGAL SYSTEM.

It is truly an amazing quirk of fate. Little did he know that he would end up becoming one of his own best examples of this breakdown. Little did he know that he would end up telling his OWN story in these pages, and then reveal that the John Doe who went through all of this is actually the writer of this book (Fate does have some very strange twists and turns at times, doesn't it?).

You probably guessed it before the story got to this point, right? Well, if not, you know it now. And so do the citizens of Arizona. For the first time, they know what their media was not willing to tell them about what has been REALLY going on. And the rest of you around the country should also realize that there is an absolute MOUNTAIN of similar situations that nobody ever reports, ALL OVER THE NATION!

And this massive problem will continue to get WORSE until there is some way the people can find out what is happening and they also become willing to roll up their sleeves and, with a courageous heart, start to make a difference! Will it happen? Don't hold your breath waiting.

Of course I could be pleasantly surprised. Citizens all over the state of Arizona, and in other parts of our nation as well, could become concerned enough about the legal system to force their state legislatures to open major public investigations, and to make sure it doesn't end up as window dressing or maybe just a little cosmetic surgery. MAJOR CHANGES *CAN* AND *SHOULD* BE MADE! Let us settle for nothing less.

And what happened in my case? I'm still a convicted criminal in the state of Arizona. It's still one big mess, as are so many other legal problems in that state. Frankly, with the way things are now, what I consider to be court assisted looting is the name of the game—a terrible statement to have to make, but I'm convinced it's absolutely true. Let's hope that changes.

And what about Arizona? Well, the new Governor, the new State Attorney General and/or the state Legislature can most certainly move to investigate this and the many other similar situations. This writer can and will supply the actual names and full details to any qualified official investigations. This can be done. Let's see what happens.

Let's hope the new people in office in the State of Arizona will be just as upset with what has been going on as you and I are. These things didn't happen on their watch. Both the "Sometown" case and the "Everson" case (and so many others) occurred before their time. They most certainly can investigate. They can put a stop to this sort of thing.

It's just a crying shame that the way the law works, names must be changed to protect the "privacy" of those who did these terrible things. But we must remember, that sort of thing fits in perfectly with the dysfunctional concept of the "game" over "truth." It's one more thing that needs to be changed.

A look at the pattern. You should also be made aware of the fact that the pattern of behavior of Mad Max is not unique. It can be found repeated in communities all over our country. I know of two such examples in San Diego. I have been told there are a number of others from coast to coast.

A number of behavioral scientists are aware of this pattern, as are some of the authorities. In the more enlightened communities, such people are not allowed to get away with it. It is, in this writer's opinion, rightfully considered as a criminal act to use the court system as a tool of extortion.

Unfortunately, far too many criminal authorities are not found to be notably enlightened concerning this problem. You must learn to understand that you will often have to FORCE an acceptable level of professional behavior onto such people and keep a close eye on them AT ALL TIMES. Permanent citizens' groups charged with monitoring responsibilities on such issues are one possible answer. What do you think?

Where we've been. You've been rudely reminded of our national debt, our government misconduct and mismanagement, crime, drugs, the tax burden, our government's drift to oppression, and the massive breakdown of our legal system. You've been told about how a well-functioning legal system is one of the most important factors (if not THE most important) in any successful, civilized society. We talked about our lack of heroes, about not having leaders we can trust, about our collective lack of values. We talked about a lot of things, didn't we?

We speculated as to what it would be like if the folks of half a century ago were suddenly transported to the nation we have become. You learned about the "gradual syndrome." And you took a hard look at the constitutional breakdown with legislative interpretation in the courts. And you read important quotes from authorities on all these matters.

Yes, you were exposed, more than you ever would want to be, to the extensive breakdown in the civil court system, with some eye-opening examples. And you got a good taste of what the criminal court system is really like, with the guilty getting off and the innocent getting convicted. You got a real taste of the disorder in the courts.

If you haven't got a good idea about the breakdown of our legal system by now, you're hopeless. If you've got the idea, and you realize the seriousness of it, and you haven't decided to take action, you're worse than hopeless—you're actually a big part of the problem! And I mean that! All of this is, ultimately, *our* responsibility—yours and mine!

In the next part of this book, we'll be dealing with the various elements that are the responsible factors, such as the lawyers, the enforcement, the courts, the incarceration arrangements, and YOU. By the time you have managed to pick your way through the irresponsibilities to the end of this next section, you'll find yourself headed for an area where we all can actually become a part of a meaningful force that can DEAL with the breakdown and its responsible elements.

It may seem like there's a lot of droppings to shuffle through before you can get to a winning horse, but believe me, it is absolutely necessary. The first thing one must be willing to do, if one is to solve a problem, is to DEFINE that problem. That's what we're doing right now. We are, most unmistakably, laying it out in clear-cut examples. When we are through with this, there should be absolutely no doubt as to what must be dealt with.

That's what this book is all about. It's here to get us informed, get us moving, and to start us making quality changes. It's all of these things and more if you will let it be so.

So, keep your seat belt on. You may even want an air bag for what's next. But hang in there. It's what must be put on the table. Then we can get down to business. Are you with me? I hope so.

Part Two

The
Responsible
Elements

Chapter Six

The Lawyers
A Distasteful Problem That Must Be Faced

This is where we begin to get into the nuts and bolts of the system, and I can't imagine a bolt that drives us nuts more than the lawyers, so that's were we'll start.

Lawyers have a long history. Shakespeare didn't have kind words for them. They didn't fare well before then and they haven't done all that well since. History tells us that most of the lawyers in Colonial America were Tories (in support of the British during our revolution). That figures.

Alexis de Tocqueville visited America in 1831 and observed that "hidden at the bottom of a lawyer's soul one finds some of the tastes and habits of an aristocracy . . . they conceive a great distaste for the behavior of the multitude." And in 1978, *Time* magazine featured a front page story about them with the title "Those *+*#!! Lawyers!"

I certainly don't need to show you how most folks feel about lawyers today. It's very obvious, even to the attorneys. Our humor reflects this. You know how it goes. "Do you know the difference between a toad in the road and a lawyer in the road? There are skid marks in front of the toad." There's the one that tells us, "It was so cold last winter, I even saw a lawyer with his hands in his own pockets." Or, "What's the problem when you've got a lawyer buried up to his neck in cement? Not enough cement!"

Then there is the story about the two ex-convicts. One decides to study hard and become a lawyer. The other one decided to go straight. I also heard that once a stranger approached Will Rogers in his hometown and asked him, "Do you have a criminal lawyer in town?" It was said that Will answered with, "Lot's of us think so, but nobody's been able to prove it yet."

And then there's the one about the sign in the attorneys' restroom in the courthouse. Wiley Miller's "Non Sequitur" showed it to us. It reads, "Wash your hands of any responsibility before returning to the courtroom."

I also recall what I am told is a true story about a Beverly Hills newspaper that decided to start a column entitled, "Great Deeds by the Attorneys." They did their best to solicit stories of worthwhile acts by lawyers. How many came pouring in? You guessed it, not even one. So, they promoted the effort even more strenuously than before. Finally they got one little story about one lawyer in another county. So, they printed it and that was the end of that bright idea.

What we're up against. I recall a gentleman from Squaw Valley who wrote to "Dear Abby" to say that he had an experience recently in a store that worried his wife a great deal. It seems a little girl came up to him crying and grabbing at his pant leg saying, "Daddy!"

His immediate reaction was to pick her up, and bring her to the checkout stand where an announcement was made on the PA system to find one or the other of the little girl's parents. The mother came and everything was just fine, but when the man got home, his wife was deeply concerned and said he should never have touched the child. He could be sued and, of course, there was even the possibility he could be jailed.

Sound far-fetched? Not at all. You've read the example cases I've given you, haven't you? That's right. You want to help a child, but everyone from unthinking authorities to greedy lawyers and clients seem very quick to target anything that moves.

Another example. I also recall a little San Diego hand-out magazine that's involved with computers. It was called the "Byte Buyer," which makes sense because a "byte" is a technical term that represents a measurement of coded information, the life-blood of computers. The term is used quite a bit in the field, as you might imagine, and is a word that is incorporated in a number of products and services that are related to this specialty.

No problem, right? That's what you think. There is a national magazine that decided to call itself "Byte" some time ago and evidently decided to claim some sort of possession of that word, as though it truly belonged to them.

Never mind that it is a technical term which has been used within many phrases, titles, and such. And never mind that you can't copyright or otherwise protect such a generic technical term. "Byte" magazine's lawyers threatened to sue the little "Byte Buyer" publication unless they changed their name.

So "Byte Buyer" changed it's name to "Computer Edge," not because they felt the big magazine owned that word, but because the little magazine just couldn't afford such expensive litigation. (Let's hope somebody doesn't think he owns the word "edge.")

Lawyers are threatening all sorts of lawsuits of this nature all the time. And all sorts of folks are buckling under simply because they just can't afford to go to court to prove they are right. They simply cannot afford justice.

Once again, how much justice can you afford? It's been estimated that at least 70 percent of the world's lawyers live in the United States. The last time I read an accounting of the numbers, there was claimed to be well over 600,000 licensed attorneys in America. And yes, there are a few of them who are genuinely trying to do a good job for their clients in a system that they're not all that fond of either. But there are also plenty who see the enormous flaws as the goose that lays most coveted golden eggs.

Many of them are not all that good at what they do anyway, except when it comes to billing. They do almost always seem to find ways of charging enormously exorbitant fees, beyond almost any profession you might care to compare them with.

And what are some of their tricks? Well, there's that song and dance of attorneys lowering client's expectations so that anything the lawyer gets will look like a job well done. And there's that great money-making technique of farming out cases to other lawyers for a "forwarding fee" or other considerations.

There are the lawyers who give the research and the paperwork to secretaries and paralegals and charge their clients as though they did that work themselves. Then, let us not forget the lawyers who love to bury the opposition in a veritable paper blizzard. Handling all that paperwork racks up time and therefore makes piles of money for attorneys on both sides.

Another trick we see a lot of is the lawyers who shuttle between private practice and working in the government in one area or another. Once he's supped at the public trough, he's invaluable back in private practice again. Now he's got all sorts of influential contacts. Now he can pull all sorts of strings for himself and for his clients, whom he charges handsomely for the service.

How have they done, serving our country in public service in Washington? Frankly, we have never had a time in our history when so many lawyers have been so deeply involved in one kind of scandal after another from the Nixon years to the Clinton administration. They are a public shame.

A hard look by the experts. Donald Robinson wrote a thoughtful article for *Parade* magazine way back in 1974 entitled, "How Well Do Lawyers Serve the Cause of Justice?" The observations and revelations are just as timely today as they were then. Clark Clifford (advisor to several presidents) was asked to comment, in the article, on the statement that, "Some authorities claim that three out of four general trial lawyers are so incompetent they shouldn't be in a courtroom."

Mr. Clifford's answer was that, "It's only too true. The British are much wiser than we. They divide their bar into two parts. They have solicitors who are the office lawyers, and specially trained barristers to do their trial work. We let any lawyer conduct a court case, and the results can be calamitous."

Another question asked if the bar associations were willing and able to police themselves. Tom C. Clark (a former Associate Justice of the U.S. Supreme Court) had an interesting answer. "Some years ago, I was asked to head an inquiry into the effectiveness of efforts by lawyers to discipline themselves. After a thorough investigation, our committee reported that the situation was 'a national scandal.' It still is." Yes, and the band-aid cosmetic touch-ups they do today only serve to bury the problem that much deeper.

An inevitable question was about the high lawyers' fees and "that only the rich or the near rich can afford justice." Yale Law Professor Joseph W. Bishop, Jr., commented that, "Lawyers' fees are getting so high today that even the rich sometimes squeal." Then he noted that "it's the two-thirds of the population in the middle that have the most trouble. If they are sued, they cannot defend themselves. They can't afford a lawyer. If they get involved in a criminal case, it can mean bankruptcy." Like they say, talk is cheap, until you hire a lawyer.

The problem is even greater today. Sure, sometimes some expended criminal defense funds get returned to innocent individuals. Most of the time their financial positions, their standing in the community, and their lives in general are in ruins. Sometimes just verdicts come down in civil courts with appropriate awards. However, the mechanisms for collection are woefully inadequate. Quite often the poor soul is left with little more than a piece of paper—a piece of paper for which he has paid dearly.

A hard look by the public. Frankly, almost all Americans are absolutely *fed up* with lawyers (and even a few of the lawyers are fed up as well). Even surveys by *The National Law Journal* keep showing that our respect for lawyers is not very good at all. (Gee, how did they ever figure that out?) One poll seems to have come up with a final figure of two percent with regard to public respect of attorneys.

Has all this animosity really been earned? Yes it has. You see, even the lawyers who agree that the system isn't working right and is often very unfair and impossibly expensive—even the attorneys who realize that justice is only just a word, they are not to be found at the barricades, shouting for major changes, angry and insistent that extensive transformation must occur and it must start right now.

A few suggest a band-aid or two. And some of them seem willing to do at least a little free work for some of the most unfortunate among us. And an even larger number express sympathy. Of course none of this is really all that threatening to the income level that this absolute mess tends to generate for the legal beagles. And none of what any of them seem to have suggested or have done shows the level of courage and unselfishness that is absolutely necessary if truly important major change is to occur. *They just aren't doing what is necessary!*

But don't think you can blame it all on the lawyers. This is supposed to be *your* country, remember? *You're* supposed to be in charge. If you don't like the way things are, you really can make meaningful changes. (That is, you can if there are enough of you out there who give a damn and are willing to make the effort. Just remember, there are a lot of fat cats out there who are counting on you not being willing to make that effort.)

A hard look by the lawyers. There are actually some lawyers who are not happy with what they are doing. In California, the Institute for Civil Justice conducted a survey of state lawyers for the Commission on the Future of the Legal Profession and the State Bar. The results of that survey are most interesting.

It would seem that a considerable number of lawyers are not at all happy with the legal profession as a career choice but precious few of them are willing to support any reforms that might make it better. And there have been other surveys and similar answers. So, here we are. That's how the majority of them feel about it. They're not *about* to make any *real* changes!

The cost. Even when you don't have to go to court personally, it's costing you. California taxpayers paid over $5.6 million for the retrial of mass murderer Juan Corona. That's not surprising. A U.S. Census Bureau survey showed that California lawyers earned a whopping total of $16.3 billion in 1992 alone. It goes up from there.

The Legal Reformer (a HALT publication) suggests that the average citizens' attorney retainer fees can be $5,000 or more and with an hourly rate of anywhere from $150 to $300 and up. As the publication has correctly observed, "most people find themselves priced out of the legal system."

All this reminds me of the joke about the lawyer who says to his client, "If you didn't commit those robberies, how are you going to be able to pay me to prove you're innocent?" Then there's the one about the guy who points a summons at a hapless citizen like a gun and tells him, "This is a very expensive frivolous lawsuit. You have only two choices. You can spend many years and a small fortune defending yourself, or we can settle this right now, out of court." Either way, he's been held up. And then there's the one about lawyer's fees being so high that, instead of hiring a lawyer, now it's actually cheaper to buy a judge.

It has been estimated that with most Americans not being poor enough to receive the sometimes available free legal aid and not being well off enough to be able to afford a lawyer, "we can't have a system of equal justice and access to justice by everyone equally." That's what Phyllis Goldfarb tells us from her professorship at Boston College Law School.

As an Associated Press story tells us, "A study by the American Bar Association found that 1 million civil legal problems a year among low-income Illinois residents were not being addressed. Only 20 percent of the overall need for civil legal help there was being met."

The legal aristocracy. From his position as the HALT Executive Director, Leonard Steinhorn had this to say. "The legal profession today is a closed system that protects its privileges, guards its right to regulate itself, and doesn't let anyone else police it." (HALT is a national, non-profit organization dedicated to the reform of the civil legal system in America.)

The profession has also sandbagged itself behind a solid wall of specialized language that is clearly designed to exclude those who are not a member of their elite group. My definition of their legal language (as described in their own style): terminological inexactitude through an often non sequitous labyrinth of polysyllabic nomenclatures.

Such a group must use whatever means are possible to destroy any and all those who would dare to offer any of the simpler legal services that could be given to the people at a reasonable rate. The HALT publication "Americans for Legal Reform" put it well. "If you provide a service for a fee, think of the economic advantage you'd have if you could put your competitors in jail . . . That is exactly the kind of power the legal profession holds—and exercises to its advantage—in America today."

Believe me, there are quite a few disquieting stories about very capable ordinary folks just trying to offer a little bit of paralegal assistance—helping people to fill out forms or do other simple legal tasks for a very reasonable fee—that are being put out of business, are under criminal charges and are sometimes being thrown in jail.

There's the case of Rosemary Furman in Florida and Robin Smith in Oregon and Dennis Ridderbush in Wisconsin. There is even the Texas Attorney General who sued an Ohio self-help book publisher. He had put out a book that helps people to save money with living trusts. There are numerous others.

Answerable to themselves alone. You should also realize that a notable number of state bar associations are mandatory-membership organizations (for *all* lawyers) and, in most states, are the only professional group that is answerable to themselves alone. They regulate themselves! That means they don't regulate themselves worth a damn! As a HALT "Attorney Discipline Survey and Report" showed, lawyer-discipline systems nationwide are slow, secretive, lenient, and unresponsive.

You should also consider the Reuters report from New York which noted that "most lawyers who have been disbarred for wrongdoing, from robbing banks to abetting murder, are readmitted to the profession when they reapply." The news service was referring to a seven-month investigation by the National Law Journal. The investigation also indicated that Pennsylvania had the highest readmission approval rate of any large state and Nevada held the record for the fewest lawyers disbarred (per capita) of any state.

It would seem that de Tocqueville was right when he spoke of our system as rigged to heap enormous benefits on the lawyers, who have truly become the wealthy aristocrats of our society. Many other writers and social philosophers have discovered this, too.

Chris Goodrich went to law school to find out what went wrong with the legal system and what he discovered went into his book *Anarchy and Elegance: Confessions of a Journalist at Yale Law School*. The *Nolo News* review of his book noted that "law in America has become a shell game designed by lawyers for their exclusive benefit. Recently, even the legal establishment is waking up to the fact that all is not well with the practice of law." The review observed that "his book peels off layer after layer of professional pretension and shows how a group of America's brightest, most ambitious graduate students end up worshiping at the altar of fear and greed."

Other books you might consider are *Lawyers and Thieves* by Roy Grutman and Bill Thomas, *The Terrible Truth about Lawyers* by Mark H. McCormack, *Lawyers on Trial* by Philip M. Stern and *What You Aren't Supposed to Know about the Legal Profession* by Laurens R. Schwartz.

The looting of the people. Well, whatever they do, they go for the big bucks. In 1992 alone, the savings and loan bail-out agency (RTC) paid $251.5 million to almost 2,000 law firms for their activities in the cleanup of the S&L thrift crisis. In one recent year Dalkon Shield awards were over $200 million.

There were also the smaller cases, like a woman with a .35 blood alcohol count who was riding in a cab and got the driver to pull over to a spot where she felt she could "relieve" herself. It was nighttime and she was drunk. She staggered around and fell through some bushes and down a small embankment. So what did she do? Why, she sued the owner of the land, of course, and she is reported to have collected an out-of-court settlement of $555,000. Fair? Of course not.

What about the attorney who shocked the city of Los Angeles with a bill of almost $1 million in legal fees for winning a judgement against the L.A.P.D. for only $44,000. And there was the case of the little old lady of Escondido, California, who was taken to the cleaners by an attorney while she was fighting for her life against cancer.

And there was the San Francisco Foundation (for the needy of Marin County) that went into the civil courts to try and change certain area requirements for aid disbursement. The way things worked out, they not only lost their case, it cost them approximately $10.1 million in lawyers' fees.

That's one hell of a dip into that charity, so much so that even other attorneys became incensed by it (Wow!). As attorney Robert Gnaizda indicated, "You had an army of 110 lawyers plundering an unguarded hope chest that was supposed to be for the poor." As he also said, in no uncertain terms, "It's a judicial and legal disgrace."

This writer also remembers a particular *Forbes* magazine issue that listed Joseph Dahr Jamail as the highest paid lawyer for that year with his earnings of at least $450 million. The magazine called lawyers the champions of the greed game. We have a federal appeals court decision that declares a twenty-five percent contingency fee charged by lawyers who help clients collect their Social Security benefits to be "inherently reasonable."

When one division of government (Social Security) screws up, another division of government (the courts) sees to it that the redress is generously shared with the attorneys (who are like a government unto themselves). What a deal! According to the *Nolo Press,* "Stephen Magee, from the University of Texas, has calculated that every lawyer costs the U.S. economy $1 million a year." This was from a study originally reported in the *Los Angeles Times.* It has also been reported that the claim of incompetent trial attorneys is now the most popular last-minute appeal made by convicted murderers.

The great refuge for the inept. As Timothy Hallanon, pioneer of legal training on interactive videodiscs, says, "Most lawyers are poorly equipped to begin practice when they pass the bar. They spend their first few years as apprentices at the expense of either their firms or their clients."

Of course there are also those like Oregon state Chief Justice Edward J. Peterson who was quoted in testimony before an ABA commission as saying, "I guess that being incompetent is not a violation of any ethical rules." Well, it certainly is in quite a number of other fields.

Judge Wayne E. Alley of Oklahoma City has gotten so disgusted at times, he has been known to say such things as, "If there is a hell to which disputatious, uncivil, vituperative lawyers go, let it be one in which the damned are eternally locked in discovery disputes with other lawyers of equally repugnant attributes."

U.S. Chief Justice William H. Rehnquist once said as part of his comments about those who plead before the Supreme Court, "It may be the attorney general of a state, the senior partner of a law firm, the head of some department who has done none of the work on the case in the lower courts but who is either too busy or too slipshod to truly digest the brief from which he is arguing." And he rightly added, "This seems to me inexcusable."

Rehnquist also has spoken about the profit motive turning the practice of law into a business, which has left many lawyers dissatisfied and perhaps less trusted by their clients. More than "perhaps," you can be sure. While sitting as the U.S. Chief Justice, Warren Burger was reported as having said that possibly up to one-half of the lawyers who appear in the American courts are incompetent. This was reported in *Time* magazine, among other places. He also spoke about how lawyers, judges, and law professors have developed a fascination with procedure (and to the exclusion of the concept of truth and justice much of the time).

You might say Burger had a tendency of making mincemeat out of inept attorneys. He reportedly told an American Bar Association meeting in Las Vegas that public opinion has put lawyers near the bottom of the barrel. If you read this book very carefully, you will discover that quite a number of very high level judges and other very prestigious individuals have finally come to the conclusion that the American legal system is, indeed, a real mess.

And what are the lawyers' answers to all of this? Well, the American Bar Association did hire a $170,000 media expert to try and mend the legal profession's public image. Beyond that, expect little more than window dressing and band-aids. I've got to tell you, this is just not a nice bunch of people. If it was otherwise, they'd be raising holy hell trying to get major, major changes in the system. They'd be turning it upside down. You can see what they're not doing. You know the answer.

Chapter Seven

Law Enforcement—
The Good and the Bad
What's Right and What's Frighteningly Wrong

Don't forget, in the next two parts and at the end of the book you will have a good chance to explore all sorts of things that can be done to reverse this nightmare. Meanwhile, we need to continue to take the necessary first step, which is to clearly and accurately define the problems with good examples. Let's face it, you can't really deal all that well with something you haven't properly defined. Once you know the territory, you can start to change the landscape.

Now it's time to cover the next element of this complex system we dare to call the American system of justice. It's time to take a look at enforcement and prosecution. You've already read a number of stories that have shown you how terrible these areas of responsibility have gotten for an ever growing number of innocent Americans. So, let's take a closer look at these functions.

A little bit of history. It has been suggested that the concoction of gin by a seventeenth century Dutch chemist was at least partly responsible for the development of formal, professional police forces in the Western World. This was the first hard liquor, and it really did a number on a number of the less responsible citizens of the time. Subsequent drunken brawls and other terrors forcefully established the need for controls and soon the first municipal police forces were established. In the New World, the first police force was established in Boston in 1837. These efforts were also felt to have been strongly encouraged by the economic and social disruptions that followed the Napoleonic wars in Europe and the Revolution in America. (It was a time of many trials and tribulations.)

It then became a problem of developing a delicate balance between the desire for personal freedom and the need for a force that necessarily creates certain restrictions on some of the less responsible manifestations of that freedom. Part of the answer was seen in the need to make the new force as professional and responsible as possible. Part of the answer was seen in making the police authorities accountable for their actions.

In harm's way. And through it all, we must remember that most of us live in at least a partially safe environment because some have been willing to face extreme danger in the thin blue line. For example, from 1794 until 1991 there were 511 police officers killed in the line of duty in the city of New York. In Chicago it was 443 officers killed in that time period. In Philadelphia and Detroit, the number topped the 200 mark.

Those are National Law Enforcement Officers Memorial Fund statistics, and although the carnage of law officers has gone down a little since then, it is still a deadly issue. (Just two years after the above exampled period, 150 police officers were killed in the line of duty in the United States in that year.)

Part of the problem is the courts (as if you hadn't guessed). One National Corrections Reporting Program listed the average time served for violent crimes in America. They were as follows: Murder—eight years; rape—five years, robbery—three years and three months. So it would seem that the greatest crime of all is the turnstile perpetuation of crime by the court system itself!

Why are our streets so dangerous? Changing social attitudes, drugs, the breakdown of the legal system (as strongly exampled in this book), and the growing use of high velocity and automatic assault weapons by the criminal elements—these are some of the reasons why. We're talking about the Israeli Uzi, the AR-15 (remodified for fully automatic fire), the AK-47, and similar weapons. And we're also talking about peripheral items such as extra large ammunition clips, bullet-proof vests, night scopes, two-way radios, and laser sights.

The cost. Now the police (when they can afford it) are having to upgrade their weaponry and their training. Needless to say, the criminals are fully participating in this arms escalation. It's a war out there.

Frankly, sometimes the police can't afford to upgrade all that much. And, sometimes, in some places, they can't seem to do any more than to just hold on by their bloody fingernails. That's the way it was in the once-bankrupt town of east St. Louis, Illinois. The police were in really bad shape. The patrol cars were old and often broken-down; most of the cars didn't even have working two-way radios; many times the paychecks had to be held up for up to six weeks at a time. (It's much better now, thank God.)

Through it all, there are a considerable number of the officers that really do try to do their very best and in the fairest and most professional way. And they put their lives on the line every single day that they go out there in the streets. Every day they do that so you can live a little bit safer.

I will never forget a poster of New York's "Patrolmen's Benevolent Association." It showed an officer lying prone in the street. The caption read, "You wouldn't sacrifice your life for a million bucks. A police officer does it for a lot less. Please help us make New York safe for all of us."

The United States is a nation of laws;
badly written and randomly enforced.

—Frank Zappa

The dark side of law enforcement. Unfortunately, there are also those attracted to the law enforcement profession who are slipshod in their work, cruel in their actions, and corrupted in their hearts. This has been and will always be a problem. It is one of those things we must vigilantly address at all times.

I'm sure you remember that Rodney King fiasco with the amateur videotaping of a beating that clearly had nothing whatsoever to do with the normal restraint of an unruly suspect. And that other one somewhat later, which showed an officer shoving a suspect's head through a window? And what about the handcuffed woman who was struck by an officer in the Newark, New Jersey, area? Someone caught that one on tape, too.

John Wheeler, the man who made this last video, had quite a time of it. Immediately after the taping he went to the police to tell them about it. He reported that they told him to leave or face the possibility of being arrested. Then, after a couple of weeks of trying to get some attention by phone, he made a copy of the recording and went to see the department's internal affairs division. Finally that blew it open.

There was yet another Rodney King type of event with Los Angeles helicopter news crews shooting the pursuit of illegal immigrants across southern California, ending with the clubbing of two of the people beside their vehicle. Riverside County Deputy Sheriffs developed that little drama. It included one deputy taking two-handed swings with his baton against a subject who was prone on the ground and obviously completely helpless.

I saw that video and studied it very, very carefully. So did a number of others. Millions more saw it on TV. So, what happened? It was decided the deputies would not be charged. How is that possible? The way U.S. Attorney Nora Manella put it, "The government would have had to prove beyond a reasonable doubt that (the officers) acted willfully and with the specific intent to deprive Enrique Funes or Alicia Sotero of their civil rights."

What we all saw very clearly was a totally unnecessary physical attack on an unresisting and unarmed man and woman. As one of the defense lawyers put it, "I don't know what it takes for a police officer to be prosecuted, but if this isn't it, then our society is in a terrible state."

And then there's the case of the female motorist who got roughed up by a South Carolina highway patrolman and the whole thing was caught on the patrolman's automatic video system, mounted on the front of his patrol car. That wasn't very smart of him, now was it?

Sometimes there's justice and sometimes there's not. You probably realize that retribution doesn't automatically happen, but once in a while we get a surprise. One such surprise was the charges brought against four sheriff's investigators and three former prosecutors in Illinois for fabrication and/or concealing of evidence that had two men on death row for the killing of a girl.

And there's those two former Massachusetts detectives who were finally caught and admitted responsibility for a string of crimes that seems to have netted them several hundred-thousand dollars. (What's the maximum on this? It seems to be around three years in prison and something like $100,000 in restitution. Cheap at any price, and they could be out a lot sooner than you might imagine.)

But then there was that monster, Jeffrey Dahmer, who "used" and then disposed of at least seventeen or more boys and young men before finally being stopped. You might also remember the little 14-year-old naked Laotian boy that the police allowed Dahmer to "reclaim," even against the pleas of concerned neighbors.

And there was that police scandal in Philadelphia where well over 100 convictions had to be reversed because it was discovered that some of the officers had planted drugs on suspects, falsified police reports, and stolen money from the hapless suspects. Not unlike another police officer in Los Angeles who admitted forging a key document in a case that also involved other officers and other cases—over 100 cases by many estimates.

Playing the drug game. It has also been observed that evidently some officers or peripheral personnel have mastered the mysterious arts of a magician. In Cypress, California eleven pounds of cocaine turned into baking soda in the police department's evidence room. It was cocaine that had been borrowed from the Fullerton police department for use in a "sting" operation.

Also, in southern California, two Los Angeles sheriff's deputies from an elite drug unit were discovered skimming drug money and laundering the stolen cash. They were found guilty, as was former Detroit Police Chief William Hart for embezzling $2.6 million from a police fund.

Three sergeants, twenty police detectives and patrol officers, and a number of former officers were arrested in Cleveland in what was described as an extensive bribery scam. Then there was that Harlem police scandal in New York involving a dozen officers accused of turning their precinct into an enormously profitable drug center.

Trying to reverse the trend. In the last few years, a number of enforcement agencies have really begun cleaning house. The effort is being made, and they are getting results. That's what we've been seeing. But the determination for vigilance must continue because, as we all know, the police do have to be recruited from humanity and not all of the inappropriate are spotted during the screening process.

Also, what about the Riverside, California, police refusing to respond to a home alarm because the woman didn't have a permit for the alarm system. The woman was beaten and raped.

(Since the incident, the police decided to respond to *all* alarms—just as there are now some changes in procedures and attitudes in the departments involved in a number of other cases exampled here. But there are those that don't change and the many that are yet to be exposed.)

There is the growing use of computers, some right in the squad cars, which can help enormously. They are also being used extensively to better facilitate fingerprint identification. There are even newer I.D. methods—everything from profile generation to DNA identification. There are new and better methods of electronic surveillance.

It must also be said that there most certainly are some procedures and methods that need a great deal of improvement. Forensic lab operations have sometimes been shockingly inferior to what they should be; lie detectors still are truly very unreliable, and, most important of all, the many new advances and improvements in most equipment costs an arm and a leg and then some. These are very real problems.

I remember that "Front Line" documentary on PBS television entitled, "My Husband Is Going to Kill Me." It was a chilling exposé. Three weeks after 30-year-old Pamela Guenther begged for police protection from her violent husband, he killed her. We certainly hope a great number of changes occurred after that, all over the country.

The border-line cases. I'm sure you've read the headlines. You know about the minor war that's going on at our border between the United States and Mexico. You're aware of the constant stream of drugs and aliens that have been and are still invading our nation. You're aware of the shooting attacks on our border patrol agents from across the border.

The Center for Immigration Research has stated that San Diego County is also the deadliest county in the nation for illegal aliens coming across the border into America. This author has visited that no-man's-land, and I can tell you that it is truly bad news down there. (Expect that zone to change, from time to time, as the authorities rush about trying to contain the problem as best they can.)

It got so bad that, at one point, the San Diego County Board of Supervisors declared a state of emergency and even asked for troops to be brought in. Appeals were sent out to President

Clinton, the then California Governor Pete Wilson, and U.S. Attorney General Janet Reno. There was no rush for any rescue. Our troops are often believed to be better employed in other parts of the world. They do seem to be just about everywhere, except in our own inner cities or at our border with Mexico. It would seem we must protect others first and foremost, before we protect our own.

There has been some effort to take back *some* control at our border. Of course every time we do something right, we seem almost sure not to do it in a full, comprehensive way, and it's often offset in every manner possible by all sorts of reverse actions (like our removal of the intense patrols in the national forest area near our border—a vitally important area that needs to be covered).

Are we ever going to get things under control? We don't seem to be able to get a whole lot of anything under control. Our government has the historic tendency of doing little, or nothing, or the wrong thing until time and circumstances have reduced our choices down to the point where there are absolutely no good choices left. (When some troops *are* brought in, there seems to be a tendency for the Pentagon to get them withdrawn as soon as possible.) So much for that.

How the government makes victims. Whatever happens, it always seems that the innocent become the victims, over and over again, as a result of the ineptitudes of the authorities. A good example is a legal extortion that occurs in a number of places around the nation when a person's vehicle is stolen. Often, when a victim's car is stolen and then recovered by the authorities, it is picked up by a contracted towing and storage firm and put in one of their holding lots.

Some time later (sometimes *much* later), the victim is informed of the vehicle's recovery and discovers that they cannot get it back until they pay a healthy fee for that towing and storage, which can sometimes mount up to a considerable sum. (I know of a little 10-year-old motor scooter that ran up a bill for more than a thousand dollars in "recovery costs.")

Why does everyone seem to put up with such ransom demands? Do you realize that there are some folks who just can't afford to get their cars back and they are sold out from under them at an auction to pay the fee? It's a case of the car being stolen once and then a *second* time with the approval and help of the authorities. I'll *never* understand why we put up with this.

There is no end of the ingenious ways the authorities have found to turn victims into victims all over again. In many areas around our nation, parked cars have become the innocent victims of drive-by shootings, hit-and-runs and other criminal mishaps simply because they just happen to have been parked (legally) in what ended up as the wrong place at the wrong time. But that's not the end of it.

One example I was told of involved such a parked car that the authorities kept at the scene for a considerable period of time while they tore the vehicle apart, getting at the stray bullets imbedded therein. The owner was simply told to come back later to claim what was left.

When he returned, he found the police had done one hell of a job destroying his vehicle and then, when they got through and left, vandals and thieves finished the job. What was left was hardly worth hauling away to the junk yard.

Were the authorities held responsible? Were they willing to pay for his loss? No! The authorities were only just doing their job. They felt no responsibility whatsoever for what they did—none at all. And similar events occur almost everywhere you look. I wonder when *your* turn is coming.

How about that case in New York when Diego Encalada bought a vehicle at an auction of confiscated autos and, three months later was arrested for possession of a stolen vehicle. He showed the cops the documents that prove he had bought the vehicle legitimately at a city auction. Did that do any good?

He was jailed until his arraignment, which turned out to be one hell of a nightmare to endure. Sure, eventually the charges were dropped. But there was no rush to give him back his vehicle or to give him his money back. After all, nobody is really held responsible in any serious way for what they did to him, right? So, why make an effort here?

There's the case of the stolen identity. The authorities claimed that Patricia Samms is really a lady named Gomez from Salem, Oregon, who owes the state of Oregon almost a thousand dollars for support costs of three children. She has had one hell of a time convincing the authorities that her name was never Gomez; she has never been to Salem, Oregon, and those three children are definitely not hers. Don't laugh. It could happen to *you* next.

There is the case of a 70-year-old lady of modest means in southern California. Her bank (Wells Fargo) made a mistake in her check's magnetic numbers and so her check bounced. The D.A.'s office went after her and tried to force her into an expensive check enforcement "reeducation" program. She had to get an attorney and went through an enormous amount of difficulties. (The authorities hadn't ever bothered to check the integrity of the magnetic numbers.)

Government warfare against its citizens. Everyone has heard all about the horrendous handling of the government sponsored confrontations at Wounded Knee, Waco, and Ruby Ridge.

My concerns are not so much a matter of who might have been right or wrong concerning the original issues. What is of greatest concern is the absolute unwillingness of the authorities to use a little intellectual creativity and to take advantage of clearly obvious openings that were available in the early stages of these serious conflicts.

I am also reminded of so many frightful scenarios like the small DEA army that converged on a home in a quiet Poway, California, neighborhood. In the middle of the night they smashed into the home of Donald Carlson, a computer executive, looking in error for some sort of cocaine stash.

Once they'd broken through and gotten in the house, Carlson had come fully awake, frightened out of his wits by what seemed like one of those violent home invasions by a gang of robbers. He grabbed a gun, intent on self-defense. He was shot in the leg. He retreated to his bedroom and tried to hide. More shots were fired at him, wounding him in the back and in one lung.

He was in intensive care at death's door for many weeks. All because the authorities had made a mistake. A questionable informant had given them erroneous information. This same sort of thing happened to a retired minister in Boston. This time the victim, Accelyne Williams, died of heart failure as the result of what came down. And yes, this sort of thing has happened a number of time across this nation. Could *you* be next?

As Peter Alan Kasler wrote in *American Survival Guide* magazine, "they killed innocent people like poor Mr. Ballew, who died sitting naked in his bathtub when they kicked-down his apartment door . . . they even taunt innocent folks while they terrorize them.

"Like Agent Donna Slusser, who, on May 25, 1994, during a bogus drug raid at an honest American couple's home, deliberately stomped to death their cherished Manx kitten and kicked its body under a tree while the horrified couple watched." Mr. Kasler further noted that during that raid, "Agent Slusser and her fellow agents ransacked the couple's home and even dumped out all their cancer medications."

Yes, these events have frightened so many, a few even did the unthinkable. They demanded that this sort of behavior be stopped. As a result, this sort of thing doesn't happen quite so often any more. At least for now. *But it still happens!*

Even the F.B.I. had slipped. A San Francisco area employee of the federal government had alerted the bay area passport office that Theodore Kaczynski was at that moment applying for a passport and that he might be the unabomber. That moment was well before he was finally caught. Was it the passport officials or the F.B.I. who blew this opportunity? We don't know.

But we do know that an F.B.I. official has admitted purging the Ruby Ridge report. We know that the agency's once-great crime lab was tainted. A Justice Department investigation charged that areas of the lab had been contaminated and that some lab reports were made incorrectly biased in favor of prosecutors. It was also charged that some of the supervisors in the lab lacked proper scientific training.

We also know that the F.B.I. had to grudgingly acknowledge that it did falsely accuse Atlanta security guard Richard Jewell of the olympic bombing and that the agency wrongly provided the Clinton White House with very confidential files of over eight hundred former members of the Bush Republican administration. Sounds like another kind of "Watergate," doesn't it?

What about the F.B.I. van that was stolen with all those assault weapons? Never mind that the contents were eventually recovered. How lax had things gotten that F.B.I. agents, gathered for special SWAT training, should have such low security with such dangerous items?

In Arizona, a former police officer was reported to have easily gained access to printouts from the F.B.I. data bank. He used the information to track down an ex-girlfriend and then he murdered her. Just one more problem for a federal agency that has, in the past, had a well-deserved, excellent reputation. (It is my understanding that the F.B.I. is working very hard to raise its professional standing back to what it once was. We hope that's the case. It's very important.)

Everywhere you turn, it's the same thing. Almost everything seems to be falling apart! Even with the corrections that sometimes do occur and the appropriate prosecutions that also have been occurring more frequently, the difficulties seem to still be far greater than our willingness to eradicate them. We really have a lot of work to do on these problems, believe me.

And then there's the Grand Jury. The idea is reported to have started under Britain's King Henry II way back in 1166. At various times it seems to have been first, the guardian of the citizens and then an infamous handmaiden of an oppressive government. For years, at its best, it was a format for investigating and reporting objectionable misconduct, particularly of an official nature. In America in colonial times such juries sometimes attempted to protect the citizenry from the tyranny of the Royal Will.

In America today, these juries are supposed to go after the bad and the seriously incompetent wherever they are, even in our own government. In a sometimes limited way, they even manage to actually do that some of the time. However, due to the juries' limited authority, limited ability (and sometimes limited courage) and most often because the public is seldom roused to action anymore, these Grand Juries do seem quite limited for the tremendous tasks they should be about.

Part of the problem may be that one can expect that most, if not all, grand jurors are nominated by judges and then the names are selected in a random drawing from this group and then they're often directed by a D.A. Since most of our problems have their basis in the non-functional or poorly functional legal system, that's like putting the fox in charge of the hen house. You shouldn't be surprised that no major, comprehensive investigation for extensive revamping of the legal system has thus far occurred through the efforts of such juries.

Reality vs. eyewitness identification. The Knight-Ridder News Service has reported that experts tell us identifications in criminal cases by eyewitnesses are wrong as many as four out of ten times. And one report states that people are inclined to misidentify others as much as a little under half the time!

Others just say it is very common to get wrongful convictions due to such misidentifications. And, Philadelphia criminal lawyer Glenn Gilman was quoted as saying, "Ninety percent of the eyewitness identification cases result in guilty verdicts when I'm sure a far smaller number should."

Truth and justice seem to be the victims in an unacceptably large number of cases. In human terms, this means enormous injustices, sometimes at a cost of innocent lives. Believe me, that really does seem to be the way it is.

And then there's the witness protection program. Knight-Ridder also reported the story of a frightening fellow by the name of James Red Dog. He tied a woman up and raped her repeatedly and, to top it off, slit the throat of her 30-year-old son. Who was this "Red Dog?" Why, he was a four-time murderer under a witness protection program.

It's that old story of how some violent criminals can sometimes "rat" on other criminals in prison and then cut a deal that gets them released, and in his case, into a well-protected witness program. In this instance he was very well protected, but the public had no protection at all. In other cases, the protection doesn't seem to be working for important *innocent* witnesses that sometimes end up dying.

It's like that case in the L.A. area of Gloria Lyons who was shot to death before she could testify that she had seen a gang member kill someone for a small amount of rock cocaine. There was no real protection for her at all. Frankly, it's often because most authorities really can't afford the expensive relocation that is often necessary. No wonder so many refuse to testify. They want to *live!*

And then there's the District Attorneys. The inventor of a very special vacuum tube, Lee De Forest, had a lot of trouble with a district attorney. His new tube was an important eventual component of radios, television sets, early computers, and even radar. He certainly knew what he was doing, and he was trying to sell stock to the public in his Radio Telephone Company.

In 1912, an East Coast district attorney charged Mr. De Forest with mail fraud because De Forest had said (in print) that it would be possible to transmit the human voice across the Atlantic. The DA was convinced that the notion was totally absurd and misleading. He railed about De Forest hoodwinking the gullible public into purchasing his stock. (Luckily, in this case, the father of radio was acquitted of the ridiculous charge.)

This example serves as an excellent sample of how many DA's and other prosecutors become single-mindedly obsessed and totally wrong. They can completely lose sight of their actual purpose of seeking out the truth. You've read a number of illustrations of this earlier in the book, as you know, and there are, as you might imagine, thousands of other examples that might be given, if I wanted to make this the size of an unabridged dictionary.

It's become a huge problem with many district attorneys, city attorneys, city prosecutors and others cut from this same cloth. It has actually been suggested that such prosecuting attorneys must be held just as personally responsible for what they do as the rest of us are out here in the real world. (My, what a radical thought.)

Short-circuiting justice with plea bargaining. I am reminded of the case of the lawyer, Henry Ramirez, who admitted having sex with a 14-year-old girl and then was allowed to plead guilty to a misdemeanor. That case is no anomaly.

The statistics show that in a majority of criminal cases, the accused doesn't really go to trial at all. His or her court appearance is usually just a matter of pleading guilty to a lesser charge as his or her "deal" with the authorities for being willing to plead guilty. (A good example of this is the nasty little joke about "swallowing the gun." It's an armed robbery pleaded down to unarmed robbery.)

Back in 1977 Robert B. McKay, former dean of the law school at New York University, was quoted in *TV Guide* magazine:

> An ever-present risk in plea bargaining... is that a person guilty of a serious crime will be let off with an inappropriately light penalty, or that a person guilty of no crime will plead guilty to an offense he did not commit because of undue pressure or just to end the uncertainty. These problems are not unsolvable. Plea

bargaining need not be limited to the attorneys; the negotiations can and probably should include the judge, the defendant and the victim where possible."

This still totally ignores the uncomfortable fact that the whole concept of plea bargaining is a clear rejection of the basic search for truth. Being properly charged for one thing and then making a deal for something else, makes a complete mockery of truth. It could actually be called a form of perjury. McKay, and the majority of the others in the profession should not be at all surprised to find that they are having trouble with many who are let off lightly and others who are unfairly penalized. When truth becomes the victim, justice can be expected to go right out the window.

You and I are not the only ones disgusted with this practice. It has already been thrown out or severely limited (sometimes permanently and sometimes not) in a number of places. Places like Portland, Oregon, and Ulster County in the state of New York and the state of Alaska and in other locations have outlawed plea bargaining. Too bad it isn't really catching on to a much greater extent.

Way back in 1976, Bert Pines, then city attorney for Los Angeles, charged that the bargaining between prosecutors and defense attorneys over sentences in return for guilty pleas undermines public confidence in the criminal justice system. I couldn't agree with him more. A plea bargain is no more than an agreement to perjury.

Chapter Eight

Self-protection and the Return of the Vigilante
A Nightmare Revisited

*Security is mostly a superstition.
It does not exist in nature ... life is either a daring adventure
or nothing.*

—Helen Keller

It certainly has become one devil of a situation, hasn't it? UPI reported not so many years ago, "One out of every three women ... will be raped." That's what Susan Murdock said (when she was director of the Women's Martial Arts Center of New York). Among her sources for that information was the FBI and the accepted estimate that only one out of ten rapes is ever even reported. (Other crimes are believed to have a low report rate as well.)

As you know, things then got even worse. Since then many police departments have set up special response teams and individuals who are specially trained to assist neighborhood block watch efforts by the citizens and other similar community efforts. Since then some things have improved a little bit.

Learn and survive. There are also countless demonstrations given and training sessions being held all over, helping people to better protect themselves. This sort of thing is particularly helpful for women, children, and older people. Those are the profiles that are most often sought after by those big, brave muggers and rapists. They don't often choose those who look and act as though they are more able to protect themselves, to run fast, or to know best how to get help quickly.

Now, more and more of us are getting into self-defense classes. There are also special senior citizen workshops, like Security Training for Older Persons (STOP) that was started up in the L.A. area. There are numerous school projects to show the kids how to identify and deal with potentially dangerous threats out there in the real world. And there are special community seminars being conducted to show how to make your home, your business and your vehicles more burglar-proof.

Easy access is considered primarily responsible for at least half of the burglaries. That's a fact that was brought out in a report by the Census Bureau for the Justice Department's Bureau of Justice Statistics. (As you may have noticed, statistics you read in this book come from professional research efforts.)

It has also been made clear that if you show high awareness and energy, a vigorous response and look like you know exactly were you are and where you are going, you are far less likely to be selected as a "mark" by a mugger or some other deviate of society.

Do-it-yourself law and order. It should also be said here that more and more folks are taking direct and dangerous action. As you might imagine, sometimes this seems to work out just fine. Sometimes the whole thing ends as a tragedy. It can cut either way, in either direction. You just never know 'till it happens.

James Taylor, a Florida construction worker, spotted his recently stolen car in a shopping plaza. He went home, got his revolver, came back, shot out a tire and held the driver until the police arrived. In California, Russ Hall spotted his recently stolen car and followed it to where he was able to apprehend the thief, and with the help of another person, held him until the police arrived.

Even the famous get into the act. Remember when the actress Jennifer Beals decked a hapless mugger in New York? The man grabbed for her purse and she put him down with a good punch. I'll bet he'll think twice about doing that again. Way to go, Jennifer!

How about that 92-year-old Kansas City lady who used her .22-caliber pistol to send a would-be burglar on his way in short order? And there was that 85-year-old lady from Muskegon, Michigan, who was facing rape and ransacking. She was able to get her hands on her late husband's gun and riddled the assailant. He already had assault convictions and was up for trial on another home-invasion charge. The courts didn't seem to be able to stop him, but Alberta Nicles certainly did.

In a number of places around the country, neighbors are working with law enforcement and other local government officials to "persuade" landlords to evict tenants who are dealing drugs. If they can't convince the landlords, they use various state laws and local zoning and/or health ordinances to take the situation firmly in hand. (If the various neighbors and officials are inclined to really understand the problem and cooperate, it really works.)

Some folks have gone to much greater lengths to solve these law-and-order problems. A group of Korean-American residents in the Los Angeles area had a very serious security problem that the local authorities didn't seem to be able to handle. As one of the leaders, Yohngsohk Choe, was quoted as saying, "If you wait for the bureaucracy to do something for you, you will wait until you die."

So, what did they do? They raised more than $400,000 to turn an abandoned bank into a new station house for the police department. Then they went forward to raise another $1.2 million or so to pay for operations. Yes, it would seem at least some of these *new* citizens haven't lost their willingness to pitch in and do for themselves (something many of the rest of us never seem to have figured out or have forgotten).

Rent-a-cops. There are also some residential neighborhoods and business districts that have decided to hire private guards to patrol their areas. They did this is Oceanside, California, and in Washington, D.C. they ended up with Black Muslim armed guards.

In other places they just come out in droves to help hunt for missing children, as they did in the San Francisco Bay area when about one hundred volunteers went door-to-door in Berkeley and Oakland to try to find a newborn baby who was kidnaped from a local hospital.

Other volunteer efforts include the thousands of volunteers who patrol the Detroit streets on what is known as "Devil's Night" when the low-life traditionally like to set everything on fire. We're talking about as many as forty thousand volunteers in some years. It's been one major effort, and it has really helped.

Getting out in the streets. Let's not forget the courageous efforts of the famous "Guardian Angels" who have done their best to make urban streets safer for us all. There's the "Town Watch" groups and "Neighborhood Watch" and the "V.I.P. Program" (retired senior volunteers) and "Crime Watch."

There are the volunteer Citizens' Patrols, using their own cars, two-way radios and/or cellular phones and hand-held spotlights to patrol neighborhoods and business districts. They have become extra eyes and ears for the police and have shown themselves to be responsible and effective.

These are not new ideas, you know. One of Rembrand's most famous paintings was called "The Night Watch" in honor of the volunteers who patrolled the urban landscapes centuries ago. (Actually its more official title was "The Company of Captain Frans Banning Cocq and Lieutenant Willem Van Ruttenburg," and it was painted in 1642, but we won't quibble over titles. The important thing is that, a long time ago, some felt they should honor these heroic efforts.)

Armed and ready. A few years back *Time* magazine reported that at least 600,000 times a year a gun is fired to protect life and property in America. This is definitely not all law enforcement activity. Believe it or not, it would seem that guns are actually used quite often by citizens protecting their lives or their property (and sometimes both).

Philadelphia bartender John Nieves was at work when six robbers entered, firing as they came in. One customer was shot in the face and then John had a shotgun pointed at his face. He managed to knock the gun aside, grab a handgun and started firing. He killed one of the violent intruders and wounded another. The rest of them fled.

A man was riding his bicycle and minding his own business when he was brutally attacked by a youth gang. He was in fear for his life, but he managed to draw a gun (properly registered) and shot one of the gang member. That immediately discouraged the whole bunch and they fled.

Seventy-year-old Cora Moore was asleep in Chattanooga, Tennessee, when someone broke into her house and struck her. Somehow she was able to get hold of her handgun and wounded her attacker. Hey, some of these little old ladies put us to shame. We should have one like that in every neighborhood.

Another would-be assailant breaking in a home, this time in Salineno, Texas, was stopped dead in his tracks by a lady determined to protect her life and the life of her two young daughters. If the guns were taken away from all of these people by our government, most of them would be dead. (Yes, there are literally hundreds more that I could tell you about.)

The moral imperative of survival. These dangerous changes in our lives and the accompanying protective reactions are even echoing in the churches of our land. Clerics and parishioners alike are finding things no longer as simple as "Thou shalt not kill." It is now better understood in many American churches that it can be more correctly interpreted as, "Thou shalt not murder in cold blood." One does most certainly have the right to protect one's own life and the lives of one's family.

That doesn't mean one should go out in the world and look for people one thinks are bad and open fire. It is not an invitation for violence. Violence is not the answer if there can be any other way. But, when you are faced with the very real possibility of a violent death, what do you do? What will *you* do?

Going after the victims. So, of course our government will always be there to help us in our defense efforts, right? Wrong! Sometimes it's there to help. More often than I would care to imagine, the officials seem to see their role as a special persecutor of the people. Don't like to hear that? Neither do I. How did I come up with that? Read on.

I'll never forget the story the late Richmond Barbour told of the letter he received about a man who had looked out of his window and saw a gang of hoodlums smashing up a parked car and dragging two teen-age girls out of the car and beating the driver with a lead pipe. The man in the window got his target gun and peppered the attackers with skeet shot which stung them. When the police arrived, they let the gang go and arrested the man who had defended the young man and the two girls.

Do you remember the case of the hero cab driver in San Francisco who had stopped a robber by pinning him against a wall with his cab. Of course the admitted crook sued the cabby and won an award of $24,595 for injuries suffered when the cab driver defended the victim and stopped the robber—another case of the world turned upside down.

There are also cases like the New Jersey honeymoon couple who were spied on by a young girl who came into their suite during a high point in their new relationship. The girl got in through an adjoining door, which the hotel neglected to keep locked.

The honeymoon couple quickly grabbed the girl and held her until hotel security could get there and take care of the situation. So, what happened? The court awarded the "peeping Jill" $2,000 because the court claimed the girl was falsely imprisoned.

In West Palm Beach, Florida, an upstanding churchgoing man had all he could take with a police department that was ignoring the junkies and prostitutes that were using an old boarded-up house in the neighborhood. Finally, in desperation, he went in the house, when no one was there, spread around some lighter fluid and burned the dump down.

He broke the law—no more than the junkies and prostitutes the police were ignoring—but he was the one they went after. He was the one they finally decided to arrest. He was the one who came up for trial in a prosecution that could give him a minimum of five years in prison.

Does anybody care? There's the lawsuit against the Los Angeles watch shop owner who shot to death the robbers who were trying to take him down. We understand the lawsuit was pending from the mother of one of the robbers for killing her poor son. What happened to Lance Thomas, the watch shop owner? He went out of business. He had been wounded five times in a series of robbery attempts and realized he was targeted by the gangs for revenge. He just couldn't keep on stopping them by himself. He wanted to live!

There was that Imperial Beach, California, man, Jaime Guzman, who shot and wounded an illegal alien who was trying to steal his car. And then what happened? Of course, the car owner was arraigned on charges.

Remember Bernard Goetz, the subway vigilante? He's that fellow who dared to defend himself against some subway hoodlums. As you may recall, he got the shaft, not from the hoodlums, but from the criminal legal system of New York. He also was successfully sued for $43 million by one of the perpetrators. Now, there's a way to take somebody down and *really* clean up. It sure beats mugging.

From coast to coast. There have also been many cases like that of Danny Palm in California. He's one of many in a neighborhood who were the continuing victims of a bully's endless assaults. With fear and violence, the bully ran that neighborhood like Attila the Hun. Yes, neighbors tried everything they could think of to break free, including forming a neighborhood defense group and calling in the police.

Most unfortunately, the authorities were of absolutely no help whatsoever—partly because of the way our laws are constructed, partly because of the way they are often interpreted in the courts and partly because the police often end up being at their best as the clean-up crew after the crime.

Eventually the neighborhood terrorism got so intense that Danny ended up having to defend himself by killing the perpetrator. It was either that or be run out of town or worse. *Then* the police got involved and Danny was arrested and convicted of second-degree murder. Eventually it was reduced to manslaughter but, believe me, he surely did pay one God-awful price to protect himself—to protect himself when nobody else was willing to come to his aid, *not even the police!*

On the other coast, Arthur Boone, who lived in a crime-ridden area of New York City, shot a couple of muggers in self-defense and was then put in the position of having to face up to fifteen years in prison for illegal possession of a gun. He thought he was going to be shot. He was carrying a gun because it was the only way he could protect himself in that area. The authorities weren't protecting him. They were only going after *him* because he dared to adequately protect himself. That's the way the laws work and that's the way they're enforced. That's the real truth of what's going on out there!

> Whenever any form of government becomes destructive . . . it is the right of the people to alter or abolish it.
>
> —From the Declaration of Independence

Taking a long, hard look. At this point, you might expect what is beginning to happen. Growing numbers of people throughout the land are beginning to look at some rather disquieting choices. Some of these people are stable, mature, and deeply concerned about everybody's well-being. Some of these people seem to be less secure in their nature and, in fact, seem downright dangerous.

Every once in a while we read the headlines or watch the TV sound bytes about militias, secessionists, and all sorts of other movements. We hear more and more about how folks trust our government less and less. It's a definite trend and we'd better start paying attention to it. Look at the results of a Channel One school network survey made with participating students in more than nine thousand American high schools. It was found that almost fifty percent of the students believe a coup like the 1991 Soviet overthrow effort is possible in the United States!

A look at history. Could it happen in America? Historians are divided on the issue. Some say it could; some don't think so. But let us consider the fact that we have already had one revolution, four presidents assassinated (with six other attempts), inner-city riots that burned sections of our cities from coast to coast, Vietnam riots that almost brought down our government and a civil war. Oh yes, we're more than capable of another revolution.

Even a number of our founding fathers were aware of such continuing possibilities. In fact Thomas Jefferson was widely quoted as saying, "I hold it that a little rebellion now and then is a good thing, and as necessary in the political world as storms in the physical."

Maybe it's just a matter of more and more folks choosing whatever they can find that might offer them a better chance for survival.

That's something to consider, you know. As Alexander Hamilton said, "Self-preservation is the first principle of our nature."

And where might all this lead to? It could lead to revolution. And it could lead to a kind of vigilantism.

Enter: The Vigilante. When the police are sometimes unable to protect us, when prosecutors do not always seek proper redress or prosecute the innocent, when the courts seem to be more and more caught up in a game that loses the original purpose, when the sentences no longer mean what they say—when it gets like this, the frustrations begin to build; the anger begins to rise.

Eventually it might become possible for some to entertain the idea of an imagined brave and righteous group of vigilantes riding hard to the aid of the beleaguered masses. For many it can be seen as a romantic idea of lost hope of security and protection, once again regained.

Another look at history. In some of our earliest settlements, in what was later to become our nation, committees were established to dispense justice. The guiding lights of such groups were usually the community leaders or religious leaders. The results of such groups were often mixed. While some were eminently fair, other were notorious. (We have all read about the infamous "witch" burnings in Salem, Massachusetts.)

During our Revolutionary War, a Colonel Edward Lynch gathered up a group of Virginians to establish their own justice system in an area that had none at the time. They drove out suspected Tories (supporters and/or sympathizers of the Crown) and other "undesirables" and they conducted some public whippings. (However, historic evidence strongly suggests that they actually did not hang anyone, although the term "lynching" and "lynch mob" were lifted from the Colonel's name and eventually came to be associated with the "necktie" parties of later on.)

In 1836, a murderous "love triangle" in early Los Angeles ended with the first vigilante committee in California forming up and taking action in place of local authorities who were unwilling to satisfy their demands for justice. A jail was stormed, an unofficial trial was held, and a firing squad concluded the drama.

San Francisco out of control. We all know about San Francisco's famous vigilance committees that were established in the late nineteenth century. The city was overrun by would-be Forty-Niners, unsavory gamblers, and similar adventurers. Many of them were totally out of control. Law and order were the casualties. Then, the committees of vigilance took charge and actually ended up establishing a fairly peaceful community.

So it was in much of the early West. As Andrew Karmen wrote in the *Encyclopedia of Crime and Justice*, "The vigilante credo was accepted by legal scholars, judges, and lawyers, as well as by men of action, during the late 1800s and early 1900s. On the whole, the legal illuminati granted qualified approval to vigilantism as a rational response to the inadequacies of the criminal justice system."

Another historic vignette you might find interesting—In 1891, a vigilante committee in New Orleans went to the city jail, removed and subsequently executed a group of suspected members of the Mafia they believed had murdered the Chief of Police. This unproven and more than somewhat rash move ended up creating some serious difficulties for a time, between the government of Italy and the government of the United States.

An interesting sidelight that is not generally known—the Mafia itself has been described as beginning as a sort of Sicilian vigilante committee to protect the general population. It's definitely not what they are today, which shows how things can evolve if you're not careful.

Has it finally happened again? A while back a friend of mine received an anonymous mailing of a newsletter that proclaimed the return of the vigilante. It was evidently produced by one of the new "committees," and it was very articulately laid out. The newsletter's banner headline mirrors many of our own feelings with the announcement that "People Are Frightened, Don't Know What to Do." Another point made suggests that "we find local judges have been taking gifts from attorneys who appear before them in court. The corruption is everywhere. Senator Warren Rudman has admitted publicly that our government is not functioning. We have finally come to the end of the road."

And you should see the part that contains their "declaration." It's the most disturbing part of all:

> We the people of the United States, in order to form a protected union, reestablish justice, insure domestic tranquility, provide for our common personal defense for our general welfare, and to secure the blessings of peace and protection for ourselves and our posterity, do ordain and establish the American Committee of Vigilance, for we, the people of the United States recognize the primary responsibility established in our founding government for the provision of protection

and the promotion of Life, Liberty and the pursuit of Happiness for all its citizens and the understanding that, as expressed on July 4, 1776 by the Congress, wherever any form of government becomes destructive (by inaction or otherwise) of these ends, it is the Right of the People to alter or to abolish it, and to institute new Government, laying its foundation on such principles and organizing its powers in such form, as to them shall seem most likely to effect their Safety and Happiness.

Since the public vote and other mandates have been ineffective in regaining protection and security for the people, this Committee of Vigilance has been established to alter the ineffective nature of the Government that has abrogated these primary responsibilities, and to do so through the creation of a functional and effective arm of protection through enforcement. This has been done, following the spirit and the letter of original American declarations and the most basic American law.

An additional few words from the document that were interesting: "We would have liked to have them keep that control if they had done the job. We are only going to do what we have to do. If the authorities are upset, let them do the job . . . and then we won't have to do it."

That newsletter was a surprise. I could hardly believe what I was reading. I don't know if this was just intended as a test, a wake up call, a legal blueprint of moves to come or what. Could this actually someday become something somewhere between justice and rebellion?

Who are these people? I don't know because they gave no names, gave no phone numbers and they gave no addresses. What I do know is that well-trained policemen definitely do make mistakes from time to time. What possibilities might we imagine for error in an amateur group, no matter how well-meaning they may be?

I soon sent it on to leading newspapers and various authorities around the nation. I felt it could be the harbinger of unsettling events to come. I was not mistaken. Since then, we have all seen all sorts of minor revolutionary activities, standoffs and bombings.

So why is this the first time you have heard of this or seen this in print? I can tell you this, there are a number of things to be found in this book that have never gotten beyond the media blue pencil. For instance, have you ever heard of *The Will to Resist* published by the

Second Committee of Correspondence of Boston? They talk about having the courage and will to resist what is clearly seen by them as a thoroughly oppressive American government.

Who are these people? They write that, "The identities of the publisher, staff and other persons and organizations involved will remain hidden so long as the threat from government persecution remains." What do you think they might mean by that? What do you think they might be doing? Why have I never heard about them in any kind of media investigation or government report? Could this be one of the reasons why so many just don't trust either the government or the media?

Chapter Nine

Looking at the Courts
An Unflattering View Behind the Black Robes

As there are actually a few lawyers who do not like the way things are going and a *very* few who are trying to bring about some real changes, and as there are a good number in law enforcement who are trying their very best to hold the thin blue line between us and complete anarchy, there also are a few judges who are quite distressed by the way things are, and are trying, as best they can, to apply some truth and justice to a procedure that is coming more perilously close to complete insanity.

More of those crazy lawsuits. The problem is far less with those few who care and try to take positive steps. The problem is more with the many who do little or nothing and continue to be a contributing part of an often out of control system. And the examples are so obvious. You'd think it would be hard for them to keep playing the game with a straight face.

It's like the fellow who was fired from the Coca-Cola Company for violent behavior and sued and initially won a $7.1 million award from the court. You see, he sued under the Americans With Disabilities Act, which states that employers must make accommodations for employees who suffer from certain disabilities. The court evidently felt that included violent behavior that resulted from excessive drinking. It's all Coca-Cola's fault, right? sure, and the sky is green and the grass is blue.

How about that bank robber who sued a savings and loan company in Oakland, California, after a booby-trapped bundle of cash popped off in his pants. He wanted $2 million in damages. I'm surprised he didn't also ask for hazard pay in addition because robbing banks can be such a stressful and dangerous occupation.

Then there's the one about the transit police in New York who interrupted a violent mugging and had to shoot one of the perpetrators. You guessed it, the mugger in question sued the transit authorities and was awarded $4.3 million. The U.S. Supreme Court has let it stand!

There's no end to it. We cannot forget Linda Ricchio, the so-called "Fatal Attraction" killer who stalked and finally killed her former boyfriend. In a civil lawsuit that occurred after the criminal conviction, the victim's family ended up in a thoroughly convoluted mess that had Vista, California, Superior Court Judge Thomas R. Murphy ordering the victim's family to pay the killer.

That's right. That's the way it came down. (Well, at least a concerned group of supporters raised the funds to pay the killer, so the victim's family wouldn't have to.) Can you believe it? Can you believe this sort of thing is actually happening in this country? You better believe it.

Do you remember the one about the killer who broke out of the Utah State Prison and sued the prison because they put him in jeopardy by letting him escape. Oh sure, they really wanted him to break out. U.P.I. reported him as saying that "Because of extreme fear of being shot to death, I was forced to swim several irrigation canals, attempt to swim a 'raging' Jordan River and expose myself to innumerable bites and many insects." I guess he felt that $2 million in damages would help him feel better.

I know you remember when that drug dealer had actor Carroll O'Connor's son so messed up on drugs that he committed suicide. The man who admitted giving the drugs to O'Connor's son and who admitted holding a cocaine party after learning of the suicide had the audacity to slap a $10 million slander suit against O'Connor because he claims O'Connor smeared his good name. (Thank God it didn't succeed.)

It's the way it is. Frankly, the fact that this case, or any of the others, would even be considered as legitimate for any serious court of law, is beyond my comprehension. But then, who's talking about a serious court of law? The examples I give you are only a small fraction of what's out there. It's my hope that this fraction will make you see just how real these problems are, just what kind of a nightmare we are really in. And who knows, a miracle could happen. You, and a significant number of others might just end up deciding that you've had enough. Now, wouldn't *that* be something?

Oppression of the people through the courts. And then there is what all governments eventually seem to do best of all, oppress the people. More often than not, that's done through the courts. Like the work-release prisoner from Tampa, Florida, who was given a fifteen-year prison sentence for slipping eight cans of Budweiser beer into the prison on a Christmas Eve. (I'm surprised they didn't hang the man right then and there!)

There's the brilliant young chemistry researcher whose discovery won him a patent and a dispute over the ownership of that patent with the University of South Florida. So, what happened to him? Wasn't this dealt with in the civil courts? He was prosecuted and convicted in the *criminal* courts and was sent to a maximum-security state prison to work on a chain gang. Even the then-governor's counsel said that, "we are concerned that it has overtones that the government overreached in this young man's case."

There's Rocky Scoggins, in prison for an estimated thirty years because he pilfered a twelve-pack of beer. Am I missing something here? I mean, besides a twelve-pack. Why are there so many like him and then we have murderers who are turned free? What do *you* think is missing here?

And how about Middlesex Borough, New Jersey's Municipal Court Judge George Psak throwing a crippled 81-year-old man in jail for refusing to pay a $42 fine for not shoveling snow from his sidewalk. As he was quoted by Reuters, "I just can't shovel myself." And, frankly, not everybody can easily afford to pay others to do it, not the way things cost today.

And in San Diego a fellow was passing out literature near the entrance of the county courthouse and Superior Court Judge Kevin Midlam sentenced him to five days in jail for violating a court order to keep him from passing out his literature near the entrance of the courthouse. He finally suspended the sentence for a year in an agreement that the man not do that anymore.

What, no freedom of speech? Of course not. His literature was not considered to be friendly to the court. It espoused what was deemed to be a controversial theory of jury nullification. If that's the way things are, I could be thrown in jail if I should try to give away copies of this book or detailed flyers about this book anywhere near his precious courthouse. So much for the Constitution.

The lawyer monopoly. We hear about how our government hates monopolies. In fact it hates them so much, it prosecutes people and breaks up big corporations in the name of its anti-monopoly efforts. But of course one of the largest monopolies of them all is the one the lawyers have nailed down for themselves. The government, through the courts, acts as their enforcers!

Just a couple of quick examples of how that works would be the conviction and the Nevada State Supreme Court's rejection of the national HALT organization's attempted friend-of-the-court brief on behalf of two Nevada paralegals who were appealing their conviction for the "unauthorized practice of law."

The judges did not like the fact that the national group didn't hire a Nevada lawyer. As the "Legal Reformer" quoted HALT's Legislative Director Deborah Chalfie, "Friend-of-the-court briefs are a way for the court to gather information about a particular case. By not even looking at our brief, they're ignoring an important perspective." Ah, but they are protecting their monopoly, right? After all, we can't have these folks come before them without using *their* attorneys and we *certainly* can't have those pesky paralegals running around helping people to fill out forms and such.

The second example is about a group of lawyers and non-lawyers that have provided free legal information and low-cost assistance in the Chicago area. A charge of "unauthorized practice of law" was made against the group when a bankruptcy trustee discovered one of its paralegals had dared to help a woman file her own bankruptcy case.

The group sued the trustees, the American Bar Association, the Chicago Bar Association, etc., and argued that the rules prohibiting lawyers from aiding such paralegals and forming partnerships with non-lawyers violated both the anti-trust laws and civil rights laws. A very miffed federal district judge, James Holderman, dismissed all challenges and scolded the group resoundingly in a footnote of over one-hundred pages. We will protect the coveted lawyer monopoly at all cost.

Getting off easy. If you only pay attention to the many instances I have given you of innocent people being railroaded by the courts, you might think all we have to do is lighten up a bit, right? Well, it's not that simple. Such things never are. When a legal system starts to fall apart, all aspects go to hell, not just one part of it. In other words, not only are innocent people being crucified by heavy-handed courts, the very clearly guilty and dangerous ones among us are getting off in fearful numbers.

There is that case in Harrisburg, Pennsylvania, about a school principal who had been sentenced to death (later reduced to a life sentence) for the slaying of a teacher and her two kids. Then the Pennsylvania state Supreme Court ruled that he must be freed because prosecutors badly mishandled his trial. The way things work, you don't seriously punish the prosecutors. What you do is turn loose the convicted killer on the rest of us.

In California, Guadalupe Estrada is shot to death in front of her children and the conviction of the killers is overturned by the Appellate justices over a question of damaging information that the jurors were not supposed to be allowed to hear. (At least that's what they implied.) Even though the justices admitted there was little doubt as to the guilt of the two men involved in the murder, there just seemed to be no other mechanism that could properly amend and yet still support the search for truth without voiding the conviction.

Again in California, Elenore Frances Buchanan's body was found in East San Diego County. Bernard Lee Hamilton was soon arrested, properly charged and convicted of the murder. Then the Circuit Court reversed his death penalty and the U.S. Supreme Court would not reinstate it. Once again technicalities reign supreme over truth and over the faded concept of justice.

It shouldn't be surprising that there's that joke going around about a young man who murders his parents and then successfully throws himself on the mercy of the court because, well, after all, now he's a poor little orphan. I wouldn't be surprised if that's really the next one somebody tries to pull.

And the shame goes on. I'm not about to get into the many details of O. J. Simpson's criminal trial. I will only say that with overwhelming evidence that makes it absolutely clear as to what happened, a jury seems to have realized that it was going to have to go out there and live in that very racially defined community after the gavel fell for the last time.

Then there was the case of Robert Lee Perkins who pleaded guilty to killing a man over 20 years ago (he'd been a fugitive for a long time) and because they said they just didn't think they had enough trial evidence, the man was simply sentenced to probation. Of course the Los Angeles Superior Court Judge, Isabel Cohen, did manage to impose a five-year probationary sentence and 250 hours of community service. I'd say that's a bargain basement price for a killing, especially with his confession to the crime.

And what about the judges who are found guilty of crimes? There's been a lot of talk about how two San Diego judges and a prominent lawyer, convicted in a gifts-for-favors scandal, were let off real easy. And there are other examples that could be given in other parts of the country.

A sad bit of humor. This sort of thing has gotten so bad that it's become the subject of skits, jokes and cartoons of every kind. Stayskal, in the *Tampa Tribune,* had an interesting cartoon showing a man who had just been held up on the street and as the perpetrator was leaving, the victim called after him, "Last spring you robbed me and got three years. Last month you nailed me again and got five to ten. Haven't you learned your lesson yet?"

Also, we certainly don't want to forget about that notorious Beverly Hills madam. I found it most enlightening that Superior Court Judge Judith Champagne squashed the efforts to reveal the names of her customers. They, of course, were participants in the crime of prostitution but there were many who were rich and famous. We certainly can't allow *their* names to be bandied about, now can we? And we most certainly can't *prosecute* them for their part in it.

Then there's that early release program for the man who was given the credit for making San Diego the methamphetamine capital of America in the 80s. Robert Miskinis got forty years on eleven criminal counts and now, after less than four years, he's free on probation. (He's supposed to have made some sort of "deal" with federal prosecutors. What a deal!)

In Ventura, California, Dwaine Tinsley was convicted on five counts of molesting his teen-age daughter. His conviction was overturned because an appeals court ruled that cartoons he drew for *Hustler* magazine under the title of "Chester the Molester" shouldn't have been used as evidence. Why not? Those cartoons don't give at least some hint as to his disposition? Does the search for truth have absolutely no place at all here?

Not to be outdone, there's the Arizona officer who checked a convicted child molester out of jail so he could take him to an elementary school to play "McGruff," the crime dog. Not only did he outrage parents and school officials by doing his best to "feel" the little kids, one of his earlier victims was among the classmates present. (In all fairness, it should be said that this seems to have been a mistake. The officials didn't check to see just who it was they were bringing to that school.)

An endless mess. There seems to be an endless number of ways that the authorities can come up with to mess things up royally. Like the way they handled things in Fort Worth, Texas, with a young white supremacist who had been convicted for the murder of a black man and ended up getting sentenced to probation only. It seems the sentence, pronounced by Judge Everett Young, was because of some sort of misunderstanding with the all white jury about what sort of punishment that could be recommended. (First O. J. and then this guy. Black or white, there is much to be ashamed of.)

Remember that movie, *A Cry For Help: The Tracey Thurman Story?* She was beaten and slashed by her husband after the police failed to protect her. Her attacker was released from prison after serving just a bit more than half of his fourteen-year sentence.

Remember Charles Keating who got off so light after causing so many to lose so much in that Savings and Loan scandal? One of the reasons sighted was a technical defect in the prosecution's presentation. Once again, they must make us all pay for a prosecutor who didn't cross all his *T*s or dot all his *I*s. So, let us never, never maintain the primary goal of gaining truth and dispensing true justice. We must play the *game*.

There's that California serial rapist who was suspected of more than two hundred sexual attacks and was paroled because he falls under California's old determinate sentencing law, which requires a definite release date (and an early one, it would seem, most of the time). Need we say more? But of course there are those who might think they've found a technical flaw in one of my many, many examples that I uncovered, and there will be those who will say that all of my examples are just a fraction of court cases and that most of them are just fine.

Never mind that there has been a lot of very careful research for this book and that the examples are only a small fraction from our files and our files contain only a small fraction of the almost countless problems out there.

Autocide. We constantly hear about the drunken drivers who kill with their cars and pick-up trucks. We also hear, all too often, about the many minor convictions and set-asides that have accommodated a continuation of the rampage that led to the killings. We hear, far too often, that, once again, the killers get off with what amounts to little more than a slap on the wrist.

I'm sure you also have heard about MADD (Mothers Against Drunk Driving) which has gotten at least some reform and could get a lot more if a really large number of you out there were to become intense, dedicated activists. But of course not all that many will take the time. There are all too many good excuses for not getting involved, right?

There are hundreds and hundreds of such examples I could give you. Let me give you just one. Phillip Cramer, a 34-year-old husband and father is run down by a drunk motorist. The drunk driver was convicted, but we are told the excuse of jail overcrowding brought about the driver's release. Her total time served in jail: thirty-one days out of an original sentence of only one year. (It should also be noted that jail space *was* available at Las Colinas women's jail at the time.)

Insanity in the courts. You've been reading about just how crazy this ridiculous system has gotten. Well, insanity is not only a condition in the courts, it can also be an ill-advised invention to be used to take control and/or money from others. You just simply have them put away.

There are many illustrations that might be given. One good example is a very sad situation we just happen to have a good deal of information about, thanks to a detailed report from the American Consumers' Association. It is an account of a particular period of time in the life of a 79-year-old La Jolla, California, resident who had retired after years of hard work and wished only to be able to relax and administer his accumulated estate as he wished. (It wasn't a gigantic estate, but it was his.) The report is as follows (with key names removed but available for any credible investigator):

> This might seem a simple matter but XXXX is a member of a very troubled family. After talking with a number of outside observers and involved persons (including members of the family), we see an accumulation of observations and opinions which strongly suggest that Mr. XXXX's older son XXXX (a San Francisco attorney) has what is hard not to describe as a great deal of hatred for his mother (Mr. XXXX and his ex-wife are still good friends) and for his younger brother.
>
> This evidently intense attitude seems to have taken a very special form following an accident when Mr. XXXX was struck by an automobile on January 28, 1993. (He was in the hospital for a while and was suffering from the usual impact traumas, both mental and physical. However, he soon showed a very good recovery for a person of his age.)
>
> Following the accident, Mr. XXXX's older son took the opportunity to take charge of the personal injury and related legal pursuits. Mr. XXXX tells us that this included his son's insistence that he sign a number of papers he was told, by his son, would help him collect more money from the accident. This is supposed to have included papers that evidently turned all of his funds and estate over to the son in a conservatorship arrangement.
>
> As a result of this family dispute, we find that the older son, through his conservatorship and then through conservatorship

appointment of others, and through a restraining order, restricting the mother's contact with the father—the older son has managed to obtain most of his goals in this very bitter family dispute. Unfortunately, it has clearly been done at the horrendous cost of the personal freedom and mental and physical health of the beleaguered father.

An example of this treatment would be when the (then) present conservator, Miss XXXX, had Mr. XXXX put into the Charter mental facility on March 5, 1993. For six days his life was a living hell of drugged compliance. It is the kind of nightmare that one could not imagine a person would be willing to subject another human being to, unless he was a genuine danger to himself and/or others.

A sanity hearing was held at the Charter psychiatric facility on March 11, 1993. The conservator, various staff members of the facility, Mr. XXXX, Dick Dunford (a Patient Rights Advocate) and this writer, of the American Consumers' Association, were all present at this hearing.

The medical staff parroted the psychiatric contentions of the conservator almost word for word—an interesting coincidence. They also listed the extensive drugging that was used in place of other forms of management. Mr. Dunford and this writer presented testimony that established an entirely different picture of Mr. XXXX and he himself made a most credible presentation of his actual state of mind.

The official and legal decision came down right then and there (from the administrative "judge"), that Mr. XXXX was NOT a danger to himself or others and that his mental state was such that he should be released immediately. It was made very clear that his incarceration in that mental facility was a very grave mistake.

So now the older son's efforts and the conservator's efforts, which seem to be so much against the best interest of Mr. XXXX, move on to other arenas—a hearing on a continuance of the restraining order against the mother, a hearing on the general plan of conservatorship and whatever else can be used in this shameful family squabble that has practically destroyed this poor old man.

This writer doesn't really care so much about the major recriminations nor the subtle nuances in this family's internal war. What we realize is that the court most likely does not appreciate being used as a weapon in this form of warfare, with the father ending up losing everything, including his most basic civil rights. We feel that most courts will not tolerate such a situation when they are finally given the opportunity to know about it.

We have been made aware, from conversations with local, state and federal officials, that this sort of thing, as terrible as it is, is an all too common phenomenon. All too many parents end up as victims of their children in any number of different ways—including as illustrated in this report. This fact, however, does not justify or otherwise condone such behavior. And it does, in fact, become the responsibility of all of us who care, to do whatever we can to stop such abuses from happening.

The aftermath. I have visited the Charter facility, and I saw some of the drug-compliant patients. How many are just being warehoused? How many are put there just to get them out of the way of their families? I get the impression that it is a common phenomenon that goes on today all over the nation and can be expected to continue.

How old are you? Might you someday be a possible candidate for such "treatment"? Hopefully, not if you have a caring and sensitive family. And what about the rest? It would seem only a few are ever rescued. What about all the others?

What happened to this nice old man? Well, as you might expect, the court (in Vista and in San Diego, California) didn't really give a damn that they were being used as a weapon in this family war. The lawyer son buried the courts with an effective paper blizzard and got pretty much his own way with regard to the control of his father's estate. Once again, truth and justice is a joke.

Children as victims of the court. You've already read, earlier in this book, of some almost unbelievable things that have been done to children as a result of the infinite lack of wisdom in our courts. This too, seems unending.

There's that former Carlsbad High School coach who was sentenced to two weeks in jail for sexually molesting a 17-year-old student. This was done under Vista, California, municipal Judge Michael Burley who was more inclined to blame the school than the actual perpetrator.

In Columbus, Ohio, Common Pleas Judge William Millard dismissed rape charges against a man who was accused of raping a 12-year-old girl *because a witness was twenty minutes late getting to court!*

Looking at the Courts

Well, at least in this case there was a public response. Of course, the judge only got a slap on the wrist—a six month suspension. I imagine he's back on the bench by now.

And let us not forget the story about little 5-year-old Jory Daniels who was taken from his parents after he was brought to a hospital with a fractured skull at the age of four months. (Yes, the father pleaded guilty to abusing the boy.) Visitation with the child revealed signs to the foster mother of very bad treatment.

The foster mother begged the authorities not to let the child get back into the hands of the parents. Bonnie Williams, the foster parent, is reported to have said that if he went back, "he was going to end up dead." Judge Jeffrey Horner was told that even though the child would be in shared living quarters of the parents, it was in the grandparents home. Social worker James Mehlfeld argued that the little boy would be okay because the grandparents and the preschool teachers would offer an adequate level of protection.

Of course, the judge bought it, hook-line-and-sinker. The little boy went home. And yes, that poor, defenseless little child ended up dead. He weighed only nineteen pounds when he was found. The San Jose Mercury News wrote the story up. But frankly, I really doubt that the courts of our nation are effected in any way by such public disclosures. Let's face it, most people get upset and then go back to their TV. That's it. End of story.

A hard look at the judges. It was the then $79,000-a-year Texas Supreme Court Justice James Wallace who was quoted a decade ago as saying, "I'm tired of being the lowest-paid lawyer in the courtroom." How wonderful it would be for so many of us who are outside the lucrative legal system to be so lowly paid.

Nonetheless, our Supreme Court Chief Justice William Rehnquist said, in his year-end message on the federal courts (at the end of 1996), "Clearly, this disparity between the salaries of the judicial and legal professions cannot continue indefinitely without compromising the morale of the federal judiciary and eventually its quality."

Of course we certainly wouldn't want to suggest that the lawyers fees be significantly reduced. After all, the poor souls so desperately need to make many hundreds of dollars to many thousands of dollars an hour, don't they? Naturally what is suggested is that the *judges* be paid considerably better so they can do as well as the looting councilors-of-law. I wish such books as Charles Ashman's *The Finest Judges Money Can Buy* were still in print.

There is a recent book that you might want to read. Max Boot, the Editorial Features Editor of *The Wall Street Journal* has written a shocking book entitled, *Out of Order: Arrogance, Corruption and Incompetence on the Bench*. As Mr. Boot told Brian Lamb on C-SPAN's "Booknotes" program, "It's about one of the most powerful branches of the American government, the judiciary, and about how they wield all this influence, all this power, all this authority and have very little accountability to go with it." Some of the shocking examples he gives in his book will curl your hair.

I think we are going to have to face the uncomfortable fact that judges are human beings. Partly for this reason, the almost absolute power of their position does seem to erode the humanity of many of these men and women and severely limit and sometimes totally eliminate their ability for self-criticism and self-correction. When judges clearly exhibit such a pattern, in their public behavior and with frequent appeals court reversals, there should be a definite, fair and practical way of removing them from their position, before great damage is done to innocent citizens. You know it is not too much to ask.

Unfortunately, this is very seldom accomplished. So now it has become a burden that is far too great to carry any longer. It is long past time to do something about it—*long* past.

Politics on the bench. One example might well be President Clinton's appointment of New York federal judge Harold Baer. He's the man who set off a major ruckus when he banned important evidence that was seized in a major drug case. This time the pressure was considerable. By a strange coincidence, he ended up reversing his ruling. It also set off some serious discussions about the "baggage" many judges seem to bring with them to the bench. It has become very obvious that the selection process is quite flawed.

Another interesting example was that of California's ANTI-discrimination proposition (209) which was blocked by President Jimmy Carter's appointed African-American judge who clearly saw it as the end of affirmative action. This judge, a former civil rights activist, had said he would most certainly stop the anti-discrimination initiative. He felt that it would abolish special programs that favored minorities and women.

Way back around the beginning of this century, a Senator from New York, George Washington Plunkitt, was quoted as having said, "With a Tammany legislature, a Tammany governor, and a Tammany court, what's a Constitution among friends?" Since then it has only gotten worse.

We regularly find political parties who dominate state legislatures, holding up the creation of much needed new judgeships and doing whatever else they can to keep governors of opposing parties from putting their people on the bench wherever they can. It's a shameful tug-of-war that is typical of the clearly politicized judiciary.

As the quality goes down, the costs go up. Back in December 1995, the Senate Environment and Public Works Committee had the courage to suggest that new federal courthouses were far too lavish and that judges must share the blame. Judge's offices were equipped with kitchens and private baths with showers—that's what they were talking about. And courtrooms with exotic wood paneling, high, impressive ceilings and marble floors. And on and on go the expensive perks. Why not? You and I, as taxpayers, are forced to pay for it. These are just a few of the modifications demanded by federal judges, even up to the Supreme Court.

And the next year, the General Services Administration and the General Accounting Office went before the Senate Government Affairs Oversight Subcommittee and clearly labeled the judges as the primary cause of the obscene costs. The costs still go up.

One shameful example. As the national organization, Citizens Against Government Waste, reported:

> Judges have demanded and received many modifications to the notorious $400 million Foley Square courthouse in New York. Although the design guide allows the use of a good grade of carpet costing around $55 per square yard, the specially designed Foley Square carpet costs $144 per square yard—adding $1.4 million to costs.
>
> And while the 1,200 wooden doors originally ordered would have cost roughly $1,300 per door set, demands for different woods and hardware raised costs to over $9,000 per set, adding $9 million to the tab. Special windows added an extra $145,403 to costs, and an underground tunnel running to a correctional facility across the street, also demanded by judges, piled on $13 million more.
>
> Floor-to-ceiling wood paneling cost an extra $5 million and hand-painted stencillings on the ceiling ran $700,000. White Vermont marble in the lobby and corridors ran $5 million.

You want more? As the citizens' group noted, "Upgrades at a courthouse in Shreveport, Louisiana, meant that walls, which should have cost $32,000, ran $165,000, and floor coverings that might have cost $109,000 rose to nearly $400,000." In addition, Boston's Fan Pier courthouse will feature a $1.6 million floating dock and surrounding 'harbor park' costing $3.2 million.

"Courthouses in Minneapolis and St. Louis will also feature indoor firing ranges—the former in spite of the fact, says GAO, that 'there are several nearby ranges available to the Marshals Service.'" So, what's the bottom line? There *is* no bottom line. It *never* ends. Recently (as of this writing) it has come to light that California, Mendocino County is bulging with municipal court judges. In fact they have so many that many have to go out of the county to find work for their gavel. But of course they still get $100,000 a year for Mendocino County service.

Another example, the first federal judge indicted in California, Robert Aguilar, resigned before he could be brought before the bench. Then, of course, the government dropped the charges against him. He remains eligible for a nice pension. Of course.

The shame goes on. Not very often does a judge realize what he's doing. I remember back when San Diego Superior Court Judge Ed Butler suddenly realized he had walked out of a store without paying for the sunglasses he'd just tried on and was still wearing. He returned them immediately and then realized it was an actual case of shoplifting in the eyes of the law. He was quoted as having at least a moment of understanding when he was reported to have said, "Just last week I sentenced a woman to three years probation for the same thing."

And I remember when the Illinois Supreme Court decided that in legal malpractice situations, lawyers' clients could not collect for economic losses caused by a lawyer's negligence. As HALT's Legal Reformer quoted State Chief Justice Benjamin Miller, the ruling would most certainly make it a smart move to "obtain counsel before they retain counsel." (Thank God it's only binding in Illinois.)

And I remember when it was reported that two Ohio Supreme Court justices got into an actual physical confrontation. It must have been something to see. It was between Justice Andy Douglas and Justice Craig Wright. (Shall we call that the Wright/Douglas debate?) With that in mind I should also tell you that judges have over half the concealed weapons permits issued by the Sheriff's Department of Los Angeles County. That's what the Sheriff's office says.

Then there's the case of 63-year-old Elmer Nance who was brought into a courtroom in a wheelchair to be sentenced to thirty years to life in prison by a judge who expressed doubts about the actual guilt of the man. (He is supposed to have murdered a 23-year-old woman.)

Remember those headlines in Philadelphia about an investigation of alleged wiretapping and kickbacks by Pennsylvania Supreme Court justices? It was also reported that the court refused to cooperate with the attorney general in the investigation. Anne Krueger asked in the San Diego *Union-Tribune,* "Should the public have the right to know which California judge was disciplined for getting tipsy from lunchtime cocktails? Or had a friend's drunk-driving case transferred to his court? Or which judge took punitive actions against political foes?"

Miss Krueger then reported that "the public doesn't have that right, now—but more people are starting to say that situation should change." And what about the examples she gave? "Those judges were among the seven in the state who were privately disciplined last year by the state Commission on Judicial Performance." What are their names? Who knows?

Yes, changes have been starting to come in this area in a few places around the country. Many more changes in many more places and a *much* more severe discipline is needed. Of course that's going to mean it's going to have to be *demanded.*

The not-so-Supreme Court. The ancient Greek philosopher Aristotle is often quoted as having said, "That judges of important causes should hold office for life is not a good thing, for the mind grows old as well as the body." That's just one of the problems of these high courts.

I wonder how many of you were paying attention back in 1979 when Bob Woodward and Scott Armstrong's book *The Brethren* came out. It chronicled some of the bitter struggles on our highest court. *U.S. News and World Report* said, *"The Brethren* may stir a move in Congress for laws providing for removal of a sick or senile Justice and barring leaks of Court materials, some scholars suggest." Well, don't hold your breath waiting. It's been many years since then, and nobody's ever been inclined to do a damn thing.

Remember all that politics we were talking about in the courts? Where might the U.S. Supreme Court stand in this? They're not going to allow themselves to be so crassly influenced, are they? They want such a high tribunal to stand above such things, right?

Well, according to their own voting records, they each have clearly shown they *do* have their own political agendas on board when they sail the judicial seas. The liberals are Souter, Stevens, Ginsburg and Breyer. The moderates are O'Connor and Kennedy. The conservatives are Thomas, Scalia and Rehnquist.

Well, at least they won't get into any other trouble, and they will stick to the way the Constitution was written, right? Let's see, Justice Ruth Bader Ginsburg is suggested as having violated federal law twenty-one different times since 1995. This is because she took part in cases involving companies her husband owned stock in. This is a no-no.

If you still don't have any doubts about the justices following constitutional law, you may want to read that section on how our Constitution has been perverted in the early part of this book. Read it and do some further research on your own. You need to come to realize that we actually do *not* have a truly constitutional government!

Cases in point. And what about some of their famous (or infamous) case decisions? Our highest court seems to think it's just fine to have drug testing for law enforcement people, student athletes, and public transit drivers (which I heartily agree with), but somehow, for some reason, they have ruled that politicians are exempt from such as that. Would you have expected anything else?

Then there's the case of the utility company that was found guilty of violating the '64 Civil rights Act. Why? Because their hiring policy required their employees to have high school diplomas and at least a minimum score on an I.Q. test. (I should hope so. It could be very dangerous around a utility company with folks who might not be able to read correctly or have reasonable judgement.)

So what was our illustrious court's decision? They found against the utility company because they claim the standards they used were illegal. Why? Because they had a "disparate impact" on various minorities. Just how the devil does such a group's lack of education or I.Q. Level end up being the responsibility of the utility?

And Florida attorney general, Bob Butterworth, has had a hard time trying to rescind the time off that is given many prisoners for early releases. The Supreme Court would not interfere with a Florida court's ruling that allows almost a full third of Florida prisoners to get back on the streets much sooner than their court sentences were intended to allow.

Why? Because the prisons are overcrowded. And, of course, we weren't going to have more adequate facilities, were we? We would much rather turn them loose again, the sooner the better, right?

And that grand and mighty high court of ours has ruled that the U.S. Department of Agriculture can force our farmers and our ranchers to pay for advertising campaigns that promote their products, even if the farmers don't want the ads or disagree with them. (And why is the government doing advertising for *any* private products?)

The U.S. Supreme Court has also decided that it is to be made easier for federal prosecutors to demand that various defendants give up real estate or various types of personal property as a special condition of a plea bargain (a lighter sentence). Now who says you can't buy your way to an easier conviction?

I could go on and on about all of it. Let this be enough for now. Next, you'll want to look at our prison system and after that, you can find out what *you* can do about what you've been reading in this book. So, stay with me. Okay?

Additional sources. Of course if there is still even the slightest doubt left in your mind about what is actually going on, let me recommend the following books for you. There is *Guilty—The Collapse of Criminal Justice* by New York State Supreme Court Judge Harold J. Rothwax. (This first one is a must-read.) There is *Whores of the Court—The Fraud of Psychiatric Testimony and the Rape of American Justice* by Margaret A. Hagen, Ph.D.

There is *Justice Overruled: Unmasking the Criminal Justice System* by Judge Burton S. Katz. There is *The Death of Common Sense—How Law Is Suffocating America* by Philip K. Howard. There is *Freed to Kill: How America's "Revolving Door" System of Justice Fails to Protect the Innocent.* And there is *The Power to Hurt* by D. O'Brien, a chilling account of judicial abuse of power. There's a lot of good reading on this list.

Chapter Ten

Crime and Consequences
A Hard Look at Prisons and Other Restraints

In our colonial and early American periods our small communities had little use for prisons as such. They chose to protect their ways and insure their security with banishment, fines, whipping, and the shame of public display in the stocks. (And there were the gallows.) Local holding cells were for the purpose of retaining suspects until the time of whatever form of trial they were using then. But, little by little, the need for longer incarcerations inexorably moved us to the requirement of a more formal prison system.

As time moved along (to the early 1800s) there developed the "Jacksonian reformers." They recognized the need for prisons but they also recognized that most prisoners retained therein would someday be coming out into society again. Therefore, there was the clear need for prison settings that worked toward the genuine rehabilitation of the prisoners (a very logical concept that many seem to have forgotten today).

It was an idea that didn't catch on very well back then either. Instead, the penitentiary developed as a concept that involved absolute silence, marching in lock step, working hard, and general isolation. By the end of this last century (the 1800s) the prison system was becoming very brutal and overcrowded.

Gradually we became a little more enlightened and things got a little bit better. But, in general, things did not move all that effectively toward genuine rehabilitation. Instead, the prison became more of a finishing school for professional criminals.

What do we want a prison to be? Let's start by defining what we are doing and explore our reasoning. To begin with, we want to protect ourselves by isolating dangerous and otherwise threatening individuals from our society, right? Many also see the need to have this represented as a punishment for doing wrong, very much as one might choose to punish an errant child. (Although, for a child, I should hope not nearly so severely as with imprisonment.)

It should not become a place that is so much better than one's lifestyle on the outside that it is almost looked upon as a reward. It should also definitely not become a training ground for greater criminal proficiency. I imagine we can all agree on that, right?

And we really don't want it to be a place of such unspeakable hell that those therein are either destroyed or become bent upon revenge against society for what is being done to them. We can agree on that, right? And perhaps we might also agree that since most will be out sooner or later (and usually sooner) a very serious attempt at rehabilitation would be an act of self-protection for all of us.

Are we doing the job right? Well, if we are, why is it that most ex-inmates seem to be doing everything they possibly can to get right back in again? Why is that? Are we missing something here? And what about light punishments for the rich and most white-collar criminals? And what about the early release of violent criminals because of overcrowding?

What do you think all of these things are telling the criminal? What do you see happening as a result?

Trying to find answers. With the high recidivism rate, experiments have begun, here and there, to try to find some practical answers. For instance, one of the first states to establish a boot camp method is Georgia. The idea seems to have been a good one in some respects but it just wasn't accompanied by appropriate practical educational rehabilitation methods and comprehensive follow-up upon release.

Discipline alone is like moving straight and fast with no place to go. So, as you might imagine, it has been discovered that the criminals put through this unbalanced procedure have been found to be more likely to continue their criminal behavior when they're released. A study by the federal General Accounting Office projected that more than half of the men released from the Georgia boot camps would be returned to prison within five years. Let us hope that older study will have inspired changes that will soon show some encouraging results.

Los Angeles' one-time chief of police, Ed Davis, reported a few years back that prisons definitely don't rehabilitate. He also noted that less than twenty-five percent of all convicted felons ever go to prison and that the judges should have their trial record published in the information packet that is sent to voters before judicial elections. Interesting idea.

What about the cable TV, body-building gyms, and other special amenities that some of the authorities are applying to the prison environment? Some say such things are very helpful as rewards for good behavior and as punishment when withdrawn. Many never had it so good on the outside. This is their reward for their errant ways? Could that be the message they're getting—not the attempted reward and punishment conditioning?

What are we trying to do? I can also recall, several years ago, a California state task force recommended sexual freedoms for county and city prisoners and access to some drugs and obscene materials. This was a task force, appointed by Jerome Lackner, and was comprised of people from his own state health department, private health agencies, the Equal Right Advocates of San Francisco, the Prisoners Union, and other interesting types.

We hear about how so many criminals have been through the system so often it's like an endlessly revolving turnstile. Well, it's been that way for a long time. A 1985 Justice Department study of about 5,800 inmates showed that as many as eighty percent have been in prison before. The findings were in a Bureau of Justice Statistics report and clearly showed an almost unbelievable recidivism rate.

Almost ten years later there was testimony before the Governmental Affairs Committee of the U.S. Senate which stated that we, the taxpayers, spent $1.7 billion a year (at that time) to lock up what has been described as increasingly ruthless young criminals. How much did our government spend on programs to try and *prevent* youth violence? Twenty-four million dollars is what the Senate panel was told. (Since then you can be sure that those figures for cost of incarceration have gone nowhere but up.)

Life on the inside. I went on a special prison tour one time. Did that show me anything? Almost nothing. Only through a comprehensive investigation, or with revelations from those who *have* to be on the inside, can you tell how it truly is. The truth seems to range all the way from country clubs to a living hell.

On the one side we have that infamous cable TV service with premium movie channels (that many of us on the outside don't have—*we* can't *afford* it), fully equipped recreation facilities and, once a week, Alaskan king crab, shrimp, and scallops. Where? Some wonderful expensive resort?

According to *Your Guide to America's Top Ten Jails* this was (and may still be) available at the Fairbanks Correctional Center in Alaska.

(The guide appeared in *Playboy* magazine.) Other top jails are in such places as Boulder County, Colorado, Oahu Community Correction Center in Honolulu and Clark County, Nevada, Detention Center in Las Vegas. The list goes on like a resort travel guide, and you can be sure there are many others beyond those top ten.

And you remember the late Richard Speck who murdered eight young nurses in Chicago in 1966? About a year or so ago a video tape turned up showing the pampered Speck snorting cocaine, engaging in sex, and bragging about living what he referred to as the good life at Stateville prison in Illinois. He also was reported to have shown a number of $100 bills and bragged, "If they only knew how much fun I was having in here, they would turn me loose."

How about Larry Hoover, a gang leader from the streets of Chicago who was charged with running a huge drug distribution network as an *inmate* in the state prison system. There is that serial rapist, Melvin Carter, who was (and may still be) living in a two-bedroom, one-bath bungalow at the Devil's Garden conservation camp (aptly named) where he was reported spending most of his time laying around, reading, and watching television.

The other side on the inside. Not so long ago charges were flying around about Georgia's prison commissioner, Wayne Garner, watching the beating of inmates. Then there are the charges by the Justice Department's Civil Rights Division that many who are mentally ill are languishing in Los Angeles County jails in cramped cells with little or no treatment. There are stories that hit the papers every once in a while about fights and riots in various prison facilities around the country. It could be over almost anything. I recall the one at Susanville in California at the end of 1997. It was a racial fight that took fatal gunfire from the guards to stop.

There is one terrible story I will never, never forget. It's the story of Rodney Hulin, Jr., a 16-year-old Texas boy who was sentenced to eight years in prison for a small arson fire that did about $500 in damage to a fence. He was put in the adult prison at Brazoria County, Texas, where he was repeatedly homosexually raped. His brutal treatment was so bad that he prayed he could somehow get out of there alive.

He asked the warden and others for help. No one seemed to give a damn. They just didn't seem to care. On January 26, 1996, the young boy was found hanged in his cell. He didn't die right away, however. He was in a coma for four months until he finally died. Let me tell you, what he went through before he committed suicide—what happened to him is all too common in the prisons. Male rape of other male prisoners is far more the rule than the exception, as are so many other abominations. And the killings are also commonplace in a number of these institutions.

And it goes on and on. Other horror stories include such accounts as given by Jeris Bragan, a 46-year-old ex-private detective who was freed from prison after a judge decided that a key prosecution witness had lied. His horror had been a duration of fifteen years behind bars.

He told local media in Nashville, Tennessee, and the Associated Press that he personally had seen twenty-nine inmates stabbed to death. He also told how he saw problem kids grow into hardened, violent criminals. His most vivid quote: "It was a slaughterhouse." And not so long ago a federal grand jury accused eight Corcoran (California) State Prison officers of staging inmate fights for the amusement of the officers. It was a kind of "blood sport." It was like something out of a nightmare.

What happens to kids and adults in the prison system is only one part of the problem. There are so many others, such as the graying of the prison population (and the associated medical costs) and the gang operations behind the bars.

And let us not forget the sexual harassment and assault of female inmates by male guards. These charges have begun to surface everywhere from the Baylor Women's Correctional Institute near New Castle, Delaware, to the Alameda County federal penitentiary in California where three ex-inmates filed a legal action claiming they were sexually assaulted, beaten, and actually sold as sex slaves while in the prison. They also have claimed that officials knew what was going on and chose to do nothing. How interesting.

And then there are the riots. There were the riots between black and Hispanic prisoners in the Los Angeles County jail, the rioting in federal prisons in Tennessee, Pennsylvania, and Illinois, and, more recently, the siege staged by inmates at barracks of the Wrightsville work farm unit in Arkansas.

There it is. It's uneven as hell. From country clubs to riotous violence and everything in between. And through it all we seem to be doing a tremendous job of producing an enormous number of dedicated, professional criminals who will be sent out to go to work on *you* and *your* family and friends—in as losers, out as professional thieves and murderers.

A look at the statistics. I've given you figures like these before from the National Corrections Reporting Program. Let me give them to you again. They showed that the average time served for murder in America is eight years, for rape it's five years, and for robbery it's three years and three months. Also, the last report I saw from the Justice Department's Bureau of Justice Statistics showed there were well over one million state prison inmates in the United States and well over one hundred thousand federal inmates. By the time you read this, the figures should be up even more.

Let's face it, most of our nation's prisons are bursting at the seams. But the lack of coordination and planning and the confusing breakdown of procedure has not only filled the prisons to the breaking point (requiring early *dangerous* releases) it has also meant that some prisons have gone in the opposite direction. System breakdowns usually don't manifest themselves in one way alone.

In Texas, for instance, officials have had an embarrassing surplus of prison cells after the largest prison-building project in U.S. history. Of course the surplus is the result of very bad planning, where we end up bursting at the seams in one jurisdiction and cells stand empty at other locations, as a result of Texas state judges who just can't seem to get it through their heads that they don't need to consider overcrowded conditions when sentencing in these areas where there are *surplus* cells. (What about having a sharing arrangement with other jurisdictions?)

The same is true in North Carolina and in other places, even as the reverse is true in so much of our country. Can't they get their act together and coordinate allocations a little better than this? Of course they can't.

And let's not leave out the women and children. The female prison population tripled in the 1980s. I shudder to imagine what the final tally will show for the 1990s. I hear the figure may now be a total of over one hundred thousand women in prisons in America.

A great number of the juvenile facilities are also at the breaking point. In many areas all they seem to be able to do is feed them and clothe them. That's all. The rest of the time they are kept in dingy cells without any help—without any hope. (A few actually do have special school programs and comprehensive counseling, however.)

And then there's the probation system. All over the country, I keep hearing about soaring caseloads overburdening probation officers and other case workers to the point where they seem to be going backwards. And The Supreme Court told federal judges to be less harsh on criminals who violate their probation by using drugs. (This was nationally reported back in March of 1994.) One study I have examined from the Justice Department showed 43 percent of felons on probation commit a crime within three years. Has it dawned on anybody that something isn't working here?

Our dangerous early release programs. There's a smug saying in the criminal class that no one ever dies of old age in a prison in America. Well, that's not completely true, but it's close. They're either killed in a fight or are given an early release. For most of them, it's an early release. Frankly, a life sentence rarely means that. Neither does any of the rest of it. Talk about truth in advertising. If there should ever be truth in our legal system, it probably couldn't survive the shock.

What do we end up with? We get people like Charles Rothenberg who set his sleeping son on fire. He served six years and five months of a 13-year sentence. We get Charles Scott Robinson who was convicted of six rape counts for assaulting a three-year-old girl. The jury wanted him to get a thirty thousand-year prison sentence so he wouldn't be out so soon. We are told he could be up for parole in fifteen years or less.

We also get people like Charles Roland Stevens, a serial rapist who terrorized San Jose State University in California. He was released early (of course). He also promptly skipped parole and disappeared. There's the case of Ruth Galanter, whose throat was slashed and was left for dead by Mark Allen Olds, a drug using gang member who has been put on parole nice and early, which has left Miss Galanter frightened out of her wits.

And there's never an end to it. We get career criminal David Ernesto Mackey just out of prison and arrested for the brutal rape of a 67-year-old woman. We get the Pillowcase Rapist, Reginald Muldrew, released and back in jail again for terrorizing a young woman. And we get Lee Jackson, released after serving a little under six years for the beating death of an Ethiopian refugee, and then, after his release, killing two old ladies.

We have Michael Kelley, a paroled rapist who killed two women in Massachusetts. We have a California parolee who was wearing an electronic tracking anklet, which didn't slow him down one bit. He was picked up for robbing and killing a woman.

Remember poor little 12-year-old Polly Klaas? She was killed by Richard Allen Davis who had a history of kidnapping, robbery, and rape and was out on parole when he killed the little girl. And yet, with all of this, as an example, the then California Governor Wilson was severely criticized by the opposition party for doing all he could to end lifer paroles.

This whole thing reminds me of that Steve Benson cartoon in the *Arizona Republic* showing a sick looking Statue of Liberty holding up an ACLU torch in one hand and a furlough program in the other as she says, "Give me your cons, your crooks, your poor misunderstood thrill killers longing to roam free."

Yes, there doesn't ever seem to be an end to it, and there won't be unless a good number of you decide that you have had enough. And not only that you've had enough. You've had enough and you are going to become dedicated to making monumental changes!

Will you do it? Who knows, maybe you'll end up surprising me and yourself as well. Who knows?

Part Three

The Legal System: A Search for Solutions

Chapter Eleven

Changing the Legal System
Making the Impossible, Possible

This is that section I hope you've been waiting for. This is where we separate the dreamers from the doers. This is where *you* can get involved.

Here is where you can remember many of the breakdowns noted in Part 1 and in Part 2 and look at some of the opportunities for your personal involvement toward genuine solutions as your *own* goal. Now we'll find out just how much you *really* care about what's been going on.

Where the leaders are. One of the first things you may have noticed in the beginning of this book is our great concern over the lack of good, solid leadership in our country at this time. I know, you can point out some who came on strong and then seemed to diminish right before our eyes. And yes, you may see a few other possibilities, if they could only have a chance in the media and with an increasingly suspicious public.

Don't waste your time waiting for it to happen, because that's not really what it's all about. You see, the leaders we need—the ones we really need to come forward are the everyday folks just like *you!* That's right. You are one of the new leaders we need (anything from a neighborhood leader to a national leader). And don't tell me it's beyond you, you wouldn't know what to do and you really wouldn't have the time anyway. Unless you're mentally retarded, it's something you can learn.

And about your time? Except for a very few of you out there, most of us can arrange for *some* time to spend on trying to really make a difference. It's all about how you set your priorities. You see, there really are seldom any truly legitimate excuses.

This means that people like you and me can get involved in our neighborhoods, in our communities, in our state, and in our nation. And I'm not asking you to do anything I'm not also doing. I've been involved for years (much of the time, almost alone, it would seem). And where have you been?

So, if you want somebody to do something about the mess we're in, just look in the mirror. It's truly up to you! If you're wondering where the leadership is going to come from, look again to yourself and to others that you and your friends can honestly support.

We are our own best answer!

> Let us never forget that government is
> ourselves and not an alien power over us.
>
> —Franklin D. Roosevelt

Returning to constitutional law. The problem is becoming obvious to more and more people every day, including to many with very sophisticated, intellectual backgrounds. But it does little good to snip lightly at their heels over the legislative judgement from our courts that ignore the written Constitution. It's not unlike what Thoreau said. "There are a thousand hacking at the branches of evil to one who is striking at the root."

One of the repair processes that may truly be necessary to fully return us to the law in our "law and order" is the development of a constitutional amendment for the reestablishment of our Constitution as it was actually written and amended. Then, as further changes are needed, we can continue to follow the amendment procedures. (What a radical idea.)

That amendment is sorely needed. An amendment that will clearly define the basic intents and purposes that have, ever so gradually, wandered away from the original blueprints. Only a constitutional amendment can immediately cut across all areas of official practice and policy.

Let us never forget, we are a people that is expected to accept the tenet that ignorance of the law is no excuse. This has been so because our laws all the way to and including our original first documents were intended to be *written*, circulated and followed as they *are*, not as they may be changed by ever-changing capricious social or political interpretation from the bench.

We must *insist* that our Constitution and our laws in general (following original constitutional purpose) mean what is actually written. This also means that a life sentence must be truly that. This also means that our civil rights must assume a level of personal responsibility that seriously considers the effect on others. That means accountability on *all* levels (and that means also with the police, the prosecutors, the judges, bureaucrats, and the politicians).

Look again at the early part of this book. You can see countless examples of what this is all about. It is not at all complicated. Truth and honorable purpose seldom are.

The growing concern. Arnold Hamilton in the *Dallas Morning News* wrote of the "winds of secession" gusting across a number of our states. It would seem there have been some serious discussions from time to time about the possibility of secession (to form a new state) all the way from Kansas to Texas, New Mexico, Oklahoma, California, Oregon, Washington, and even in New York.

However some discussions are actually now touching on the possibilities of secession from our nation itself! Now that *really* worries me. Has our government become so oppressive against our people that this is being seen by some folks as the only possible solution? Is it getting that bad? Can we not find more reasonable solutions?

Will we end up with national secessions and committees of vigilance and all sorts of other frightening actions because we are not willing to have the courage to fight for reasonable solutions? You tell me.

Getting involved. Constitutional amendments are one tool that can be used to create meaningful positive changes. But it can get out of hand as well. Yes, I sincerely believe we do need an amendment of clarification to reinstate original meanings and remove legislation from the bench. But, shall we also have an amendment to guarantee a balanced budget, to better consider victims' civil rights, to restrict or eliminate unfunded mandates, to guarantee term limits, to require supermajorities in Congress for the passage of any tax increases?

Some of these may be possibilities, but what about school prayer, English as the official language, abortion, flag-burning, etc.? Some of these issues can be very divisive and might be better dealt with in some other manner, wouldn't you say? Or are amendments the only way? Not always.

Amending the Constitution. You may want to read about the procedures that must be followed if you're really going to get serious about such things. Here is Article V of our U.S. Constitution (with my underlining of the three methods that have been given to us):

> <u>The congress,</u> whenever two thirds of both Houses shall deem it necessary, shall propose amendments to this Constitution, or, on the application of <u>the legislatures of two thirds</u>

<u>of the several States,</u> shall call a convention for proposing amendments which, in either case, shall be valid to all intents and purposes as part of this Constitution, when ratified by the legislatures of three fourths of the several States, or <u>by conventions</u> in three fourths thereof, as the one or the other mode of ratification may be proposed by the Congress; provided that no State, without its consent, shall be deprived of its equal suffrage in the Senate.

What does this mean for you? If you're serious, this means starting local citizens' committees to study this matter and explore the method or methods you wish to follow. It also means communicating with your fellow citizens through the local media. (Sometimes this brings you responsible cooperation and sometimes it's a very difficult task. It depends on the attitude of the decision makers in your local media.)

It also means networking with other individuals and groups in other communities and other states and around the nation as a whole. It means working together with folks who share this common interest. It means working together in spite of the differences some may have in other areas. Let's see what you really can do.

Order in the court. What it takes to get it back. We kid ourselves with such lofty clichés as inscribed on the facade of the Supreme Court building in Washington, D.C. It reads: "Equal Justice Under Law." It is truly a bitter joke in the face of what we have. It should be replaced with, "How much justice can you afford?"

It is widely known, in and out of the dubious legal profession, that almost nothing is equal anywhere. It is confusing, disorganized, and just simply doesn't come even close to anything equal to . . . to whom or to what? That's the problem. There is not even an effective benchmark from which to proceed. (Remember, our Constitution, under judicial legislation, can no longer serve as a truly dependable benchmark.)

We simply have to apply the courage and wisdom necessary to clearly face the fact that our legal system is careening in all directions. We will also have to be able, unafraid, to accept the conclusion that the wheels of justice must be given a *serious* realignment. We must become strong enough, as groups and as individuals, to really make these absolutely necessary changes.

What is the law? It's hard to tell anymore. However, we can take a stab at some of the original definitions. This will help you and any group you join or start to understand the underpinning, at least a little bit.

Our most basic source for law in America is our constitution. (One of the first things that might be suggested we do is to push through that amendment of clarification to reinstate this document to the purpose of its original intent.) Another basic source for law in America is with our legislative statutes. (We must force our lawmakers to reshape our laws to bring us truly into the twenty first century.) Another source is with administrative rules in various government departments. (There must be a much greater accountability here. Such a change *is* possible.)

Another basic source is our system of precedents, sometimes referred to as "case law." (We must constantly fight against the tendency of case law to take precedents over constitutional law, which happens as often as it can be gotten away with.) And, the most important source of law in our nation is, of course—*you*.

Don't let them snow you with that pap about their knowing the law and the system and you being the dutiful little ignorant supplicant who must stay out of what they declare you don't know anything about. Let's face it, *they* have made an absolute *mess* of it!

We also have what is called an "adversarial system." This procedure goes back to the Middle Ages (and even before that). It was a time when disputes were often decided with trial by combat. This was fashioned into a courtroom custom of an adversary combat of words that somehow was magically expected to reveal the truth as the preferred outcome. (I can get better odds at a Las Vegas crap table.)

It was primitive and only managed to work correctly once in a while, when you had good and intelligent people in charge. As we have come down the ages to modern times, we find less and less of the good and the intelligent and more and more of the lawyer opportunists and judges with arrogant egos. We will take apart this "adversary procedure" in more detail and with more energy a little later on in this book.

The bitter jokes that must be ended. There are so many. There is the hypocrisy of the legal requirements for film credits which are pushed aside where they can't be read as they roll by, to make room for station promos and trailers. There are the legal statements that it is felt must be added to some radio ads and are run off so fast that absolutely no one could possibly determine what was being said.

There is an enormous number of clearly proven perjuries that are swept aside as they play the adversary game in the courtrooms. There are the judges who seem to have the egos of minor gods and make the decisions of a mental retard. There are the prosecutors who seem

Changing the Legal System

to relish the exercise of abuse and oppression without regard for truth.

Ordinary citizens need to monitor these very obvious abuses. Every community needs such independent citizens' groups (and without hidden agendas) to bring these things to light and make absolutely sure they are properly dealt with. It is something that you and I *can* do.

Monitoring the courts. We must watch what happens in our courts, and we must watch it very closely all the time. When things go wrong, you and your group must be ready to go to the media and to your legislators (if necessary) and anywhere else you have to go to stop the unbelievable stupidities right in their tracks. You must hold them *fully responsible* for what they do!

I know, in some states there are panels or commissions or such that are even sometimes empowered to deal with seriously incompetent judges. As I am sure you realize, everything from nothing to a slap on the wrist is the usual end result—not always but usually so.

A few examples of such incompetence would be appropriate. A Montana man was arrested in northern California for a parking violation and highway patrol officers discovered drugs—almost $5,000—and a stolen handgun. The 9th Circuit Court of Appeals overturned the conviction that followed because the court felt the authorities knew the accused had been recently paroled from a prison sentence involving drugs. The court decided that the arrest and search were illegal.

What would you do? If, after looking over all the court records, you and your group felt this was a very bad decision, what could you do? You could push for legislation that would more clearly define the right of the police to check out traffic violations or any other kind of violations whether they believe the person has a record or not. (Some decisions are already moving in that direction.) If that doesn't work? If such a law should ever be found to be unconstitutional (with our legislative judiciary), a new crime amendment might be necessary to deal with this and so many of the other insanities in the courts. Can you help to get some judges voted out or, if they're there until they die or retire, can you find adequate cause to push for removal on the grounds that the judge is unfit? Do it!

What about the thousands that there was no room for in this book and the many thousands who endlessly continue to ruin lives everywhere? Go after them! Go after them all! Don't stop until you get every last one of them! Make them just as accountable for what *they* do as *we* are supposed to be for what *we* do!

I know, it's a radical idea. But it's an idea whose time has definitely come. Let me tell you, we either start doing things like this, and with one hell of a lot of energy and dedication, or you'd better just start getting used to having an oppressive government that becomes more and more like the former Soviet Union.

More things to change. Here's another great example of something that should *never* have happened. As you might imagine, in many parts of the nation state laws mandate that permission be obtained from one or both parents before a child can obtain a driver's license or have decorative body piercing done or before various dental work is done or most medical treatments or other similar services can be performed on the child. This is normal and necessary to enable parents to have the important adult supervision and control that is so absolutely necessary in a functional family, and this is most certainly understood by practically everyone.

However, not so long ago, the California Supreme Court in its infinite lack of wisdom decided that an unmarried child (a girl) who lives at home and is under the age of eighteen can get an abortion *without* any parental consent and even without a *word* to the parents. What the hell is happening here? Have these judges completely lost their minds?

What can be done about it? Plenty, if you're willing to put up a good fight. Frankly, it will probably take a state constitutional amendment to force the court to adhere to a more sane behavior on this issue, to bring back a reasonable measure of parental control in California families.

Responsible citizens of the state should also organize to do everything possible to remove all such irresponsible judges from their posts. You either do that or you'll be faced with an endless stream of idiotic decisions of this nature that never stop coming down on us all. If you're not in California, don't feel too smug about it. You're next. About half the states have parental-consent laws that the American Civil Liberties Union may be expected to disrupt in a similar manner. And what about normal family controls in the other states? You see, nobody is safe without putting up a fight.

The jury is out on juries. The antiquated adversarial system also gives us very amateur juries that sometimes award phenomenal amounts in trivial matters and sometimes convict with almost no reasonable evidence or even with none at all or go in almost any other direction imaginable. This was well illustrated in the ABC documentary "Guilty or Not?" (seen from time to time on the Discovery Channel "Justice Files" TV series).

Changing the Legal System

The program noted that as many as ten thousand wrongful convictions occur per year. It was also observed that eyewitness misidentification often results in false convictions. Also it was not hard to realize that many of the problems were with some very unsophisticated juries that just don't have the training in observation and logic that really is necessary to do the job in a professional manner.

From time to time citizen or judicial task forces or study groups are formed in various states to study the feasibility of improving the quality of juries or changing the structure or functions in one way or another. It is usually a vain attempt to try to improve the quality of performance. Citizens need to form such a committee with the audacity to study the possibility of doing a major revamping of the *entire system.*

One of the positions that I personally take concerning this mess is reflected in the attachment I included with my Juror Affidavit reply when summarily commanded to be available for duty (at $5. per day). It went like this:

> My attitude about the American legal system as it is now constituted (which I have had sufficient experience with) is such that you would definitely *not* want me on any jury under *any* circumstances. Among other things, I consider the adversarial system to be an absolute disgrace.
>
> The so-called search for truth is relegated to a procedure not unlike a Las Vegas crap shoot. Sometimes it works, by chance, and sometimes it doesn't. But almost always the adversarial "game" must be played *without* a truly proper regard to actual truth or the basic concept of justice (which we have all found to be a privilege that quite often cannot be adequately afforded).
>
> I could say more—much more, but you can be sure, you really don't want to hear it. I'm sure you get my drift.

Yes, if enough of you returned this kind of message to the court, they would have to make some genuine changes. But of course, enough of you won't really do anything like that, now will you?

Remember your purpose. With all of your efforts—with citizens' groups monitoring the courts, informing the public and pushing for significant changes—with all that you can do, never ever lose sight of the primary goal. When considering the men and women in any government position from the administrative to the legislative or the judicial, we must make them just *as accountable for what they do as we are supposed to be for what we do.*

And for those who think this idea is irresponsible and unrealistic, let me add the words of U.S. Supreme Court Justice Louis D. Brandeis (from Olmstead vs. the U.S. in 1927):

> Decency, security and liberty alike demand that government officials shall be subjected to the same rules of conduct that are commands to the citizen. In a government of laws, existence of the government will be imperiled if it fails to observe the law scrupulously. Our government is the potent, the omnipresent teacher. For good or for ill, it teaches the whole people by its example. Crime is contagious.

A hard look at the lawyers. I am reminded of Parker and Hart's "Wizard of Id" Sunday comic strip with a kid being asked by the king what he wants to be when he grows up. The little dickens replied that he wants to be a crook. When asked what his second choice was, he answered, "A lawyer." The king then looks at the reader and thinks, "The kid's got a one track mind."

Even Ted Geisel, the late creator of the famous Dr. Seuss children's books, had an intense dislike for lawyers. Near the end of his life, I am told he began a book about lawyers. He grew so angry and his book evidently became so angry that he was said to have finally recognized that it just wouldn't work. So far as we can tell, most unfortunately, no trace of that book remains. It was never published.

Our lawyer-controlled legislatures. Peter Stone is quoted as saying, "I have come to the conclusion that one useless man is called a disgrace, that two are called a law firm and that three or more become a congress." Well that's not far off.

Even though the number of lawyers serving in Congress today is a bit lower now than in recent history (according to the American Bar Association), it is still the dominant number, beyond all other occupations represented. As it stands now, it's just a little under fifty percent. (And in some state legislatures it's *much* worse.)

That's a lot of lawyers in one place. But do you really wonder why? Just you remember, that's the seat of power—that and the judge's bench. That's where they must go to gain control and to maintain control. They know exactly what they're doing, and don't you forget it. What can you do about it? What you can do is to see to it that *no* attorney gets into office or back in office, in *any* legislature, either state or federal. I know, that does seem a bit extreme.

Changing the Legal System

Well, it's a problem that has gone to the extreme. This may be the best immediate answer at this time. Think about it.

Cutting the cost of lawyers. As *Parade* magazine reported a while back, attorneys in this country evidently file at least eighteen million civil lawsuits each year. As you might imagine, it was also noted that this was creating a strongly negative effect on our economy. The article further reported that "the mere filing of lawsuits against them has forced industrial plants to shut down, doctors to abandon their practices, playgrounds to close and dads to stop coaching in the Little League. The defendants decided they simply could not afford to fight all the lawsuits, even though they might well win."

Of course there has been some minor efforts to get legislation going that would cut the cost of litigation by limiting the amount of punitive damages and even requiring the losers to pay the costs of the lawsuits. Now that's an interesting concept. (not at all unknown in other civilized parts of the world).

What about "double-dipping"? You don't know what that is? That's when estate lawyers collect big fees from serving as executors of an estate *and* also for acting as attorneys for that *same* estate. It involves a number of activities that usually overlap and allows the disreputable lawyers to get it comin' and goin'. If you're in a state where this is a problem, you can be a part of a strong push to get legislation passed to change this situation, to make it downright illegal to charge twice like that. It's up to you.

Let us not forget the uncomfortable fact that there are at least two million auto accidents in America each year that involve personal injury. You will also find that more often than not the accident victims are taken to the cleaners by their attorneys to the point that many of these unscrupulous attorneys end up with most of what was awarded.

That is often referred to as the "contingency fee rip-off" and it is yet another thing that can be brought under control by state legislation. Of course it won't be easy. You'll be facing more lawyers in the legislature than you ever wanted to know existed. But the right kind of public spotlighting of those who oppose such corrective legislation can go a long way toward reform.

There are also those rip-off copies of patented products and copyrighted and trademarked items that must be dealt with in prohibitively expensive civil litigation. Often that means the thieves are never brought into court. Why? Who can afford it? What can be done? Much can be done. You can *change* the system. What I will *never* understand is that what we are dealing with here is something that seems to me to be a clearly *criminal* act. So what do we do? We push for national legislation that will make it a criminal matter. That's what we can do.

Some sheepish concessions by the ABA. Some time ago the American Bar Association's Standing Committee on Ethics and Professional Responsibility issued a Formal Opinion (93-379). In it they lightly deplored a number of common billing practices of lawyers.

Some of the naughty things mentioned were the adding of surcharges for expenditures on behalf of a client, the billing of more than one client for the same hours spent, receiving various discounts from assisting colleagues and not passing the savings on to the client, and the old favorite, the general padding of the bill.

Surely we cannot do away with such time-honored traditional practices, now can we? Oh yes we can! But that will probably only be when enough of you have taken it upon yourselves to see to it that relevant legislation has been introduced and passed to change this situation. You might also want to consider federal legislation that will make it mandatory for the lawyers to put everything into plain English. Let "Eschew Obfuscation" be your guide. (That means, "Avoid making anything difficult to understand.")

Another possibility. It was noted in the Nolo press that, "It is nowhere written in the stars—or in the U.S. Constitution—that only lawyers can deal with basic legal issues and that their services must be bought at exorbitant rates." They went on to note that good, quality methods can be set up to make sure the law is truly affordable to everyone.

The Nolo press wrote of six fixer-uppers that should be seriously considered. They are (in abbreviated form) as follows:

1. License mid-level legal services providers, paralegals who can meet state licensing requirements.

2. Expand Small Claims Court. Limits should be raised.

3. Make the courthouse user-friendly, from the clerk's office to the law library to the courtroom and . . . forms and instructions should be available for all basic legal actions.

4. Help people help themselves. Non-lawyers need help preparing paperwork . . . through a low-cost legal advisor program.

5. Write laws in plain English. (It's about time!)

6. Help people settle lawsuits out of court. Mediation, arbitration and other cost-effective ways to avoid the pain and

high cost of contested lawsuits should be offered at a reasonable cost.

If you want more information on this, I believe the Nolo Press may have copies still available of "Legal Breakdown: 40 Ways To Fix the Legal System." Write or call them for details. They can be reached at: Nolo Press, 950 Parker Street, Berkeley, CA 94710. Phone: 1-800-992-6656.

The need for far more volunteer lawyers. I remember Supreme Court Justice Sandra Day O'Connor's impassioned plea to the lawyers of our nation before the American Bar Association meeting in Atlanta. She was asking, practically begging, for more lawyers to donate time to the poor.

It is a plea that has been made many times by many people and few have ever responded. In most of this nation, the poor still have their access to much needed legal help severely restricted. And, as always, those in the middle-income level still find that they often are quickly sent to the poor house by the legal profession. They are cleaned out. And no one in that profession is making a truly serious attempt to make a major change in that situation.

Disciplining the arrant lawyers. Question: What's the main difference between baseball and the legal profession? Answer: In baseball, when you're caught stealing, you're out.

Let's face it. In law, there is so much that is like stealing, it isn't much of a stretch to move just a little bit further in that same direction. Since discipline in such matters is so unsure (and sometimes non-existent), it does seem like a most inviting open door to many in that "profession." (Just you remember, power does not corrupt nearly as fast as immunity.)

So is anyone anywhere making *any* attempt to rectify this situation? Is there anyone or any group willing to face the incompetence and the blatant dishonesty? Well, the American Bar Association, realizing the problem has grown to such public proportions, has offered a few public relations ploys.

The ABA has formed commissions and has released suggestions for improving the profession's image with various polite suggestions concerning the discipline issue. Among their suggestions is the idea of local bar associations being willing to give up lawyer regulation to the highest court in each state. Their idea is that somehow this will remove any potential conflict of interest or other unfair influences that might be perceived by the public when lawyers are in charge of disciplining their own.

Of course they really don't want anyone to consider the fact that judges have been lawyers as well and are steeped in the traditions of that brotherhood. Although there are a few judges who have become outspoken mavericks, most have been found to be very cautious about disciplining their own and, in some cases, are not willing to do so at all. Once again it's another suggestion of letting the fox guard the chicken coop.

There are a number of concerned, educated, and highly capable individuals *outside* of the legal profession who could serve on *citizen* judicial discipline commissions. They could have the power of a grand jury and then some, but the members should *not* be appointed by judges or others in the legal profession. (They could also be empowered to investigate the judges as well.) What do you think? Would you be willing to push hard for something like this? Just you remember, like everything else worthwhile, it won't happen without a considerable amount of effort by a number of dedicated people. That's what it takes.

Can you sue the bastard? Another approach is for clients who have become the victims of their lawyers to sue those lawyers. I see that insurance actuaries have shown that malpractice claims issued against lawyers have been increasing at a rate of 20 percent annually. Unfortunately, it is a very difficult process. Very few attorneys have been willing to specialize in legal malpractice. Quite often you need to look for such an attorney outside your own local area.

You may want to ask your local bookstore to order the Random House book, "If You Want To Sue a Lawyer—A Directory of Malpractice Attorneys." It was written by the HALT organization and is considered to be a quality effort that could be of great help to those in need.

To catch a thief. What about the lawyer who is clearly a thief by any definition of the term? In about forty-seven states there are some funds that local bar associations have set aside for the reimbursement of clients who suffer theft by lawyers. Of course, as I am sure you suspect by now, a great number of victims receive very little or absolutely nothing because often such programs are so poorly run, with both procedures and funds available.

There may be a disciplinary or grievance committee in your state. There may also be some sort of arbitration process available. If all else fails, there are always the media (which isn't often interested) and the police (who feel they have better things to do much of the time). There is also the IRS. If a substantial amount has been taken, they might be interested. It isn't often that such income is declared on the return.

One possible solution. A "Legal Reformer" report of the "Americans for Legal Reform" group published some of the comments from the final report of the Connecticut Commission on Legal Ethics a while back. The comments were by the Connecticut Supreme Court Justice T. Clark Hull who served as the Chairman of that commission. Some of these interesting statements were as follows:

> I personally differ somewhat with my colleagues on the Commission in harboring a deep rooted doubt that lawyers can ever successfully regulate other lawyers.
>
> The failure of the legal system to deal promptly and effectively with lawyer ethical misconduct can only further erode the confidence of the public in the law, the courts and the legal profession.
>
> The events of the past several years unfortunately highlight the damage inflicted upon the public and the profession by the wrongful acts of those few lawyers who willfully flout established standards of ethical conduct.
>
> Embezzlement by lawyers must be stopped. To this end procedures must be put in place to detect wrongdoers, to remove them swiftly and permanently from the profession and to provide methods for full and prompt financial reimbursement of the innocent victims of lawyer misconduct. The public interest demands no less.
>
> Much empirical evidence exists as to inadequate bookkeeping practices and sloppy or nonexistent records. Some evidence exists of improper use by lawyers of clients' funds, such as temporary borrowing for the lawyers' own purposes. Overwhelming evidence exists of criminal conduct on the part of a very few lawyers, with tragic and drastic results to their clients and to the profession and ultimately in every instance to themselves.
>
> The Commission recommends that the consequence of intentional and willful embezzlement or criminal misuse of clients' funds shall be certain permanent disbarment.
>
> Concentrated efforts to prevent attorney misconduct are lacking. Programs that might provide early warnings of potential wrongdoing are not in place. The Commission believes that these deficiencies must be remedied. To this end it proposes

the creation of an Office of Attorney Ethics, broadly empowered to develop, implement and supervise ethics education programs, to operate systems directed toward the early detection of wrongdoing, to oversee the grievance process and to supervise a client-victim restitution program.

Wherever you are in our nation, if you like any of these ideas, you can initiate a citizens' effort in that direction. Don't expect it to happen if such an effort isn't made, however. It's still going to come right down to *you*.

Other ways and means. From time to time, companies start up that are involved in serving the disenfranchised—the victims of lawyers. One I can recall is a group called "Legalgard, Inc." This is a company that investigates lawyers' bills on behalf of clients. It is my understanding that they have found "irregularities" in as many as 80 percent of examined documents.

Last I heard, they were still in business and, in the northeast can be reached at 412-269-9811, in the southeast at 404-303-9260 and on the west coast at 818-713-9041. If you're somewhere else, someone at one of those numbers may be able to give you a closer contact.

Since even the American Bar Association statistics have shown that usually less than one percent of consumer complaints about lawyers, nationwide, ever led to severe punishment such as disbarment or to voluntary resignations—since this is so often what we have to face, perhaps suits against lawyers under consumer protection laws is another way to go. It's something to consider.

Something else to consider. "Americans for Legal Reform" has also come up with a Client Bill of Rights—things you most definitely should be entitled to when you need the services of a lawyer. They are as follows:

To be treated in a business-like manner.

To receive copies of all important paperwork and telephone calls and to be kept informed about what's going on with your case.

To have your telephone calls returned promptly.

To the truth, even when it hurts.

To your lawyer's best effort.

To have your lawyer comply with the Canon of Ethics.

To be treated with respect.

Operating outside the profession. Now we get down, once again, to that monopoly that the lawyers and their bar associations maintain in the legal profession. They speak of stopping what they classify as the "unauthorized practice of law" and they claim that the law forbids the rest of us from giving legal advice or assistance, yet I have trouble trying to find any prohibitions of this nature that are actually defined by statutes. Am I missing something here?

As HALT's "Legal Reformer" has indicated,

> ... with study after study showing the great unmet need for affordable legal services and non-lawyer paralegals gaining widespread popularity among lower and middle income consumers, bar associations, legislatures and supreme courts across the country are beginning to take a second look at "alternative legal services." But while some states are considering ways to allow paralegals to operate in the open; others are looking at ways to shut them down altogether.

This means that, once again, if you want it, you'll have to fight for it. These nice lawyers are not going to hand it to you on a silver platter.

Want to know more? You can order "The Independent paralegal's Handbook" from Nolo Press. Call them at 1-800-992-6656. Or possibly you might like to get in touch with the "National Association of Independent Paralegals." You can call them at 1-800-542-0034.

It should also be mentioned that "Americans for Legal Reform" does its best to sponsor bills before various state legislatures to try to put an end to the strangle-hold lawyers' cartel that is bleeding us all white. One such bill would establish a "legal technicians" category of professional help. These individuals would be trained and licensed but they would definitely not be lawyers and would not be charging those unbelievably exorbitant fees. If you want to get involved with them, you can call (toll free) 1-888-367-4258.

The lawyers fight back. I remember the story of Richard Lubetzky. He is a law school graduate who became a legal reform activist with CAL Justice (a California group). He passed the bar exam but the California Bar Association would not admit him to its association, and therefore, he was not allowed to practice law. (Yes, the bar associations have that much power.) They said he lacked good moral character (which should be considered as a recommendation in an association of lawyers). They actually had no other reason to make that claim of refusal other than by the fact that he was very active in the battle over lawyer-discipline reform.

Lubetzky had to go all the way to the state Supreme Court to win his right to practice law. Were those who pulled this trick on him held responsible for what they had done? Of course not.

I also recall that well done ABC story on "20/20" about lawyers. The main question was whether or not they are worth the price you pay. As Barbara Walters said, lawyers are certainly easy enough to find but, "Have you priced one lately?" She further noted that they're multiplying as much as four times faster than the population as a whole. And even with all of that they still don't come cheap. Are they worth it? As Walters observed, "Critics say no."

John Stossel added that the system is definitely out of reach for many people. He also brought up the fact that even the Bar Association had admitted an estimate of at least a hundred million people who can't afford a lawyer. Since then, folks in some states have actually found that their local bar associations have reluctantly moved toward allowing a minimum of non-lawyer participation in a very limited sort of way, but that doesn't amount to all that much.

In this particular program they included an interview with Jerome Papania, a legal assistant who had become a serious target of the legal community. Mr. Stossel noted that Mr. Papania was helping folks with such things as simple bankruptcies, uncontested divorces and name changes. As it was explained, most people seemed to like this sort of help. Of course the lawyers didn't like it. The police raided his office and took him away to jail. As John Stossel reported, "Jerome was charged with the unlicensed practice of law. He faces a maximum two years in jail."

The District Attorney, Richard Ieyoub, got into the act and announced (on the documentary) that they felt they had sufficient evidence to come to the conclusion he was involved in "the unauthorized practice of law."

As you might imagine, he was convicted. Whatever happened since then, I'm not sure. However, I do know that this sort of thing has been going on in various places all over the nation. The lawyers have an iron grip on the legal system (and on your wallet) and they have an arrangement, under their version of the law, which allows them to use the police and the courts as their enforcers. The mobs would just love to have something that works just half as good as this. It's a great racket.

It should also be noted that NBC has done some fine work exposing problems and breakdowns in our nation. "The Fleecing of America" segment on the NBC Nightly News is a good example of some of their best investigations. And there are others. Look for them and tell your friends about them. When the media does a good job, it needs your support.

On another battlefield of the war. HALT's "Legal Reformer" reported that, "Under federal law, people are entitled to declare personal bankruptcy by filing a petition with the federal bankruptcy court. The petition follows a standard form with listing of 'assets,' 'exemptions,' and other information. People can do it themselves with some help. Naturally, people who are bankrupt do not have a lot of money to pay for lawyers.

"Independent paralegals have found they can help people through bankruptcy for a small fee. In an effort to protect their turf and high fees, bankruptcy lawyers are trying to get an amendment to the federal bankruptcy statute which would enact grave penalties for non-lawyers who help people through the process."

These kinds of efforts can be found rising up out of the legal cesspool from time to time. After all, they have to protect their exclusive right to get deep into your back pocket, right? Of course it's true that there has been *some* legislative movement toward the overhaul of the antiquated bankruptcy system. And yes, more still needs to be done—*much* more.

Another example. "The Legal Reformer" has had many terrible tales to tell about ordinary Americans just trying to help other ordinary Americans. Another one I will never forget:

> It is hard to report about Peggy Muse, an independent paralegal in Oregon, because we don't know where she is. Last we heard, the Sheriff was looking to cart her off to jail. She runs a paralegal self-help office for people in divorce, change of name, simple wills and other services which paralegals offer all over the country. In Medford, Oregon, the bar association went after her for "practicing law" and the judge convicted her.
>
> According to Peggy she had no lawyer when she went before the judge and she asked for time to replace her original lawyer who quit on her. The judge said "you had one once and that is enough." She refused to participate in the trial because she had no lawyer. After she was convicted, sentenced to jail and fined $25,000, she appealed but lost in the state courts. She asked for time to go to federal court but the judge said no and the bar association put in a petition to have her jailed immediately.

That sort of thing can't happen in America, right? Not in the America that you and I remember. But then, this isn't that America anymore, is it? If this book teaches you nothing else, it most certainly should teach you that we are fast becoming so many of the terrible things that we have fought wars over for 200 years to keep others from turning us into.

Had enough? Let me quote you a story from the "Nolo News" a while back.

> An independent paralegal based in Kalispell, Montana, recently attempted to represent a physically handicapped man who couldn't afford a lawyer. Jerry O'Neil relied on an 1871 Montana statute (MCA 25-31-61) that allows a party to a justice court action to be represented by anyone.
>
> But O'Neil's pleadings were drowned out by the sound of the state supreme court backpedaling. First, the Montana Supreme Court ruled that, despite the clear language of the statute, "any person . . . may act as attorney," it was a "one time only grant of privilege" for a non-lawyer to appear.
>
> Not satisfied with interpreting the statute to mean the opposite of its plain language, the supreme court recently decided to eliminate it by judicial fiat. This has taken the form of a proposed rule of court, Rule 13, which does away with the clear statutory right of non-lawyers to represent people in justice court.

And as if that wouldn't be enough, there is the specter of California's powerful trial-lawyers' lobby that seems to orchestrate state legislative opposition to legal reform measures that the voters have overwhelmingly supported, and to do so in ways that tend to completely circumvent our original system of government.

Yet another example. I also have a letter that was sent out to state lawyers some time ago from the "California Lawyers Political Action Committee." The letter states that, "Our Board members have raised over $30,000. We know that contributions are fundamental to politics. The groups that make contributions generally have better access to those who make decisions in our political process."

It goes on to say,

> Bar leaders formed this PAC to preserve the independence of the legal profession. In the furtherance of this purpose, the Board has stated that it will oppose unreasonable regulation and deregulation of the legal profession and support maintenance of the unified Bar. This is not a PAC for Democrats,

Republicans, or other brand names. It is a PAC to financially assist those elected officials who are willing to listen to our concerns.

It then went on to note that,

Recently, the concept of unregulated "legal technicians" has been actively promoted by an alleged consumer group known as HALT (Help Abolish Legal Tyranny). They have also announced a plan to try to remove fee arbitration programs from state and local Bars.

HALT wants to put them under the control of a separate state agency with non-lawyer arbitrators authorized to issue binding fee dispute decisions. We do not know what will be next, but based on past experience, you can bet it will be yet another anti-lawyer proposal.

At the bottom it is signed by Leonard J. Meyberg, Jr., Chairperson.

There it is. It's right from their own mouths. There should be no doubt left as to what is really going on here—no doubt at all. Now you know what you are up against. You are up against pretty much the same thing almost anywhere in our nation.

Exploring other alternative methods. There are several computer programs available that can help you do it yourself, up to a point. Among them is "Home Lawyer" which, it seems, was put together by Hyatt Legal Services. Another program is "Do-it-Yourself Lawyer" from Expert Software. And there is "Personal Law Firm" by Bloc Publishing.

You might care to look for these and other programs of this nature in your local software store or in appropriate catalogs. You can also inquire about programs like this from Nolo Press.

There is also legal assistance by telephone. You can call 1-900-835-2529 or 1-800-835-3529 (for charging with your credit card). And yes, you do get to talk with a lawyer and, the last time I checked, it was costing no more than $3 per minute. Not bad, not bad at all. (Let's hope it also involves some skillful advice.)

Another alternative. Customers of Wells Fargo Bank received a notice a while back that stated, "Wells Fargo has adopted a Comprehensive Dispute Resolution Program . . . for certain disputes with account holders. The following amendment to your Consumer Disclosure Statement sets forth the terms of the program. Your continued use of your account will constitute your agreement to this program."

And then it goes into all the details.

Such mediation and arbitration programs are becoming more and more prevalent as everyone, from the public to the business sector, becomes more and more fed up with the endlessly escalating legal costs. So you see, you're not completely alone out there. There are some others who don't like the way things are and they're doing the best they think they can do to improve the situation.

Of course much, *much* more needs to be done. An ever increasing number of us have come to realize that the entire legal system, as it is now, needs to be *scrapped!* That doesn't mean everything needs to somehow be thrown out overnight. That wouldn't be intelligent at all.

What's needed is some gradual repair work right now (as I've suggested) and then a major overhaul of the entire method, one segment at a time, little by little, until finally we have our country back once again. It can't be done overnight. There are no quick fixes. You've got to be willing to be in there for the long haul. You've got to truly develop a courageous heart.

Persecution or prosecution? Much needs to be done to identify those who have laid down behavioral footprints that are dangerously criminal in nature. Those with such a history need to be worked with early on.

And then there are those who cannot be so readily identified, who are perpetrators sometimes turned loose due to mistakes of the prosecutors. And then there are those who are clearly innocent and are subjected to an almost mindless persecution due to inept prosecutors. There is a lot that needs to be answered for.

What do you do when the criminal system is criminal? What you do is change the rules. On the legislative level, if possible; on the constitutional level, if necessary. A few slaps on the wrist and the removal of an especially bad apple once in a while, does not get the job done. Band-aids will do almost nothing to clean up the mess.

Once in a while a bad prosecutor is taken to task (somewhat), as was the case with Assistant U.S. Attorney Edward Weiner and Special Assistant U.S. Attorney Hugh McManus and a few others from time to time. In these two noted examples it was a matter of legal sanctions (minor slaps on the wrist) for not sharing evidence with the defense attorneys as they are supposed to do. And, of course, the terrible injustices continue almost everywhere.

Mark Sauer wrote about Murray Weiner's nightmare in the *San Diego Union-Tribune*. It was about how a respected business owner was left to rot in jail for almost four years because of a totally irresponsible prosecution. His innocence was finally established and he

Changing the Legal System

was eventually freed but not until he had gone through those years of pure hell.

Then the rude revelation came. He lost a lawsuit against the district attorney's office (through the county) as Mr. Sauer put it, "on grounds that the district attorney's office is now immune from lawsuits alleging that prosecutorial misconduct or zealotry led to a false conviction."

As Murray Weiner put it, "They can be morally wrong, they can manipulate evidence and witnesses and make false statements to the court resulting in a false conviction, and now you can't do anything about it." That about sums it up. As Mr. Sauer quoted the defense attorney, "The problem with this (Supreme Court) ruling is that now no one is accountable as a policy maker." Let's face it, there should never, *ever* be any reason for excusing responsibility for such behavior—for such wanton persecutions.

Remember the Sometown story? That was a particularly good example because it was loaded with errors and willful stupidities from beginning to end. There was the amateur police investigation, the erasing of taped evidence by the police, the lack of witness accommodations at the court, the lack of adequate court records of the proceedings, and there was the mistrial due to prosecutor errors.

There was the accuser's offensive against a key defense witness, the Soviet-style retrial without the accused and without key witnesses, bad attorneys who don't seem to know what they're doing, the prosecutor's possible suppression of evidence favorable to the defense, lack of investigative processes on the breakdown of law and order in the area, lack of media interest throughout, winning the appeal and finding the whole thing thrown right back into the same court again, for a *third* trial which turned out to be yet another bad example of the dysfunctional system. And throughout, no jury allowed.

Unbelievable? It sure is, but it happened. It is happening all over the country, and some of the situations are life and death matters. And this will continue to happen until everyone is held responsible for what they do. That means *everyone*. That means the police, the prosecutors, the attorneys, and the judges. That means *everyone!*

And don't you forget, we are not asking for any more than what they like to demand of us. Nothing more. Nothing less.

We all must be willing to move heaven and earth, if necessary, to see to it that the rules are changed so that truly they *will* all be held responsible for what they do. Of course it will be a hard thing to push through, but it absolutely must be done! You know it and I know it and they know it, and some of them will do just about anything to stop you.

And on and on it goes. Another good example (or maybe I should say, another bad example) is of an Orange County, California, prosecutor who got Thomas Thompson sentenced to death for a murder the prosecutor claims he did all alone. A couple of years later, David Leitch was also on trial for the same murder and the prosecutor then said this other man was also there and was also involved. He was also convicted.

According to the U.S. Circuit Court of Appeals, the prosecutor needn't be consistent in such matters. Well, how about that? There shouldn't be any doubt left as to the depth and scope of the comprehensive breakdown that's involved here. Once in a while, as we've noted before, someone is slapped on the wrist. As was one San Diego prosecutor who was accused of lying about his involvement and dealings with unidentified informants. He was placed on administrative leave.

We're going to have to go well beyond that. Never forget, to be sure you have responsibility, you must be sure you have full accountability. This includes everybody. Remember my story about that D.A., Ed Miller? He let so many slip by (like that Tucker case) and finally he fouled up just one too many times and enough people got upset with him, and he was out. That's the way you've got to do it.

What about witnesses? You would think if you had witnesses that would take care of everything, right? Well, it ain't necessarily so. As you may recall, earlier in this book, we went into the lack of dependability of witnesses. There are processes that might be followed that could help in instituting an effective quality control in that area. As things are now, there is a growing segment of behavioral scientists, judicial experts and others who are beginning to suggest that, as they function now, witnesses may not really belong in court at all. Mostly it seems to be because of what they have discovered.

Among other things, it seems that fear of violence can negatively effect the ability to accurately remember what happened. It also seems that the confidence of a witness has absolutely no bearing whatsoever on the degree of dependability of the witness testimony. And, it seems that many whites have a hard time accurately identifying blacks. Research also tells us that a hold-up victim tends to focus primarily on the weapon, not the perpetrator.

There's lots more, but you get the idea. What is needed here is some serious reeducation in the fine art of observation—some serious retraining of witnesses—and a much better handling of them in the courtroom. The problem of witness availability needs to be addressed as well. Some law enforcement authorities have instituted a fly-in program to bring witnesses in from far-away points. You see, there's a lot that *can* be done.

The shame of plea bargaining. One of the most disgraceful and dishonorable practices in our courts is the use of plea bargaining. There's no other way to look at it. It's the reduction of a charge to a lesser charge for the promise of an admission of guilt to that lesser charge.

The excuse is that it's supposed to be expedient and is immediately successful for *some* sort of conviction. The truth is that truth is the first victim. When the charges can be changed, as in some sort of grotesque game, the truth no longer has any relevance whatsoever. It's gone. In its place you have nothing less than an agreed-to perjury!

With that, true justice is hardly a meaningful factor anymore. Of course, with our current despicable system, things are so enormously fouled up that it's looked upon as just about the only way they have of getting any kind of conviction at all. That's how bad it's gotten.

The jury is still out on juries. Grand juries are mandated by our Fifth Amendment and have hardly changed since the beginning. Since all federal criminal cases are supposed to begin with a grand jury indictment, the mindless "game" often played in that setting can make true justice somewhat of a gamble, to say the least.

It has been said that if our federal grand juries had to function as a few of the states' grand juries do (such as with California) the prosecutors operating before the federal grand juries would have to make any favorable evidence available to the jurors. That's just one of the many changes that have been pushed for. There are many others as well.

Some state and county grand juries in our country have found that their recommendations are often ignored by public officials or, at the very least, given a polite brush-off. Media disinterest, and therefore public disinterest, sometimes encourage this state of affairs. Sometimes it's also the juror selection process and the operational procedures that lose the public confidence.

Judges who nominate the jurors are not necessarily good judges of the character or the competence of their nominees. They, along with many prosecutors, are often not all that aware of the proper function of the grand jury either. A citizens' group of exceptional caliber and size could be a worthy replacement of the judges who select, provided enough checks and balances are intrinsic within the structure.

Similar changes are also needed in the regular court juries within the states as well. The general public (if confidence is raised by massive changes) needs to take a much greater responsibility in jury participation. Perhaps, if the adversarial system can be retired altogether—and it can—then the function of judge and jury can be combined in a new form. It can become a proud group of full-time professional arbiters whose sole purpose is to seek out the *truth*, the *whole truth*, and *nothing but the truth*.

No more games. Now *that's* something worth fighting for.

Tort reform in California. Signe Wilkinson of the *Philadelphia Daily News* put it so well in his editorial cartoon showing a courtroom scene and the complainant saying, "The cigarette that I was forced to smoke dropped ashes on the silicon breasts I was forced to implant and they melted all over the hamburger I hadn't cooked so that's why I deserve $325 million."

How on earth has everything managed to go so terribly wrong? How did this happen? Well, way back in 1944, as we were winning the Second World War, we began to lose in our courts. That's when the then California Supreme Court justice Roger Traynor began to practice his theory that liability cases should be considered as an opportunity to set public policy and to do so firmly against the business community.

And did it ever. The idea spread across the country, wiping out our constitutional and common law in every direction. This is what we have come to. It not only works today against the business world, it can be used in any irrational way you can imagine against almost anybody or anything. There seems to be no end to the possibilities.

Employment for the mentally handicapped? We have all heard how felons have sued for injuries during the commission of a crime, for medical expenses and sometimes for pain and suffering. Drunks have also used that same pain and suffering ploy to push for big settlements in accidents that they were responsible for. Let's face it, the inmates of the mental hospitals are alive and well and fully employed in the operational levels of our American legal system.

As Dick Thornburgh, former U.S. Attorney General and ex-governor of Pennsylvania, wrote in the *San Diego Union-Tribune*, "The direct cost of our civil justice system nationally is more than $152 billion a year—60 percent of what this country spends on public education, kindergarten through 12th grade, and 2.5 times what is spent on police and fire protection. Under our system of civil justice, plaintiff lawyers get a third of the take."

He also noted that at least two-thirds of the medical claims generated from auto accidents are phony. This ends up costing you hundreds of additional dollars a year for your auto insurance. He also added that, "According to a 1991 study by the Rand Corporation's Institute for Civil Justice, just one area of tort law—wrongful employment termination suits—reduces California employment levels by as much as 4 percent to 5 percent." If you're not in California, don't snicker; it's most likely just as bad where you are, believe me.

So what are you going to do about it? Are you going to continue to just sit there and take it? Or, are you finally willing to get together with others to push very hard for corrective state and national legislation? There are some folks out there who are already trying to do what they can to clean up this mess. They just need one hell of a lot more folks like you willing to come on board and help out. That's what it takes.

Other efforts. Of course even the courts are trying to do a few things here and there to try and patch things up a bit. Now and again teleconferencing is being tried to move things along when clients, lawyers and witnesses may be many miles apart at critical times. There is also a new program that some jurisdictions are attempting, called the "fast track" system. It is designed to reduce the time it takes for a civil suit to go to trial. And I can recall a Vista, California, Superior Court Judge (Herbert B. Hoffman) who was boycotted by the district attorney who refused to bring criminal cases to his court for various reasons.

Also I recall the report that was commissioned by the chief judge of the State of New York, Judith Kaye. Recommendations included the opening up of the lawyers' disciplinary proceedings to the public, the establishment of mandatory fee arbitrations, the raising of fines against lawyers who've filed frivolous claims, requiring client retainer contract letters, and the creation of more mediator programs for disputes between clients and lawyers.

Of course none of this is being done in a way that will have the necessary major impact on the system as a whole and it certainly doesn't address most of the problems. How about simplifying the legal process and putting everything in plain language? How about the use of non-lawyers for simple document services? And on and on it goes.

From time to time there are also a few bills presented in various state legislatures and in Washington, to try and get some genuine tort reform. There are also initiative efforts made from time to time to put measures that address such reforms on various state ballots. How do such things go? For the most part, not very well. What they need is a large and angry population right behind them. That's what they *really* need.

The other Arizona story. I also recall reading in the American Bar Association Journal (way back in 1977) that,

> During 1975 and 1976 nearly three hundred practicing lawyers in Phoenix and Tucson, Arizona, participated in an experiment simulating innovative and highly expedited procedures for initial appellate review. The results of the experiment strongly suggest that a vast majority of appeals can be resolved soon after trial without transcripts, without lengthy formal written briefs, but with heavy emphasis on oral argument.

This would suggest that Arizona was planning to move forward. Who knows the wonderful things they might end up doing, right? Wrong! Instead, there's been one scandal after another. As you recall, Arizona Governor Fife Symington was convicted of a felony and forced to resign. His replacement, Jane Hull, then did her best to defend her state.

She was quoted by Luna I. Shyr (Associated Press) as saying, "I would hope the rest of the country doesn't judge us on a few little things." The wire story noted, however, that "those 'few little things' go back a decade, to then-Governor Evan Mecham. Mecham was impeached and removed from office in 1988, and later was acquitted by a jury of fraud and perjury charges."

The article also noted the infamous "AzScam" sting which netted seven legislators and other "little things." And then of course there is that Sometown story and that Phoenix divorce case. One could fill a book with this sort of thing. So, what does it all mean? It means that the citizens of Arizona should be mad as hell about what's going on. (However, since the media there isn't world famous for its crusades, precious little may ever be done, unless enough of the citizens say *"enough"* and back it up with appropriate action.)

And, as I always say, if you're not from Arizona (or from whatever state I might be talking about at the time), don't feel smug about it. Wherever you're from, you have more than enough problems of your own. The dregs of our society seem to be in charge of our legal system just about everywhere. Frankly, nothing would work at all, if it weren't for the few judges and very few others who are genuinely trying to make some sense and justice out of the disorder.

The empire strikes back. And of course what's happening is that the lawyers are massing against such efforts in record numbers (and with a lot of money). As Dan Walters reported in the Sacramento Bee (in California), "Few in California politics can remember a time when trial lawyers, insurance companies, business and professional interests and consumer groups weren't enmeshed in 'tort reform,' as the political warriors call it. The reason is simple: money—big money."

He went on to say, "The state, in effect, decrees who can sue whom, what actions expose one to liability, what can be collected by the prevailing party and what fees can be charged by the attorneys. Untold billions of dollars in jury judgments, out-of-court settlements, premiums for auto and other forms of liability insurance, profits on new products, corporate stock issues and attorneys' fees hinge on the rules of the tort game."

He also noted that, "The wars are fought in the media, in the Legislature and at the ballot box. And politicians love it because they can milk everyone involved for 'contributions' to finance their own campaigns." Wherever you are in the nation, this is what you can expect to be up against. That's why it's going to take a lot of folks working very hard against these lawyers. That's why *you* have got to get involved.

The battle for tort reform around the nation. Bill Rechin and Don Wilder do a newspaper strip called "Crock." I'll never forget the one where a man is told that his lawyer says he's found something that could make it possible for him to reopen his case. The man asks, "He found new evidence?" The other fellow answered, "No. He found your checkbook." Well, that's the way it seems to be in the criminal courts and in the civil courts as well. As I've said before, it's more a matter of how much justice you can afford than anything else.

Believe it or not, some folks still think it's just the big boys who are taking the punishment from the system. Au contraire, it is shared by us all. Everybody can get a chance to be destroyed by our irresponsible legal system. And practically everything costs us more because of it. (Legal liability insurance costs a small fortune, which is passed on to the consumer.)

You should be warned, a larger number of you than you might ever imagine will someday have to face the full brunt of it with your *own* day in court. It doesn't matter where you are in this nation. You're no longer safe anywhere! Don't you forget it!

And some of the fault must also be laid at the feet of some very unscrupulous types who are more than willing to go after anybody to get whatever they can. I'm not only talking about attorneys who are willing to do that. I am also talking about some questionable clients. And there are those almost unbelievable lawsuits, like the manufacturer of a wading pool who is sued because his pool was listed as sixty-four inches in diameter when it was found to sometimes be only sixty inches. (Of course it's a matter of how much you *inflate* the thing.)

And there was that suit against Toys 'R Us and Tonka because ads said their "Easy Bake" oven can do the baking in under ten minutes but didn't explain that it would also take a little bit of time to mix the snack powder and pre-heat the little oven. (And maybe they also might have included the time to buy the item and take it home? Come on!)

Coming in on a wing and a prayer. Remember that case where a flight attendant was claiming he had been physically manhandled sufficient to justify a $5 million suit against Reverend Robert Schuller? Well, a couple of witnesses came forward to make it very clear that the issue involved no more than a pat on the arm.

Was that yet another case of somebody trying to hit the jackpot, no matter what it took to do it? So it would seem. It seems to be one more good example of why we need to change the laws so that the loser in such a suit has to pay all the court costs and attorney fees on *both* sides. (And yes, the losing *lawyer* should be included in that penalty as well.) Ready to push *that* issue in your legislature?

Still other efforts. Some administrators and judges seem to think that audio or video taping in the court works better and more accurately than with the old stenographic method. Unfortunately, that assumes it will be done with reasonable intelligence. If it's done the way it was in Sometown, you can forget it. You can end up with no court record at all.

The National Association of Realtors developed a system that brings aggrieved parties together in an attempt to bring disputes to reasonable resolutions. Now, more and more real estate contracts include clauses that mandate disputes to arbitration.

The whole idea is to get things as far away from expensive lawsuits as possible. Remember, with those lawsuits, only the lawyers can always be expected to go home winners (or rather to the bank and then home). More and more communities have established alternative dispute resolution programs to settle civil cases without the enormous cost of going to court. Such programs often have volunteer mediators who are experts in the area under question or are exceptional in other ways (at least that's the way it's *supposed* to be).

Other breakdowns to repair. You recall that poignant part of this book where I gave you so many horrible examples of what has been done to our children? In case this problem just hasn't sufficiently gotten through to you yet, let me throw another one at you.

There is that story in the Chicago area where a little 3-year-old boy was found dead by hanging, allegedly by the mentally ill mother who had the child returned to her care. Oh yes, they had a task force investigation, and, oh yes, the report recommended a complete overhaul of the system that somehow had let four judges take the child out of safe foster care and send him to his death.

Of course the judges weren't held to blame, even though those judges should have cut right through that stupid "game" they play and demand to have an adequate investigation and a complete and detailed report as to exactly what was *really* going on and exactly where any possible danger might actually lay. However, at least the attorneys on both sides were slapped on the wrist by the eventual investigation for agreeing to orders and procedures that gave the judges practically no information at all concerning the potential problem.

What was done? Very little. Is this sort of thing still happening? You can bet on it—all over the nation. So, are you planning to become a part of a group or start a group that will *never stop pushing* for truly *major* changes in the way this legal system operates? You can see what needs to be changed, can't you?

Is our legal system getting away with murder? The record shows that there is very little deterrent to murder in our nation. A fairly recent federal Bureau of Justice Statistics survey reports that the average sentence for murder in our country is just fifteen years and the actual average time served is only 5.5 years. I know. I've told you before and I'm sure you realize, it really does seem to be close to this figure most often. (You've seen some of the other statistics earlier in this book.)

What can we do about this? For the immediate future we should be demanding laws that mandate *truth* in sentencing. (It's an approach that's being put forward and adapted a little bit here and there, but it's needed everywhere and in clear and absolute terms.)

For the long run, we are really going to have to change the entire legal system. What we have now has to be *scrapped!* There's no way around it. It must be done. And it must be replaced by something that will really have a very good chance of ferreting out truth, without games, and truly allowing real justice to occur. Only a dream? Only if you do nothing to make it happen. (Keep reading. I will be showing you some interesting alternative ideas later on.)

So, where are we now? Well, there has been some progress, not much but some. Violent sexual predators can now be confined in mental hospitals, possibly for the rest of their lives after they've completed their prison terms. And there are a few groups beginning to gain a little headway against the inane legal system itself.

However, don't be deceived. Most of what is happening represents some cosmetic surgery and a few band-aids. That's about where we are now. Let us not forget the O.J. example of good DNA evidence with that bloody glove, that bloody sock, the bloody footprints, the blood on the Bronco, blood here, blood there. The trail was clear and definite. There was everything but a home video of the murder, and you know the verdict.

Who will judge the judges? Once in a long while, a rare bar association or a citizens' group manages to conduct a poll among lawyers and sometimes with the general public, to rate the performance of the local judges. (Performance is the right word when you consider the "game" that is played in the courtrooms.)

Most judges don't like that very much. They consider it to be an irrelevant popularity contest. They tend to put all sorts of pressure on those who promote such projects and see to it as best they can that it is never done again.

Maybe the best approach would be to have a very sizeable and professional citizens' group monitor the courts very closely and do very detailed evaluations of the goings-on. And, of course, they must make the results public. That means the group must truly earn credibility and the local media must be willing to cooperate in allowing public accountability.

The next step, of course, is to work very hard to defeat any really bad judges (and there are more than just a few) when they are up for re-election, and with other judges who seem to be appointed forever, have them removed for just cause. It can be done. It has been done. But it isn't an easy thing to do, and you've got to be sure you are correct with what you do.

Let's see more headlines like, "Riverside Judge Faces Charges of Misconduct," in California and from Tennessee, "Former Judge, A Fugitive, Is Found in Mexico." Let's not forget the judges convicted on bribery charges in San Diego. And what about Chicago's not-so-great reputation? And what about the rest of the nation? What about those who are yet to be uncovered? I once again ask, what are *you* doing? Are you just reading the headlines and hoping for the best?

And then there are those cases like that of Gerald Gallego, known as the "sex slave" killer. You know, he's the one who was sentenced to death in two states. As you might expect, his death sentences for two of his Nevada murders were overturned by a federal appeals court because it was felt that misleading jury instructions were given concerning the possibility of his parole.

Never mind about the one responsible for making the error. Nothing will be done about *that* individual. You can count on it. Of course a new penalty trial must now be held. But what about some genuine quality control in the original court? When are we going to turn that into a serious consideration? Where do *you* stand on this issue?

Politics and the judges. Former Supreme Court nominee Robert Bork wrote a book a few years ago (entitled, *The Tempting of America— The Political Seduction of the Law*) in which he noted that, more and more, the high court decisions seem to have a clear political influence involved. You may recall, I started out this book with a hefty little section dealing with such judicial legislation.

Mr. Bork spoke of these judges seizing political power and creating legislation rather than following constitutional interpretation because they felt they are morally wiser than the people's legislatures. How nice. Once these federal judges are in, they are in for life (or until they retire), and you can't vote them out if you don't like their legislation.

It's no wonder that both major parties have had their turn at holding up judicial appointment for fear of even more uncontrollable political activism from the bench. As Charles Levendosky, editor of the *Casper Star-Tribune* in Wyoming wrote toward the end of 1997, "The Senate Judiciary Committee is holding justice hostage." He wrote of over one hundred vacant federal judgeships going unfilled.

This means many thousands of civil cases that are left completely dead in the water. And this means, as Levendosky wrote, "In our criminal courts nearly 16,000 cases are caught in limbo." Everybody ends up suffering, and it is simply because so many of the judges are like loose cannons, leveling whatever gets in the way of their ideological preferences. This whole mess has *got* to be changed.

What must be done? You're not going to be able to reeducate those idiots no matter how hard you try. They already know what's best and you, frankly, are little more than an ignorant peasant. (At least that's what they seem to think.) Once again I tell you, what's needed here is that amendment to the Constitution—that amendment of reaffirmation which reestablishes the clear and obvious meanings within this precious document and disallows any further legislative variation.

If changes are to be made, make them with amendments, as I've said before. That's the way we are supposed to do it in this country. If they can't handle that, we can always offer them a one-way ticket to a dictatorship where their ideas might be more welcome. I'm sure there's a place for them somewhere in this world—but not here.

We must also be willing to get tough with those few judges who are actually caught in various illegal activities. We must no longer handle things like we did with former San Diego Superior Court Judge Michael Greer who was convicted in a bribery scandal not so long ago.

What happened to him? Why, he was sentenced to probation, and I understand he is receiving a generous pension. How nice. Who says crime doesn't pay? The question is, are you going to put up with this sort of travesty any longer?

An isolated case? Hardly. You and I have been reading all sorts of headlines, from time to time, about judges caught in some sort of scandal or other. And there are the many little cases you may never hear about, such as with former Judge Robert McDonald who was convicted of drunk driving more than once and avoided jail through one of those infamous behind-the-scenes plea bargains. Some Californians heard about that one but hardly anyone anywhere else did. Just as Californians don't hear of the local scandals from other parts of the country, unless it's a big case.

Just as you folks in Chicago probably never heard about how the California Judges Association knocked out an important rewriting of the rules of behavior in their Code of Judicial Conduct a few years back that would have made the code far more mandatory than advisory. And, I am told, there is plenty going on in the Chicago court system that would make interesting reading to Californians.

And, let's face it, sometimes bad things are happening in local courts that even the people living right in the middle of that community have no idea about. It just isn't being reported. Well, in spite of it, there is a move on to make laws that will put some *real* teeth in the discipline and removal of bad judges. (I wonder how successful *that's* going to be.)

Where you fit in. The problem is it's an effort by far too few trying to do far too much. It's an effort that clearly needs you, dear reader. I know, I never give you any peace on this point, do I? I keep hammering it in, don't I? I can't help it—you *have* to get involved!

Want to have judges chosen by a genuine merit system? Want to hold them to a limited tenure? Want to make sure they are fully accountable for what they do? Well then, get to work. You're the one who can make it so. (But, for God's sake, don't turn them into even more political animals than so many of them have now already become.)

You might also choose to start your own local group to attack some of these problems or you might wish to consider an existing group. You might want to get in touch with "Judicial Watch." You can call them (toll free) at 1-888-593-8442. There are a number of other groups you'll see listed at the end of this part of the book and at the very end of the book. Keep track. Take notes. See what you can get involved with. See what *you* can do.

Don't think it'll do any good? Well, once in a while something worthwhile has a genuine chance. (It would be more often if *you'd* get involved.) It wasn't so long ago that a legislative measure actually managed to be approved in the House of Representatives (over the strenuous objections of the Clinton administration) that would require the federal government to reimburse citizens for the legal costs of unwarranted criminal prosecutions. If it would ever have managed to pass in the Senate and override a presidential veto, it would be a miracle. (Unless, of course, a lot of people got behind the issue and truly pushed like hell.) What do you think?

Divorce from a failed system. I have been made aware of the dilemma of Timothy Lee Dean and Janet LaFramboise. He was sent to jail because he wouldn't pay the required child support after the divorce. While in jail he was involved in a fight that seriously injured his left eye. Now he's out and broke and in desperate need of a cornea transplant. She never received more than a few dollars and now it looks like she never will again and now nobody can do anything about it.

Then there was that movie, *Scattered Dreams: The Kathryn Messenger Story*. That was the docudrama starring Tyne Daly and Gerald McRaney. It showed us one woman's fight for custody of her children after she and her husband were wrongfully jailed in Florida. It was one hell of a mess. Oh, there's lots more. I'm sure you're aware of that. So, what's being done about it? Well, in California judges must now document why joint or sole custody is given to a parent with a proven history of domestic violence, drug abuse, or alcohol abuse. (Oh, I guess they can still put the kid in serious jeopardy. It's just that they must now document it. How nice.)

Another new law says that those who collect alimony should become self-supporting in what they describe as a "reasonable period of time" (whatever that means). In some states there has actually been some serious efforts to set things up with volunteer lawyers helping low-income couples, establishing help centers for child support cases, and far more serious sentencing programs have been initiated for domestic-violence offenders.

The California Judicial Council has put together a document called, "Family Law Court 2000." It suggests a number of changes that could make a difference. The document is available on the following website: www.courtinfo.ca.gov/onlinereference/fc2000.doc. You can also write to Michael Fischer, Administrative Office of the Courts, 303 South Tower, San Francisco, CA 94107.

But just you remember, these are just little things being done here and there. They've hardly touched the surface. If anything more is going to be done, a lot more folks are going to have to join in the effort.

Do-it-yourself law. When we think of this, we usually think of making out our own contracts and other legal forms and we think of small claims courts, but sometimes it might be meaningful, and a lot cheaper for everybody to consider this approach for amicable divorces as well.

Without this approach, a divorce could conceivably end up not unlike that Peter Kohlsaat "Single Slices" cartoon of a newly divorced couple walking along and talking about how now that their divorce is final, their lawyers have all their money. They have no house, no car, nothing. And then they start to reminisce about how it has turned out to be like when they first met (broke then, too). Kind of romantic. Ha!

Well, no matter how one looks at it, we are in desperate need of major divorce reform. It's such a mess that it sometimes seems as though innocent men and women are made needless victims as a routine procedure. This is another area that needs some genuine public effort.

And of course there are also Small Claims Courts (or Special Sessions Courts). Sometimes there are good judges there doing a good job and sometimes you have those who are putting in their time and just don't give a damn. You've got to sort out what you've got in your own areas and deal with it. And you've got to push for a greater maximum monetary limit.

Where to go for help. And there are places where you might find out exactly what you need to know to handle many of your legal needs by yourself. As Ralph Warner wrote,

> I quit practicing law almost twenty years ago. During my five-year career, I was appalled by the fact that everywhere I looked, from divorce to landlord-tenant disputes to road accidents, it was obvious that lawyers were concealing and complicating simple information so they could sell their services at a high price.

He went on to reveal that,

> By writing and publishing self-help law books through Nolo Press, I could sell the same information lawyers did, but simplify it as much as possible and price it so everyone could afford it.

Nolo Press has lots of good material like that. As I've told you before, you can reach them by calling 1-800-992-6656 (or locally in Berkeley, California, by calling 510-549-1976). I'm sure they'll be happy to send you one of their catalogs. (No, I don't get a kick-back.)

Additional help that you will really need (in fact, we all need) is with a much greater effort toward plain-language law. Very little has been done to simplify that incomprehensible polysyllabic Latin nomenclature that masquerades for intelligent communication in the legal profession.

This is done purposely to sandbag the ramparts against upstarts like you and me who would like to take care of simple things ourselves without having to end up with a major production with legal fees that break our backs. We've got to *push* for this change.

Other possibilities. A few years ago, a number of lower cost legal services started up around the country. "The Law Store" opened up in some of the Montgomery Ward stores (now the service has been changed to "The Legal Service Plan" at 1-800-323-4620), "Lawco" started in Los Angeles, a savings and loan association started providing legal services at reduced fees from an independent law firm, and legal insurance plans began to show up here and there.

Most of these groups have faded away but there still might be one or two available in your part of the country. You'll have to ask around. See what's available in your community. If nothing is available and it's important to you, you certainly are free to explore the possibility of starting a discount legal service (or possibly a paralegal service, if they won't throw you in jail for it). It's up to you.

Oh, and I've recently discovered another group you might want to consider. It's called the "Legal Club of America" and with over 6,000 attorneys nationwide, they are offering notably lower hourly fees and a number of important free services. Membership fees in this "club" are not high. Check them out to your own satisfaction. Call 1-800-305-6816 or reach them on the web at www.legalclub.com.

Another idea that seems to be developing here and there is neighborhood justice centers (or dispute settlement centers) where minor community disputes can be mediated outside of the costly and crowded court system. Such centers are applauded as a truly inexpensive and often very effective alternative for everything from employer/employee disputes, landlord/tenant problems, consumer/merchant difficulties, husband/wife disagreements and some of the smaller juvenile problems. Do you have something like that in *your* neighborhood?

Another way to go when you don't want to just end up making the lawyers rich is to consider utilizing the services of members of the American Arbitration Association. They have offices all over the country. If you can't find one in your area, you might write them at 1150 Connecticut Avenue NW, Washington, D.C. 20036 or call 202-296-8510. They probably can find you some help in your area.

The dark side of representing yourself in court. If this was anywhere close to being the country we all used to think it was, we should be able to go into court and represent ourselves if we wanted to. Unfortunately, going "pro per" can be a very painful, eye-opening experience in most jurisdictions.

True, there are some judges and other court officials who admire the gumption of the few amateurs who dare to tread on the treacherous quicksand of the civil and criminal courts and are quick to try and help them along. But don't hold your breath waiting for such as these to show up. They are truly an endangered species.

As Ralph Warner noted about self-representation in the Nolo News, "From beginning to end, the legal process makes it hard—sometimes impossibly hard—for intelligent and reasonable people to accomplish what should be routine legal tasks." He revealed an example of the prejudice that clearly works against the poor guy who dares to exercise his right to represent himself in a court of law.

As he observed, "When he asks the court clerk what papers to file, he gets a blank refusal of help. Telling him anything about the divorce process would be illegal, the clerk says—the unauthorized practice of law. Get a lawyer, he is told." And, as he further observed, "The clerk is likely to be so unhelpful that the couple won't even know if they are in the right room. They will be told to sit towards the back of the courtroom as part of the audience (lawyers, of course, sit up front near the judge). Their case is likely to be heard last, to accommodate the busy schedules of the attorneys representing clients."

As also noted, when you apply for a driver's license or file a tax return, officials most often at least try to help. In fact there are instructions, pamphlets, etc. But it's a whole different story when you go to court. If you're on your own, you're *really* on your own.

If all of that isn't enough, Warner also warned that "bias against someone without a lawyer may cloud a judge's judgment about the merits of the case." This is yet another major area that really needs to be cleaned out thoroughly. You've got to be able to have a decent chance with the clerks and in the courts with or *without* a lawyer. We've got to put an end to this prejudice. That's all there is to it.

Some attempts are being made. The shameful legal practice of forcing the dead to enrich the lawyers is being offset, little by little, by the efforts to get people to set up special trusts for their estates that will avoid the probate scandal altogether. (There are some attorneys who are helping in this effort and a few at a reasonable fee.)

There are also a few examples (very few) where city attorneys have developed alternative programs of informal hearings conducted by paralegals under professional guidance to deal with minor misdemeanors. If it's handled right, it could be a genuine step in the right direction.

Remember, there are far too few within the system that are willing to give you and me a reasonable break. That's just the way it works. So, somebody's got to *change* the way it works. Guess who that "somebody" is?

Joining in with others. We have already given you some resources you can use and told you of some groups you might be interested in. Now let me give you some additional groups to choose from, should you be interested in joining in with others. Believe me, it's a great way to get started. (A longer list is at the end of the book.)

There is "Citizens Against Lawsuit Abuse." They will be happy to send you a free kit to help you be a part of efforts to help limit frivolous lawsuits. They can be reached by calling 1-800-558-2252. There is also the American Tort Reform Association, 1212 New York Ave. NW, Washington, D.C. 20005. They can also be reached by phone at 202-682-1163.

The "Association for California Tort Reform" can be reached through the toll free number: 1-888-882-6363. They can also be reached on the Web at www.actr.com/actr. The "Doris Tate Crime Victims' Bureau" is at 1-800-784-2846. And, the "Safe Streets Coalition" at 919 18th St. NW, Suite 800, Washington, D.C. 20006. (I've seen this group in action.) You can also call them at 202-822-8100.

You also may recall such excellent ABC documentaries as the "Turning Point" episode, "Dead Drunk: License to Kill" with Barbara Walters. It showed how repeat drunk drivers still manage to beat the system a lot of the time, stay on the road, and too often end up killing others. This is a program that is repeated from time to time because it is still such a serious issue.

The show points out the inadequacies of the laws and the courts. And, as Barbara Walters pointed out, "Nothing seems to make a dent with repeat offenders." One group is doing all it can to make a dent in this problem. It's a group I know you've heard of—Mothers Against Drunk Driving (MADD). They can be reached at 1910 "K" Street NW, Washington, D.C. 20006. You can also reach them through 1-800-438-6223 or at 202-467-6233 and you can visit them at their Internet website at: http://www.madd.org.

You may have noticed that we made some very brief quotes and wrote some very short descriptions and comments on several of the fine ABC documentaries that have been done on this subject. We were in touch with Veronica Pollard, Danielle Carver, Felicia Stoler, and others at ABC, trying to get them to agree to a more extensive reporting on at least one of their programs, "The Trouble with Lawyers."

You might be surprised, as we were, to find that they were totally unwilling to cooperate with us in any way whatsoever. They turned us down flatly. So, as a result, we have had to limit our coverage to brief quotes and comments of critical review and not give you the more in-depth presentation that such a program truly deserves. I don't understand their paranoia but, I must admit, it is something I have discovered in a few areas while researching for this book.

A special group I know you will want to get in touch with is "Americans for Legal Reform" at 1612 "K" Street NW, Suite 510, Washington, D.C. 20006. You can call them toll free at 1-888-367-4258. This is an organization that is dedicated to reforming the civil law segment of our legal system. They are very dedicated and have a number of local chapters around the country (just as MADD does).

Another group you may also want to reach is "Judicial Watch," at 501 School St. SW, Suite 725, Washington, D.C. 20024. You can call them, toll free, at 1-888-593-8442. As Larry Klayman, the Chairman and General Counsel of the group says, "We're the public interest group that not only talks, but actually does something about corruption in government and the court system."

Getting things started. If you'll ask around, I'm sure you will find other groups that will be of interest to you. In fact, you may find a local group that has recently been started by one of our readers or maybe you will be the beginning of such a group. Hey, it's up to you. You can make it happen.

Create or be a part of something that is monitoring and learning about your local courts and develop a good rapport with your local media. You should also learn how to do local, regional, and national cooperative networking with other groups and individuals with the same and similar interests. It's amazing what you might all be able to do together.

Remember, this book is where we detail a number of the problems, and we also serve as a workbook for solutions. Use it that way. Let it help you to get started. Let it help you to get involved. (And if you are one of the few who does get involved from time to time, use it to help you to be even more effective.)

Share this book with others. And share the enthusiasm. I know, there's a lot to take on. But if enough of you get involved, you *will* make a difference.

Ending a failure and beginning anew. I am totally convinced that there are very few truly honest people in this country who do not now feel that to make justice *really* work, we need new tools and new directions. As California Superior Court Judge Perry Langford said at the time of his retirement from the bench, "For the last few years I have become so disillusioned that I have no desire to be around anymore." He has joined a small but growing number of men and women in American law who have had it with this mess.

Langford made it very clear when he added, "The judicial system needs to be profoundly reformed. We really need to take stock, starting at the bottom. A whole lot of it should be thrown out, if we really want to be honest with ourselves." Notice the word, "profoundly"? A person doesn't usually use that word unless they're talking about some major, fundamental changes of *real* significance. I don't think he's talking about cosmetic changes or a few little nudges here or there.

Arbitration as a beginning. This is not something that can be changed overnight. This is something that is going to have to take a great deal of careful planning and with a lot of practical public input. And there is already a beginning. It's called "arbitration."

Arbitration is the settlement of a dispute by one or more individuals chosen to hear both sides of a legal dispute and come to a decision. Unlike mediation, it is usually mandatory, often as a part of business contracts previously agreed to. It can be found in required labor-management procedures as well and it's also coming more and more into favor with minor civil disputes, all the way down to family squabbles and neighborhood disagreements. When the arbiter (or arbiters) are primarily interested in learning the facts and finding the truth and when the adversary "contest" is not at all a part of it, it can be a truly honorable and very inexpensive way for people to really work things out. (In other words, what the courts should be and seldom are.)

Some may consider it as a new idea for cleaning up some of the many problems of the civil courts. You may be surprised to know that various forms of commercial arbitration have been used for many hundreds of years in America and in Europe and in other parts of the world as well. It is not a new idea, but like many good ideas, it is one of those things we seem to have to learn about over and over again.

Maybe one of these days we'll start to take it seriously? Maybe we will explore the possibility of considering it as a mandatory first step in *most* civil disputes? Well, we will if enough of you decide to take it seriously and make important moves in that direction.

Other major changes are needed. In addition to quality arbitration on the civil side, important changes are desperately needed in the more complicated areas of civil litigation and in the nightmare we consider as our criminal court system. Even back in 1988, the Supreme Court Chief Justice, William H. Rehnquist, said before the Australian Bar Association, that "the adversary system of justice is designed to establish the truth, so to speak, by letting each party go at the other hammer and tongs without regard to cost or delay. But we are gradually learning, I think, that the abstract ideal of justice has more components than this—indeed, that perhaps procedures which are both simpler and less time-consuming, while they may lose something in the pursuit of totally accurate reconstruction of events, may more than make up for this lack by the reduction of costs and delays." Now you've got the word right from the top.

As Ralph Warner wrote in the Nolo News, "Let's take many types of disputes out of the adversary system altogether. Maintained largely by legislators who fund their campaigns by contributions from fat cat trial lawyers, the adversary system often produces unjust or corrupt results. It tarnishes the very idea that our legal system is designed to deliver justice."

A hard look at the adversary system. It's a procedure common to common law countries (like the United States) wherein the defense and the prosecution square off at one another and do battle. As before noted, somehow, we are expected to believe that truth is, in some miraculous way, going to rise out of the rubble and make it possible for a Solomon-like judge to dispense some sort of divine justice.

(We have clearly seen what the chaotic result has been. The legal profession is going to find out that we are a lot more connected to the real world than they evidently think we are, right?)

It was a fairy tale system that had its beginning way back in the ancient medieval times when it was evidently thought that, somehow, truth and justice would emerge from such a game of conflict. That's the way they thought back then. Now some of the thinking is beginning to change.

Another procedure, common to what are called "civil law" countries, has the court joining much more closely with the prosecution and the defense to actually *investigate* the case before it. It's not a great deal different from what we're supposed to have now. It is an improvement, however.

A new idea whose time has come? Now the idea is beginning to form up for the actual *elimination* of the adversarial approach, altogether. Many see it as a fresh breeze on a hot summer day, which has been long, *long* overdue.

What do we replace it with? Let's look at an interesting possibility. Let's consider mandatory arbitration for most civil litigation as a starting point (and, hopefully for many, an ending point as well). This would be on the lowest level of the various state civil court systems.

Next up, would be the *Initial Court* (a state court) for civil and criminal issues. In such a court you would have a professional Judicial Examiner (a "juris peritus"—one who is skilled in the law and who is going aggressively for the truth). This must be someone who can pass a sophisticated exam and face an initial citizens' panel of review, openly and publicly. (And there must no longer be a lifetime tenure—on *any* level of the system.)

There would also be a Truth Advocate involved (with a team of investigators if necessary). This would be someone who has a solid background in science and general investigation procedures. This must also be someone who is not the slightest bit interested in either side, only in the *facts*, the *truth*, and the realities of the case. It should be someone who is hired by an open, public committee under the guidance of a professional personnel manager, and can be easily fired if his (or her) performance is not up to an acceptable standard.

In a sense, the Truth Advocate is the fact-finding leg man for the Judicial Examiner. In practice, they are intended to work as an efficient team, searching out all the possibilities to determine the full nature of the truth. There would also be an officially sanctioned public monitoring of the court proceedings and a public committee appointed by a variety of inside and outside elements, reporting to the court, and to the people, on this level and the upper levels as well.

Onward and upward. The next level up would be the court of *Judicial Review*. Here is where the appeal is made to three Judicial Examiners with direct involvement from an official Citizen Oversight Panel made up of professionals and other quality observers from *outside* the legal profession and another Truth Advocate (a different one). This proceeding would also be publicly monitored, as would *all* court activities on *all* levels (with *no* adversarial contest involved).

As with each level, if an involved party or an Examiner or an Advocate insists that it be done, the case must again be reexamined by the next highest authority, in this case, the court of *Special Review* (a regional court, neither federal or state—run by a special regional panel). Here you not only have three Judicial Examiners and a Citizen Oversight Panel, you once again have a Truth Advocate to reinvestigate whatever and wherever necessary.

Next, if a constitutional issue needs to be addressed (because it has not been satisfied in a lower court), or a special judicial review sees even the slightest possibility of irregularity that they are not able to satisfactorily resolve, the case moves up to the Federal level and to an identically equipped *Federal Special Review* court. Then next would be a *Secondary Court of the U.S. Supreme Court* with Judicial Examiners (and a special professional participant from the private sector). At least one Citizen Oversight professional and one Truth Advocate should also participate.

Finally, if any constitutional issue has been raised and has not been resolved satisfactorily, or, once again, a special judicial review sees any possible irregularities they are unable to satisfactorily resolve, the case is finally heard in the *Primary Court of the U.S. Supreme Court* (equipped as the Special Review court was). And remember this, on all levels and in all courts, it is definitely not a contest. It is a serious search for *truth!*

It also should be noted that the decision for any higher review, at any point in the process, might also be determined by a minimum of 1/3 of the vote (or nearest fraction thereof) of *all* those involved with the charges and/or disputes, voting in favor of such a review. This includes *everyone,* even individuals facing judgement in the court. (If more than one person is facing judgement in any single action, the vote of all such parties shall be shared as an appropriate fraction of one vote.)

All official participants in all courts must have had extensive training and testing commensurate with the special skills required of such individuals. Then their selection, from this group, should be

Changing the Legal System

made by a sizable and very public citizens' committee that also meets a high standard of excellence. And such official participants must always be subject to public review and periodic testing to better guarantee the highest quality of performance that is possible at all times.

What have we been talking about? No more prosecutors, no more defense attorneys, no more "games." We're talking about a new idea featuring a team of scientifically trained investigators and every opportunity for the accused and all possible witnesses to give full testimony to a panel of what amounts to "Truth Judges."

Is this how it should be done? Not necessarily. This is just one idea. It's an idea that might be a real starting point or it might just motivate an even better approach. But we have to start somewhere, right? So let's look this over and whatever else might be suggested out there. And what about adding "not proven" (with further investigation possible) to the present conclusions that now usually end up as only "guilty," "not guilty," or "no contest"? And what about perjury, which is seldom taken very seriously? And there is so much else we should consider.

Let's gradually and carefully work ourselves out of this mess we are in and try to move toward some sort of reasonable alternative. But always remember, any alternative will be only as good as the efficiency of the process, the honesty and professionalism of its participants and the close monitoring and other checks and balances that must be built in and be functioning well.

We must acquire a genuine passion to develop truth seeking to a fine science. Remember that, and we might actually get somewhere with all of this. We might really do it.

∽ Chapter Twelve ∽

Changing the Enforcement
Making It Work

As you well know, the crime rate has been very high for a very long time. Then it began to drop. Not an enormous amount—it has a long way to go—but the drop has been significant. Why has that happened and what can we do to keep this trend alive and well? Let's take a look and see.

To begin with, they say that less than half of the serious crimes are ever reported to the police and an even greater percentage of the lesser crimes don't reach the authorities. We are told approximately twenty million serious crimes are committed each year in America, and of that number, only around 500,000 perpetrators ever seem to go to a federal or even a state prison.

Believe it or not, that's an improvement. Enough of you have reacted and many politicians have finally responded to your concerns and fears. There are now sometimes longer sentences in prisons that are getting tougher.

In some areas we are finding limits being placed on the discretion of judges and even on some of the parole boards. There has been a significant expansion of some of the police forces in our nation. Something else that is very important, a new approach in law enforcement management is beginning to take hold. It involves the disbursement of responsibilities down to the precinct level in what is sometimes being called "community policing." There are new intervention programs to head off serious problems *before* they happen.

Now what we need to do is to further encourage all these positive efforts and push *hard* for a more universal adaption. Your input is really needed in these areas.

Changes in the streets. Another thing that is being considered in various places around the country (and is once in a while being implemented) is the development of new design techniques by city planners, architects and developers to build and to remodel with features and layouts that discourage criminal activities. The most obvious involves lighting and the less obvious might involve everything from access control to surveillance cameras.

There are crime-free housing complexes that are being developed out of former problem areas. Official community efforts along these lines involves a lot of promotion and other forms of public relations. Participating landlords and managers must also be a very real part of the solution. They'll need to go through training sessions and have their sites altered, if necessary, and inspected. And much more needs to be done in these areas, you can be sure.

A number of cities are beginning to implement teen curfews. Opposition forces contend that good teen-agers are being penalized for the misdeeds of a few. What they don't seem to understand is that an even more important factor is the good teen-agers' *safety*.

There are also some landmark efforts such as the "Take Back the Streets" program, which is designed to train and pay the more responsible of the homeless to do patrol duty in the parks and other urban areas as extra eyes and ears for the police—an interesting idea.

Citizen involvement in general. There are a number of activities I have already mentioned that you might want to take a second look at. A few urban police departments have implemented an effort called, "R.S.V.P." This involves getting retired but physically active folks trained and on the streets doing various kinds of traffic control, minor ticketing, observation and reporting, and other similar tasks. This frees up the regular police for the more serious needs.

Let us not forget the Neighborhood Watch activities that can involve us all in our own immediate neighborhoods and there are the Citizens' Patrols made up of screened and trained volunteers who patrol in the night to become extra eyes and ears for the police and sheriff departments. They're usually equipped with two-way radios and/or cell phones. They do a great job.

There are a number of other programs, some of them very sophisticated and comprehensive and, I might add, quite effective. A good example would be the "Safe Streets Coalition." You can write to them at 919 18th St. NW - Suite 800, Washington, D.C. 20006 or telephone them at 202-822-8100 to find out what it's all about.

There is also that great TV show, "America's Most Wanted." Not so long ago, after ten years of programs, they celebrated their five hundredth capture. It's everyday people like you and me who have recognized and reported the finding of all of these wanted criminals. It's yet one more way that you can get involved and become part of the solution.

Of course, there are those who have felt it necessary to obtain tear gas, or pepper spray units, or Mace, with special identifying dyes, or maybe one of those hand-held zappers or Taser units. There are towns like Thousand Oaks, California, where radar checkers have been issued to volunteers in their efforts to curb dangerous speeders in various neighborhoods. A few other towns have been trying the same thing. It might help.

Law enforcement counter-attacks. Once in a while a private company actually donates something of real value to our men in blue. One such donation was a new surveillance reproduction system that produces really clear enlargements from surveillance video tape used in banks and some liquor and convenience stores.

We encourage those who use such monitoring systems to upgrade their local law enforcement assistance in this manner as soon as possible. Of course, not everybody is going to be able to make a donation like this. Most commercial establishments are going to have to consider buying better equipment for their own businesses.

Good surveillance equipment is a key to effective apprehension. That's why some police departments are supplying their men and women in the field with special video cameras. Unfortunately, budget constraints are keeping this effort to a minimum. Community support groups are suggested for the purpose of raising the additional funds needed for such projects.

Budget problems are also responsible for the enormous number of fugitives that never seem to get caught, even sometimes when they might be found without a great deal of effort. However, every once in a while a task force of regional, state, and federal agencies works closely together and manages to bring in many thousands of wanted criminals in a relatively short period of time. It certainly is something we should try to do more often.

New DNA techniques can now often prove that a tiny sample of blood or a hair follicle or semen came from one particular individual. This means that such DNA methods are becoming as accepted as fingerprints. In fact, they are already being referred to as "molecular" fingerprints. (You also might find it interesting to know that more than 25 percent of the more than twelve thousand DNA cases analyzed by the FBI since 1988 have given us irrefutable evidence clearing major suspects.)

Lots of fascinating 3-D software are being developed that can recreate principal events in question, right before your eyes. It's absolutely amazing and it's just the beginning.

Using the legal system to fight crime. Other efforts worthy of mention are to be found in the use of civil injunctions concerning geographic location and association of gang members and other dangerous individuals. This seems to be working, at this point, but somewhere down the line someone might manage to convince an airhead judge that somehow such dangerous criminals are being unfairly deprived of their right to associate with whomever they wish, wherever they wish, regardless of what they always end up doing.

There is also the use of zoning laws, building codes, and health regulations to shut down drug houses, places of prostitution and similar unsavory endeavors. These civil remedies are often a part of the new community policing approach and is also sometimes coupled with special community support from such groups as the "Safe Streets" and others with similar commitment. Remember it most often requires community support and assistance from people just like you and me.

Working with the kids. In an ideal world, the kids would always be the most precious thing in all our lives, all the time. Unfortunately, in this far less than perfect real world, the kids come up short far more often than not. And we all pay a big price for this!

One of the many problems involves what, in some areas, is called the "Juvenile Dependency court." This court (under whatever name it may have in your area) often concerns itself with children who have been neglected or abused in any number of other ways by their own families.

This is one more area of our legal system where the truth is often buried deep beneath the procedures—that "game" they seem to feel they must play. When the authorities can't cut through such idiocies, terrible things can happen to the little children (as you may remember reading about in an earlier part of this book).

In some states, there are what seems like some genuine efforts to try and improve this situation. Are there problems in your area? Have state and national experts convened with concerned citizens to properly sensitize the court system and protect these most vulnerable children? If not, you have a good job cut out for yourself.

Don't think you can't do anything. You *can* change the way the courts work. You *can* do a lot of other things that will help. You could be like Barbara Rivas, who rolled up her sleeves and got right into things. She became a Violence Prevention/Intervention Coordinator.

She became a Safe Schools Coordinator. She developed a very special curriculum for kids who were assigned to Juvenile Court Community Schools. She formed Junior Support groups made up of children who had gotten into trouble and had found their way out. Miss Rivas also brings some of those who turned things around in their lives, into the schools to talk about their experiences and how they finally got their acts together. That is one busy lady. That is one beautiful person.

Sometimes we read about reductions in serious crimes in America. But in most areas it seems that juvenile arrests are up, the kids' drug use is up, their drunk driving is up, and their weapons possession (and use) has become an even greater problem. We desperately need more programs, all over our nation, for the growing numbers of kids at-risk. We desperately need more folks like Barbara Rivas.

There is nothing better than two good parents. As the Director of the National Fatherhood Initiative, Wade F. Horn, has publicly stated, "In 1960, the total number of children living in fatherless families was fewer than eight million. Today, that total has risen to nearly twenty-four million. Nearly four out of ten children in American are being raised in homes without their fathers and soon it may be six out of ten."

Horn further noted that our culture has evidently been willing to accept the idea that fathers are unnecessary. What a sad thought. It goes along with so many other terrible things that we have somehow managed to get used to. Mr. Horn suggests that we must learn to understand the critical role that fathers can play (and should play) in the lives of their children. As he put it, "not just as 'paychecks,' but as disciplinarians, teachers, and moral guides." In other words, both mothers and *fathers* need to be there for the kids. (Of course, those mothers and fathers must be loving and responsible in their interactions.)

Mr. Horn was the Commissioner for Children, Youth, and Families and Chief of the Children's Bureau within the U.S. Department of Health and Human Services and also has served as a presidential appointee to the National Commission on Children (among many other numerous accomplishments). I have a feeling he just may know what he's talking about.

The parents really do have a lot to keep track of today. There is everything from dangerously negative peer group pressures and violent and rather pornographic TV and films to such strange, new worlds as cyberspace porn on the Internet.

There are some efforts to try and tone down the TV and film contents and there are efforts from the on-line industry to "patrol" and clean up the information highway. Of course, without your help, I'm not sure just how far all of this will go.

Remember, the police can't do it all for us. We've got to get in there and be part of the solution. Some are doing that now. It's helping. Many more are needed. It's essential.

We must stop perpetuating crime. I'll never forget the news reports about Lawrence Singleton ending up with a mistrial for a murder down in Florida. Remember, he's the low-life who raped a 15-year-old California girl several years ago and then chopped off her arms and left her for dead. Well, he got out and went at it again, this time with a successful murder.

Well, why not? Over half of all the adult offenders in this country who were serving criminal sentences are now on probation. (At least that's what a Justice Department report tells us.) An alarming number of them end up as *repeat* offenders. (Well, at least it can be reported that Singleton was finally convicted of murder this time and got a death sentence.)

Efforts to keep these dangerous individuals in prison are underway, but it's going to take a lot more involvement by a lot more concerned citizens to make a truly significant and lasting difference. To start with, a life sentence is supposed to be for *life!* What part of "life" does the befuddled court not understand?

Controlling the loose cannons. One of the most frightening examples of things getting *way* out of control would be the mistaken identity killings in Arizona by bounty hunters. I know, it's Arizona, and law and order there is one big joke, or is it? A totally innocent young couple was gunned down in their home, in a hail of gunfire. That's not funny.

Even though the authorities arrested the killers, it was after the event. Let's face it, the proper controls just weren't there beforehand. This did not have to happen. As Arizona's Maricopa County Attorney Rick Romley was quoted by the Associated Press, "It created an image that this is the Wild West." Gee, why would anyone ever get that idea?

Some effort is now being made to put a little better screening and more control on bounty hunters. However, this cannot be expected to have a truly significant impact unless the general public pressures officials everywhere to make some truly comprehensive changes.

New police guidelines. I recall the case of the West Palm Beach police officer who was accused of beating a hitchhiker to death and the public concern and call for a national registry of bad cops. You see, the officer was evidently just not that stable. In fact, he had been in a drug treatment program in Tennessee. (The record of this had been kept closed.)

Then there's the one about the little party for an honors student and her orderly, under control friends. No booze, no drugs. Just a few kids and chips, dips, and balloons. You guessed it, the police decided to raid the home, and with all the dramatic force you might expect, since they were accompanied by "reality cop show" cameras and crew. The multi-million-dollar lawsuit should give pause to those out of control Los Angeles cowboys before they try to do something like that again.

And you've heard about how the Louisiana State Police stop, search, and seize the personal property of large numbers of innocent interstate drivers? This abuse of proper law and order was originally intended to help in the drug fight and then it kind of got out of control. It's a classic case of the improper use of the forfeiture law— the misuse of probable cause. Thank God, "Dateline NBC" brought this to everyone's attention. (They've done some good work in these areas.)

It also should be said that New Orleans has gotten a new police chief with a mandate to clean things up and he has done a very credible job of it from what we hear. You see, things *can* be turned around.

There is still so much to be done. Like the police scandals that surfaced in New York (as with the torturing of a Haitian immigrant). There were also those video tapes of beatings by cops in California and all sorts of other revelations all over the country.

We've got some very good law enforcement people who are doing an exceptionally good job, but between ineffective courts and a few bad cops, they have an extremely difficult time of it. They need changes and they need your support.

We need to bring the forensic labs up to the highest possible standards and keep them there. We need to implement the new DNA advances in every jurisdiction. We need to establish and maintain a good trail of integrity for gathered evidence. (The O.J. trial showed how sloppy the security and records can get in such matters.)

Sometimes we need to have a noticeable improvement in the quality and sophistication of the field decisions that are made by officers. (Some of them just don't seem to have any clear idea about the law or the art of careful observation.)

We also find that some of the efforts in various state legislatures around the country are not as successful as you would think they would be in passing laws that will see to it that there is adequate punishment for police misconduct. Even so, there has been a little success in these areas. If you want more to be done, then all you and your friends and neighbors have to do is get involved. (It always comes back down to that, doesn't it?)

Police autonomy and responsibility. In order to survive in a reasonably safe and orderly manner, we all have had to surrender a part of our absolute freedom. As an example, when we come to a corner with traffic lights, the travelers on each road must be willing to stop and share the access in a timely manner, when required to do so.

We also have had to surrender some of that freedom to a force of police who are charged with the responsibility of maintaining law and order. In doing this job they must have a certain amount of independence. However, there always needs to be accountability. That's why media attention on their behavior, citizen input, and a truly independent civilian review board can be a very important thing.

How is the community support for the police in your area and are there effective mechanisms in place to guarantee accountability? Remember, they need your support and you need accountability. It's a two-way street, with or without traffic lights.

Chapter Thirteen

Changing the Incarceration
Making a Better Result

What is the purpose of prisons? Why, it's to protect the law-abiding citizens by removing convicted criminals from society and punishing them, right? Well, let's see what happens.

The statistical evidence does seem to rather clearly show us that when the prison population rises, the crime rate drops. The statistics also seem to indicate some deterrent effect. So, this solves the problem? Well, only to some extent and only in the short term. We're still not solving the underlying problems and we are spending an enormous amount of money.

Most prisoners are eventually released. And the recidivism rate, half of the male inmates in many states, continues the problem and eventually sends many of them right back to prison again. So, we should keep them in there longer? If that's all we do, it's just doomsday deferred, wouldn't you say?

A good look at most of the incarceration facilities show us that there is little rehabilitation going on in there. Mostly it's just negatively reinforcing the original criminal behavior. In other words, we're only making it worse.

Of course, when some criminals are found to be endless repeaters and a clear danger to society, there is really no other alternative but to do everything we can to keep them locked up for the rest of their lives. But what about the others? Maybe we need to make some changes?

With all of this in mind, what might we consider as the primary goals here? Possibly we could consider them to be as follows:

1. Protect society.
2. Create an effective deterrent/punishment.
3. Initiate effective rehabilitation.
4. Make the system cost-effective.

Keep that list in mind as we go bravely forward into this subject. Who knows, maybe we can end up discovering something we can do that might even work.

Making changes. We still see quite a mess out there. (Remember the Justice Department report accused an Arizona sheriff of brutalizing inmates?) However, it's not all bad. In some places they are taking away the luxury perks and replacing them with a system of reasonable discipline.

There are also some new high-tech procedures being applied. The Epic Solutions software company has come up with some special computer programs such as, "Book 'em," "Hold 'em," and "TAG 'em." These allow authorities to compose dossiers with photos, marks, fingerprints, affiliations, arrest records, crime scene details, and all sorts of other interesting, helpful information.

Such programs allow authorities to track a suspect all the way through the system. We're talking about all sorts of details, like jail behavior, visitor information, court dates, and medical records.

In some places, they are replacing old-fashioned shackling of inmates with what is called a "stun belt." It will really stop an inmate from escaping from an outside work crew and also save money. Among other things, fewer guards are needed.

Other areas of concern that are being addressed by some officials include limiting the "media glorification of criminals." It's really amazing. Some of these serious capital offenders are made into gruesome celebrities with interviews, book deals, TV specials, and all sorts of other things like that. And they just love it!

Some First Amendment advocates are against any limitations placed on prisoner interaction with the media. However, more mature minds realize that a three-ring circus is definitely counter-productive.

Everything from chain gangs to private prisons. The size and cost of the problem is getting so out of hand that in some places they are ready to try just about anything. Remember the announcements from Florida, Arizona, and Alabama about the revival of chain gangs? I was *really* surprised when I read about pending *female* chain gangs in Alabama.

Private prisons have become big business in some places. As you might imagine, of the nineteen states that have them, Texas has the most of all. Well, I guess there surely is enough room down there. Is that a solution? Well, it's a holding tank, of sorts.

It doesn't sound too much like any sort of permanent solution and, at times, they have had real problems in some of those facilities. The laws are still unclear about such approaches. (The law is unclear or unworkable in almost *every* area.)

What about rehabilitation? Which is it going to be, hard time or rehabilitation? Something's got to be done. Untold billions have been spent building new prisons and operating them. The population explosion in those institutions just goes on and on.

Some interesting things are being tried anew. In some places they are starting gardens that are developing into small farms. It has proven to be a very special kind of reeducation that seems to work with some prisoners.

There are also a few efforts being made to develop some genuine academic excellence in the incarcerated population. This hasn't gone very far yet, but it does show some promise. We also could learn from other nations that have done rather well with inmate industry. It certainly could take some of the financial burden off the taxpayers, if it's done right.

Efforts in this direction include inmates in Oregon making denim wearing apparel, prisoners in Nebraska making maps in Braille, and Nevada inmates working on everything from limousines to antique automobile restorations. In California there is everything from plant care and custom embroidery to airline reservation services.

It's actually just a small beginning, but that's where you have to start—at the beginning. You will be pleased to know that deductions are taken out of such inmate income for everything from room and board, taxes, crime victim compensation, and family support. At least that's what I'm told. I'm also told that this could be proving to be a very valuable lesson in discipline and good work habits.

What about learning all about computers? It all adds up to a growth of self-esteem, which is the beginning of genuine recovery.

Then there's parole reform. This is another one of those areas that needs change. There have been some really disastrous early release programs and other similar calamitous endeavors that have certainly had their impact, but those, most definitely, are not the changes this writer has in mind.

There are also some "book and release" operations that fare no better. All such efforts do is leave the clear impression in the criminal mind that laws of responsible behavior are little more than a fiction for derisive humor and can be ignored. Well, what else would you expect?

Such programs were never meant for *real* criminals, right? Only those who have just made a little mistake are supposed to be considered for such lenient treatment, right? Some of them are, most certainly, new in the criminal trades and, by these lenient actions, are more than a little encouraged to continue down that dark path.

Who was it who decided regular booking officers and/or low-level judges were somehow going to be endowed with wonderful powers of a gifted behavioral scientist? Since when have they been so well equipped to separate the wheat from the chaff?

Possibly it might not be so unreasonable to require that inmates be held for the full term of their sentences—that ten years means ten years—that "life" means *life*. (What a radical idea. Imagine that. Holding the system to its word.)

So, is that all there is? I should hope not. Let's hope that we can also implement all sorts of good programs like counseling, training, placement, and such interesting endeavors as the Parolee Partnership Program and other efforts of that caliber.

Other movements. Unlike so many of the American prisons, with their killings, rape, and drugs, Japanese prisons are clean and orderly with little violence. They treat their prisoners with an unbending discipline and rules that we might think of as cruel. However, it is far less cruel than the way things end up, under the current arrangement in so many of *our* facilities.

We've started to do a few things right. We're starting to withhold government S.S.I. welfare payments to addicted prisoners. If fully implemented everywhere, it could save more than $125 million over a five year period. That's what I hear.

There's the movement away from the fancy living conditions. In Colorado, I understand there is now a definite change from frills to austerity. And it is with a level of serious discipline that promises an even harder time for any prisoners who don't toe the line. (It's about time.)

There is also a growing call to put the offenders to work. The back-breaking cost of building and maintaining all those prisons has prompted the cry. Let's face it, something has got to be done. Another call is for the development of alternatives for the more nonviolent felons. We'd better be careful what we do in that area. We could get ourselves in trouble very quickly.

Then there's the idea of the "boot camp." You've heard about them. They've been tried in California and in a number of other states as well. Sometimes they seem to be working reasonably well (especially for young offenders) and sometimes not.

Georgia was one of the first states to try it out. Unfortunately, it was found that inmates placed in such arrangements were even more likely to continue their criminal behavior after release. This revelation was from a General Accounting Office study.

It showed that there is definitely more than one kind of "boot camp" and definitely more than one result possible. Georgia's experiment wasn't one of the better approaches. There was little concern for preparing the prisoners for a law abiding, successful future on the outside. (Let's hope they've learned from this result.)

Another "boot camp" approach, this time in the state of New York, proved to be much more successful. There was notably less recidivism. Why? Well, New York put some real emphasis on substance abuse programs, education, and vocational training as an integral part of the program. (It might also be noted that these operations usually cost less than the regular mainstream prisons.)

Another new idea whose time has come? What can be learned from all of this? Why would it not be possible to develop a modified "boot camp" concept that could give us disciplined, almost totally self-sustaining facilities that would also include intelligent rehabilitation programs for those who really should qualify for such considerations? No, this is not a pipe dream. There are enough examples of these elements in force as separate factors. We can see the potential. We can see the possibilities here. This just might be something that can definitely be done and done very successfully.

Yes, it will be quite an effort. Again, it means a lot of folks willing to get out there and really campaign for such a major change. It's a comprehensive concept. It's a responsible approach. It certainly should be worth your consideration, wouldn't you say?

If you still should have any doubts about the need for such changes, please consider that letter by convicted killer Alan Holland who wrote about his killing of a little old lady, "because she didn't shut up when she should have." He also wrote about how he was looking forward to his life in prison with three meals a day, no bills to pay, plenty of recreational activities, and lots of television. (And guess who's going to pay for it.)

He and lots of his buddies need to be taken off the backs of us taxpayers and put to work with a program of no-nonsense discipline and no fancy perks. Of course, there are others who can genuinely be rehabilitated. The modified program we're talking about can be designed to do the job. So, are you ready to help move things in that direction?

Chapter Fourteen

Your Role in American Law
Personal Responsibilities Reexamined

The danger we face. Sometimes the *Media Bypass* magazine shows us a side of things that is seldom reported. One thought provoking article, "Government Oppression Sparking Freedom Fires," by Gerald A. Carroll, has a few things to say that you just may want to pay attention to. One of his interesting quotes is from the Jackson, California, "Mountain Trader." In part, it goes like this:

> We have all been raised to believe that government is right and that we should be good citizens and obey the rules. But we have seen our guaranteed rights become privileges. We have seen dishonest politicians and petty bureaucrats take control of our everyday lives to the point where they tell us what we can or cannot do with our land. They tell us who we must hire in our businesses.

Ben L. Hiatt is the author of this quote, which also states that "we Americans are a proud and independent people and we tend to resent anyone telling us what we must do and what we must think. We will tend to go along with the government, but only up to a point and for a great many proud and independent Americans, that point has been reached and is very nearly surpassed."

As Carroll added, "The United States began as one that emphasized individual rights and freedoms, instead of centralized, overbearing oppression thinly disguised as representative, constitutional government." He further stated that, "Genuine people with genuine fears are being hurt in a variety of ways by what they feel is an unfeeling, mechanical government apparatus that has run amok."

Carroll also quoted J. J. Johnson's testimony before a U.S. Senate subcommittee hearing on militias. Among other things, Johnson noted that "the only thing standing between some of the current legislation being contemplated and armed conflict is time."

And he quoted Dr. Eugene Schroder's contributions to what is described by some as the "new American freedom movement." His remarks included the observation that,

> Quietly, yet rapidly, the small town values of community and common purpose are vanishing. Instead of strength in numbers, we as a nation are increasingly being split into smaller and smaller competing factions, with the cry of "every man for himself" ringing throughout the land. It seems the phrase of "divide and conquer" has taken the place of "One nation under God, indivisible, with liberty and justice for all." Americans are retreating behind locked doors in their individual homes, afraid to enjoy the sunset for fear of the darkness it brings.
>
> When and where did it all begin to crumble? How and why has America, which was once a nation whose strength united was so much more than the sum total of its parts, begun to break apart into bitterly opposing special interest groups?

How did it happen? Remember that "psychology of gradualism" I told you about in the beginning of this book? That's how it happened. Are we really becoming as broken up as he indicates we are? Well, you must have read and listened to at least some of the many reports that have been published about the "Balkanization of America" haven't you?

To properly raise the hair on the back of your neck, I will end this little bit with a final quote from Gerald A. Carroll, who is also the author of the book *Militia Nation*. He made it very clear that "the militia—the 'enforcement arm' of the citizens' uprising—appears to be growing stronger and stronger with each day." (I believe you can probably reach *Media Bypass* magazine at 1-800-429-7277.)

Where does this leave us? It leaves us all in the very difficult place of having to do something about our many problems and to do so effectively and to do so *now*. Let's face it, it really does seem that if we do not, it will eventually be done for us by the less responsible; and it could get ugly—very ugly.

We need to start by effectively addressing the serious and oppressive breakdowns in our legal system, the bulwark of our function as a nation. We also need to deal with the many other related areas of equal concern, such as the bureaucracy and our political system as it operates today. We need to develop a meaningful *evolutionary* process, not a bloody *revolutionary* one.

What's really going to be hard for some of you to understand is that your own momentary financial well-being is not an accurate indicator of our condition or our future as a nation. We have all too many examples over the past seven thousand years of recorded history to remind us just how fragile and temporary human security really is. Take it seriously. Don't let any current comfort lull you into believing otherwise.

The price of non-involvement. March 13, 1964 was the fateful day when Kitty Genovese brought home to the American people the terrifying cost of not caring enough to get involved. In the early hours of that morning, it was reported as many as thirty-eight of her neighbors heard her screams and cries for help. The neighbors just watched from their windows as Kitty was stabbed to death. In fact it was a full half hour later before anyone even bothered to call the police. People all over our nation were shocked. But did we actually learn anything by that example? Some seem to have. A few get involved from time to time and manage to make a significant difference every once in a while. Still, most will not.

The grizzly headlines are still there. A young man in Wichita, Kansas, bled to death from gunshot wounds because it took so long to finally find someone willing to call for help. A little 13-year-old girl waded into a fountain after visiting the St. Louis Zoo and was raped right there by two older boys as thirty-five people in the area watched and did nothing. In Houston, bystanders wouldn't help two toddlers found floating face down in an apartment swimming pool. When they were finally rescued it was too late. In early 1998, people watched from their apartments in the Denver area while four men beat a taxi driver to death.

And let us not forget the neighbors in a New York housing project who ignored the obvious signs of serious abuse that led to the torture death of a little 6-year-old girl. Let me tell you something, this happens a hell of a lot more often than you might ever imagine. I wouldn't be surprised if it is happening from time to time, right in *your* community.

These few examples cover different years in several areas. They could fill this book if we had the room. You have only to pick up the paper to find the latest examples or you can watch everything from TV docudramas on the subject of non-involvement or watch the replay of old movies like *High Plains Drifter* or *High Noon*.

Cowardly little communities still exist. This writer is aware of such neighborhoods in relatively recent situations. One that comes to mind is an outwardly peaceful residential block in a southern California city where a kid goes bad with drugs and with his rowdy buddies. One neighbor tried to rally support to stop the noise, vandalism, and marijuana cultivation and, for his efforts, the neighbors just wouldn't get involved. In fact, one neighbor was willing to testify against the effort of control for, as she put it, the safety of my children and my pets.

However, it must be said that things are beginning to turn around more and more. But lots more involvement is needed by lots and lots of people who just wouldn't dream of getting involved. Evidently far too many are still willing to wait it out until that dream becomes a living nightmare.

Political non-involvement. I'll never forget that great political cartoon by Mike Thompson of the *State Journal-Register*, showing two guys walking along and talking. One says to the other, "Our government's messed up and it's because our politicians are all a bunch of lazy, do-nothing, apathetic, responsibility dodgin' slackers!" The other fellow asks him if he's going to vote to change things. The answer, of course, is, "Naaaaaw, why bother?"

Another cartoon, this time one of Bob Thaves' " Frank and Earnest" strips. Our hero is evidently signing in at a cryogenics lab where people are frozen. He's saying that he's not interested in anything long term. As he put it, "I'd just like to sleep during election years."

Think that's funny? Well, according to the educational TV series, "Government by Consent," the United States has the *lowest* voter turnout of *any* Western nation. That's not surprising. One report I saw by the Committee for the Study of the American Electorate had only 20 percent of voting-age citizens casting ballots in states holding primary elections at the time of the poll.

That's down from around 30 percent in 1972 and, frankly, it isn't any better today. As Dr. Norman Vincent Peale put it, "Americans used to roar like lions for liberty, now we bleat like sheep for security." Let us not forget what Sen. Sam J. Ervin once said. "If men and women of capacity refuse to take part in politics and government, they condemn themselves, as well as the people, to the punishment of living under bad government."

I also found an interesting comment by David S. Broder in the *Washington Post*. He wrote, "The real problem is that we have not found any effective method to instruct White House and executive branch officials on their duty to obey the law, because we have failed as a society to express our contempt and disgust for those who violate their oaths of office with such impunity."

One of the more chilling observations came from Cuban refugee Dr. Miguel A. Faria, Jr. He was quoted in *American Survival Guide* magazine as saying that "unless the American people awaken from their current state of apathy and regain control over their own government . . . the future certainly will be, as Orwell predicted, a human face with a boot forever stamped on it."

Excuses, excuses. Amy Onorato did an interesting piece in *Women's News* with the tongue-in-cheek head that reads, "The Country Is Falling Apart and I Only Have Time to Watch It." She points out four of the many excuses people give for not getting involved. They are as follows:

1. I do not make a difference!
2. I do not have the time!
3. I am not informed enough!
4. Only radicals do it!

You don't make a difference? As she wrote, "by default, we have banded together in silence to create negative movement. We have all made a difference!" That's right. Things got this bad because *you* and so many others *did nothing!* (Or else, perhaps, you did a few "feel good" things that never amounted to all that much.) Just remember, there is only empowerment through involvement!

You don't have the time? Of course you don't. It's really a matter of prioritizing your time. Other things are much more important, right? That's what *you* think. You're not informed enough? Well, you're reading this book. That's a start. But don't stop there. There are other books I've recommended you might want to read. There are some informative TV news specials, documentaries, local study groups and yes, even talk radio. And you can join a community discussion group or start one of your own if there's not a relevant one available in your area. There are an almost endless number of ways you can learn.

Only radicals get involved? That probably will be the case until lots more ordinary every-day responsible Americans like you decide to really get involved and stay involved. What do you think the chances are of that happening, hmm?

The psychology of non-involvement. Edmund Burke said, "custom reconciles us to everything." So it does. The breakdown of the legal system has become so commonplace that it has become accepted. And, after all, one cannot really do anything about the way things are, right? *Wrong!*

Of course you could be like that character Fig in the comic strip "Crock" by Bill Rechin and Don Wilder. One time someone asked him what was wrong and he said he'd been sitting on a sharp rock for a year. When he was asked why on earth he doesn't get up, he replied, "I might sit on a sharper one next time."

Sound ridiculous? Of course it does, but there are a lot of folks out there who would rather accept the oppression put upon them now than to do battle against such oppressions and thereby possibly risk even greater misfortunes being put upon them. So, do you think you are safer in the long run opting to watch the violence on television rather than looking out the window?

If you don't feel that way about things—if you *are* really involved, or seriously plan to be, then show this book, and some of those others I've recommended, to some of your many friends who remain in the sleep-walk mode. See if you can help change a few minds. (It won't be easy, but it will certainly be worth it.)

The anatomy of failure. How might one follow the dysfunctional thinking process of such people? I guess you could start with their refusal to see or otherwise acknowledge a problem. If that doesn't work—if they can't avoid noticing what's going on—perhaps they will be able find a way of playing it down as relatively unimportant.

If that doesn't work, they can always go through that dance about not being able to make a difference anyway. Who knows, maybe they could really make it into a self-fulfilling prophecy, if they tried very, very hard not to try to do anything at all. If that doesn't do it for them, as a last resort, they could always invent all sorts of complex reasons why they just can't really get involved. (We humans are masters of creative justifications.)

Who knows, they might end up convincing themselves that they did a good thing by not doing anything. They might even warp their reality sufficiently to enable them to end up being actually proud of themselves. How wonderful it must be to have one's feet so firmly planted in mid-air like that. Whatever else you do, keep in mind the Ashleigh Brilliant Pot Shot, "Before I can do anything important, I have several unimportant things to do that simply won't wait." After all, "It is usual nowadays to ignore what should be done in favor of what pleases us." This last quote is by Titus Maccius Plautus, one of the great playwrights of ancient Rome. (We all know what happened to the Roman Empire, don't we?)

Getting involved right now. Let's say you're one of the marvelous few who is now determined to go at it full tilt. If you are, get ready for some action. First, you must determine the goal or goals you want to work on. Let's call it your "mission statement."

Do you want to start by getting together with others in your community and educate yourselves as fully as possible on the nature of the problem or problems you plan to tackle and on the ways you might be able to attack such problems? Or, do you already feel sufficiently educated in such matters and are now ready to "hold their feet to the fire" (as talk show host Roger Hedgecock would say)?

And do you have a workable goal format to begin with? What do you want to do? Do you want to put amendment pressures on Washington concerning constitutional issues? Do you plan to develop monitoring and reporting teams for the courts in your area? Do you want to go after the lawyers? Do you want to work on eliminating the adversarial "game" and establish a system of public truth seeking that replaces the "contest" approach with logic and science? Do you want to hold judges and prosecutors accountable?

Let's face it, you can't just jump in and do *all* these things. You've got to pick your target and then really focus on it. What will some of the first things be that you will have to do? You'll have to get a number of people interested in joining the effort (try newspapers, talk shows, etc.), you'll want to develop a working group, get it organized, find out the talents and skills of its members, and set up a logical sequential pattern of activity that will truly move you forward.

As you get involved, expect that once in a while someone will try to get into it who is bringing along some less than desirable baggage. The person may have an inappropriate political ax to grind or the individual may be an opportunist of some sort.

When you run into people like that, you will need to deal with the problem early on. To begin with, you should have a statement of purpose and conduct that can be signed by everybody who comes on board. It should be something that clearly describes where you're going and why and that it must be done with intelligence and maturity and in the spirit of cooperation. In other words, it's a serious thing and it's a team effort. And you must always do your very best to keep your lines of communication open with everybody. This should be true not only with those you will be working with, it should also be true with officials, with the media, and with the general public as well.

These tasks sound impossible? They're *not* impossible. You *can* do it. Unless of course you are going to opt out as one of those who feels you really can't. If that should be the case, just you remember, "There are those who make things happen, those who watch things happen, and those who wonder what happened." Don't you be one of those who always ends up wondering what the hell happened.

Remember, if Shakespear is right and the world is but a stage, what are you doing out there in the audience?

Part Four

So Many Problems—
So Little Time

Chapter Fifteen

The Drug War That Never Was
Facing the Truth

Anatomy of a human frailty. As seven thousand years of recorded history will attest, we are very imperfect beings. Some of us really do try to get our acts together and some of us even manage to succeed, up to a point. But some find it very difficult to overcome various negative patterns and addictions that can cause great harm in our lives and, almost always, in the lives of those around us as well.

One of the most obvious examples is so clearly seen in that horrendous struggle with various addictive drugs. I see so many kids and young adults today who are not so unlike the walking brain-dead of the late night fright-flicks. What is just as disturbing, most folks just seem to walk on by and ignore them as best they can. Others end up having to deal with them, and they try to do so in as simple a way as possible without having to really come to grips with what they have managed to accept as the new "norm."

It is such a sad and shameful place for us to come to. It is also a most unfortunate place for the poor victims. As Hosea Ballou wrote, "Real happiness is cheap enough, yet how dearly we pay for its counterfeit."

An historic overview. We have always wanted to feel good. Early records suggest prehistoric people discovered that eating certain plants, when one is ill, might help in returning good health. Some of these early "drugs" really were effective. Some were not. Some were downright dangerous.

An ancient Sumerian clay tablet, created at around 2000 B.C., shows a list of eleven or twelve different drug "prescriptions." By around 1500 B.C. the Egyptians had advanced these efforts considerably. One of their scrolls from that period lists at least seven hundred "drugs" for more than eight hundred "prescriptions." Later on, the ancient Romans established the first apothecary shops (the first drug stores).

Some of these concoctions were quite effective and some were not. Some were not at all safe for human consumption. The most insidious were the ones that addicted the user and then slowly killed the hapless victim. (It would seem we haven't learned much since then, have we?)

The 60s and 70s gave us the drug oriented counterculture. They even had their own magazine, *High Times*, which openly promoted the use of illegal substances, and more currently, featured Beavis & Butt-Head, Howard Stern, and almost anything else that offered the appearance of mindless, low down, and filthy behavior.

And where are we today? If you've read the papers, watched the news, followed some of the relevant documentaries, or even just paid attention to what's going on around you, the truth of what is happening is very clear and inescapable for you.

We read and hear of people from almost every background imaginable getting tangled up in the web of drugs. This writer even made a list to see just how pervasive this problem really is. And who were these people? It covers them all, . . . politicians, doctors, soldiers, truckers, housewives, policemen, blue-collar workers, teachers, executives, teen-ages, celebrities, reporters, firemen, grade-school kids, White House staffers, writers, pharmacists, cab drivers, entrepreneurs, engineers, pilots, homeless wanderers, and just about anyone else you can think of.

Maybe it's not so surprising that ABCs "World News Tonight" reported a 60 billion dollar loss to American industry in the first year of this decade due to drug use. It's also an estimated annual loss in the same amount according to the U.S. Chamber of Commerce. (Yes, employee drug screening and educational programs are helping to turn it around a little bit. But only a little bit.)

The problem is everywhere. Even Yves Saint Laurent decided it was "cute" to come out with a new perfume called "Opium." As if that wasn't enough, some well-known and otherwise respected personalities have even decided to endorse the idea of legalizing one of the "gateway" drugs that gets people started. Oh yeah, we're in great shape.

A hard look, whether you like it or not. A California state study showed as many as 11 percent of the state's pregnant women involved with substance abuse (a report that appeared in the *New England*

Journal of Medicine). A later study showed one out of nine new moms on drugs and/or heavily into alcohol.

A report by the American Public Welfare Association suggested that much of the increase in foster-care is because of the drug abuse by the parents. Another study, presented at the American Association of Suicidology, found that at least 50 percent of the victims of suicide, who were under thirty, were discovered to be heavy drug users.

It reminds me of some of the dialog in "Pyotr's Story" by Spider Robinson (as published in *Analog* magazine). One of the characters was saying, "How do you figure a thing like heroin, Mike? It seems to weed out the very stupid and the very talented." It could have also been said that it might well be so because both groups are generously represented by another characteristic they have in common, . . . as the very vulnerable. The character further observed, "Tells you something about the world we're making. The very stupid and the very sensitive can't seem to live in it."

One study by the Robert Wood Johnson Foundation and Brandeis University indicated that substance abuse is linked to five hundred thousand deaths a year in America. And now drug acceptance is infesting the preteens. Kids as young a nine are trying out marijuana. The Partnership for a Drug-Free America indicated that it's still not an enormous number as yet. Maybe not yet, but give it time.

We never seem to learn. Still, even with all of this, the drug apologists who would legalize pot (the opening gambit for many drug addicts), often would like to convince you that alcohol and minor drugs really don't lead to violence. They sometimes also suggest that making such drugs readily available would actually reduce the violent need to obtain such drugs.

I guess that means that under such threats of violence we had better make such things available to these addicts or else. If acquiescing to such threats doesn't turn your stomach, perhaps you might like to consider the fact that such arguments were used to help end prohibition and alcohol has clearly grown to be an even greater problem today.

We are constantly being cautioned by medical authorities that people under the influence of drugs or alcohol can and, all too often, *do* become violent. In fact, a fairly recent report by the National Center on Addiction and Substance Abuse tells us that 80 percent of the adults in United States prisons are there because of criminal activity linked to drug and alcohol abuse. I think you will find that a surprising amount of this is clearly linked to violent behavior while under the influence.

As Judge Frederic Link said, while speaking of crime on the campuses of American schools, "If it wasn't for booze, methamphetamine, cocaine, or marijuana, I'd be out of a job." Of course not many in government seem to understand the problem.

I'll never forget the former postal employee who had gotten a $30,000 loan from the Small Business Administration to open up a little store in the St. Louis area that provided just about every bit of supportive paraphernalia that any drug dealer or addict might ever want. (I guess you could say it was a case of your taxpayers' money at work.)

We should not forget the 1998 International Olympic Committee that didn't seem to care at all about participants use of marijuana. As the Canadian Olympic Association chief, Anne Letheren, is reported to have suggested, almost everybody smokes marijuana in Whistler, B.C. Some drug war.

It reminds me of that Gamble cartoon in the *Florida Times-Union* that shows what looks like a plague of locust (labeled as "the drug epidemic") descending on a lone and harried policeman who is trying to swat the little devils, one at a time. Could it be that somebody is trying to tell us something? Could be.

Pot-pourri. Arizona and California have the dubious distinction of leading the way in the liberalization of drug laws (now along with four other states). They have started by legalizing marijuana for medical purposes as long as some sort of health-care practitioner says it's all right.

Now pot growers are trying to consider themselves as medical suppliers. The goal is to provide the weed to anyone who is claiming to be sick or otherwise in need. Some have expressed it as their duty to help the poor and the sick. At up to $400 an ounce at times, whoever the sick may be, they'll be poor soon enough. (And with some of the health problems associated with pot, the sick could be in for quite a time of it.)

All of this is encouraging the growing support for the weed among college students of America (along with growing numbers of grade-school kids and young adults). We just won't pay any attention to such spoil-sports as drug advisor McCaffrey with comments about those new pot laws putting our teens at risk. We don't want to hear about things like that, right?

This writer also reads reports in the press from time to time that you would find interesting. I recall one in March of 1998 about a fellow named Skipper who had convinced authorities he needed to eat marijuana at mealtime to overcome nausea and loss of weight because of his AIDS problem.

So, what happened to him? He got hooked on meth. Why am I not surprised? Because marijuana is such an effective "gateway" drug.

Some of those who are responsible. You're going to be reading about some of the serious medical and psychological problems associated with using marijuana in just a short while. But first I would like you to know about some of those who would put the children of our nation in such jeopardy.

The drive in California to legalize pot for medical use was reported to have received $195,000 from the International Brotherhood of Teamsters. Other backers included such rich moguls as Laurance Rockefeller, Richard Dennis, and George Soros. Another surprise is the support given by Men's Warehouse's George Zimmer.

You are helping indeed, Mr. Zimmer. There are a number of medical authorities who feel that such support puts an ever growing number of our youngsters at ever greater health risk. I guarantee it!

And just in case you think the support only comes from do-what-feels-good-liberals, this writer almost fell out of his chair when he read some time ago about William F. Buckley, Jr., coming out in favor of the legalization of that weed.

Don't get too discouraged, you should also be aware that not only do the supporters seem to cross most political boundaries, so do the critics of such legalizations. However, the big problem still remains that the vast bulk of the American population just doesn't seem to care, one way or the other. Anything can happen and it's all right, just as long as they have some money and no one interferes with their television reception.

The brain-dead move forward. What happens when something like that is no longer subject to total restriction? One good example would be the Netherlands, a land of some pretty strange walking-wounded. In the 70s the cops stopped enforcing the laws against pot and by the 80s the use in that country had tripled and was even being sold openly in the coffee shops.

It's a lot harder to get reliable statistics on drug abuse in America, but even with some uses of some things in some groups seeming to drop a bit from time to time, it has continued to rise with "gateway" drugs for many of the young in our country. What we see in the streets, in the quality in some of our work force, and in the general demeanor of a number of our young people tells us the situation may be worse than any survey is going to reveal.

What about the other drugs? Pot seems to be leading to other drugs and one of them that our nation's anti-drug czar, Barry McCaffrey, is worried about is methamphetamine. He believes it may be shaping up as the next major drug threat. (It's sometimes referred to as "the poor man's cocaine.") It also should be noted that various news services have reported that it is believed illegal drug activity now amounts to over 8 percent of all world trade! And it may be as much as 10 percent!

There it is. It's real. It's bad, and is definitely not going to go away by itself. When you get right down to it, it can be summed up most effectively with one very simple statement. *The drug problem is us!*

I am reminded of that "Evolution" cartoon by Marlette in the *Charlotte Observer* showing the evolution of our species. First there is a monkey-like creature sniffing and snorting on the ground. Next there is a slightly less primitive critter who is almost upright. On and on it goes until we come to "modern man" who is walking fully upright. However, the next example shows man down on all fours again, sniffing and snorting you-know-what.

Is this how it's going to go for us?

The pot of fools gold—the marijuana deception. Does anyone care anymore? I remember attending a "Beach Boys" concert just a few years back and I had to leave. The enclosed arena was thick with the sick-sweet smell of pot. I am told the same thing is true at pop concerts and "rock" shows all over the country. Does anybody do anything about it? Evidently not. About all one can do is just leave.

I am also told that an extra quality marijuana called "lawyer bud" is commonly sold to lawyers, accountants, and other white collar professionals. No one seems to think anything about it. And do you remember when property near Ronald Reagan's ranch was seized by federal agents after a marijuana crop was found on the land?

I can remember when some allergists did a test of the air in West Los Angeles and found that as much as 40 percent of the airborne weed pollens came from the hemp plant that you know of as marijuana. It doesn't take an astrophysicist to figure out what's been going on in that neighborhood now does it?

Oh, but it makes you feel *good*. And it has all kinds of medical benefits, man. Oh, sure it has. I guess that means you're not about to read that National Institutes of Health report that quoted top drug scientists who seriously questioned the value of using marijuana to relieve pain and cure nausea when there are other medications that are even more effective and don't haze the patient mentally in the process.

You don't want to know about such compounds as "AM404" from Daniele Piomelli's lab at the Neurosciences Institute. It is reported to give you the benefits without the bad side effects and other dangers of pot. We don't want to hear about any of the other alternatives either, right? We'd rather watch the eyes of our teens grow dimmer.

You may not go for all that nonsense about how great pot is, but a lot of folks buy that fairy tale, and most of the rest of you just check out of the whole issue by taking no stand at all and doing absolutely nothing. So, maybe it's time you looked at some hard facts about the weed.

Medical facts about marijuana. A couple of days after California voters approved of the medical use of marijuana, Channel 13 in Los Angeles put on a well researched report (in their 10 P.M. newscast) on the new, more potent grade of marijuana that is in use today and is aimed at our teens and pre-teens. They also showed that our baby-boomer parents don't seem to be very concerned about the problem. They don't seem to know or care about the dangers.

Doctors came on to state that people do become highly addicted to the drug. And what else does it do? The program noted that research does seem to show that usage damages the central nervous system, inhibits emotional development, creates a loss of motivation, shortens the attention span, creates respiratory problems and promotes prenatal brain damage.

Still not convinced? The U.S. Department of Health and Human Services concluded in a report that marijuana distorts perception, damages short-term memory, and impairs judgement and complex motor skills. It was also reported to alter the heart rate and is known to lead to everything from lethargy to severe anxiety attacks.

Also THC, the active ingredient in pot, has been found to damage cell membranes and Dr. Donald Tashkin, a UCLA research physician, has noted that those who smoke three or four joints a day often suffer noticeably from chronic bronchitis in a manner similar to cigarette smokers who go through at least a pack a day.

The New England Journal of Medicine had an article about gynecomastia—breast enlargement in the male. An interesting conclusion was that there definitely seems to be a direct correlation between heavy pot smokers and such male breast enlargements. And the American Council for Drug Education states that there is definite evidence that marijuana affects the ability to drive a vehicle and that those high on pot are involved in an unusually high percentage of traffic accidents and fatalities.

It has also been suggested by new evidence that marijuana may weaken our ability to fight disease. Research at the University of Illinois in Chicago have found that the THC in pot seems to weaken the immune system. Columbia University researcher Dr. Wylie C. Hembree III has noted that heavy and sustained use of marijuana negatively affects male smokers' ability to produce normal sperm.

Science Digest magazine reported conclusions published in an American Lung Association Bulletin to the effect that marijuana smoke is more damaging to the heart and lungs than tobacco smoke and that one study found that a single marijuana cigarette produced as high a level of carbon monoxide in the smoker's blood as ten to twenty tobacco cigarettes smoked in a single day.

The facts go on and on. An American Medical Association "Drug Abuse" handbook for doctors states that marijuana smoke contains larger amounts of cancer-causing hydrocarbons than tobacco smoke. It also noted that lung damage can appear within three months and that bronchitis and emphysema are common in regular users.

University of California (L.A.) researcher Dr. Donald T. Tashkin published his conclusion in the *New England Journal of Medicine* that those who smoke three or four marijuana joints a day may well be putting themselves at as much risk of getting lung cancer as smokers with a pack-a-day cigarette consumption.

The committee from the Institute of Medicine of the National Academy of Sciences reported that marijuana most certainly does significantly impair motor coordination, the ability to detect a flash of light, to follow a moving object with your eyes, negatively effects oral communication, hampers short-term memory, and the ability to learn.

Dr. Philip Landfield of Wake Forest University (in Winston-Salem, North Carolina) has revealed that the active ingredient in pot causes a definite loss of brain cells in rats that is like a similar effect attributed to aging. Dr. Robert Heath of the Tulane University School of Medicine was quoted in *Science Digest* magazine as saying that regular use of marijuana may end up widening the gaps between nerve endings in the brain. This may be compromising very important functions like memory, emotion, and behavior.

University of California researchers came out with the observation that prolonged doses of the active ingredient in marijuana shrink the frontal brain lobes of test monkeys. The National Institute on

Drug Abuse presented findings of pot-induced damage to the region of the brain involved with memory and emotion.

University of Hawaii scientist Barbara Siegel noted the distinct possibility of mercury poisoning associated with the smoking of marijuana. Also, some marijuana may, from time to time, be found to be salmonella-contaminated. This according to one report from the Centers for Disease Control (as reported in the *New England Journal of Medicine*).

Dr. Harold Kolansky and Dr. William T. Moore reported in the *Journal of the American Medical Association* that marijuana smoking on a regular basis can cause grave psychiatric ills, including psychosis. This is indicated even in young people who were known to be previously very stable.

It is also very well understood by behavioral scientists that youngsters need to learn how to deal with the normal anxieties and stresses of life as they grow up in order to develop a reasonable degree of mental maturity. When this process is short-circuited by the use of pot as an escape every time there's a problem, you eventually can and often do end up with an adult who has the metal maturity of a child.

We all know about how marijuana is often the "gateway" drug to even more dangerous drugs. There is even a Scripps Research Institute report that suggests that pot may actually prime the brains of some users for those harder drugs. Dr. William Pollin, as director of the National Institute on Drug Abuse has testified in Washington to a Senate Labor subcommittee that a study on this issue definitely indicates a strong link between a start-up with marijuana leading to cocaine and heroin use.

As Dr. Hardin Jones, professor of physiology and medical physics at UC, Berkeley, California, has stated, marijuana is "the most dangerous" of drugs because the user is least aware of its effect, which can be devastating. The medical evidence goes on, and on.

I wonder if any of those well-known personalities and wealthy individuals who exercised their irresponsible support for the legalization of marijuana have any idea at all about how they are helping to severely damage so many of the young people of our land. I truly wonder how *any*one can be so stupid or so callous about our children.

Medical facts about illegal drugs in general. In the 1800s, the only big Western nation that didn't have any real meaningful laws controlling narcotics was America. As you might imagine, morphine, opium, cocaine, and opiates in general were wide open to abusive use.

It didn't do us a lot of good. Little by little we began to see the frightful legacy this was creating in our country and such things as cocaine began to become one of the most feared drugs. In fact, as Lloyd Shearer reported in *Parade* magazine, "In 1910, President Taft sent a report to Congress describing cocaine use as 'the most threatening of the drug habits ever to have appeared in this country.'"

Federal laws were passed against the hated drug within four years and intensive education on the threat, in our schools and in our families helped to reduce the demand. Too bad we have such a short memory. To bad we just can't seem to learn from our own history.

Some good examples. In Dallas a 16-year-old is critically wounded and a 14-year-old is shot to death and authorities said they had been selling crack cocaine and something went wrong. A New York school bus driver is caught buying crack cocaine and is arrested. A train is derailed near Chester, Pennsylvania, and a control-tower operator was believed to be responsible and was tested and found to have marijuana and cocaine in his system.

The National Transportation Safety Board found that cocaine used by a pilot on a commuter flight in Colorado was a contributing factor in a crash that killed nine people. In Mountain View, California, parents of a teen-age girl were found to have taught the girl how to cook cocaine into crack cocaine and how to personally use cocaine. Parents in Odenton, Maryland, were charged with selling their 2-month-old baby boy for $3,500 and three ounces of cocaine. In Corpus Christi, Texas, a baby-selling ring was broken up that evidently was swapping small amounts of cocaine for babies of female drug addicts.

Dr. Edward Mohns, founder and director of the Alcohol-Dependency Treatment Program at La Jolla's famous Scripps Clinic says, about crack cocaine, "It's the most addictive substance we know of on this planet."

Getting to the heart of the problem. Dr. Henry Tazelaar, a Stanford University surgical pathologist, who coordinated a special study on the matter, has stated that those who use cocaine can actually suffer permanent damage to heart muscle tissues. This, in turn, makes them more susceptible to cardiac arrest.

An American Heart Association meeting in New Orleans brought out the fact that cocaine constricts arteries and clogs them as well with blood clots. It was further reported that while this is happening, the body's increased demand for blood occurs because the drug raises the blood pressure and increases the heart rate. What is the result? As you might imagine, it's often death from a sudden heart attack, linked to cocaine use. That's what the hospitals report.

Dr. Sidney Cohen, of the Neuropsychiatric Institute, UCLA School of Medicine is quoted in *Health Scene* as saying that "dependence of the cocaine type produces an array of psychophysiological and physical disorders, many of which can be life-endangering." Dr. Cohen further stated that cocaine can actually kill even those who use the drug infrequently.

The destruction of the brain. Your heart and your brain are two of the most important elements of your existence. Your heart brings life to your body and your brain brings life to your conscious being. And your body can be destroyed in many ways by drug related heart problems and the havoc that can be done to your brain by drugs can truly destroy your being, a little bit at a time.

If you should ever have the opportunity to see one of those three-dimensional computer images of a healthy brain and one of a brain that has been damaged by cocaine, you will see, most graphically, just what this means. The normal, healthy brain shows vibrant colors—the bright blues, yellows and strong reds of a strong blood flow. The cocaine brain is filled with dark holes, showing the lack of a healthy blood flow.

What does this mean? It means that you have difficulty concentrating on things and your memory is noticeably impaired. You lose interest in sex. You become aggressive and paranoid, and you could end up having hallucinations. In simple terms, the more you use the drug, the more chance you have of losing your mind—going crazy.

And the chances are you don't think there's anything wrong at all. You feel just great. Only at the beginning. The end could leave you brain-dead or possibly a full-blown example of a cocaine-related death.

Birth defects and other problems. Let us not forget the warning of Dr. Gilbert Chavez, an epidemiologist at the federal Centers for Disease Control. He tells us that women who are on cocaine early in their pregnancies are almost five times more likely to end up with babies that have really serious birth defects. A similar warning was echoed by Dr. Kenneth Lyons Jones, Jr., at the University of California in San Diego. He clearly stated that even light cocaine ingestion threatens the fetus.

If you're on that drug, you really don't care do you? Of course not. I guess it's going to be up to the rest of us to care and back it up with direct intervention. (That's something volunteers can be trained for. That's something people can do.)

Next, we hear from the national Centers for Disease Control that tuberculosis may be linked to the use of crack cocaine. And the violence caused by this insidious drug is another nightmare that we read about in the papers all the time. Frankly, I could fill this book several times over with examples concerning just this one drug alone.

The meth in the madness. Other drugs are doing their bit as well. Take methamphetamine as an example. Sometimes severe meth intoxication ends up overflowing the emergency rooms. If you manage to survive, expect to have long-term health problems with this one. As Dr. Robert S. Brown of the University of Virginia and Thomas Streed of the San Diego Sheriff's office found, there seems to be noticeable brain damage in prisoners who are admitted long-term users of meth.

Other methods of madness include PCPs and LSD. As the late Dr. Richmond Barbour had written, "People high on PCP are indeed madmen. They are unbelievably strong, have no restraint, and are unable to feel pain." Sometimes the only way the authorities are able to stop such a life-threatening rampage is to shoot the poor soul.

PCP is short for "phencyclidine." It's a concoction of eleven different chemicals that create a devastating psychoactive drug. It's sold under at least seventy different names, including "angel dust" and "crystal." It's an addictive, living death under any name.

Frankly, it can knock out an elephant. It can put a human in a stupor or send him (or her) on a delirious, violent rampage. High enough dosages bring on comas, seizures and death. It's most certainly a devastating way to commit suicide.

LSD (lysergic acid diethylamide) is that stupid drop-out drug of the hippies and flower children of the 60s. They had themselves convinced that it was the mind-expanding "acid" when all it really offered was a sometimes mind-shattering delusion filled with schizophrenic-like psychoses, paranoia, and all sorts of horrendous flashbacks. (If you have any doubts, ask the National Institute on Drug Abuse about it. They'll explain it to you.)

And then there is heroin and designer drugs. We hear about victims dying of an accidental overdose of heroin. We hear about the intense addiction that was involved. We hear how potent such drugs are and how fatal they can be. Sometimes it's the weakened system of the user. Sometimes it's because of that "black tar" form of heroin. (I've heard of Mexican black tar heroin being blamed for a condition similar to what has been called "flesh-eating bacteria.")

But then one can always turn to one of those synthetic street "designer" drugs. One of them, called MPTP, tends to leave many victims with irreversible Parkinson's Disease. Other synthetic concoctions do other dramatic damages. Some, of course, will just kill you right away and that's the end of that.

I could go on forever about all this stuff. I could tell you about the AIDS explosion, to an ever increasing degree because of needle-sharing addicts. (It has been suggested that probably over one-third of the drug addicts in America are infected with the AIDS virus. That's several hundred-thousand people!) I could also tell you all about the wave of mental illnesses that have been linked to abuses of drugs and alcohol. And there's so much more.

Somehow I have an idea that you really don't need to hear any more about these sorts of things. I have a feeling you may have this picture clearly in mind now. Let's hope so. Let's hope so because now it's time to do something about it.

Chapter Sixteen

Drugs: A Search for Solutions
Turning Things Around

Losing the Battle. In 1985 the General Accounting Office reported that the "war" on drugs was having little effect on narcotics operations. A few months later, the then Attorney General Edwin Meese spoke of America's drug problem as being, "a national disaster in the making."

In 1986 the House Select Committee on Narcotics Abuse and Control received the border report that our government is losing the war to stop the ever-increasing flow of drugs from Mexico and other Latin American nations. In 1987 the then FBI director, William Sessions, said our continuing substance abuses show that Americans are really not yet serious about trying to solve the problem.

In 1989 Chicago educator and author Jawanza Kunjufu made it abundantly clear that American leaders are not really serious about combating drugs. In 1991 the then New York City Police Commissioner, Lee Brown, stated that "we are not winning the war on drugs." In 1994 we discover that the Social Security Administration's Supplemental Security Income (SSI) was being used by abusers to finance drug and alcohol binges.

In 1996 Linden Blue, a trustee of the Hudson Institute and former vice chairman of General Atomics, offered a telling question about our drug problem. He asked, "Are we so weak and intimidated that we can no longer solve our most pressing problems?" In 1997 the California state Senate voted to eliminate the state law that mandated the loss of one's driver's license when one is caught smoking pot.

And then, of course, there is that shameful legalization of pot for what is laughingly referred to as "medical use." As I write these words, thoughtful people all over this nation are speaking out about the drug war that never was.

Introduction to the counterattack. Folks are reaching in every direction. I remember when Alabama was considering a $75,000 lottery exclusively for those who turn in major pushers. And then there was Jerry and Jennifer Miracle in Detroit. Police seemed indifferent to their neighborhood drug problem at the time, so these two hand-made signs and posted them in their neighborhood, urging neighbors to unite and report crack houses.

Since methamphetamine manufacturing was discovered in better neighborhoods as well as in poor, run down areas, some property owners were alerted and a few communities began to pay attention. Some of the signs they were looking for (with the help of landlords and officials): red residue on the furniture and sometimes on the walls as well, burns in rugs and carpets that don't look like cigarette burns, strange chemical containers in the trash, and strong chemical smells emanating from the property, a lot of fans being used and/or an air-conditioner that is run all the time, smoke detectors that have been covered with plastic or foil or have been disconnected or removed, large packages and containers (drums, boxes, etc.) being delivered and removed all the time, shutters and drapes that are closed all the time, and rental payments that are always made with cash.

Pay attention to this. If you spot many of these signs, call the authorities in your area and ask for the local narcotics investigators. They probably will get right on it. If, for some reason, they don't seem all that interested, call the local media, elected officials and/or higher level enforcement officials.

Other things you can do. If you and your neighbors are really sure you've got a meth lab or a crack house or a general drug dealer doing business in a nearby building, talk to the police and the landlord. Since some landlords just end up renting again to another drug operation (because they're paid off or they just don't pay attention), work with local code enforcement and develop community pressures. Help to make sure you end up with responsible, law-abiding tenants in those places.

You might also want to check into the "Safe Streets" project. They can help you to organize so you can get this done with a minimum of difficulties. (You'll see this group listed in the first appendix at the end of this book, with a phone number you can call any time.)

One neighborhood in the Los Angeles area used video cameras to help clean up their area. It was in the heart of Hollywood where dealers used the streets like a drive-in drug store. Then landlords and others in the area got together and saw to it that banners were hung and cameras were installed.

The drug dealing dropped dramatically. And, since then, other neighborhood activists and local business associations have picked up on this approach. With the help of public and private funding, in concert with local law enforcement agencies, this can be a big help for you, too, if you need it. Do some checking; see what you think. (It could be considered a part of that new idea we like to call the "video vigilantes.")

Sometimes the effort also involves neighbors and special associations (with the cooperation of local officials) tearing down crack houses and other abandoned drug magnets. Sometimes the neighbors either don't get the local support they need or don't feel they can wait for it, and they just tear it apart or burn it down on their own. Frankly, I just can't endorse this approach. It is almost always much better to do it with official support, believe me.

You can also do what Michael Ryan reported on in *Parade* magazine a while back. It was about how Hawkins, Texas, set up some strong controls to insure that their kids won't be destroyed by drugs. Among other things, they announced that if any of its junior or senior high students wanted to be involved in any extracurricular activities (such as sports), they would have to agree to mandatory drug testing.

Did everybody get all upset about this? No, they didn't. As Michael Ryan reported one of its supporters saying, "We can either stop it before it starts or get them into the kind of program that brings them to a point where they really want to stop." Way to go, Hawkins!

There are also some good programs for the workplace. This can also be of great help. You can call the Center for Substance Abuse Prevention, Work Place Helpline at 1-800-967-5752. Additional information on how you can be a part of the answer can be obtained from The National Institute on Drug Abuse at 1-800-729-6686. Check them out, and some of the others listed at the end of this book. They are there for you.

I sure do give you a lot of homework, don't I? Well, there's so much to be done. Most folks seem to want somebody else to do it. That's why this book is so thick with problems and things to be done. I don't ever again want to hear anybody tell me somebody else should do it, and they don't know what to do anyway.

Prison and rehabilitation. *Parade* magazine (Sunday newspaper supplement) is so very good about showing what can be done to make things better. They do it with the drug issue, and they do it with so many other things that effect the quality of life and the safety of us all.

Not so terribly long ago, Bill O'Reilly wrote in *Parade* about drug rehabilitation programs in our prison system. Among other things, he reported that "if we really want to win the war on drugs, say some experts, we should pay attention to a new approach to rehabilitation in prison."

He exampled the Alabama approach (the first of its kind in the nation) wherein inmates with drug problems are given the opportunity (upon conviction) to enter a special drug treatment program. They are informed that if they decline the opportunity, there is little chance they'll ever get out on parole. In other words, they'll have to do hard time the whole time!

It was further noted that "more than 90 percent of Alabama's drug-addicted convicts go through the rehabilitation program." And it is evidently a very comprehensive, well organized program that seems to be getting some genuine results.

How good is it? As one of the doctors pointed out to O'Reilly, "the parole failure rate for those who have undergone in-prison drug rehabilitation is nearly 20 percent lower than the rate for those who did not go through the program." Encouraging.

Other evidence is mounting from across the nation that is telling us many comprehensive long-term substance abuse programs do work. They aren't cheap but they are effective. I guess, because it takes so long and costs so much, it just isn't happening in very many places.

Why does it take so long? To a great extent, because drug dependency is usually accompanied by pre-drug or drug-induced emotional disorders that are often quite complicated and deeply embedded within an unstable psyche. Let's face it, there's no short road to nirvana.

The psychological focus. Even back in 1993, there was a presidential commission recommendation that all fifty states adopt tough anti-drug laws that include meaningful education and comprehensive treatment. However, even though the call was made (then and before and since), there has been a limited emphasis in that direction.

I recall when Dr. David Izenzon started Potsmokers Anonymous in New York. It involved a nine-week program for people unable to break their dependency on marijuana. The good doctor seemed to have developed a strategy that has a reasonable measure of success.

I remember when "ABC News" reported on District Attorney Charles Hines' tough residential drug rehabilitation treatment program in Brooklyn, New York. It was reported that it cost three times less than a year in prison, and it showed an encouraging percentage who were evidently successfully rehabilitated.

I am aware of the El Cajon Municipal Court Substance Abuse Assessment Program (in California) where the recidivism rate is half the state average. How does it work? The offender is sent to talk to two addiction counselors. These are people who are former substance abusers, and they know all the excuses. They assess the situation and work out a treatment program.

Isn't it terribly expensive? The full program is around $130,000 a year, but the cost is recovered by the fees paid by the participants. It also saves everyone money in the process because there are so many recovered offenders that will no longer jam the system.

So, why aren't some of these great programs in massive use across the nation? Maybe Dr. Guido Belsasso was right when he was quoted by Richard Louv as saying that "... what the U.S. government is doing amounts to lip service." It also could be said that the rest of us aren't doing a lot about such things either.

Of course, substance abusers are often the first to tell you that it isn't really hurting them, and they can quit any time they want to. Such chemically induced delusions, and other perceptual changes make it almost impossible for many abusers to recognize what is actually happening to them. Let's face it, even so-called normal people can create elaborate justifications for practically anything. Imagine what a drug addict can do in this area.

Possibilities with medication. In 1985 Dr. Todd Estroff told a Dallas meeting of the Society for Neuroscience of a possible way of controlling addiction to cocaine. His reasoning went this way. Cocaine immediately stimulates a very large increase of dopamine in the human system. This is felt to be a primary reason why it offers a short period of pleasure for the user.

Since the brain has a real problem with such large amounts of dopamine in the system, the natural production of dopamine falters and falls off. This abnormally low natural production may, in fact, create the craving that occurs for more cocaine.

Now scientists have reduced the craving and withdrawal problems with a drug that seems to bring back some of the natural dopamine production in the human body. (Dr. Estroff is with the Fair Oaks Hospital in Summit, New Jersey.)

Two years later it was announced that a study by Scripps Clinic and Research Foundation discovered that the drug "bromo-criptine" may be effective in getting addicts off of cocaine. The drug notably reduces the craving. (It's a sort of follow up on that earlier New Jersey study.)

In 1989 doctors at the University of Minnesota told of tests with "carbamazepine," that showed a marked control of the cocaine desire in subjects and Harvard Medical School researchers discovered that "buprenorphine" also suppressed the craving.

In 1991 Dr. George Uhl, a scientist at the National Institute on Drug Abuse announced that a brain protein gene has been found and isolated that is extremely sensitive to cocaine. Knowing this could lead to blocker and other gene therapy that could break the addiction.

In 1993 research scientists at the College of Physicians and Surgeons at Columbia University in New York announced that they had found a catalytic monoclonal antibody enzyme that might be able to seek out, bind, and then break the cocaine molecule into two inert and harmless by-products.

In early 1998 Physician Leadership on National Drug Policy reported that around 40 percent of drug addicts find success with abstinence-oriented treatment programs. A few other reports seem to indicate an even better result.

As we near the end of the century, there seems to be all sorts of medication and treatment procedures that can successfully treat cocaine addiction. There also seems to be some progress with drugs and programs that can counter other addictive substances as well.

So, what are we waiting for? Why are these and other similar medications not in massive use in this country? Is there something we're not being told or have we decided to just give up? You tell me.

Saving our children. They tell us that the typical American family of our idealized past has all but vanished, to be replaced with either one parent only or no parent at all in the home, during a reasonable amount of the time. Sure, there are families who remain whole, close and are very, very special. But we cannot escape the uncomfortable fact that this beautiful image is less and less a part of our real world today. And you can see the results of this. You can't escape it.

What do we do about it? Well, some folks have tried a little bit of this and a little bit of that. They've done about all they can do with a general population that just isn't getting involved. And naturally, there are those who never really grasp the true nature of the problem, never bother to learn and seem satisfied to settle for a few "feel good" things to do that make them feel better, even though it accomplishes precious little or nothing at all in the end.

There have been coloring books to teach kids to say "no" to drugs. There have been video games and CD-ROM programs that try to show kids what's right and wrong and why and give them some reasonable tools for survival in this dangerous and uncertain world.

These things help but they seem so little, so late, and without the intensive community dedication that is so absolutely necessary. Frankly, so many of these efforts seem more like frantically trying to rearrange the deck chairs on the Titanic, as though that would somehow help to keep away the reality of the disaster.

So, what *do* we do? A lot more than we're doing now, that's for sure. Among the many things we might consider is to pay attention to the teens who are telling us to learn how to target substance abuse problems and potential problems a lot earlier in life.

It is suggested we should focus much more on what has been going wrong in young people's lives. Maybe we need to find out why so many kids have been turning to alcohol and drugs in the first place.

Other suggestions include the need for more youth clubs and other community activities for young people. There needs to be a major emphasis in the local media and with everybody in general for more parental involvement, for more adult responsibility. (What's going on in *your* neighborhood?)

When a kid is involved in drugs, alcohol, or crime in general, he needs to be put in a really heavy-duty rehab program. It needs to be something truly comprehensive and something that reaches out and makes significant changes in the contributing environment. Have you got something like that in *your* community?

For those of you who have a problem kid and don't know where to turn (and you never saw the movie Toughlove, starring Lee Remick and Bruce Dern), let me recommend an outstanding organization that might be able to help you to help yourself. Toughlove is a self-help group for families of children who are substance abusers.

There's a manual for parents, and there are support groups in various parts of the country (or you can start one in your area if you like). You can call them at 1-800-333-1069 if you want more information or you want to get involved. It's something worth considering.

Various YMCA's have special programs to help keep latchkey kids busy and on the right path. Find out what's available in your area. (If there isn't anything where you live, find out why not, and then turn around and make it so.)

Remember, for many of the baby-boom generation, there is a lot of denial concerning drug use with *their* children. This was shown not so long ago in an important survey by the Partnership for a Drug-Free America. Consequently, there are a lot of kids out there dulling and sometimes destroying a very precious thing—their minds.

Others coming forward. Some professional athletes have come forward from time to time to get involved in various anti-drug programs, media promos, and other involvements. Remember that "All-Stars to the Rescue" TV crusade against drugs that was aired a few years ago? That's a good example. Unfortunately, such involvements are seldom more than short-term hypes that are here and gone before we know it.

Some kids have been helping other kids. You see, youngsters often tend to model themselves after other kids who are about three years older. Such older kids can really help these younger ones to stay away from drugs and alcohol. They can be an enormously effective influence if they are the sort that others will tend to look up to.

There are lots of ways these contacts and influences can be facilitated. Sometimes it can be through special school programs. Sometimes it's with targeted community activities. It can also be at special teen summer camps. Are there comprehensive involvements of this nature in *your* area? If not, what do you plan to do about it?

What to do in your own family. Ken Barun wrote a great article in *Parade* magazine entitled, "How to Help Your Children Stay Off Drugs." He observed that "no one has more influence on your youngsters than you do. So educate yourself to the dangers of drugs—then teach your children."

He also listed five major areas for you to get involved in. (1) Build up your child's self-esteem. (2) Monitor their friendships. (3) Promote alternatives to drugs. (4) Teach your child about drugs. And one last thing that's very important to remember: (5) Parents have to toe the line, too.

What do you look for as warning signs? The Partnership for a Drug-Free America lists a number of things, including the following:

> Chronic eye redness, sore throat or dry cough.
> Chronic lying, especially about whereabouts.
> Wholesale changes in friends.
> Stealing.
> Deteriorating relationships with family members.
> Wild mood swings, hostility or abusive behavior.
> Chronic fatigue, withdrawal, carelessness about grooming.
> Major changes in eating or sleeping patterns.

Loss of interest in favorite activities, hobbies or sports.
School problems, slipping grades, absenteeism.

I might also add to that list:

Serious concentration problems.
Dilated pupils.
Loss of motivation.
Trouble with relationships in general.
Paranoid behavior.

I'm sure you remember that terrible tragedy when the actor Carroll O'Connor lost his much loved son to drugs. Well, he wrote a special article for *Parade* magazine, too. In it he said that "it's time to admit that our approach to the drug problem has failed."

He made it very clear that we must work on education. He also said, "I advocate a program of selective arrests to go after drug dealers." He added, "Spend more money interdicting the drug invasion: use the regular military forces, and use also special forces and military intelligence."

He also clearly advocated drug education for parents. Let's face it, parents have got to find out how to deal with this menace and then become dedicated and get involved. Mr. O'Connor concluded with his advocacy for "immediate discussion." As he put it, "We must begin a real and honest dialogue . . . challenge me. Let us start."

How else can you get involved? You could call Communities Against Substance Abuse at 1-800 580-7200, or you could go on the World Wide Web and connect with www.drugfreeamerica.org or www.whitehousedrugpolicy.gov.

The education solution. Many of our answers are going to be in our schools. I know, with a few of the schools it does seem to be a curriculum of reading, writing, and reloading. And even with the vast majority that are not so inclined, there is still the drugs—there is always the drugs.

I remember so many frightening reports about this. I remember people like William Raspberry reporting in the *Washington Post* that "in Detroit, one-fourth of our kids drop out between eighth and ninth grade; 90 percent of the kids who face the drug-court judge are dropouts, 92 percent are functionally illiterate—and they have about a 75 percent recidivist rate, so they keep coming back into the system."

Mr. Raspberry said that "the true solution is right under our noses." He made it very clear that we must keep them from dropping out in the first place. Well, some of the schools of our nation have been working on that problem, but with so many academic problems and so little community support in many areas, we're not developing the extensive solutions here that we desperately need. It's just not happening.

Some efforts still go on, however. A recovered alcoholic anonymously donated a scholarship at the University of South Florida's Sarasota campus for drug addicts and alcoholics who are genuinely trying to put their lives back together. And the D.A.R.E. program is being used in many schools to attack the problem. Unfortunately, it hasn't seemed as effective a program as it needs to be. Maybe after some changes are made? (Let's hope they're being made now.)

Then there are those programs that feature kids who are ex-drug users. Some have become very effective persuaders. They may be making a real impact. Too bad they seem to be so few in number. (It always seems to wind up being a case of too little and too late, doesn't it?)

Drugs and the media. Many good efforts have been made by the media—TV documentaries, newspaper articles, magazine features (as in *Parade* magazine), and radio talk-show efforts. But, as with all other segments of our society, it has not been hitting home hard enough, often enough, nor is it aimed in a demographically appropriate manner much of the time.

Let's face it, the sophisticated psychological persuasion of Madison Avenue advertising agency brains haven't really been *fully* engaged in this battle. It just isn't happening to the degree that is needed.

There is also the unfortunate fact that there has been a certain amount of glorification of drug use in the fashion industry, in some movies, and with some of the more rebellious radio and TV "shock jocks" and the like. They think they're "cute." They think they're "in." They have no idea of the number of lives they probably are responsible for losing.

A while back, General Barry McCaffrey, director of the Office of National Drug Control Policy, proposed a new and more powerful use of mass media to cut down the drug use among our kids. It will take more money than is allocated, and it will need far greater sophistication than we've seen so far; but it could possibly really work if it is done by the professional advertising industry in the right way. And, of course, it needs to be a long, sustained, and truly *massive* effort.

Also, it's too bad, but the public service announcements just aren't cutting it all that much, so far. Some aren't produced that well, and they aren't often properly targeting the right audience. And those

PSAs are almost always too few and not often well placed because the media often finds more immediate financial gratification with payed commercials in the most appropriate positions and with that needed frequency.

Market forces are squeezing public service spots off the air or into secondary time slots in just about every format. If you want to change that, you're going to have to organize an effective citizens' campaign for media enlightenment. If they eventually find that enough folks are deeply concerned, most of our media will react in a responsible way. They usually do. But they do need your input.

The Office of National Drug Control policy has launched an extensive market test of a broad-based anti-drug campaign. But you need to keep the pressure on Washington to continue that effort, and you need to encourage media to reexamine their policy on public service announcements. And it wouldn't hurt to push for more serious programming aimed at this major national crisis.

> *The biggest problem in the world*
> *could have been solved when it was small.*
>
> —Witter Bynner

Having a full-scale war on drugs. Being the human beings that we are, we really seldom care to deal with things until they get completely out of hand. Then we want someone else to come along and solve the problem. That's what happens with most things and, as we all know, that's what's happened with drugs. We've really done a number on ourselves on this one.

Now we are going to have to either start learning how to wave by-by to our civilization or *really* get our act together and turn this thing around. It's as simple as that. Or, I guess I should really say, it's as complicated as that.

Remember way back in 1988 when a House panel in Washington declared that Congress just can't "micro-manage" that "war" on drugs and that a great effort had to be launched with an administration drug coordinator (with a nice fat bank account) to develop a new, and hopefully, successful approach in the drug "war."

In 1989 (a banner year for proclamations) John Lawn of the DEA spoke about the control of our borders with a cheery, "Even if the military stood shoulder to shoulder around our country, we manufacture enough illegal drugs in this country to satisfy every illicit appetite." In that same year the Pentagon announced that two Coast Guard admirals will be leading a sweeping campaign to bring a halt to drug smuggling on both the Atlantic and Pacific coasts.

In 1991 our dear government announced it was establishing a national center that will train volunteers from all over the nation in effective strategies for combating substance abuse. And in 1998 the Pentagon recommended permanent cancellation of armed military patrols along our Mexican border.

I know, it was in response to the accidental shooting death of a civilian. So their answer is to pull back? I sure hope they're not planning to deal with other types of war situations like that. So, what should have been done? Well, if this is really a drug *war* then there should be a no-nonsense, wide, no-man's-land set up on this side of the border and *no* civilians allowed anywhere in that zone. That's it. Let's get serious about it.

You may not realize it but figures I got just a few months ago show that the Pentagon's drug enforcement budget now approaches $1 billion a year, over four thousand National Guard troops are or have been involved in approximately thirteen hundred anti-drug operations, and 89 percent of police departments now have paramilitary units with almost half trained by our soldiers, sailors, and airmen.

With all of those alternating shouts and cringes, have we actually managed to accomplish very much? Not a hell of a lot. Not actually. Even with all of this, and all of what you have read in this section on the drug problem, and even with all the rest that there isn't room enough to put in this book, . . . with *all* of that, you would really think we might actually consider a true *war* on drugs in the *fullest* sense.

You'd think so, but our government, in its infinite lack of wisdom, would much rather give aid overseas and send our troops to other countries to help *them* out. For God's sake, let's not get serious about solving our *own* problems right here at home. That would be truly unthinkable.

What is needed: A <u>real</u> declaration of war. "For the first time in recent history, America is being invaded successfully. Not by a foreign power bent on enslaving us, but by those bent on making a filthy profit by smuggling and selling illicit drugs that have already poisoned and could ultimately destroy our society." That is a quote from a joint statement by a group of U.S. mayors just a few years back.

You might also want to consider what Carl Rowan wrote on the subject in a Field Newspaper Syndicate release. "No Soviet missile ever could do so much damage in America's high schools, colleges, and other communities as does the cocaine from Bolivia and Peru, or the marijuana from Colombia, the heroin from Iran and Pakistan."

I recall Sandy Bauer's column, "In One Ear," from the Knight-Ridder News Service, when a very interesting review was made of the John Chancellor book, *Peril And Promise: A Commentary on America*. Bauers noted that, "Chancellor sees the American public as talented but complacent. We respond with creativity and vigor to an emergency, but tend to ignore ordinary adversity. He speculates that what the nation needs is a national crisis—a peacetime Pearl Harbor—to get us back to work."

Even Daryl Gates, back when he was the L.A. Chief of Police, asked the president to declare a national emergency because of this massive drug abuse problem. Well I'll tell you something, a growing number of us are becoming more and more convinced that only something on the order of a declared national emergency (just a little short of full martial law) will *ever* get the job done.

Some of us are convinced that this should be coupled with a truly massive, comprehensive "systems" approach that will properly take into consideration the enormous complexity and pandemic nature of this problem, as "systems" approaches are designed to do.

Don't think we can do it? Yes we *can!* It's only a matter of enough of you becoming willing to become a bit fanatical about this and learn all about it and work on it and work on it and *never give up!* What we need is nothing less than your fervent commitment and the appropriate accompanying action.

As U.C.S.D. drug specialist Dr. Marc Schuckit was quoted in a Neil Morgan column, "To win against drugs, each of us has to take the drug epidemic personally." *That's* for sure.

One of the major efforts in all of this is going to have to be the changing of the attitudes of our fellow Americans. What I mean is that most Americans just don't seem to take any of this all that seriously, or they do but prefer to retreat from involvement. Or perhaps they just don't care.

Many will say, "I just wouldn't know what to do." Of course they can learn but that would evidently be just too much of a stretch for them. Others will say, "I just don't have the time." Of course they don't have the time if they don't set their priorities that way. Others will give you all sorts of other excuses. Remember, we humans are masters at justification—justification for not only what we do but also very definitely for what we decide we don't want to do.

And might we be able to change the attitudes about the drugs themselves? Why not? Look what we've been able to do with tobacco (although we still have a long way to go with our youth). Tobacco is now perceived as a great health hazard, but these other drugs are much more dangerous—are a *much* greater threat. Of *course* we can do it!

We can and must learn to perceive this drug threat as just as serious as we did the bombing of Pearl Harbor. We must become *that* dedicated. We must be willing to make *that* much of a commitment.

Let these words from Carlos Andres Perez in the News and Events of the Institute of the Americas make an impact on your mind. "Drugs may be the most formidable threat that humanity has faced over the course of its existence."

Don't let your concern become a velleity—a mere wish that doesn't lead to the slightest action. Let's see what you're really made of. *Let's get going!*

Chapter Seventeen

Politics
What It's <u>Really</u> All About

> *The more you read about politics,
> the more you got to admit that each party is
> worse than the other.*
>
> —Will Rogers

The truth about the American politician. He (and sometimes she) can be so charming and interested in your problems when it's advantageous to be that way. When no special advantage is seen, that individual can often be revealed as a truly crass and thoughtless lout in many ways, owned by an irresponsible combination of inflated ego and campaign funding commitments. And even though that surely is not all of them, for many of the lot, that is what they often seem to eventually become. It's not a pretty picture.

Let's face it, when big money rolls in to support a politician's campaign, don't you think that if there's any way possible for the politician to give extra consideration to big contributors' wants and needs, that politician will find a way to justify special attention to those wants and needs? Come on now, let's be realistic. Of course that's what's going to happen.

What is that sort of thing called? Well, when one is not trying to hide behind a wall of polysyllabic nomenclature, it is quite simply called a legal way to bribe a politician. It's that simple.

Our reactions to the nature of the beast. As Lou Cannon once noted in the *Washington Post*, "Voters are saying they don't trust either party." Considering the way the whole mess is organized and operates, it's no small wonder.

As Don Bauder once noted in the *San Diego Union-Tribune*, "politics is the one field in which non-performance is rewarded, not punished. In politics, only rhetoric counts. In politics, nobody is expected to deliver on promises." Of course not. Not enough of you folks seem to be willing to hold them *really* accountable for what they do or don't do. What else can you expect?

So what do we get? As Groucho Marx said, "In America you can go on the air and kid the politicians, and the politicians can go on the air and kid the people." And in another of his famous quotes, he said, "Politics is the art of looking for trouble, finding it everywhere, diagnosing it incorrectly and applying the wrong remedies." Then there's Hubert Humphrey who said, "We believe that to err is human. To blame it on someone else is politics." That's what we get.

We must eventually come to finally understand that, even though we all take turns being wrong sometimes, we have allowed far too many politicians into office to make a career out of doing that practically all the time. It shouldn't surprise us to discover that we have a chameleon figure leading a hollow society. We made it possible.

We get frustrated and we make jokes about them, like the Frank & Ernest cartoon by Bob Thaves with one character saying, "Do you think air bags are really dangerous?" and the other character answering, "Only if they get elected."

The other thing we sometimes do was amply illustrated in the *Chicago Tribune's* "Still Life." It goes like this: "Of course I know who I'm going to vote for . . . I'm voting for whoever the guy is who's running opposite the one I'm voting against!"

Where is there someone we can vote for? Responsible people who might be interested take one look at what it takes—what they have to go through, and then back away just as quickly as humanly possible. I gotta tell you, most of the best and the brightest don't want any part of it.

Many of the good and talented among us feel that government has really lost its luster, in a big way. They see what it costs in obligations to finance their elections. They see the special interests moving in on them. Once they are in there, they see the almost impossible task of accomplishing much of anything. They see how the little that does get done is often so misshapen by compromises that whatever the situation might have started out being, it often becomes worse than before.

In other words, it has become obvious that major changes must be made in the political process itself, if elections are going to ever have any real significance ever again. That means, the system needs an overhaul, *now!*

How to get in power and stay in power. It's simple, really. You just either have to be very wealthy or have a very "understanding" relationship with big campaign donors, lobbyists, and other nefarious types. You can be sure, the biggest and richest auction in America is a major election.

You've been reading about some of the more current political donation scandals in the papers, so you know what I'm talking about. But is that only just a problem of the moment? And what about the lobbying?

A good example that answers both of those questions could well be the associated press report about how big corporations, associations, unions, and other special interests were calculated to have spent a minimum of $400 million in just the first half of 1996, doing whatever they could to influence lawmakers, bureaucrats, and other Washington influentials.

That's a whopping amount but it's from a careful analysis of the first disclosures under what was then the new lobbying law. If that doesn't stick in your craw, look how politicians, over the years, have learned so well how to develop an ever growing dependent voting group through what has become our welfare system. (One thing we're finally beginning to reform, thank God.)

As George Bernard Shaw once noted, "A government which robs Peter to pay Paul can always depend on the support of Paul." Sometimes it's like what Samuel Johnson said, "Power is gradually stealing away from the many to the few, because the few are more vigilant and consistent."

Even with those welfare reforms we've had, much of the political establishment absolutely depends on keeping a majority of blacks, Hispanics, and other minorities shackled to the "welfare plantation." This is a legal way of buying votes, plain and simple. It's also an awful way to treat human beings who have a lot more potential than to be a slave in such a degraded system.

It doesn't come cheap. By just about all accounts and records it does seem that the repetitious, slick, quick, political TV commercials have the most influence of all on the outcome of elections. And, by all accounts and records, such TV commercials cost a fortune.

Spend millions and millions and millions of donated dollars (at what cost?) and tell the voters what they want to hear, and create the right distractions, and pull all those other rabbits out of the hat and the "spin doctors" will have their politicians sitting on the high perch in no time at all.

Way back in 1968, Henry J. Taylor said it best of all, "Politicians rely on the public's short memory. They bounce distracting balls into the air by talking about the future. They try to make the public forget the boobland decisions and broken promises for which the nation pays so dearly.

"That's not democracy; it's a swindle on the democratic principle. Aren't our leaders ever to be held to account for anything?" Well, it's still a good question. Aren't they *ever* going to be held accountable?

Remember when fairy tales would begin with, "Once upon a time . . ." Now they all seem to begin with, "If I am elected . . ." or as Will Rogers put it, "If everything the politicians promised during a campaign came true, there would be very little reason to want to go to heaven."

Who was it who said, "What this party needs is a forward-looking candidate who has the vision to avoid issues even before they arise?" That could have been a sound-bite from either party. Like it or not, between the Donkeys and the Elephants there seems to be an *awful* lot of bull.

The cost of being a politician. Now let's think about the enormous expense of all that bull. Let's think about the *true* cost of being a politician.

It costs a fortune to run, so, only the wealthy or the compromised usually manage to slam their way through the monetary barrier. Everyone demands everything once you're in and some offer enticing incentives for your "special" considerations. It is found to be almost impossible to accomplish anything of any exceptional value once you are fully emerged in the choppy seas of the "beltway mentality."

So what happens? Most of our best are eliminated right at the beginning. What you have left are those who are not so fussy about what it takes. What you have left are only a few idealists and one hell of a lot of opportunists.

What are the opportunists like? That all depends on who bought them and what their oversized egos are demanding. You usually get some special interest legislation, a notable hidden cost to the taxpayer, and the continuing growth of a generally oppressive government.

You also can expect to get some people who have no better behavior in their private lives than they have with their public manipulations. They haven't the slightest idea about the obvious and natural connections between their private lives and their public responsibilities.

Viscount Morley wrote that "those who would treat politics and morality apart will never understand the one or the other." They only understand what they have turned both into, to their own special advantage. *That* they understand.

Do you really believe a man who will sneak around and break the most important personal contract in his life (with his wife) will miraculously be absolutely clean and pure when considering his public contracts and other outside responsibilities? If you really do believe that, I've got a line on all sorts of bridges, gold mines, pyramid clubs, and lottery tickets you might be interested in.

(Come to think of it, many of you do seem quite interested in some of those really big state lotteries. Those state run lotteries where you have a better chance of being hit by lightning than coming up the big winner.)

Maybe our changing moral requirements suggests what Stayskal might have meant with his *Tampa Tribune* cartoon showing someone running out of a bank with a gun and a bag of money. A bystander says, "Hey! That was Senator Truall!" His companion replies, "Well, what he does in his private life shouldn't concern us."

I really do believe that we must rise to the words of Thomas Jefferson. "When a man assumes a public trust, he should consider himself as public property." And what should we do with public property that has been thoroughly blighted? You get the picture.

The escape to situational ethics. It never ceases to amaze me how easily many people (and particularly most lawyers and politicians) can create such beautifully deceptive justifications for just about anything they want to do. Often it comes down to a special "editable" version of ethical standards that can be changed to suit one's mood as easily as one might change one's underwear.

A good example of this strange philosophy can be seen in Anita Hill's statement concerning Clinton, where she says her accusation against Clarence Thomas is different from the accusations made against the president. Then she reveals her motivation for such a statement with her request for us to consider the administration's policies toward women before judging his personal behavior.

Well of course the two are different to some extent. No two situations like that are ever *exactly* the same. It's the way in which they *are* similar that makes it really interesting. When she talks about considering policies before personal behavior, you get a marvelous example of that situational ethics we were talking about.

A further example of this sort of thing was quite well illustrated by Signe Wilkinson in the *Philadelphia Daily News* with a cartoon showing three strident ladies with N.O.W. buttons and big signs. The first sign reads, "Dump Clarence Thomas!" The second sign says, "Dump Bob Packwood." The third one notes, in much smaller letters: "If the charges are absolutely true, be very, vary disapproving of Bill Clinton." You get the picture.

No choices—no empowerment. I am reminded of the Richard Locher illustration in the *Chicago Tribune* in which we see a couple strolling down the street, past various election posters. The wife says, "That's the beauty of America—freedom of choice." The husband answers, "Yeah! Now if we only had some choices to choose from."

Even though "no man is good enough to govern another man without that other's consent," as Abraham Lincoln said, there is so precious little opportunity for that consent to be enthusiastically given by anyone these days. More and more folks are getting fed up with voting for the lesser of two evils so much of the time.

Frankly, that obvious lack of quality in the political landscape has been a reoccurring bane of humanity for an endless period of time. As George Bernard Shaw observed it, "He knows nothing; he thinks he knows everything—that clearly points to a political career."

Robert Louis Stevenson put his finger on one of the causes when he wrote, "Politics is perhaps the only profession for which no preparation is thought necessary." It certainly doesn't seem to be, and training most certainly should be an absolute requirement, don't you think?

Another cause is, of course, the rotten preliminary processes that quickly eliminate most of our best—that keep our finest from ever reaching that place where they might actually make a difference. Let's face it, friends, it's a stacked deck. And the jokers take the pot.

The politics of economics—the looting of America. As Bob Thaves' "Frank and Ernest" noted, we may think our economy's humming along, it's just that we're not sure what tune it's playing. But we are beginning to get the drift of some of it. As Adlai Stevenson once said, "There was a time when a fool and his money were soon parted, but now it happens to everybody."

Harry Hopkins had it right way back in 1938. "We shall tax and tax, and spend and spend, and elect and elect." And of course we will couch it all in more palatable language. As any good politician will tell you, when it comes to "spending," that's when they have to use their own money. When they are using *your* money, well that's called "investing."

The process is not unlike those who would chop wood out of the bottom of a boat to make a grand construction above deck. And when the ship begins to sink, such a person will usually be able to make you think it's all someone else's fault and that he, or she, will somehow manage to save the ship, even as it begins to slip beneath the waves. Such a person is usually referred to as a politician.

Economics 101. How good they are at hiding their foolishness behind such complex economic ideologies. There is "Monetarism." That's the idea that too much money floating around in the economy will lead to inflation, along with a general economic upturn, and that not enough money in circulation brings on deflation and a general economic downturn. So their answer is to depend completely on the Federal Reserve authority to firmly control an orderly release of the supply of money at a constant rate. (Looks a lot like something that's happening right now, doesn't it?)

There is "Keynesianism." That's the idea that during economic down-turns, the government should move in and stimulate the demand for goods and services by spending, spending, spending, even at the cost of a budget deficit. (This sounds familiar too, doesn't it?)

Then there's what is sometimes referred to as the "New Classical Economics." It offers the contention that the market produces the best solution to our economic problems and that the people should be allowed to act in their own best interest. It is argued that most of the government involvement is very ineffective and often makes things an even bigger mess, so the government should keep out of the marketplace. (We hear this discussed a lot, right?)

And there's "Supply-side economics." The idea here is that the economic policy should be to stimulate "supply" rather than "demand." This then should be done through the government's tax policies, such as with the cutting of marginal tax rates. (Heard about this before?)

There is what is called "Reaganomics." With this approach you also cut the marginal tax rates to encourage investment, which would be expected to encourage more business, which would bring about more jobs and higher incomes. This in turn could be expected to produce more tax revenue so as to help in the reduction of the deficit and the balancing of the budget. (Sounds like the deficit and balanced budged issues we're dealing with now, doesn't it?)

What is this federal deficit? Well, simply put, it's when our government spends more money than it takes in. This makes it necessary for our government to borrow money in order to continue such spending. As the deficits get larger and larger, piling up more and more loans through the nation's supply of private investment, there is less and less money available for business growth and other private uses. It sometimes becomes more and more expensive to try and pay loans for college and home purchases, among other things.

Who ends up owing such huge deficits? While we spend the money in Washington like a bunch of drunken sailors, your kids and generations yet unborn are left with the bill. It has become a crushing debt that we so lightly put upon our children and our children's children. It is a terrible thing to do, wouldn't you say?

I guess you could say that our posterity are those in our future who will have to try and manage to survive in spite of us. If you should doubt the insanity of what has been done and what is continuing to be done, read some of the definitive articles that are being published from time to time and watch some of the documentaries on the subject. Sometimes the evening news will have an inclusion that shows what's happening. A good example would be NBC's "The Fleecing of America" segment.

The shadows beneath our economy. Our enormous national debt is obviously the main factor. Other things might not be quite so obvious. By way of example, the way government economists define our economic position and progress is a dubious process that is, to many, highly questionable.

In the last few years we have routinely been told that we are enjoying unprecedented prosperity and almost zero inflation. This is according to such indicators as the "gross domestic product." A northern California public policy group called "Redefining Progress" suggests that indicators such as the gross domestic product (GDP) are not necessarily all that accurate.

The group seems to have drawn support from over four hundred economists nationwide and many others as well. They suggest that the statistical examples used to compile the GDP are not always very realistic. In other words, they sometimes are really a long way from real-world economics.

What about inflation? This writer can tell you that just about everything in his life has been going up, up, up—everything from professional labor, groceries, and cable television, to ever-growing tax obligations. Others everywhere tell me the very same sad story. Are the government economists reporting on another country on a different planet? It would certainly seem so.

The way they talk you would think that we are still the richest nation there is, right? *Wrong!* According to a system developed by the World Bank for determining national net worth, Canada and Australia rank as the wealthiest of nations.

Where is the United States in all of this. Last time I looked, we were in 12th place. (Many also tell us that Japan may have surpassed the United States to become the world's top patron of industrial research and development.)

The system calculates a nation's standing from values assigned to the nation's natural resources, its capital investment level, and by the productivity of that nation's people. Sound impressive? Well, maybe so, but at times it does seem like the various competing economists are spending most of their time jerking us in one direction and then another.

Maybe I should remember what Laurence J. Peter said. "An economist is an expert who will know tomorrow why the things he predicted yesterday didn't happen today."

Noting the bloat. Through it all, there are three things of which we are really sure. Our national debt is enormous, our government is far too large and oppressive, and our taxes are confiscatory. (What *else* should we expect from a humongous government?)

It's not something that just happened yesterday, you know. I can recall Charles Peters writing in *The Washington Monthly* (way back in 1992) about a group of farmers who received 66 million dollars from the Bureau of Reclamation and a whopping 379 million bucks from the Department of Agriculture, the first to pay to irrigate land that then produced surplus crops and the other amount was used to limit the production of those surplus crops. They got it coming and going, and you got it right in the wallet, of course.

All this from a government that, even today, has over *twice* the number of employees in the U.S. Department of Agriculture than there are farmers. It is also my understanding that more people work for our government, in all jurisdictions, than in the entire manufacturing sector of America, combined! *What on earth have we created?*

Then there's the U.S. trade deficit. A little after the first quarter of 1998, the Commerce Department reported that the U.S. trade deficit in goods and services with foreign nations reached a six-year high in March. That's how much imports were ahead of exports. It amounts to over 13 billion on the wrong side of the ledger.

And then there's the corporate welfare. You and I, as taxpayers, pay in subsidies, grants, and special tax breaks that benefit fast-food giants, big candy manufacturers, chicken processors, and other food corporations and all sorts of other huge businesses. I also recall figures like $278 million in technology subsidies from our government to Amoco, AT&T, Du Pont, IBM, Citicorp, General Motors, and General Electric from 1990 through 1994. (You can read about it in Michael Moore's book, *Down-size This!*)

And of course when sports teams hold a community hostage with the threat of leaving the area, local taxpayers usually buckle under and pay up to those hugely profitable corporations, in the form of condemnation of desired properties, publicly financed facilities, and/or other considerations. (The last time I looked there was as many as thirty teams threatening to bolt unless they got new stadiums.)

And the waste goes on. From time to time Citizens Against Government Waste publishes a report called "Government Waste Watch." Among the abuses noted in the report, there have been such things as, $36 billion in unneeded inventory is being stored by the Department of Defense; an estimated $27 billion is lost annually to Medicare and Medicaid fraud; $9 billion has been spent on the Superfund program over twelve years cleaning up just eighty of the nation's 1,275 hazardous waste sites—40 percent (or $3.6 billion) of which was spent on administration and management; $1.2 billion in oil royalties have gone uncollected by the Department of Interior.

"And $12.6 million was taken from the Social Security Trust Fund to pay federal employees who work full-time on union activities; an estimated $2 billion in food stamp overpayments go unrecovered each year; Department of Interior bookkeepers 'paid' $800,000 for a $150 vacuum cleaner, $700,000 for a $350 dishwasher, and $79 million for an $800 mobile radio unit; 163 federal job training programs costing more than $20 billion compete against one another to serve the same client population; a cosmetology school received $2.8 million in federal funds over three years to train 673 aspiring beauticians, but only 19 ever received state licenses—at a cost of $148,000 per license."

That's just a small sampling. That sort of thing is going on right now, just as much as ever. There is no end to it, unless of course you decide to *make* an end to it. That's up to you.

Come and get it! Everybody seems to be getting into the act. There are special publishers and promoters of every type and stripe popping up, offering all sorts of ways to load up at taxpayers' expense.

Politics

A few samples: "Uncle Sam wants to help you. Every U.S. citizen entitled to $100,000 in free services!" This was an ad from an outfit that calls itself "Government Information Service."

Another ad shows, "How to Collect $$$ from Uncle Sam." A new book written by a former Federal investigator tells how every American can collect their share of the $250 billion that will be handed out this year by Uncle Sam." That's from someone named R. Emil Neuman. A mass mailing wants to show you, "How to buy from the government... dirt cheap!" It offers, "A comprehensive guide showing the average person how to buy hundreds of items for 10 cents to 50 cents on the dollar." This was offered by "Financial Reports" from Omega Publishing.

Another ad shouts about a, "Revolutionary new government funding program!" It talks about free money, free government benefits, free low % loans and free cash grants. This is from an entity called, "Government Funding Assistance." One from Peters & Associates tells about, "Free grants—$3 billion a year!" And the Wellington Company headlines its promo with, "Free money from these insider government agencies!"

There's lots more. But I don't want this book to end up as a whole library unto itself. It all reminds me of Dick Turner's "Carnival" cartoon of one cop saying to the other, "And when a company misuses other people's money, Higgins, the charge is not 'impersonating a government agency.'" Oh, for the Proxmire "Golden Fleece Award." We need you now more than ever.

Our looming national debt. Once again, "It is usual nowadays to ignore what should be done in favor of what pleases us." Sounds like me or one of the others who is trying to get people to pick up a little responsibility here. As I said before, that was written by Titus Maccius Plautus. He was one of the great playwrights of ancient Rome. And we know what happened to Rome, don't we?

> *Blessed are the young,*
> *for they shall inherit the national debt.*
>
> —Herbert Hoover

Is that the way it's going to be? It's just a real shame that the future generations of our nation can't be here now, so they can also enjoy what we are doing with their money. Too bad that all we're going to leave them with is the bill.

As Larry Burkett wrote in his book, *The Coming Economic Earthquake* (a national best-seller), "In the early sixties, no one would have believed our economy (or any other) could absorb nearly $4 trillion in debt and still survive." Well, according to our super-smart Marilyn Vos Savant, "as of February 20, 1996, our country's liquid assets (including such things as currency, checking accounts, savings accounts, money market funds, certificates of deposit, and treasury bills) totaled $5.616 trillion. The national debt totaled $4.988 trillion as of last October" (Reported in *Parade* magazine).

As of April 1, 1999, the national debt had risen to $5,666,007,565,054! And yes, that first figure is 5 *trillion!* You can imagine where it is now. To begin with, it takes the taxes of everyone west of the Mississippi river just to pay the *interest* on the debt. At this rate it is estimated that a little beyond the turn of the century, it will take the current tax level from almost *everyone* just to pay that interest.

Still don't get it? Well, let me put it to you this way. If you had gone into business at the time of Christ and lost $1 *million* a day, every day, seven days a week, from then until this very moment, you would not have managed to even reach *one* trillion dollars! Now have you got the picture. I hope so.

It is written that a "debacle" is a disaster or fiasco. And it is written that an "apocalypse" is the writing or otherwise prophesying of a cataclysm. I offer a new word, "debacalypse," as a prophesied disaster or fiasco. That's what we're talking about here.

Forget the momentary surpluses that were created by governmental "creative bookkeeping." As Wright, the political cartoonist for the *Palm Beach Post* showed it, one should, "Never offer a beer to an alcoholic, a joint to a pothead, or a budget surplus to a politician." Let's face it, federal aid to education should start by teaching basic arithmetic to the politicians in Washington.

Breaking the budget. When there is a little surplus in the budget every once in a while, even when often fictionalized, it will be very, *very* hard to break the politicians of that nasty habit of spending, spending, spending in every conceivable direction. As radio commentator Paul Harvey said a while back, twenty-five hundred new government bureaucrats have been added each day since Clinton first went into office. Mr. Harvey also noted that the Clinton tax increases are not only the largest ever in America, they are the largest there has ever been in the entire world!

That seems hard to believe, but I don't think he's kidding us. Then there was that $1.73 TRILLION budget. It was said to contain massive amounts of new government spending, to be paid for by $90 billion in new taxes on businesses, smokers, and possibly anybody else they can hang it on. And it's a time-bomb. Once again, it's bigger government instead of smaller government.

Another cartoon by Wright in the *Palm Beach Post* shows a crumbling and dangerous inner-city in the foreground and the White House in the background. A dialog balloon over the White House says, "It's settled, then. We bail out the Soviet Union!"

The foreign trade deficit. Our American trade deficit has been anywhere from $100 billion to $200 billion, off and on, for some time now. Every once in a while it looks a little bit better and then we take another bath again.

I'll never forget when it was announced in October of 1997 that Communist Mainland China had suddenly become the nation to enjoy the largest of all trade deficits owed to it by the United States. At that time I think it was around $5.2 billion and rising.

Well of course we want to support the slave labor Communist system as much as we can, right? I know, maybe if we infect them with free enterprise, they'll change. Well, let's hope so, but don't hold your breath.

The cosmetic, public relations solutions. Lyndon Johnson had his "Programming, Planning and Budgeting Systems." Richard Nixon had his "Management by Objectives." Jimmy Carter had his "Zero-based Budgeting." Ronald Reagan had his "Grace Commission." George Bush had his "Total Quality Management." Bill Clinton has his "Reinventing Government."

They all had the answer, didn't they? Sure they did. And government just got bigger and bigger and bigger. Why, I can even remember the old "Hoover Commission" of *many* years ago.

We also must consider the most uncomfortable and seldom stated fact that we just can't keep growing forever. Someday we're going to have to face this fact. Knowing how Washington operates, that probably won't happen until it's too late—way to late.

Escape to bankruptcy. Consumer bankruptcies seem to be setting records. The second quarter of 1997 showed 367,168 filings, the biggest ever, at that time. More current records don't look all that much better, believe me.

Sometimes it's because of this wonderful economy that so many seemed not to have found. Sometimes it's just a profound degree of ineptitude. Sometimes it's a con artist cleaning the slate before his next "project." (As you certainly must know by now, our legal system has become a marvelous refuge for the worst of scoundrels.)

Some go in under Chapter-7. This allows the debtor to keep a notable amount of his or her property. Non-exempt assets are sold, and the funds are apportioned out to pay bills, sort of. Then the debtor comes out with no debts. Of course, if he had a business, it's closed, but that's okay. The debtor has wiped out all of his debts. Never mind that this has left others with uncollectible losses.

Of course there are other chapters. Not fair? Gee, where did you ever get that idea? Remember this, too, is a part of our legal system. Fair is not part of the vocabulary.

One answer that a growing number of folks are getting involved with is what is sometimes referred to as "the underground economy." They buy and sell with cash only, without receipts, and without any records whatsoever. Sometimes this is done as barters and doesn't involve money in any form. It's a risky business. I certainly don't recommend it.

And then there's the Infernal Revenue Service. It wasn't always like this. There actually was a time when the tax men were not considered as a reincarnation of the dreaded Gestapo.

> *What a man has honestly acquired is absolutely his own, which may be freely given, but cannot be taken from him without his consent.*
>
> —Samuel Adams

Those days are *long* gone. The problem is nobody seems to have learned the lesson of John S. Coleman who said, "The point to remember is that what the government gives it must first take away." And take away it does. The I.R.S. was allowed to work *outside* of the laws of our nation. It worked under Napoleonic law (with an initial presumption of guilt) instead of under the American common law system where you are supposed to be presumed innocent until proven guilty.

I know, we're supposed to have softened the behavior of that infamous agency. Well, that may have finally happened, to a degree, but they still have a long, *long* way to go.

And then there are the tax laws. What a mess! As Jonathan Weisman reported in the *Congressional Quarterly* a while back, we are being warned by experts about the enormous complexity in the tangled new U.S. tax laws. It was part of an effort called the "Taxpayer Relief Act," and there couldn't be anything further from the truth.

As Mr. Weisman wrote, "Harvard University law professor Daniel Halperin has suggested that the Federal Trade Commission investigate whether the Taxpayer Relief Act's name violates truth-in-advertising regulations." The professor further stated that "some of the changes indicate the IRS has lost control of the system."

It's the tax code from hell. There's hardly anyone who understands it. In fact over half of the American taxpayers have to pay professional tax preparers to do the paper work. Even then, many of the tax preparers are somewhat lost and the Internal Revenue Service itself can't figure it out. If you don't believe me, try calling them for advice.

One study showed that callers were given wrong answers 8.5 million times. And of course *you* are held liable for *their* errors if you should take their advice. So why don't you read up on it yourself? Sure. It's somewhere between 6,000 and 9,451 pages and over 2.8 million words. (When the federal income tax began in 1913, the tax code was comprised of 16 pages.)

A special quote comes to mind. It was written by Frederic Bastiat, and it most certainly applies here. "It is impossible to introduce into society a greater evil than this: the conversion of the law into an instrument of plunder." We have most certainly done that in a big way.

The American Gestapo. We all know about the I.R.S. Let's face it, there has been revealing testimony before Congress and any number of horror stories printed in the media and discussed on TV. Unless you've just returned from a half-century hibernation, you know about the American Gestapo.

I'm still not going to let you off easy. I'm going to rub your nose in a little bit more of it. I just want to make sure you know what you're *really* facing here. I don't want there to be even the smallest possible doubt.

We've all heard about hapless small business owners who have had just about everything they own seized by the I.R.S. with what they call a "jeopardy assessment," wiping out the business and just about everything else in sight. And then the I.R.S. finds they made an error. Oops.

So, they give back whatever they have left, which usually isn't much, or a small compensation is eventually made possible. But meanwhile, the business was destroyed, the hapless taxpayer's life has been destroyed, and any reasonable recovery is often next to impossible. In some instances, the citizen-victim just crawls in a corner and fades away. In some cases, the victim actually commits suicide!

Sounds a lot like Nazi Germany or Communist Russia, doesn't it? Unfortunately, it's what we once called The United States of America. Wiley Miller put it well in one of his "Non Sequitur" cartoons. A judge is telling a white collar criminal, "You have been found guilty of extortion and racketeering and are hereby sentenced to work for the I.R.S."

A bit of nostalgia. And this sort of thing has been going on for years. Do you recall what happened to one of our most beloved comedy teams many years ago? After years of support of our government and its efforts in World War II, Abbott and Costello were dealt a blow from which they never recovered.

They had put their trust in a man who was supposed to take care of the books and handle the taxes. He did not take proper care of the tax responsibilities, and he also stole from the comedy pair. And then, the I.R.S. decided to make an example of them, even though they were not really to blame for what had happened. The I.R.S. cleaned them out—absolutely ruined them.

Now, back in around the mid-90s, Jim Wright, a former speaker of the U.S. House of Representatives, wrote a very revealing column for the *Fort Worth Star-Telegram*. He wrote of Internal Revenue agents swarming into the offices of a little family oil exploration company in Fort Worth, armed to the teeth. "They abruptly sealed off the building, banished its astonished owners to the lunchroom, and posted armed guards to keep them out of their own offices."

They conducted a day-long search of all records and seized all files and all documents, the computers and even private correspondence. They stripped the place clean. As Jim Wright reported, they had paid their taxes, "and never had any serious problems with the IRS." But now, without their records and computers, they were practically out of business.

As Mr. Wright noted, "The Fourth Amendment to the U.S. Constitution was supposed to protect private citizens against this kind of arbitrary action. It says: 'The right of the people to be secure in their persons, houses, papers, and effects, against unreasonable searches and seizures, shall not be violated.'"

Since when has the I.R.S. worked within constitutional law? In fact, they are not a truly legal entity in this nation, in any way shape or form. Let's face it, Napoleonic law (guilty until proven innocent) is what they have operated under. It is a totally lawless process in this nation! Now that's what's *really* been going on!

By the way, this example and others were seen on C-SPAN, with testimony before the Senate Finance Committee's IRS Oversight Hearings not so long ago. It was one frightening experience. As with other examples this writer knows of, one instance given involved a heavy-handed "mob" of armed and ready forces descending on hapless victims with the style and intensity of the KGB. It's almost inconceivable that something like that can happen in America. But is it really all that much "America" any longer? Think about it.

As if that wasn't enough, there were all sorts of additional horror stories told of I.R.S. abuses destroying innocent lives on MSNBC's "Weekend Magazine with Stone Phillips." This has been very revealing, as has the C-SPAN coverage and some of the newspaper and magazine articles. Thank God for the elements in media who are willing to take on such monsters in our midst. I hope it made an indelible impression on you.

Investigating the I.R.S. When an internal audit was done of the I.R.S. operations (as reported in 1998) it was found that the agency systematically trampled taxpayers' rights to rake in all the money it could. Then there's that business about collection quotas. It's against the law, of course, but it was found that field auditors were nonetheless prodded by their bosses to reach what is called, "statistical bench marks." Yes, the pressure was there and agents have even admitted it!

That investigation by the Senate Finance Committee, this last year, revealed (as you know) that the I.R.S. is guilty of an enormous number of other serious abuses of its power as well. Some of the little known "extras" that came to light included the admission that the agency prefers to zero in on low and modest income taxpayers because they usually can't put up much of a fight. And it was found that I.R.S. people routinely snoop around in the tax records of famous people, people they don't like and even potential mates.

Jeff Jacoby wrote in the *Boston Globe* about how the I.R.S. was discovered to be sending out around 30 million tax penalty notices every year with almost *half* of them turning out to be erroneous. He had a few other interesting things to say as well. "How about the Philadelphia chemical firm that was penalized nearly $47,000 because the IRS determined that its tax payment of $4,448,112.88 was a dime short?"

He also brought out the fact that as many as 3 million women were wrongly fined each year because they got divorced or re-married. And, "The number of taxpayers whose old-age benefits will be cut because the IRS doesn't properly record their tax payments—10 million."

Back with the Senate and House tax committees we found a disquieting revelation that evidently the Internal Revenue Service had been singling out conservative tax-exempt organizations for audits. Frankly, this should be no surprise to anyone. It's all just another disreputable part of politics.

Have you heard about how I.R.S. examining agents have been getting bonuses for especially good assessments that their audits somehow manage to squeeze out of hapless taxpayers? I am told, if any such assessments are proven to be wrong or otherwise illegal, the agents *still* get to keep the bonuses!

The sad story just goes on and on. There is that fine old couple (Mennonites by religious persuasion) that has a little farm and a little produce stand they have been operating somewhat informally and with much bartering. Naturally they got in lots of deep trouble with the I.R.S.

They discovered that they would have to fabricate some of the information in order to fill out the tax forms the way the tax collectors want it. With total dedication to complete honesty, they simply announced that they would rather go to jail than lie. As the Associated Press reported the husband as saying, "They can take my body, they can take my property, but my integrity, I don't want to part with."

Then there's the story about the 84-year-old woman consigned to a wheelchair and forced to live off her savings as best she could. She underpaid her federal taxes (of $515) in the amount of 60 cents. Naturally she got a bill for interest and penalties totally $50.28. *That,* for a 60 cent unintentional underpayment. And, as I am sure you are aware, we could go on almost forever with stories like these.

Then there's that "Berry's World" cartoon about a guy talking with a tax agent. It seems the taxpayer owes $600. The taxpayer wondered how on earth he was going to scrape up enough cash and he says, "I guess I didn't estimate my withholding tax right last year." The agent says, "Too bad you don't owe more . . . if you owed them $600 thousand they'd probably settle for ten cents on the dollar!"

That's the way it happens. How totally dishonest it is to hold the taxpayer responsible to the extent of interest and penalties for not *guessing* right on quarterly estimates that are, after all, only estimates in the first place. But then, what can you expect from an outlaw agency that doesn't have even the smallest vestige of a conscience and hasn't been held responsible for what it has done, in most instances, for countless years.

Declaring war on the I.R.S. Back in 1981, former Senator Eugene McCarthy came out publicly and said that our constitutional freedoms are being seriously threatened by the I.R.S. Over a decade later, Edmund Fitzsimmons came out with the book *De-Taxing America* in which he suggested ways he felt we can legally stop paying income taxes. (Well, it may or may not be legal, but that seldom stops most governments from imposing their will. And you can be sure, it's the same for our government as well.)

The Tax Avoidance Digest suggested that "you fight it quietly... you disappear... make yourself invisible to the computer...." Frankly, that's also rather risky advice. Irwin Schiff wrote the book *How Anyone Can Stop Paying Taxes*. A good example of what can happen is what happened to him. A U.S. Tax Court ruled that he will have to pay $44,200 in back taxes, plus penalties of $48,948. Schiff also wrote the book, *The Federal Mafia—How It Illegally Imposes and Unlawfully Collects Income Taxes*. A lot of good that did him.

Other tax protesters are routinely hauled into courts and are routinely found guilty. Of course the I.R.S. is never found guilty of *its* lawless operation. Oh no, we can't do that, now can we? In any case, there actually are some books that might be interesting for you to read. One is *A Law Unto Itself: Power, Politics and the IRS* by David Burnham and *Unbridled Power* by Shelley L. Davis.

If you really want to go to war against our gigantic tax code and the I.R.S., there has been a whole movement established to abolish the I.R.S. and/or the current tax laws and there are lots of other serious efforts out there as well (not the minor cosmetic tinkering our politicians are applying). Look in the appendix section at the back of this book, and you'll find all sorts of names, addresses, and phone numbers. The rest is up to you.

In case you're wondering, this writer was audited a couple of years ago and, in my situation, it went just fine. There was nothing found to be out of line, and there was no additional amount owed or anything. So, my concern is definitely not from personal experience. My concern is strictly a matter of the unspeakable horrors that have befallen so many others.

Even though some behavior modification is being forced on the I.R.S. under new congressional law, no one seems to be held responsible for what was done; and little is actually being initiated to make the *major* changes that are clearly necessary.

The tax system and Social Security. The Social Security Act was passed in 1935. It was the largest single "tax" project of the entire New Deal. Little did they know that the day would come when government "borrowing" and the lack of good investment would put the entire system into dire financial jeopardy. Little did they know that the way they operated would gradually change until it became just one more oppressive government agency.

What can you expect from a government, really. Governments, their agencies, and their faceless bureaucrats are seldom held responsible for their deeds. It is a most uncomfortable historic reality that must be dealt with endlessly if any measure of freedom or dignity is to remain with the people.

The Social Insecurity Administration—How it really works. It is the largest single program in the entire federal government. It is also a kind of "pyramid scheme" that is clearly beginning to come apart, even as we find that the Social Security taxes are actually higher than the federal income taxes for about two-thirds of the American workforce. It is also argued by some as an opportunity to rob the poor children of tomorrow to care for the elderly of today.

It has also been found to be stacked in a way that encourages the elderly to quit the job market and depend on Social Security. You see, until the age of 70, S.S. payments are reduced by $1 for every $3 that is earned over an $11,160 minimum of yearly income.

Another little known fact is that the huge amounts that many married women have paid in over their lifetimes have been more like "donations" to the system. What they eventually collect has been based on their husbands' earnings, not on what they, themselves, have earned. That's what they tell me. (It's hoped that will have changed by the time this book reaches the bookstores.)

The big issue that's gone public is the sorry fact that all the money paid into Social Security isn't properly invested to make a reasonable return. Any surpluses, after paying retirees, is put in low-return Treasury Bonds. That just means the government borrows the money cheaply and spends it like a drunken sailor, as it always does.

As Charles Krauthammer reported in one of his columns, "In fiscal 1994, President Clinton crowed that he had reduced the federal deficit to $200 billion. In fact, the 'operating budget' was about $250 billion in deficit, but the Treasury counted the year's roughly $50 billion Social Security surplus to make its books read $200 billion." One could say that the president "borrowed" the Social Security trust fund to the tune of $50 billion. That makes that trust fund a very cruel fiction in many ways.

More abuses of the system. I remember when the report came out about how a little under 10 percent of the convicted prisoners in Butte County, California, were found to be receiving Supplemental Security Income (SSI) disability payments from the agency.

Then we heard about how drug addicts and alcoholics were drawing disability payments on a regular basis to help them support their substance abuse habits. Then we found out how Social Security was losing a small fortune to out-and-out disability frauds. And there was the immigrant SSI fraud. There's never an end to it.

Do you remember when it was discovered, not so long ago, that our dear government unfairly terminated important disability payments for a whole lot of poor kids, and then misinformed their parents about their legal rights and even discouraged some of the parents from appealing the improper government action?

Social Security vs. the people. There's the case of Charles and Penny Hauer, a loving couple who adopted thirty-five disabled children. Maybe you've heard about them? They were on the Rosie O'Donnell show, where they were presented with tons of clothing and toys.

You guessed it. Social Security sent the Hauer's a notice requiring the cash value of the gifts and suggesting that it could qualify as added income and get the children's supplemental Social Security benefits taken away. However, after the TV news-documentary "Extra" featured their problem, the Social Security people must have decided it would be a much better public relations move to decide that the gifts were given to the parents, so the youngsters won't lose their much needed benefits.

Of course they didn't actually give up on the Hauers. Since the home they had sold, when they bought their present home, fell out of escrow, Social Security found the opportunity to penalize them by cutting the benefit checks by 10 percent.

You want to help out? You'd better not. Give them some money to help them along and the caring folks at Social Security will strip them of their meager benefits. You can count on it. That's the way it works.

Another example is in the rules that can now penalize physicians who treat elderly patients outside of the federal Medicare program. And do you remember when about 700,000 Americans were shortchanged by about $850 million because of a programming error on the Social Security computer?

How about Robert Hoffman who was declared dead by a computer entry error, something that happens from time to time. Mr. Hoffman had one hell of a time with the Social Security people even after he made it very clear that he was truly alive. Checks were still not coming, and then they came in excess and even after he did his best to get that properly corrected, the officials *still* couldn't get it right. I don't know if it ever did finally get straightened out.

An interesting example in full detail. I have a long and very detailed letter in front of me that I believe can really show you what's going on, on the inside. It also illustrates the true mindset of these people. Here it is, word for word, as written to the Medicare Specialist at the Western Program Service Center of the Social Security Administration.

Dear sir (or Madam):

Possibly with the mistaken notion as to the purpose of Social Security and its Medicare adjunct, and possibly with the hope of honest fulfillment and human consideration, I send you this communication. In this letter, I lay out the problem, as it was and as it is.

As I noted in my letter to Jannette Wright, of my local Social Security Office (on 5/30/97), "I had excellent health insurance that covered everything quite well. And then I turned 65 (October 15, 1996) and found myself (with government arrangements what they are) totally without any private insurance whatsoever.

I contacted the Social Security office and originally got the impression that I was covered under Part "A" (hospitalization) and Part "B" (medical) for the government insurance that is supposed to kick in at that point. (The records should show such initial coverage.)

Then I was informed that I did not qualify for the normal coverage under Part "A" (unless I bought into it), but that I could opt for private insurance for that coverage if I wanted to do that. I thought that would be just fine, so I said I would be happy to do so."

In that letter I explained that, "Next, I went out and did a long and exhaustive search for the needed private hospital insurance. I talked with the big insurance companies and I got some of the independents to search their data bases for me. I did manage to get Standard Life for the supplemental, but I couldn't find private hospital insurance anywhere for someone like me, who is 65 years of age."

I further noted that, "After many months of intensive searching, I finally came to realize that there is absolutely *no* permanent private hospital insurance available to me at all! Believe me, if I had any inkling that my small personal estate could be put in such precarious jeopardy, there is no way I would have allowed the cancellation of that Part "A" and gone back out in the world with no protection at all in that area. That would be a terribly foolish thing for me to do.

"Now I am back and asking what happened and how can I get back into this Part "A" that I now understand is necessary. And I am astounded to hear that I will probably be penalized with additional cost to get back on board—a situation that never would have happened if I had been given the straight scoop right from the beginning."

I concluded that letter with the following comments. "You must understand that you folks are the experts on these matters. People like me don't really know anything about these things beyond what you tell us and what we read in your brochures and such. Frankly, I was depending on all of you and I have now ended up here. This was not my idea, believe me.

"Now I need help from you all—this time the right way. If what I am now told is correct, I somehow need to get back into your Part "A," but it is so expensive that the increase you want me to pay, because I didn't stay in the plan (I was sent running around looking for the end of a rainbow, I guess)—that increase is a very difficult and totally unfair burden for me.

"Somehow, I don't think the health care system was designed to do things like this to people. I would also like to think that you folks will be able to reverse this situation and consider safeguards so that people like me don't fall through the cracks like this again."

Next, the local Social Security office required me to send you a notice of my withdrawal of termination of the Part "A" coverage, with my request for said coverage. I sent it to you as soon as I was told to do so (on 7/17/97).

The local office's response was sent to me on July 28, 1997. This reply stated that, "In order for the Social Security Administration to act favorably on your request, the agency would need to establish that your withdrawal from Premium HI was based on an error, misrepresentation or inaction by a government employee which resulted in your withdrawal action."

My immediate reaction was that this was very appropriate and that there would be no further problem then. I should have known better. In the very next paragraph it was made very clear that, "After investigating this matter, we have concluded that no such misrepresentation or misinformation occurred. Consequently, we cannot favorably act on your request to withdraw your withdrawal from Premium HI."

A full year later was then mentioned as the next possible time that I could re-enroll and I also discovered that this would be with a notable penalty for having come back "late." And, also included with this letter, was a copy of their "Special Determination" report of this "case."

In the report they included testimony by a Mrs. Campbell, who originally interviewed me. I can only guess that they weren't paying a great deal of attention to what she reported because this one just got right by them.

You see, Mrs. Campbell testified that, "I make very sure that the individual completely understands what they are signing up for. If they indicate that they have not checked elsewhere, I recommend they do, so that they either can get a smaller premium via private insurance, or realize that Part "A" is not unreasonable."

This, of course, was a blatantly false and totally misleading advisory. There is *no* such private insurance available out there for this type of coverage. If I had known this I would *never* have taken the steps to opt for such a mythical coverage. I was totally depending on her advice and her own words now tell you what she said.

The report acted as though Mrs. Campbell hadn't said what she actually said and thus concluded that, "Mr. XXXXX provides no evidence that he was actually given advice which caused him to withdraw from Premium HI. Although he asserts such advice was given, he could not provide any information concerning the specific content of the advice. He could not provide any information concerning when, where or who gave him the advice."

Then the report makes a kind of tongue-in-cheek statement to the effect that, "While Mr. XXXXX may have been advised to see if he could find a private health insurance, this certainly does not constitute advice to withdraw from Premium HI." Well, you can believe that it most certainly *was* the primary motive for my withdrawal. I had no idea that there was *no* such private insurance out there and I couldn't imagine that anyone in the Social Security Administration would suggest such a thing if it were not so. Yet, someone did, didn't she?

It is my understanding that this report was somewhat unusual. I am told that normally, government agencies tend to stonewall themselves in a much cleaner manner which then allows it to be simply the government's word verses a citizen's word. (You can imagine how *that* goes.) I realize that the somewhat less careful construction of this report was unexpected good fortune for me. Now there can be no doubt whatsoever as to the false information imparted and my motivation for withdrawal due to that false information.

Next, after some additional pressures applied, I received a notification from your Western Program Service Center (dated October 29, 1997), in which you stated, "As requested, we have reviewed your case and decided that we can start your hospital insurance coverage beginning October 1996. However, you will have to pay the back premiums for October 1996 through November 1997 in order to receive coverage. The total amount of premiums for October 1996 through November 1997 is $4,288." (This amounts to a kind-of retroactive coverage for something I was denied during that period and something for which there was no need during that period either.)

That communication was truly unbelievable to me. Others tell me it is quite normal when you have a government where individuals therein are seldom held responsible for what they do. But, to me it is still unbelievable.

First, your misinformation sends me on a wild goose chase and then I am stalled off when I try to return. Now you want to charge me for all that time? It is time that would never have come out like that if it were not for *your* agency's original error and *your* agency's unwillingness to allow me back in.

You created the problem. I didn't. And as I said in my letter to your department (on October 29, 1997), "I am sure you don't intend to have me pay for coverage that I never had. That would be absolutely criminal. I am sure you want to start my coverage right away from this time forward, a time that exists in the *real* world."

Next, I finally ended up trying to enroll in the early part of this year (1998), *without* having to pay retroactively. It was my understanding that, if accepted, this service would commence on July 1, 1998. Is that correct?

I had done my homework and I knew what the premium was supposed to be, so you can imagine my shock when I received your notice with a 10% monthly penalty added to the premiums for having come in so late. All of this in spite of the fact that *you* folks are the ones who made it come out this way, not me. I will not stand to be penalized for *your* errors! You're trying to do it to me again!

I am also beginning to realize that there is truly a vast difference between what you all claim is the wonderful things you are doing for the old folks and what is sometimes actually happening. I ask you to correct this error as soon as possible. I look forward to your reply.

That's the story. Copies of this communication were sent to the Social Security Commissioner Kenneth S. Apfel, Congressional Representatives Bob Filner and Brian Bilbray (who have been trying to help get this mess straightened out), the Congressional commission on Medicare, and to a local attorney who had also been trying to help out.

So, is that all? No it isn't. The continuation of this fight evidently encouraged the agency toward even more punitive measures. They cut off the regular medical coverage as well (which he had dutifully paid) leaving the fellow with absolutely nothing.

After appropriate efforts were made, the medical coverage was returned, only to be taken away yet again. No one seems able to stop this scandalous behavior.

So far the government is totally unmovable. This is not unexpected. It is their usual posture on most things of this nature. But now we have the facts in this book, backed up by the Social Security Administration's own document.

Now what do you think of your precious Social Security? You just better hope they don't foul things up with *you* some day. If they ever do, you're going to have quite a time of it (unless enough of you decide to do a little housecleaning in that agency).

If this long letter does nothing else for you, it should show you how to make your case when you have been wronged. Put the facts together in full detail and in proper chronological order. Sometimes such efforts can help. Who knows, maybe someone will give it a little public exposure.

Bureaucracy—everybody's nightmare. It has been said that bureaucracy is a process for converting energy into solid waste. As Paul Harvey has told us, twenty-five hundred new government bureaucrats have been added each day since Clinton first went into office. That's an awful lot of solid waste.

They also say that a citizen visiting Washington is like a victim returning to the scene of the crime. What a convoluted, non-sequitur philosophy they have back there in Washington. As Kelvin Throop III noted in *Analog* magazine, explanations for some humorous definitions reveal a great deal of the problem.

Three examples were, "Promotion from Within: A system of moving incompetents up to the policy-making level where they can't foul up operations. Reappraisal: An abrupt change of mind after being found out. Taking Forceful Action: Doing something that should have been done a long time ago."

It's enough to drive you nuts. And it doesn't encourage mature, sane behavior in the bureaucrats and politicians either. As a matter of fact, a few years back, *Parade* magazine revealed that there are more psychiatrists per capita in Washington, D.C. than in any other city in our nation. I believe the figure was 27.8 psychiatrists for every 100,000 people in our capital city.

There are dozens and dozens of the exceptionally dysfunctional bureaucratic operations in many different areas of irresponsibility, shown throughout this book. And I'll bet you can come up with some extremely frustrating examples of your own.

I remember Lawrence Hebron's article under "Ideas and Trends" in *Business Week* magazine, where he wrote that the problem "lies in a concept of government that knows no bounds. It stems from a theory of unlimited state power and responsibility." He also made note of Washington's influence over us in great areas in both our public and private lives.

He also spotlighted how all this imposition was requiring additional, personnel, and long hours of labor just to try and comply with all the new requirements and to become at least somewhat familiar with the extensive regulations. In the end it's simply burying most of us.

Our Congress itself is one of its own worst examples. There is practically an army of aides, advisors, councils, assistants, etc., just to enable the politicians to pick their way through the bureaucratic labyrinth. It's like creating a similar problem to try to solve the original problem. Doesn't seem like a very smart move to me.

Then there is that governmental gobbledygook—spoken and written "bureaucratese"—which seems to have been designed to elevate bureaucrats beyond the comprehension and control of the average citizen. It's a very effective lawyer's tool, used most enthusiastically by most governments. And let us also not forget their prime directive of massive self-preservation and the rock-solid tendency for the institutionalizing of rigidity. In short, it's a mess.

All this reminds me of the Stayskal cartoon in the *Chicago Tribune* showing a Washington bureaucrat giving instructions to his secretary. "Here's a White House memo asking us to cut down on waste. Make six copies. File one and cross-file the others. Send copies to our staff in triplicate. Ask them to file one, cross-file one and send one back initialed. Make six copies of the initialed memo, file one and cross-file the others. Send a letter to the White House outlining what action we're taking. Make six copies for our files and send it in triplicate to our staff. Have them initial one and file the others. When the initialed letter is returned make six copies and . . ."

The problem is everywhere. The Immigration and Naturalization Service (INS) is another good example. (Or rather, I probably should say, another *bad* example.) We've all heard about illegals having a field day with our medical services and with our welfare services in general, even as many native-born citizens are somehow unable to qualify for those same services.

Things don't work all that well in just about every area of that service. Another good example that I know of is of a husband and wife who own a little store and have been unable to find a qualified and trustworthy person to manage it. However, one of the wife's sisters is a C.P.A. with extensive education and experience in business management and would like to come to America and take the job. (She is from the Philippines.)

So, the husband and wife attempted to qualify the sister in one of those special programs that was said to be able to bring her in to take the job. Evidently the "authorities" had other ideas. First they said she was not going to be paid enough. So, the husband and wife raised the offered salary. Then they said the sister was "over qualified." This they said at a time when many companies were downsizing, leaving many white-collar workers "over qualified" for new jobs that they were now routinely having to take.

In other words, it didn't really matter what forms were filled out or how much accommodation was attempted. They just decided she was not to be allowed in. What happened? The couple is going out of business at a loss. That sort of thing goes on all the time.

The Uncivil Service. Another thing many of you readers may have heard about is how easy it is for very incompetent and otherwise unqualified workers to get themselves into government jobs, under the civil service system, where it is anywhere from very difficult to absolutely impossible to get them removed. The accountability factor is near zero. It really is, and you and I pay the price for this serious oversight in many different ways.

As Jay Solomon, former head of the General Services Administration said once in a *U.S. News & World Report* interview, in Washington, "No one is responsible for anything." Other quotes of note include, "The government lacks accountability." And, "I couldn't eliminate some duplicate, unnecessary positions, because they were mandated by legislation."

He also spoke about the many incompetents in top-level federal jobs. He said, "Many of them rise through favoritism, some through political appointments." When asked how you get rid of such incompetents, he replied, "It's hard. The civil service system doesn't allow it."

This problem isn't just in Washington. It's in states, counties, and cities all over America. The incompetence is accompanied by a confusing maze of licenses, permits, and special regulations that are sometimes absolutely impossible to deal with.

What about the mix-ups in identities that bring down everything from ruined credit to actual arrest warrants? Most of the time it's a mis-entry on a computer by a bureaucrat. Most of the time, it's a horrendous mess for the poor victims to try to clean up. Let's face it, those responsible don't give a damn. Nobody's going to hold *them* responsible. They are certainly not interested in putting things right. Of course not.

Playing Post Office. We're all aware that *something* is wrong in the Postal Service. The work-place shootings were so numerous that when it happens anywhere, it is often referred to as, "going postal." And there are many other things going on.

As you may realize now, at least 34 percent of all businesses in America are now based in the home. That's what they say. As you might imagine, they usually don't like to use their home address, so they get a box, often from a service other than the post office, so they can receive UPS, Fed-X, and other similar type packages that the post office won't accept. (The post office doesn't "recognize" the competition.)

However, the Postal Service doesn't seem to like those independent box services either. They back that up by not forwarding mail to or from any such service. They also have recently decided on an additional designation that is now being forced on such box holders. It really doesn't matter how close to the line you are and how expensive such changes might be for you, as things will be, you will be forced to add "PMB" after your box number.

We are told that after a break-in period, mail without that designation may not be delivered to such boxes. That's going to be just great. Many who have such boxes report that often those who write to them even sometimes forget to include the box number itself, but it was still correctly delivered. Evidently not any more. (Are you going to tell your congressman about this?)

If a private mailing service tried to restrict forwarding from its competition or tried to force other special requirements that would limit deliverability to their competition, they'd be up on charges. Not so with the Postal Service. They're exempt from anti-trust laws.

And so it goes. I could go on and on about these bureaucratic problems, but I think you get the idea. However, if you want to learn more about the maze of laws and bureaucracy you might like to read Philip K. Howard's book, *The Death of Common Sense.* Another good book, that could help you to translate from the language of government back into English, would be William Lutz's *Doublespeak.*

Are you still with me? I know, it's been a long haul, but you realize all this is important. You know what it takes, don't you? Remember, you're not only being shown many of the details of a number of the problems, you are also discovering things you and others can do about it. That's right. The ball is in *your* court now.

Chapter Eighteen

Politics: A Search for Solutions
Cleaning Up the Mess

The most crying need in the humbler ranks of life is that they should be allowed some part in the direction of public affairs. That is what will develop their self-respect.

—Henrik Ibsen

The beginning of the movement toward reform. Franklin D. Roosevelt put it well when he said, "Let us never forget that government is ourselves and not an alien power over us." Well, that's what's supposed to be. It's supposed to be you and me. However, that isn't necessarily how it evolves when most of the people decide not to be involved.

That's difficult to understand when you realize the hard-fought path that has brought us to this much gentler way of involvement that is possible in our nation. One could call upon everything from the laws of Hammurabi to the first democratic ancient Greek city-states, the run-in at Runnymede, and to our war for independence, to show the slow and sometimes very painful growth of humankind toward the sophistication of modern self-determination.

Don't we realize what enormous human sacrifices were made to give us this opportunity? What have we done? Have we lost our democracy, or just misplaced it?

There are at least a few who are asking such questions but fewer who have decided they must begin the serious effort to bring us back on track. Now we must do all we can to increase those numbers, many fold, over and over again, until "we the people" have become an irresistible tide!

It all starts with the question What do we expect our government to do? We want to "reinvent government," right? We want, among other things, to make drastic cuts in the bureaucracy and make *all* who are in government, in *all* areas and on *all* levels, much more efficient and really responsive to the citizenry. As David Osborne describes it in his book *Reinventing Government,* it is the desire to have, "a shift in the basic model of governance used in America."

Of course truly notable changes in our government can't happen without notable changes in basic policies, including sharp reductions in the overpopulation of policy mandates. If you want to bring us back from oppression, governmental ambitions must be drastically scaled back and, in some cases, entirely removed.

We'll have to face it, it's like trying to get a junkie off of his drugs. Those in power don't really want such a drastic operation. Maybe a little cosmetic work, for political expediency, but nothing major—nothing *really* important.

Now you know why meaningful innovations in government have such a high failure rate. Now you know why you must get together with others, study the problem, and attack it with a sophisticated strategy and a lot of sustained energy. It will take nothing less.

Forward, march! You remember some of the early skirmishes? There was that attempt to bring federal spending in line and the old guard administration wouldn't budge. In fact, as you may recall, we had two governmental shutdowns. Yet, in spite of it all, a few good things did manage to get rammed through by the new kids in Congress.

There was a sort-of balanced budget push. There was that anti-crime package called the "Taking Back Our Streets" act. There was a little tinkering with Social Security but, of course, the most basic problems were not solved. There was that Common Sense Legal Reform act that limits punitive damages and business liability. (That one cuts both ways.) There were other things as well. And there were things that didn't get off the ground, such as a constitutional amendment to limit terms in the House and the Senate.

Well that was then and this is now. We sure haven't gone very far, not really. Balanced budget? Sure, if you want to combine the increase in tax revenue (because business is better at the moment) with "creative government bookkeeping" which takes some items "off-line" and the rest out of our Social Security savings.

What about that "Contract with America"? Not enough of you really held those politicians' feet to the fire long enough and intensively enough to force major changes to keep on happening. So what do you do now? You put that pressure on, and if your representatives in Federal and State legislatures don't make some really heroic moves, you start working immediately to get a much better candidate to run against him. And I mean you've *really* got to do it!

Reforming the political system. As Mathew Henry noted, "It is not fit that public trust should be lodged in the hands of any, till they are first proved and found fit for the business they are to be entrusted with." In other words, good business sense, morals, and professional ethics *do* matter.

But not much ever happens in that area, to clean up the filthy mess. One time in California things got so bad that even the Assembly Ethics Committee recommended that all legislators and their staff and all lobbyists take courses in ethics from time to time. Other efforts to require and/or instill a genuine value system have been attempted elsewhere in various states and on the federal level as well. As you may have noticed, nothing has changed.

Even at the very top it is vitally important that the leadership shows the very highest in standards in both personal and professional areas. After all, they serve as roll models. Many youngsters and even many adults look to their behavior as justification for their own actions. You know what I mean.

You've got to drive this point home very forcefully, everywhere you go and especially in the media. You've also got to be willing to do all you can to replace those in Washington who very clearly cannot live up to such reasonable standards. It's your responsibility—yours and mine. It's got to be done!

Cutting down the bribery. We all know the political golden rule, right? Those who supply the gold make the rules. It's sometimes called campaign financing. For those who believe in truth in advertising, it's a legal form of bribery much of the time.

As Common Cause reported at the end of the first quarter of 1998, the national Democratic and Republican parties raised a record $90 million in unregulated political contributions for the previous fifteen month period. In America you get the best politician money can buy!

The year before, an ABC/*Washington Post* poll showed that 63 percent of Americans that were polled oppose the way campaigns are financed and 67 percent don't think Congress will reform the system. A CBS/*New York Times* poll found that 50 percent of those polled felt we need fundamental changes and 39 percent said the system needs to be completely rebuilt!

Don't kid yourself, what can be done, will have to be done by a really large citizens' movement. As it is now, strongly financed political action committees drown out individuals and small citizens' groups, and enormously expensive sound-bite TV spots bury most chances for media involvement on a community level.

The answer is that considerable numbers of citizens have got to roll up their sleeves and get strongly involved. Involved in what? For one thing, involved in cutting donation levels at least in half and then again after the next election, and so on until it has been *really* cut back. No, it's not an abridgement of the freedom of speech. It's just the opposite. It's a sincere effort to keep mountains of money from gagging the rest of us who might *also* like to have some free speech. (Free? That'll be the day.)

As the funds are being severely cut back, it might be of great value to require the TV networks to give significant free and equal air time to the political candidates. No this isn't some sort of hair-brained scheme of this author. It's the excellent idea from no less than Reed Hundt, Chairman of the Federal Communications Commission.

If the not-so-Supreme Court decides the whole business is some sort of abridgement of free speech, a serious national constitutional amendment campaign must be launched all over this nation. It will be quite an effort, if it should be proven to be necessary, but it's really worth it. As Robert Kuttner of the *Washington Post* observed, "The domination of U.S. politics by special-interest money keeps the issues that matter most to voters off the agenda." It's something that has to be stopped.

Another area that needs to be cleaned out has been spotlighted by George F. Will, another *Washington Post* writer and national columnist. He wrote about many thousands of nonprofit groups that, "get billions of dollars of federal grants and contracts." He noted that "many recipients spend money on lobbying or other political activities." No, federal funds are *not* supposed to be used to support special-interest political lobbying and candidate financing.

Some of the example groups listed were, "Planned Parenthood, which does nicely at the federal trough, intervenes in elections with mailings targeting right-to-life candidates." There's the National Council of Senior Citizens, which Mr. Will reported, "gets 96 percent of its funding from the federal government." And boy, have *they* ever been involved in political assaults. (As it also might be said of A.A.R.P.)

You would think, since it does most certainly seem that so many of them are actually breaking the law, that this will be an easy one to clean up. Don't bet on it. Lawlessness never stopped the government or special interests from doing whatever they want to do and fight you toe-to-toe to stop you from stopping them. We've just got to become large enough in number and totally determined to put an end to this sort of thing. Accept nothing less!

While we're at it, let us not forget the line item veto which was struck down by the Supreme Court. Looks to me like another job for an amendment. And possibly it would not be such a bad idea to put several of those required amendments on the agenda for a constitutional convention. (It's about time we also faced up to the "motor voter law" fraud, too.)

Refining the elective process. Mark P. Petracca and Karen Moore featured an interesting article in the *San Diego Union-Tribune,* dispelling the myths concerning term limits. (Mr. Petracca was listed as an associate professor of political science at the University of California, Irvine. Miss Moore was a political science major and graduate of U.C., Irvine. They co-authored a special report concerning term limits. The article is from this report.)

They cite such criticisms as the lowering of the number and quality of office seekers and the general quality of government, if we should be so brash as to institute term limits. Then Mark and Karen noted that "seven cities in Orange County have had term limits in effect for years." And they conducted a survey from which they discovered that "77 percent of the elected officials in term-limited cities agreed that term limits do not decrease the quality of local government."

This agrees with what I have learned from other sources. It's not really a bad thing at all, except for the professional politicians. It's not so good for them. And yes, there are still a few diehards who seem to think that term limits are somehow unconstitutional. Somehow, they seem totally unable to come to terms with the presidential term limit that has been in place since near the end of World War II.

What we need now is term limits as a *national* issue for *everybody, everywhere.* But then that will take a lot of folks making a major effort. It always comes down to that, doesn't it?

A primary problem. What about the primaries? We find ourselves with restrictive selection committees in some areas, making choices (in caucuses) that most citizens feel totally locked out of. We find ourselves with primary selection processes in other areas, where early maneuvering of would-be candidates, deep within the bowels of the party, determine who will eventually surface. These are the things you face, to a greater or lesser degree, in both parties.

Among the many suggestions made is that primaries or caucuses be held with a strictly limited framework containing possibly five "Super Tuesdays," each three weeks apart. It has also been suggested that we have staggered primaries with the elimination of "Super Tuesday." Others say, no, no, we must shorten the nomination process and change it entirely to a national, same-day primary. Of course none of these suggestions address the problems I mentioned above. (After all, we wouldn't want to *really* open things up, now would we?)

Stanley Schmidt, the editor of *Analog* magazine, did an interesting editorial in one of his issues. He boldly suggested that "campaigns should be conducted entirely by means of candidates explaining their positions themselves, in their own words." His reasoning is that it is alleged, "people judge what they see and hear far more on presentation than on content. If true, (it) represents a very serious problem. People who understand it and concentrate hard on presentation have an excellent chance of using it to get themselves into powerful positions, and they stay there long enough to do a lot of damage."

Mr. Schmidt shows that maybe what we need are "schools that will teach everyone to see through the tricks, to cut past facades, and think critically about what people are actually saying—and to judge them primarily by that, not by how they look, or how glibly they speak." We can't have that! We're right in the middle of the dumbing down of many of our kids (even while some of us do our best to reverse this trend). Now you want to give them the opportunity of actually becoming genuinely intelligent? What a novel idea!

Another idea to consider. In Pickens County, Georgia, the local ballots are blank for the two major parties. For over four decades, local offices have been held only by independents. Possibly an even better way to open things up for the rest of us would be to follow the Nevada experiment. In its best form it would have "none of the above" as an alternative choice. Then, if the majority select it, that part of the election will have to be done over, excluding the unacceptable choices.

This could be a really creative end-run around the closed-shop they call the primary election and the limited choices known as the general election. Remember, if you like the idea, you can be sure most professional politicians will *not* like the idea. You'll have a big fight on your hands. But don't let that stop you.

Oh, and while you're at it, why not get rid of that archaic Electoral College that actually selects the president and vice president.

You don't think it matters? Well, so far, three times the Electoral College went *against* the popular vote. It happened when Andrew Jackson lost to John Quincy Adams, Samuel J. Tilden lost to Rutherford B. Hayes and Grover Cleveland lost to Benjamin Harrison. It could happen again.

Another issue that should most definitely be considered is the false political advertising that seems to be totally out of control. This is something I will never, *never* understand. There are laws concerning false consumer product advertising but there seems to be no control whatsoever with regard to the equivalent in the political arena.

Once again our dear judges claim that the First Amendment should be stretched, beyond recognition, to somehow manage to cover just about anything that one might say or do. The politicians just love this, as you might imagine. Sometimes legislating from the bench is just the ticket for them.

Seems like another job for an amendment effort, doesn't it? Perhaps that amendment that's been suggested to redefine a number of elements in that hallowed document, back to the original meanings. (Then, if judges or politicians want to make a change, they can do it the *right* way, the way the founding fathers intended for it to be done.)

Voter responsibilities. First of all, I have never found any rule or regulation that says you can't launch your own personal effort to find a reasonable candidate, convince him or her to run, get others involved and help him or her to campaign. Yes, you *can* get involved to that extent, or to any other extent that you wish to. It's *your* choice.

There are also other things you can do. You can become a part of one of those "Lead or leave" campaigns that presents committed pledges for support and action to members of Congress by disgruntled voters. You can also stop pushing for more selfish self-interests and start considering the shared, constructive concerns we hold in common with others, even though such efforts can't line our own pockets. I know, that's a radical idea, but I really think it's a good one, don't you?

You can write to your senators and congressman. I have done that and the following is the main thrust of a short letter I sent to one of my reps in Washington. I told him what this voter thought his priorities should be, which included the following:

> A term limit amendment, the 50 prime cuts in government costs (as suggested by "Citizens Against Government Waste") which could save up to $182 billion over the next five years, massive renovation of our legal system (where one usually is

only as right as one can afford to be), a serious consideration of at least a modified "flat tax" provision, a genuine war on drugs that would be considered as seriously as the war that followed the attack on Pear Harbor (both which involve the security and survival of our nation).

Then, after you and your friends have made your concerns known to them, monitor their progress, ask them repeatedly about their actions and generally give them as hard a time as it takes. You've got to do it that way. Believe me, if you don't, nothing will happen. That's the nature of the beast.

And, for God's sake, get out there and *vote!*

Getting even more involved. That old political war horse, Sam Ervin put it this way, "If men and women of capacity refuse to take part in politics and government, they condemn themselves, as well as the people, to the punishment of living under bad government." Now you know how we got this way.

I sincerely believe that there are a number of people within this civilization who have exceptional intellectual potential. Within that number, I believe there are a few who have actually realized a degree of that potential.

Among those few, some remain immature in many ways, some have developed as genuine predators, some are gentle but unmotivated, some have taken refuge in pure science or other escapes in an effort to distance themselves from what they perceive to be the general chaos, and a *very* few seem to be really trying to help this still very primitive species toward a positive, forward moving evolutionary development.

Since it would seem very little can be done within this civilization without an exceptionally effective involvement within the political structure, very little of positive consequence has been done by those few exceptional individuals who truly want to make a difference. This is because the political structure is formatted in such a way as to eliminate most desperately needed, exceptional individuals from any effective participation.

This can be changed. We can have term limits in all areas. We can have massive political funding reform. We can have balanced public media presentation of all candidates. We can eliminate the backroom political maneuvering. We can do all of this and more, if enough of you decide to make it so.

Now and then
an innocent man is sent to the legislature.
—Kin Hubbard

Again, *Parade* magazine with its continuing constructive public service has addressed this issue as well. In an article in that Sunday newspaper supplement, Colin Greer wrote about, "Why You Should Run, Too." Some wonderful examples were given. They were really inspirational. And an instructional list was offered on "How to Run for Office." It covered the following:

1. "What is your purpose?" What would you really like to do if you should win?

2. "Be sure you're ready." Realize that this is a major undertaking. It will take a lot of your time and energy—more than you might imagine.

3. "Assess which office you want to run for." Pick a realistic goal. Make it a run for something that is possible and where you might really have an opportunity to make a difference. Take a hard look at potential obstacles.

4. "Learn about community issues." Study good books and other references and dig into the issues that really matter to those around you. You can learn a lot if you're willing to make the effort.

5. "Identify issues you care about and work actively on them." Be an active, involved individual. Speak out. Write letters. Go to meetings. Volunteer and be a real part of genuine solutions.

6. "Contact the political party of your choice and community leaders." Become an influence in the establishment. Join forces with others you think well of. Get to know them and let them get to know you.

7. "Write a campaign plan. Get organized." Outline what it's going to take. Solicit advice from experts, when you can.

8. "Form an advisory committee." Build a team of friends and professionals and others who really want to help make it all happen. Work with that team and learn from each other.

9. "Build a list of supporters." Campaign first to gain many friends and others who might be willing to get involved and help you run for office. Remember, you'll need a lot of help. You can't do it alone.

10. "Identify how you can raise money." Try to estimate, as best you can, what it will take to run a good campaign. Then you and your supporters will have to reach out there for

contributors who are willing to give you some financial assistance.

Just you remember what Walter Page said. "There is one thing better than good government, and that is government in which all the people have a part."

Handling breakdowns in the system. You've got to learn how to raise hell and how to do it in the right way and in the right places. You might start by demanding a pledge from the lawmakers. You might want to consider the following elements for such a pledge.

1. Before any government financial allocations are to be made, the lawmakers must be willing to consider exactly where that money is coming from—where it's *really* coming from, and to do so *publicly*.
2. When a lawmaker proposes a new law, he (or she) should always include a proposal to *eliminate* at least a minimum of two existing laws which are obsolete, ineffective, unnecessary, or otherwise inappropriate.
3. Lawmakers must be willing to consider whether it's the people or special interests who want laws being considered. If it is not in the people's interest, the lawmakers must be willing to vote *against* such laws (unless there are exceptional extenuating circumstances which then must be publicly justified).
4. The lawmakers should promise to do *all* that they can, to "sunset" as many questionable financial "monsters" as can be ferreted out.
5. All lawmakers must consider their constituents *first, last* and *always*. They must not forget that they are the elected *employees* of the voters.
6. Every elected official must pledge to a *high* moral and ethical standard which, if breached, will initiate their *registration* from office.

These are just a few of the many possible suggestions. Take them and use them if you like and add lots more to the list if you wish to. If you can start a noisy little group (or a big group, if possible) that is willing to require such responsibility from your elected officials, and is willing to monitor their activities, and raise public concerns if they don't come through for you, and even work hard to replace them, when necessary, . . . if you are willing to do all of this, you just may get somewhere, especially if others are doing the same in many other parts of the country.

That's part of the handling of breakdowns, because the very first area where the breakdowns manifest themselves, is in the person of the elected officials. Other breakdowns can be managed by citizen monitor groups, fact finding groups, and other "whistle-blowers." You have the power to put together whatever you need. You really have.

A few final thoughts on this. All parties share responsibility here, and every one of our citizens most of all. No one party or one philosophy can be found that is absolutely good or absolutely bad. No group of citizens should ever think they have all the answers either.

A couple of good examples might be American conservatives who must consider *real* ecological responsibilities, even though many of them might not feel it to be necessary, and American liberals must consider *real* fiscal responsibilities, even though many of them might not care to do so.

To put it plain and simple, *everybody's* got to learn to get their act together.

Reducing the size and cost of government. Paul Tsongas put it thus, "The great political tugs and pulls of the past 35 years have concerned the distribution of the golden eggs. In the 1980s and 1990s we must focus on the health of the goose." Our government has, without doubt, become an oppressive leviathan that is ready to eat up all the money there is if given the chance. Soon your goose will be cooked, and there will be no more eggs.

We have got to cut back—go on a governmental diet. We've got to get rid of the waste and the unnecessary. Just you remember, you may be able to live high off the hog now, but what about your children and your children's children? We're not *really* reducing our monstrous national debt. What will you be leaving them with?

Gingrich told government employees to "bring us items so dumb that you wouldn't want to tell your mother you were busy doing it." He also said he wanted to get rid of some of those "stupid" federal government regulations and have a "correction day" once a month for bad law elimination in the House.

Well, I don't see it happening, nor do I see any major improvement. So, go after the new speaker and go after all the rest of them—the Democrats and the Republicans—all of them. Tell them to get busy or get out! (And be ready to *put* them out.)

Remember, sometimes the more drastic steps are the best for such a major operation as this. As nationally known business consultant, Peter F. Drucker said, "The only truly effective way to cut costs is to cut out an activity altogether. To try to cut back costs is rarely effective. There is little point in trying to do cheaply what should not be done at all."

Some of those programs are there to help us, right? Please, not *that* much help. I have a sneaking suspicion that we can really learn to solve far more of our own problems than you might imagine. This is especially true when you consider the uncomfortable fact that the vast majority of our problems have governmental origins.

Cutting out the fat. The Grace Commission report uncovered enormous waste in the federal budget. One figure I saw was a whopping $424 billion that could be cut without causing hardly a ripple. Several years later, the citizen's successor to the Commission, the "Citizens Against Government Waste" organization, started coming out with periodic lists, one of which I have in front of me right now. (You've read some of the earlier examples.) It shows fifty-one samplings of what can be cut, if we really have a mind to do so. A few samples of these examples are as follows:

- Eliminate the Market Promotion Program (MPP)—5 year savings: $434 million.
- Reform Federal Student Loan Programs—5 year savings: $14.4 billion.
- Impose a moratorium on construction and acquisition of new Federal buildings—5 year savings: $1.6 billion.
- Reduce funding for Overhead and Duplicative Research at the National Institutes of Health (NIH)—5 year savings: $4.9 billion.
- Reform national parks concession management—5 year savings: $60 million.
- Bring federal retirement benefits in line with the private sector—5 year savings: $33 billion.
- Pare the number of political appointees—5 year savings: $363 million.
- Reduce the Agency for International Development (AID) Assistance—5 year savings: $3.5 billion.
- Eliminate funding for pork-barrel highway demonstration projects—5 year savings: $3 billion.
- Reduce congressional franking by 50 percent—5 year savings: $100 million.

Whew! And that's just the tip of the iceberg. All I can say is God help the "U.S.A. Titanic" if we don't get back on course. Of course you can get on board and help make that happen, can't you? Sure you can.

There are so many areas that need our attention. There's that big federal pension that offers such a nice golden parachute for so many of those we kick out of office. I was only able to get some of the older figures but even they are way out of line.

It shows immediate entitlement to pensions that range all the way from $35,000 to more than $100,000 (as calculated by the National Taxpayers Union). At that time *Money* magazine reported that taxpayers would have saved as much as $56 billion in one year alone if private industry's pension levels were the rule.

What about that $41 billion in unnecessary gear that was reported stockpiled by the Pentagon not so long ago? The figures are from the U.S. General Accounting Office, which also includes such interesting little tidbits as the five hundred aircraft identification markers they don't need but have warehoused while going ahead and ordering one hundred more of the same thing.

What about the rampant fraud that has been found recently in the Women, Infants, and Children nutrition program and in the food stamp program? You've read the headlines. How have we allowed this to happen? Isn't anybody watching the store? They sure as hell aren't watching the cash register.

> *Good positions are always open in government and industry for people who can tell lies convincingly.*
>
> —Ashleigh Brilliant ("Pot Shots")

Reforming the Civil Service. Most of you folks probably already know about the endless problems with government bureaucrats who don't seem to care about anything except perhaps that they're in charge, no matter what kind of harm that may do. And you know, no doubt, about the efforts that seem to be launched, from time to time, to reform the Civil Service, so that people like that can actually be fired.

Cosmetic window dressing, that's what it is. Once again, if there is going to be any chance of bouncing these duds out on their keisters, an awful lot of angry citizens are going to have to lay the law down with both houses of Congress. It's the only way you're ever going to get anything close to personal accountability in the Civil Service.

We must instill personal accountability. And we must do this not only in the Civil Service, but in *all* branches of government on *all* levels. I mean everywhere, from the police, the elected officials, the bureaucrats, the prosecutors, and the judges, to the administrators, and the lawyers.

"Decency, security, and liberty alike demand that government officials shall be subjected to the same rules of conduct that are commands to the citizen. In a government of laws, existence of the government will be imperiled if it fails to observe the law scrupulously. Our government is the potent, the omnipresent teacher. For good or for ill, it teaches the whole people by its example.

"Crime is contagious. If the government becomes a lawbreaker, it breeds contempt for law; it invites anarchy. To declare that, in the administration of the criminal law, the end justifies the means—to declare that the government may commit crimes in order to secure the conviction of a private citizen—would bring terrible retribution.

"Against that pernicious doctrine this court should resolutely set its face."

Those words are from U.S. Supreme Court Justice Louis D. Brandeis. And, do you know when he said that? In 1927! Is it any less valid today? I should hope not. Just remember, power does not corrupt so fast as it does with immunity.

Reforming Social Security. You remember what I told you about the Social Insecurity Administration? Remember the abuses? Remember the financial condition and how it got that way? That's right. It's a serious mess.

Remember, in about a decade, an estimated 75 million "baby boomers" are going to start retiring and totally inundating the Social Security system. It's a wreck waiting to happen, and a little cosmetic surgery isn't going to do it.

Investment strategies must be examined. Bad management must be dealt with. Partial-privatization plans like that of Sen. Moynihan and Sen. Kerrey need to be looked at. Other possibilities need to be seriously studied. And this must be done quickly and thoroughly. There's no time to waste.

Reforming the legal system. The American legal system is by far the *biggest* problem of all and the most important one that needs to be dealt with in a *massive* way. If you have read the seemingly endless examples of this problem throughout this book you know what I mean and you know what must be done. If you or friends or family have been laid low by this archaic system of injustice, you know what I mean; and you know what must be done.

For those few of you who still haven't got it figured out, go back to that section on "Changing the Legal System." Read it through

Politics: A Search for Solutions

again, very carefully. I know, it's a massive problem and it does seem almost impossible to do anything of any *real* consequence. I know.

It's the biggest problem of all for three good reasons. The first is that it is so pervasive throughout our entire civilization. It involves everything from our most basic constitutional law and all civil and criminal law in America, to law enforcement, the shocking abuses of our bureaucracies, the lawyers, the courts, our political system, and just about everything else.

The second good reason is that the legal community, the lawyers, judges and most of the politicians, control it all and are not about to let you or anyone else mess with the exceptionally profitable situation they have right now. Oh yes, they will make grand gestures with a little fiddling here and there. They will make small changes. But that's it. They will *not* stand for any real basic changes. That will have to be *forced* upon them, which they will see to it will not be an easy thing to do.

The third good reason is that most Americans do seem to have evolved into harmless little teddy bears (or Beanie Babies?) whose primary function, when put upon by unfair events, is to crawl in a corner and whimper. We have all been conditioned to this, or some similar ineffective behavior, gradually over a long period of time. We have allowed ourselves to become the ultimate wimps. We no longer have the guts to *really* clean up a big mess like this. Or do we?

I guess we'll just have to find out, won't we? If we do have what it takes, it will involve a sizable number of responsible citizens who are willing to join or establish groups, become better educated about the problems and about the possible solutions and who are willing and able to develop an effective battle plan. It's something that we absolutely can do. It's only a question of how many of you will pick up the gauntlet and, with determination and a courageous heart, move forward on this.

Remember, some of the things that must be done include holding them all to full and personal accountability, having independent performance evaluators over judges, prosecutors, and lawyers and with public disclosure and evaluation conclusions with *teeth*, creating a very professional and sizable group of pro bono citizen advocates for the countless victims of the system, phasing out the antiquated adversarial method in the system in favor of a genuine search for truth, and ending the totally unconstitutional judicial legislation once and for all.

I know, it seems to be that fabled unreachable dream. Well it *isn't* unreachable. You *can* do it. It's just a matter of whether there are enough of you out there who are willing to make such a wonderful, historic effort.

Reforming our tax system. You've been following the news, I'm sure. You know that finally there is some attention being paid to the monstrous tax system and the American Gestapo (sometimes known as the I.R.S.). Wonder of wonders, there even are some things being done about the problem. (You see, sometimes something *can* be done.)

Now it's important for you to see to it that those changes are not allowed to be applied timidly or to be gradually frittered away over time and that many important additional changes are made. You've got to get in their face and stay there.

One of those groups that's doing just that is the "It's Our Money, Not Theirs" project of the National Federation of Independent Business. It's an organization that isn't afraid to tackle the problem with a campaign to retire the massive tax code. (Contact information can be found in the Appendix, List of Organizations.)

There are some very fundamental things that are wrong with the way it is now, besides the extensive errors and strong-arm tactics. That massive tax code is so unwieldy that even the best C.P.A.s have problems with it, not to mention the I.R.S. itself, which at times doesn't seem to have *anything* right.

It might also be questioned as to whether our government or any government should have the right to loot one or more classes of people in order to buy the votes of others, and I must also say that I don't believe that governments should have the right to loot the wealth of our future generations through extensive deficit spending so that the chosen ones of our current time can have their unearned luxuries. We've got a lot to consider here, don't we?

Remember the key changes that must be made. Once again, I believe it was Thoreau who said that "there are a thousand hacking at the branches of evil to one who is striking at the root." You and your friends have got to go for the roots. You've got to hit dead-center on the basic areas where these problems originate.

One of the first basic problem areas is with the public attitude. We've got to change a lot of minds. We've got to convince a lot of people about problems they may not want to hear about and don't want to deal with. We've got to get them fired up, as I hope you are now.

Then we've got to go for those really meaningful changes. Again, just to keep you from forgetting, here are some of those key changes that *must* be made.

Politics: A Search for Solutions

1. We need a reaffirmation amendment to our Constitution, to get us firmly back to following our laws, *as written*. No more judicial legislation.
2. We must eliminate that terrible adversarial system of law, in favor of a new, direct approach to finding truth and truly dispensing justice.
3. For the first time, we must hold *everyone* in government *personally* responsible for what they do and don't do, even as we are similarly held responsible in the private sector.
4. We must have massive reform of political financing. What we have now is a form of graft, pure and simple.
5. We must launch a major effort to reduce government spending on all levels everywhere.
6. We should hold all elections just before or immediately following the national annual tax payment deadline.
7. We need a "none of the above" box below choices on the voter ballots, with the requirement of new elections with new candidates for all offices where "none of the above" gets the simple majority.
8. We should require term limits for all elective offices everywhere, in all levels of government, including with judgeships.
9. We must have independent performance evaluations (with teeth) for all judges, prosecutors, and lawyers.
10. We've got to establish an entire system of independent citizen advocates for victims of government in all areas, elective areas, the bureaucracies, our courts, everywhere in America.

How's *that* for a shopping list?

Chapter Nineteen

Other Problems to Consider
Repairing America

> *What is it that gives a young man strength,*
> *gives him the courage, to stand up in front of a column of*
> *tanks right there in front of the world?*
>
> —former President Bush, praising the Chinese
> demonstrator who stood alone in front of tanks
> to briefly stop their advance through Beijing.

Because you are the ultimate victim. I shall try not to fool myself too much into believing that everyone out there will rise to the need simply because it will help the many unfortunate Americans who are being ground to dust by a dysfunctional system. But possibly it would not be asking too much to hope that at least a reasonable number will come to realize that, in the long run, they will also be eventually included in the growing list of victims.

Would it be possible for a reasonable number to put aside their predispositions of not wanting to know, of not wanting to be involved, of not wanting to learn and to make a meaningful effort? Eric Hoffer may have been right when he said that "far more crucial than what we know or do not know is what we do not want to know."

Can enough of us decide to really want to know and to roll up our collective sleeves and become a significant part of the solution? They say the average lifetime is probably not much more than 638,280 hours. (That's 2.4 billion seconds.) Seems like it's about time to get started, doesn't it?

What you've read is just the beginning. Those many horrors detailed in this book and the suggestions given for solutions are only the beginning—a good beginning, to be sure, but only a beginning.

Other Problems to Consider

The difficulties permeate every area and every level of our society. This is the case because, most unfortunately, our government has come to permeate every area and every level of our society.

By way of example, in 1890, to fight business monopolies, the Sherman Antitrust Act was passed in Congress. In 1914 the Clayton Antitrust Act was passed and the Federal Trade Commission was established, to further discourage "unfair" competition in business. So, what do we end up with? We end up with our own government becoming the largest and most powerful business monopoly the world has ever seen.

We can see it in Medicare, government run gambling, government printing, various forms of price fixing, extensive private property regulation and confiscation, letter mail control, the tightly controlled legal system, and on it goes in every area throughout our lives. You can't escape it. You can't escape the largest monopoly ever conceived.

The fiction of private ownership. Let's look at some of these other "problems." Let's start with your assumed right to own property. By way of example, let's take on Urban Renewal, and to do so, let us first look at the background—a little bit of history.

As you may be aware, the signers of our Declaration of Independence were businessmen and property owners. They put a great deal at risk. They had a lot to lose. However, they clearly felt that their liberty and their right to their own property was a goal that made it well worth the risk.

It was a grand and shining idea that was to be constantly under attack, from the "robber barons" of yesteryears to the modern city planners of today. It didn't matter to the greedy ones that this was a fundamental right of great value.

Back in those early days, and for a number of years thereafter, there were quite a lot of folks who had really strong feelings about their homestead, their property, their own. And even into modern times there are those who still echo this sentiment. As Walter Lippmann put it, "The only dependable foundation of personal liberty is the personal economic security of private property."

But that was then and this is now. Things have changed—*really* changed. Do you remember, way back in the 60s, when a courageous ex-Marine barricaded himself in his little home in the Los Angeles area to try to keep the "authorities" from taking it away from him? Our dear government authorities used their powers of eminent domain to seize his home and demolish it, to make way for a private motion picture museum that was never built. How nice.

He just never could get it through his head that the fighting he had done, at the risk of his life (as a Marine), to protect our liberties, our personal security, and our property really had little meaning anymore. He couldn't understand how his property was only his until someone with the right government support was able to force the sale of that which was coveted by others.

It could have been almost anyone's home if it was inconveniently in the way of somebody's grand plans, realized or not. And although there was a lot of sentiment in favor of the beleaguered ex-Marine, not much more was done than to show a little moral support. I mean, after all, we certainly can't *really* get involved, now can we? And, after all, it wasn't *my* home that was being seized. That's right. *Not this time.*

Enter, Urban Renewal. Abuses abounded and set the stage for one of the most effective looter's tools ever devised. It was the innocent sounding and so blindly well-meaning concept of Urban Renewal for America's cities. And who could be against it? After all, it is meant to uplift the poor and the downtrodden of our inner cities, right? We're going to tear down the slums and build wonderful new things. Isn't that just absolutely wonderful?

It all started with a federal Housing Act, sponsored by former U.S. Senator Robert Taft of Ohio and passed by congress on July 15, 1949. It was intended to provide federal aid for slum-clearance projects and for building low-rent public housing. Title-1 of the new Housing Act was designed to encourage municipalities to acquire and resell substandard areas at prices below cost for private redevelopment.

Well, that may have been the way it started but that most certainly wasn't where it ended up going. Sometimes what they did was very profitable for the "chosen ones" and sometimes their projects fell flat at great cost to the taxpayers of course.

The bottomless pit of Pittsburgh. Back in those infamous 60s, the city of Pittsburgh put together a grandiose project that swept through private property like the four horsemen of the apocalypse. They built their Three Rivers Stadium, a retail center, a new convention center, and a grand highway system that chopped residential neighborhoods to pieces. Oops, sorry about that, but we do have to build our grand things, right?

How grand was it? The retail center laid an egg and starry eyed civic leaders now want to forget about that stadium and build two new ones and construct another retail mall. Now we know what is meant by that saying, "Those who do not learn from history are doomed to repeat it."

Other Problems to Consider

Actually, regardless of the success or failure of any of these projects, the single most important issue still remains, the right to be secure in one's property. We understand having to sell to make way for a public school or a much needed road or some other necessary public project. What we should never allow is the looting of private property for someone else's *private* benefit.

You tell me what you would call it, when a person's home can be condemned and taken from him (or her) and sold to other private interests for the profit of those other private interests? And I'm not talking about slums. We've left that fiction behind a long time ago.

Would you like *your* home to be put to a forced sale and taken by some public agency and resold for the private benefit of someone else? Are you willing to concede to this "land reform?" Well, it would seem you have. We all have.

Once again:

> *It is impossible to introduce into society a greater evil than this—the conversion of the law into an instrument of plunder.*
> —Frederic Bastiat

The way the agencies function. Under the Urban Renewal program, Redevelopment Agencies (or similar entities) are established by eager officials, often in concert with avaricious business men and associated opportunistic developers. These agencies then use the power of eminent domain to force the sale of private property for public use.

Now, of course "public use" is being conveniently redefined to mean the taking and holding of private property by such an agency for the purpose of transferring said ownership to other private interests that adhere to the overall concept for that area that they now have in mind.

One of the many games they play is to hold what they like to call "public hearings." These propaganda ploys, along with stacked media promotions, help to solidify their position. They also allow comments and arguments from the public that may not be favorable to such projects. This is to give the false impression that there is actually some sort of democratic process going on.

Such hearings have, at times, been overwhelmed by objections. However, if the officials are determined enough to follow through with their schemes, no matter what, then you can be sure that is exactly what happens, as it does in almost all instances. Democracy has no place here—none at all.

This is supposed to be for "blighted" areas, right? Never mind the fact that their own lack of proper and enforced zoning laws or public health enforcement brought it about in the first place, if such a "blight" even happened at all. Never mind that the word *blight* now often refers to just about any use of just about any private property that does not conform to their new grand scheme of things. Never mind about any uncomfortable little observations like this, right?

One of many good examples of the convenient changing of the definition of *blight* would be as it was applied in the *very* up-scale community of Coronado in southern California. The so-called "blighted" area included everything from the grand beach estates of retired admirals to the internationally famous Hotel del Coronado.

This sort of thing has finally gotten to be a bit of an embarrassment. In fact, in some areas of the country, it has gotten so bad that special legislation has been passed that restricts the use of such redevelopment designations in what is referred to as affluent areas.

Naturally that just protects those who are well healed in fine estates and various businesses that are similarly endowed. Most of us cannot ever expect such considerations in our well kept homes and small businesses. *You only own your property just so long as someone who knows how to go about getting it doesn't want your property.* Don't you forget it.

Other examples of blatant abuses include the private, closed-door policies of the Boise, Idaho, downtown renewal operations. The city council had closed the door to public discussion. The Gannett newspaper-radio-TV corporate group evidently didn't like this sort of thing at all and subsequently created open town meetings through which the people had the opportunity to force at least a small degree of citizen participation.

Most areas don't seem to have such public defenders. The other side has all sorts of effective weapons to bring to bear on the situation. One such resource had even placed at least one very revealing display ad in a major metropolitan newspaper. The ad promoted Bergen and Lee, Inc., a public relations outfit. The ad noted that they have provided, "publicity, publications, and community relations for redevelopment projects since 1967."

There are also quite a number of professional "planners" who specialize in such projects. There are a number of developers who like to jump in on such opportunities as often as they are able. Let's face it, there seems to be no end of opportunists in this field.

And of course there are a number of very effective professional lobbyists and financial advisors that haunt the halls of various state

Other Problems to Consider

capitals and Washington, D.C. on behalf of some of these agencies and their related associations. And of course, these agencies issue their revenue bonds which banks and savings and loan associations are quick to cooperate with as they eagerly feed at the trough.

The H.U.D. scandals. You probably are aware that the federal control and implementation of Urban Renewal or Redevelopment (or whatever you want to call it) has been under the Department of Housing and Urban Development (H.U.D.) for all these many years. I'm sure you're aware of the seemingly endless scandals that agency and a number of its people have managed to get themselves involved in.

A quick overview of relevant headlines and subheads that have been generated over this last dozen years or so, includes:

> Key HUD Aide Suspended Over Criminal Charge.
> Proxmire's Golden Fleece Award Goes to HUD.
> Kemp Assails Flaws in HUD Subsidies Costing Millions.
> Probe Reveals Favoritism in HUD Program.
> HUD Scandal Indictment Targets Ex-aide to Pierce.
> Congressional Audit Asserts HUD Problems Unresolved.
> Crony of Ex-HUD Boss Is Guilty.
> Ex-HUD Aide Faces Fraud Charges.
> HUD's Terrible War on Neighborhood Halfway House Dissenters.
> HUD Probe Ends With No Charges.
> Ex-Cabinet Official accused of HUD related felonies.
> HUD Denies It Took Action On A Union Hit List.

But then, what can you expect from a government department that is involved in a looting process of this nature? You really shouldn't be surprised.

San Bernardino Urban Renewal. I know I've thrown a lot at you, but I really feel that you need to take a look at a few good samples of Urban Renewal in operation, so here's some more despicable examples.

I think most folks are at least somewhat familiar with how Hispanic homes and other properties were taken away from so many in Chavez ravine in the Los Angeles area and put in the hands of the private, profit-making Los Angeles Dodgers. What most folks don't know is what's happened in some of the nearby lower-profile towns, like San Bernardino, California.

San Bernardino had a nice little downtown area with a local department store and all the usual shops and special amenities that small town America is famous for. A small amount of the outlying area included a few spots that had been allowed to run down. (No one ever bothered to ask why this was allowed by the officials in charge.) Most of the downtown, however, was in quite reasonable shape.

Then, some self-appointed community "leaders," with the willing assistance of local politicians, decided to declare the whole area blighted and formed a Redevelopment Agency to take the place over, tear it up, and put in a big new shopping center, one with access directly to and from a neighboring north/south freeway (and no access to or from the rest of the downtown area).

A wellspring of disapproval rose from the community. This writer was among those who tried to convince the officials that destroying the right to private property for the private benefit of others was totally immoral and cutting off the rest of the downtown like that would destroy it. They weren't interested. As far as they were concerned, no such area depletion would happen.

To hell with the democratic process. The idea of such a project was put to a vote on the ballot and it was turned down by the voters. Did this stop them? Hell no! They just told us all that it was only an advisory vote, and they didn't have to consider it. In other words, damn the people! Full steam ahead!

So the project went forward. Lots of good people lost their homes and businesses. Many were older folks who had taken years to build up their local clientele. The forced sale and relocation was the end for them. But who cares, right? After all, a few eggs have to be broken if you want to make an omelet. Well, that's what one of the local politicians told us.

In came the many big businesses and franchises that we all know so well, including J.C. Penney's and Montgomery Ward. And, it might be added, a local department store, The Harris Company, was part of the original push for that redevelopment and, wouldn't you know, found itself whole and not forced to sell and allowed to be a key part in the new mall project—which so effectively cut off the rest of the downtown area.

The end result. And what happened to the rest of the downtown area? It went steadily downhill and became a *true* slum in its appearance and with all the accompanying crime that one might expect. In fact the problem spread beyond the downtown area. It became a city-wide problem.

In recent years we have seen San Bernardino reported as having the highest big-city crime rate in the state of California. Right about that same time *Money* magazine pegged the violent crime rate for San Bernardino as the sixth-worst in the nation.

Then "Zero Population Growth" issued "The Children's Environmental Index," rating 207 U. S. cities. Among those at the bottom of the index was, you guessed it, San Bernardino. Most unfortunately the area has really earned its dubious title of "The Armpit of the Inland Empire." How sad.

Who was responsible? Politicians like Donald G. Mauldin, Al Ballard, and John Quimby. Business men like James A. Guthrie and Leslie Harris. Administrators like A. Merle Sessions. And the list goes on and on. What about your own community? Who are those who are responsible for the mistakes made in *your* town? Do you care? I hope so.

San Diego Urban Renewal. Although all such projects destroy citizens' property rights, it's much easier for folks to accept the crime if the results are successful enough. The "malling" of San Bernardino that turned out to be a mugging is not the only end result. San Diego trashed your rights of property ownership, too. However, in this case, they ended up with one of the late developer Ernest W. Hahn's more profitable private commercial developments.

Oh yes, they held public hearings. That was only window dressing of course. That didn't really mean anything. No one was able to protect their property rights. Even with that, the agency officials were mostly inclined to play their cards very close to the chest. So close that one city councilman, Fred Schnaubelt, resigned from the city's Redevelopment Agency because they wouldn't even give *him* requested data on the downtown project. (That eventually got cleared up, sort of. But it shows you how they prefer to operate.)

Of course with the commercial success of the new downtown area, the media was very much inclined to join in the celebration. It was much more convenient to just forget about the real cost in one of our most basic human rights. And as is most often the case, as goes the media, so goes the public. Hey, after all that wasn't *their* homes or businesses that were taken, right? It was *other* people's property.

Losses and tragedies under Urban Renewal. The losses are far ranging, all the way from the historic and the artistic to the many personal tragedies. Very much in the mistaken tradition of destroying almost anything that isn't new, many irreplaceable architectural gems and historically significant buildings have been routinely leveled.

This has also been true for many great examples of fine art murals. There was the "Picasso's Eyes" mural in San Diego that fell to the wrecking ball. There was a twenty-foot metal sculpture that was mistakenly razed by redevelopment dolts in San Jose, California. This sort of thing has been happening from coast to coast.

California coastal conservation has no meaning to these redevelopment fanatics either. Especially since the courts have gone along with them (as they almost always do) and declared that Urban Renewal projects are exempt from the regulations of the Costal Zone Conservation Act.

There also have been so many little stores and mom-and-pop shops that have been completely erased by these so-called grand projects. An interesting example is of a store owner in National City (in California) who complained that his business has been destroyed by officials that wouldn't issue him appropriate licences because he was forced to move by a redevelopment project and has now found himself in an area that has been targeted for *future* redevelopment.

Bulldozers descended on a close-knit little Hispanic community in Addison, Illinois. It was clearly not blight, but it was Hispanic. To the officials that seems to be one and the same. And a southern California headline read, "El Cajon Redevelopment Leaving Some Homeless." Are they just discovering this? That's nothing new.

There was that subcommittee of the Downtown Coordinating Council of San Diego that issued a disturbing report on the human cost of the Horton Redevelopment Project. As the report noted, "Redevelopment in San Diego and current national economic and social conditions have exacerbated a wide range of urban problems." Well, the economic problems seem to be temporarily better. At least there's that.

In Oceanside, California, snack shops, bookstores, arcades—twenty businesses in all—were forced to move or just go out of business. They were in the way of "progress." Many did have to go out of business. They couldn't afford the higher rents elsewhere, and they had now lost their neighborhood customers that took such a long time to develop. That's just too damn bad, right? After all, where do you think you're living, in the United States of America?

It only gets worse. Now there is almost nothing left of your property rights. Just a couple of years ago the city council of National City approved the condemnation of a small used car lot so it could be sold to a big dealer (Ball Automotive) for their planned expansion. More recently, in Hurst, Texas, the city used its power of eminent domain to force a group of homeowners to abandon their properties to allow for the expansion of a big neighboring shopping mall.

Even more frightening is a report by the *New York Times* News Service on this situation. The news report quoted University of Colorado professor of law Richard Collins saying that "state and federal courts have been reluctant to restrict governments' power of eminent domain." He said the courts have upheld a number of rulings involving transfer of land to private ventures.

When it comes right down to it, with most of our problems, it's the *courts* again as usual, isn't it? That's where the vast majority of the difficulties originate in our beleaguered nation. That's where we have to go to get to the roots, instead of aimlessly hacking away at the many branches.

The vultures of Urban Renewal. Some are genuinely evil people. There are always a number of those who will be very quick to move against the less fortunate like any true predator would. But there are also quite a number of people who think there is absolutely nothing wrong with what they are doing.

Justice Louis Brandeis understood this. He wrote that "experience should teach us to be most on our guard to protect liberty when the government's purposes are beneficial. Men born to freedom are naturally alert to repel invasion of their liberty by evil-minded rulers. The greater dangers to liberty lurk in insidious encroachment by men of zeal, well-meaning but without understanding."

In one category or the other there are so many like those I've mentioned. And there are so many others. Some make it an important part of their business, like Victor Gruen Associates, Inc., who like to design the new constructions from the remains of what was taken from others. There are those like the late Ernest W. Hahn, who created a shopping center dynasty out of this sort of thing.

His centers went everywhere. They were built in New Jersey, Maryland, Virginia, North Carolina, Tennessee, and Florida. You will find his handiwork in Tennessee, Texas, Iowa, Minnesota, Montana, and Colorado. And if that isn't enough, you can look in Utah, California, Nevada, New Mexico, Oregon, and Washington state as well.

Who might be some of those in your area who have taken full advantage of the government's evidently limitless power to loot its citizens? You should find out. In fact it should become general public knowledge as to what these people *really* did. Not the pretty things they put up. They should be forced to face the truth of what they were *really* a part of.

Way back in 1988, the *Wall Street Journal* reported that "the Supreme Court and the Reagan administration have begun to repair fifty years of erosion of a fundamental right granted American citizens by the Constitution, the protection against unwarranted seizure of their property by agencies of government." As you can see, *that* never got very far.

If anything is going to ever be done, *really* done and done right, it's going to have to be people like you and me raising all kinds of hell and *forcing* them to return our liberties. The democratic processes are there. The appropriate procedures are available. What's missing is a determined people who will no longer allow these terrible things to happen in this country.

Fighting back as a consumer. Moving on to other areas of concern, we find ourselves having to do battle from time to time as consumers. If we don't, we lose. If we do demand that what we buy should be as advertised and reasonably functional, then we may have a chance. But we have to be willing to fight back.

Sometimes it ends up with a situation where nobody wins, unfortunately. It happened to this writer when he made the mistake of buying a new Chrysler 5th Avenue car just a few years ago. It turned out to be a real lemon. The list of problems was endless. It involved everything from stalling, things falling off the car, electric wiring shorts, sectional separation, electronic system burn-out, smog check failures, and ending with the paint peeling off in sheets.

In the beginning, when it was under warranty, I went to various Chrysler dealerships to correct the problems but quickly learned that if I wanted to get things really fixed right I would have to go to my own friendly neighborhood mechanic. I even went to the trouble of testing a dealership with the rubber pad that wouldn't stay on the brake peddle. They couldn't even fix a simple thing like that so it would stay on. I ended up fixing it right with a special super-glue that worked just fine.

I wrote to Chrysler about my problems. No answer. I wrote to Lee Iacocca personally. No answer. I eventually wrote to Robert Eaton, the new Chairman and C.E.O. No answer. I couldn't take advantage of the state's lemon law because I hadn't had my car in to their dealerships enough times. (I had to bring it where it would *really* get fixed.)

When the paint began to peel off in sheets, I found out that this was a problem that Chrysler had that year with a primer coat and a paint job that would not maintain adherence. So, I applied to Chrysler for a new paint job and, true to form, was refused. I was, as usual, on my own.

So what did I do? I made up a nice pair of window signs for the car that explained how this lemon came to look this way. It became clear that Chrysler automobiles may be just fine as long as not too much ever goes wrong. But, if you get a real lemon, God help you.

What was the result? I know for a fact that at least a few dozen people who had been considering a Chrysler product changed their minds. So far, it's the best I can do. People can see what's left of my car anytime they want to and then make up their own mind about that car company.

I remember one media quote from Robert Eaton where he says, "We want to give customers what they asked for—and add features that will delight them." We're waiting.

Not getting involved. When one faces the threat of losing one's liberty all at once, a person will often rise to fight. When one loses it little by little, no single unit of loss is usually great enough to make it noticeable, or if it should be noticed one or a few small losses are not great enough, for most folks, to motivate any action.

Then there are those who feel they are powerless and will probably never have any real empowerment because there is so little that they could ever do. As Edmund Burke observed, "Nobody makes a greater mistake than he who did nothing because he could do only a little." And one could go on and on with all the excuses in the world, almost none of which ever really ring true.

Many of you already knew about many of the oppressions and blunders of the courts, the bureaucracy, and our government in general. You've heard and read about some of the armed raids. You are aware of normal, everyday, *innocent* people who run afoul of terrible errors and end up disappearing from view.

But hey, nobody's come for you yet, and our economy has never been so good, so why should you get involved, right? That's other people's problems. It's sort of like what Pastor Martin Niemoeller wrote many years ago. The Pastor was a "guest" in the Dachau concentration camp during the time of World War II. This is what he wrote:

> In Germany, the Nazis first came for the Jews, and I didn't speak up because I wasn't a Jew. Then they came for the trade unionists, and I didn't speak up because I wasn't a trade unionist. Then they came for the Catholics, and I didn't speak up because I was a Protestant. Finally they came for me, but there was no one left to speak up.

If you still feel you've got lots of wonderful good reasons for not taking up the cause, take heed of the words of John Stuart Mill. "A man who has nothing which he is willing to fight for, nothing which he cares more about than he does about his personal safety, is a miserable creature who has no chance of being free, unless made and kept so by the exertions of better men than himself."

Always in the audience? Never on the stage? Oh yes, the non-doers do a magnificent job at developing marvelously creative whining strategies every time they get grazed or otherwise hit by any of the growing oppressions. This is their method of trying to get others to help them out while still managing to do as little as possible themselves. And some of them are so good at it.

I know. You don't like reading this, right? Hopefully, it's because you have come to realize that *there is only empowerment through involvement.* Hopefully, *you* are planning to be a part of great and historic changes. Right?

But there are so *many* out there who need to read this book, and other books as well, and need to read these words before you now. So, as part of your involvement, you're going to do all you can to get as many as possible to read these words and, hopefully, become motivated to rise to the occasion, right?

Can a person not feel the futility of living one's life with so little to mark its passing? Are you satisfied with reaching comfortable insignificance as a lifetime goal? Can there not be a greater reason for us having been here?

It is my fervent hope that these words will not fall on deaf ears and closed minds. It is my greatest wish that all of us—without concern about race, gender, or other divisive polarizations—can learn to work together, to make a difference, a *real* difference. We can do it. Shoulder to shoulder, *we can do it!*

Really getting involved. There are some folks who are getting involved—really involved. I remember the "Magnificent 13" young volunteer patrols on the New York subways. Back in 1979 there were more than eighty involved in that effort. And remember how Bridgeport, Connecticut, mobilized almost the whole town to fight their very bad drug problem?

How about the "Zebra Squad" of Houston, Texas. In one two-year period they calculated they had been responsible for the capture of over two thousand parole violators. And then there are the various Citizens' Patrols. They're usually trained by and work closely with local police as an extra set of eyes and ears. In a number of areas they have proven to be very effective.

There are also those groups called the Retired Senior Volunteer Patrol (RSVP). These folks are graduated from a special abbreviated academy run by local police. Then they go out on the streets in the daytime to do ticketing work, traffic control, check on shut-ins, and do all sorts of other valuable services. I've told you about most of these groups before, remember?

Other Problems to Consider

Then there was that group that started at the San Diego airport (Lindbergh Field). They were on hand to remind officials to be sure ID's were being checked before passengers boarded. (Many illegal aliens had been using commercial air transportation to disburse throughout the United States.) Then certain self-proclaimed Chicano activists descended on them and started a minor riot. Because the authorities were as blind as authorities usually are, both groups were thrown out of the airport facility.

That was what the activists wanted of course. It took major and costly legal action to reverse the decision on that one. Yes, sometimes the correct thing can eventually happen in the court system. But it's still a gamble and a damn expensive one at that.

You are also probably aware of the radio talk show hosts all over America who have been bringing listeners to Washington, D.C. to hold the politicians' feet to the fire—to get them to put through major tax reform, political reforms, etc.

One of the originators of this "hold their feet to the fire" movement is a very positive and energetic radio host by the name of Roger Hedgecock. He's heard mostly in southern California, but he's had some national radio exposure as well. And you can be sure, wherever he's heard, he's out there getting involved and doing his best to get his listeners involved.

Then there are also folks like Oprah Winfrey, who believes in trying to make a difference by helping others. She's involved in major charities and all sorts of other positive activities. In other words, she doesn't just tell others to do it. She has become one of her own best examples.

Other celebrities get involved from time to time. There was William Shatner hosting a benefit screening of the fourth "Star Trek" movie for the benefit of the Juvenile Justice Connection Project and there was the "Golden Door" founder, Deborah Szekely, developing the Inter-American Foundation to train community group leaders to build muscle for miracles. And let us not forget retired General Colin Powell's "America's Promise" volunteer movement. It's alive and well, thank you, and trying its very best to make a difference for everybody's benefit.

A few have tapped their creative side and become Video Vigilantes. They've documented everything from illegal dumping to drug dealing (with long lenses from safe vantage points). Some have even become "stringers" for local exposé TV shows. Lots of possibilities here.

All of these efforts, and the many others that are out there, are very helpful, you can be sure. However, it should be noted that they are still far, *far* too few in number, and some of them are more involved with hacking at the branches of the problems and not really getting at the roots. Frankly, we need a small army to tackle those damn roots.

You know what we need. A good list can be found at the end of the section entitled "Politics: A search for Solutions" under "Remember the key changes that must be made." Don't forget, some of those solutions might be put in one or more constitutional amendments; others can be handled in different ways. All must be vigorously fought for.

Your involvement. I have always believed that if the people will only lead, the leaders will have to follow. Can't you be a part of that? Let's face it, a life without a cause is a life without an effect. Doesn't your life deserve a special and really worthwhile purpose?

We are entertained by our fictional super-heroes. We love to watch them trounce the bad guys. We have always loved to watch Superman, Wonder Woman, Bat Man, Hercules, and Xena, the Warrior Princess. We like to see them win the day.

Few of us seem to realize that we can be our *own* super-hero. *We* can rise to the challenge and, with a courageous heart, we can really change things for the better; we can right the wrongs; we *can* really make a difference.

We can be the super-heroes of *real-life* situations. Rewrite your own life's script and do it *your* way. Become the hero of your *own* story!

A Diane Stafford feature in the *Kansas City Star* brought the advice of Stephen Covey to my attention. He's the Chairman of the Covey Leadership Center, and he's made out a preparatory list for those who would become leaders. The first thing is to become a model of *principle*-centered leadership. Next is to remember you will always have much to learn. (This book is a start.)

Next, you must develop a positive, well organized and energetic attitude. You must be dedicated and responsible, and you must understand the feelings of others and learn to motivate them in the very best possible ways. And don't worry. If you don't think you can develop the right stuff for a leadership roll, get involved with those who have become or are becoming good leaders. Get in there, one way or the other.

Really making it happen. Getting *really* involved is also a very satisfying thing. You meet and get to know lots of wonderful new friends, and you end up doing a lot of good for everybody. I guess you could call it open heart without surgery. Not a bad feeling, wouldn't you say?

Have neighborhood town meetings. Talk with the media. Get on the Internet. Develop a speakers bureau to talk to service clubs and other community groups. If you get things going to the point where you're putting together a big rally, try to get one or more known speakers willing to stand with you in your efforts. There are all sorts of folks you might be able to dig up. See who you can find. (Yes, and this writer will always do his best to be available, whenever he can.)

Be willing to go all the way with this effort. Remember, serious mountain climbers don't go just halfway to the top because that's only as far as so many others can reach. They go *all* the way. In other words, you can fly, but that cocoon has got to go. Heed the words of Norman Cousins, who said, "Never underestimate our problems and never underestimate our capability for meeting those problems."

The media. All through the book you have seen examples where the media have come forward and exposed a number of our serious problems. You have also seen examples where the media completely fell down on the job, sometimes to the severe detriment of others. Media, as with all other areas of human endeavor, are also imperfect. As with everything else, there is always much to be proud of; and there is always much room for improvement.

By way of example, sometimes TV news goes after things in a very good way. This book notes a number of exceptional shows such as CBS's "60-Minutes," "The Fleecing of America" series on NBC, and there are a number of others. Believe me, this all helps.

I also recall Bill Moyers' series on PBS stations, "Moyers on Addiction: Close to Home." His own son's battle with alcohol and drugs served as a most understandable inspiration for the series. I just wish more well-known personalities would address such issues without having to wait until it hits them personally.

The media—mostly TV and newspapers—is, understandably, one of the main battlefields in all major efforts to get us back on track again—to clean up the mess. I recall back in 1985, when the Department of Justice pushed a TV campaign to "report, identify and testify" when a witness or a victim of a crime. I would imagine it helped.

A year later members of Congress were asking the TV networks to join the effort against illegal drugs with a comprehensive anti-drug campaign aimed at the youth of America. Again, it wasn't that big a deal, but I'm sure it must have helped at least a little.

What is really needed? Perhaps a *major* campaign with rallies and other major events and all sorts of creative efforts by as many producers, writers, and celebrities as can be found. Something that becomes a truly major event lasting for several months and with follow-ups later on to encourage extended efforts. Something that both broadcast channels and cable channels can become involved in and something newspapers and magazines can develop features about.

Will they be willing to make such a major non-profit commitment to our future? And will the TV and film folks be willing to make the changes in programming that can help to establish a more positive environment for our very impressionable children? Can that really happen?

I am reminded of one of Dana Summers editorial cartoons in the *Orlando Sentinel*. It's the one showing four panels depicting various emotionally charged events. The first shows someone holding a drowned child in Bangladesh. The second shows the bodies of Kurds in Iraq. The third shows a starving child in the Sudan holding up an empty bowl. The fourth shows a small whale stuck in the ice and efforts being made to free it. Only that fourth one is being covered by the media, and it's being done as though it's the Second Coming.

I am also reminded of the major elements of most of the commercial TV programs we see. After the no-brainer sitcoms, what's often left is an intense amount of primitive violence and lots of irresponsible sex. You don't think young, impressionable minds are not adversely affected by such things? Then why are TV ads so profitable? I have a sneaking suspicion it's because, like television in general, *they are effective!*

For those who have just fallen off the turnip truck and don't really know what's going on, let me refer them to some of those Jerry Springer shows where everybody seemed to end up clobbering one another. When they weren't doing that, they were having such people on as one young woman who was bragging that she had sex with a record number of several hundred men within a few short hours. (And they showed video tape!)

With people like Jerry Springer, Howard Stern, and others of their ilk, we end up with what I could only describe as television for Neanderthals. Let's face up to it. We aren't *solving* the problems. We're helping to *create* the problems. (I say "we" because you and I, in large enough numbers, can effect the sponsorship and general success of such shows. We really can.)

I am further reminded of one of Holbert's panels in the *Boston Herald*. It shows a Hollywood executive sitting at his desk. Behind him are posters of some of his super-violent TV shows and films. He is reading a paper which headlines one of those school massacres by a young teen-ager and he is saying, "Whoa! How does this kinda thing happen?" (I don't really think I need to add anything here, now do I?)

It's even gotten to be too much for people like Ralf Moeller, the star of the "Conan the Barbarian" syndicated TV series. He was quoted by the Newhouse News Service as saying that "the kids are taking guns and killing their classmates and friends. We have to change our thinking." Right on, Conan!

Our educational system. I'm sure you can recall those new "three-Rs" of our modern American education—Reading, Writing, and Reloading. Not at all funny and, thank God, not actually a problem for a large number of our schools. But it does seem to be a problem with a few of them, and they're not necessarily drug-infested inner city schools. It seems to be able to happen just about anywhere, as you know.

I am told of one report by the Bureau of Justice Statistics and the National Center for Education Statistics that informs us that almost twice as many teen-agers tell of gangs in their schools than six years previously. Also they report that violent crime in the schools increased nearly 25 percent in that same period.

The problem is real. We are going to have to probe very deeply and find out exactly why such kids become so dangerously violent. I know, a good part of the problem is a lack of proper adult guidance and inspiration in the home and a notable part of the problem is the intensely pervasive nature of our violence oriented entertainment industry. Drugs are also a big factor.

There may be other things, too. We'd better find them out—all of them. Then we'd better learn to do something about them. We'd better learn fast.

Other problems involve the so-called dumbing down in our schools. Various scholastic tests seem to suggest that this is a genuine problem. Longer school hours, specially trained teachers, and special, innovative methods are clearly needed.

There are new teaching projects such as "Micro-Society," as developed in a Lowell, Massachusetts, magnet school. Such methods seem to be magnificent, highly motivational teaching procedures. I've seen the faces on some of those kids. The enthusiasm is almost unbelievable.

Have you ever thought of bringing "Structured Brainstorming" to the upper grade schools and to the high schools? If it's done right, nothing else around there will ever be the same again. I mean, it's that good. What about teaching teachers how to motivate? What about the introduction of a comprehensive value system? All of this and so much more can be done. It really can.

Speaking of a value system, a concerned group of clergy, educators and others (a part of a 24-member nonpartisan panel) wrote a very special report that was issued by the Institute for American Values. It was titled, "A Call to Civil Society: Why Democracy Needs Moral Truths." It's a call to reset our nation's moral compass.

It was a recognition of a truly desperate need for all of us to find ways to agree on a workable public moral philosophy. It was noted that without such a guiding philosophy our nation would be doomed to continue its moral decline. The group and, in fact, many thoughtful people throughout our land, are convinced that without such a guiding light, our democracy will not long survive.

A few schools are trying to address this need. The Markkula Center for Applied Ethics at Santa Clara University in California established a model undergraduate program to study the art of ethical decision-making. Then, with such skills in place, they teach ethical behavior to high school students in San Jose who in turn will pass the learning on to the elementary level.

There's a lot to such programs, and this writer strongly suggests that schools all over our nation would do well to make serious inquiries about this and similar efforts. Parents and community leaders should also not be shy about getting involved. Believe me, this sort of thing is really important.

The political system and beyond. It was George Washington who said, "The basis of our political system is the right of the people to make and to alter their constitutions of government." What do you think that suggests?

It was Thomas Jefferson who said, "What country can preserve its liberties, if its rulers are not warned from time to time, that this people preserve the spirit of resistance?" What does that suggest? And, in more recent times, Clifford Graves said, "It's been my experience during twenty-plus years as a bureaucrat that nearly all significant changes in public policy emanate from citizens action. Rarely does an elected official come up with an original idea." What do you think about that?

You see, it's not just me ranting about what we gotta do. The call is echoed all through history. It has *always* been the people's responsibility. And now it's *our* time.

One just might start with the crying need for a new declaration of principles for our political system, for our legal system, and for our public and private behavior in general. First we had a problem with "all the President's men." Now we have a problem with "all the President's women" and, as if that wasn't enough, Chinese Communist political contributions were made to the benefit of an administration that somehow manages to approve giving the Communists important space-age technology that helps make us a ground-zero target once again. And it really does look as though most Americans really aren't all that upset about such things. Clearly we need a whole new set of principles. What has been happening is *totally* unacceptable. Don't you agree? My God, I hope so.

The illegal system. You know what to do here. Much of this book deals with the dilapidated legal system. Just don't forget the words of John Galsworthy. "Public opinion's always in advance of the law." It is truly our responsibility to scrap the antiquated mediaeval system that we have and develop truth-seeking to a fine science.

We can put footprints on the moon and little robot scouts on Mars but somehow we can't seem to bring our legal system out of the dark ages? If it weren't so terrible it would be laughable. As H. L. Mencken observed, "The penalty for laughing in a courtroom is 6 months; if it were not for this penalty the jury would never hear the evidence."

I know, we are supposed to be governed by laws, not people. That is one of the biggest fictions ever foisted on the poor, unsuspecting public. It's *people* who make the laws, *people* who screw around with the interpretations of the law, and it's *people* who bungle through the legal processes of the law. And we end up with this mess! The imperial court system of America has much to answer for what it has done.

As far as constitutional law is concerned, regarding the way they're handling it, our Constitution should be written in pencil. That would make it more convenient to warp it any which way, as the perception of social change wafts past the minds of the legislative judges.

Remember that quote from New York State Supreme Court Judge, Harold Rothwax? Take another look at it. "Criminal justice in America is in a state of collapse. We have formalism and technicalities but little common sense. It's about time America wakes up to the fact that we are in the fight of our lives."

Are you ready to do something about it? By God, I hope so!

Wanted: A return to accountability. It was just recently that our Supreme Court came down with a decision that extended an almost absolute immunity to cover local officials, very much as they have for government officials on regional, state, and federal levels. In other words you can sue city hall but the people who are actually responsible for what was done wrong are completely immune.

That's the way our very questionable government wants it. What I have been hearing the people want is to have those damn fools held just as responsible *personally* for what they do as all the rest of us are held responsible for what *we* do. Sounds reasonable, doesn't it?

They whine, oh, we couldn't operate that way. I should hope to hell they couldn't. That's the whole idea. And yes, I know it won't be easy for them. It isn't easy for us either. I have a retail business that requires a million dollars of liability insurance. My comprehensive homeowner's insurance includes extensive liability coverage. My car insurance also includes liability coverage.

The only way we can ever really civilize the bureaucratic beast is to *hold them personally accountable!* That's what it will take, and that's what has to be done.

The return to original principles. Machiavelli was considered as quite the expert on all things political. The fifteenth century Florentine wrote that republican forms of government gain much benefit when they return to their original principles. He noted that the best of them "have the longest existence, which possess the intrinsic means of frequently renewing themselves."

The fate of a nation is in your hands. Edmund Burke had it right. "The only thing necessary for the triumph of evil is for good men to do nothing." Future generations will look back at us all and see what? Will we have begun great changes?

> *The death of democracy is not likely to be an assassination from ambush. It will be a slow extinction from apathy, indifference and undernourishment.*
>
> —Robert M. Hutchins

Will it be good-bye, America; or will it be a new beginning?

Special Notation: And now, after all of this, I also ask you to read the "Epilogue" at the end. It will mean a great deal to me if you will read it. Thanks.

—Jonathan

Epilogue

> *We sometimes get all the information,*
> *but we refuse to get the message.*
>
> —Cullen Hightower

Well, there you have it. Is it going to be good-bye? Is that all that can finally be said for those of you not understanding the full, real nature of freedom? Or will you not be leaving me? Will you discover the truth? Will you learn what Goethe meant when he said, "None are more hopelessly enslaved than those who falsely believe they are free."

Do you see how, little by little, America has been going away? Can you not imagine why Frank Lloyd Wright wrote that "government can be a kind of gangsterism and is in Russia and is likely to be here if we don't take care of ourselves pretty carefully." Can you not see what has been happening?

> *I believe there are more instances of the abridgment of the*
> *freedom of the people by gradual and silent encroachments of*
> *those in power than by violent and sudden usurpations.*
>
> —James Madison

Are you going to remain quiet? Can you not imagine the need for a major personal change in the important priorities of your life? Will you just be satisfied to say good-bye and be done with it all? Is that all there is?

I do not ask you to do anything that I have not been trying so very hard to do all of my life. But it is so lonely out there. There are so very, very few of us out there.

When I come forward to make a major personal commitment on behalf of some abandoned soul in desperate need, he or she is so surprised. So few seem to understand why anyone would make such commitments. What's in it for you (meaning me)? How can this be happening?

Is it that rare? Oh yes it is. When the Sometown extortion came down heavily upon me, I found out, for the first time, how one really feels in such a situation. Half of my friends politely distanced themselves from me, for, after all, what could they do? A few expressed sympathy. A few even tried to think of something they might be able to do to help, even though they had no experience helping others this way, so they were totally ineffective.

You are almost always left out there alone. And that's why evil events dominate in so much of human experience. Most folks will not take the responsibility of major commitment to others in such matters. They will not make the effort to learn and to take the time to be involved.

Are we going to make a major change in our attitudes? Or is Henry David Thoreau right, "Men will lie on their backs, talking about the fall of man, and never make an effort to get up." What will come from all of this?

I can find no other reason for our endlessly violent and destructive world history other than the uncomfortable truth that we allow it to happen. It is such a sad and absolutely unnecessary heritage of a very imperfect species that evidently is mostly unwilling to rise to a higher level of moral dignity and is most often without a strong and courageous heart. So, the pain and suffering goes on, ... and on, ... and on.

Are we willing to continue to live like this? Are we willing to be little more than blobs of protoplasm that try to suck up a little self-satisfaction and then return to dust? Is that all there is?

Do I hear a resounding *no?* Are you ready to stand tall and face the truth that each of us is either going to be a part of the answer or we shall remain as a part of the problem? We can do it, you know. We *can* make a difference! There was only sixty-six years from the time of the very first powered flight and the moment when man first set foot on the moon. We can do almost anything! We *can* make a difference!

If enough of us get involved, you won't be alone. I'll do what I can, too. I'll continue to do all I can, as a writer, to educate and to motivate. I will also make myself available for rallies and other major efforts. I'll do every damn thing I can. Will you do the same?

Someone asked if a nice donation should be made to the effort, how could it be used? I don't really expect this, but if we would ever be so fortunate, I would establish a non-profit organization to facilitate organizational and coordination efforts all over the nation and install a central web site and help to cover the costs involved in necessary travel and accommodations in the planning and motivational efforts to move us all to great tasks and even greater results.

It would also be an enormous help if some of our more concerned TV and motion picture stars and sports and music stars would be willing to come forward and become a part of the effort, as I've previously suggested. And there are so many others who could help. What about the leaders of corporate America and those from the academic world and executives in the media?

And this is not just a movement for America. This is a concept of commitment and action that can be of value to humankind all over the world. It is an idea that can belong to everyone.

Make this effort *yours*. Make it belong to *you*. Make it yours and we *will* make a difference. We *will* have an American renaissance. And I will be very proud of you.

We are like water, soft, flowing, and nourishing; easy prey for the opportunists among us and the institutions they often control. Yes, we are like water, but who can stand against the raging flood?

Appendix A

Organizations of Interest

Categories Listed

Changing Politics
Civil Law Reform
Court Reform (in general)
Crime (in general)
Criminal Law Reform
The Drug Fight
State Drug Abuse Authorities

Government Reform (in general)
Highway Law
Juvenile Problems
Legal Education for Citizens
Senior Citizens' Concerns
Taxation and Debt Reduction
Voters Education

Changing Politics:

Center for National Independence in Politics
129 N.W. Fourth Street - #204
Corvallis, OR 97330
Phone: 503-754-2746

Citizens to Reform Congress
(Project of the National Center for Privatization)
P.O. Box 96511
Washington, DC 20077

Common Cause
2030 "M" Street, NW
Washington, DC 20036
Phone: 202-833-1200
FAX: 202-656-3716

National Taxpayers Union
325 Pennsylvania Avenue, SE
Washington, DC 20003

Appendix A

> Public Citizen
> Suite 605, 2000 "P" Street, NW
> Washington, DC 20036
>
> We The People (Project of the American Policy Institute)
> 6137 Lincolnia Road
> P.O. Box 11839
> Alexandria, VA 22312

Civil Law Reform:

> American Tort Reform Association
> 1212 New York Avenue, NW
> Washington, DC 20005
> Phone: 202-682-1163
>
> Association for California Tort Reform
> (No address given.)
> Phone: 1-888-882-6363
> Net: http://www.actr.com/actr
>
> Citizens Against Lawsuit Abuse
> (No address given.)
> Phone: 619-295-6059 or 1-800-558-2252
>
> Coalition for Fair Liability Laws
> P.O. Box 162771
> Sacramento, CA 95816
> Phone: 916-774-0717
> FAX: 916-774-0642
> Net: http://www.cfll.org
>
> Americans for Legal Reform (HALT, Inc.)
> 1612 "K" Street, NW - Suite 510
> Washington, DC 20006
> Phone: 1-888-367-4258 or 202-887-8255

Court Reform (in general):

> Judicial Watch
> 501 School Street, SW - Suite 725
> Washington, DC 20024
> Phone: 1-888-593-8442 or 202-646-5172
> FAX: 202-646-5199
> Net: http://www.judicialwatch.org

Crime (in general):

> Safe Streets
> 919 Street, NW - Suite 800

Washington, DC 20006
Phone: 202-822-8100
FAX: 202-822-8149
E-mail: woottonssa@aol.com

Criminal Law Reform:

Doris Tate Crime Victims' Bureau
(No address given.)
Phone: 1-800-784-2846
FAX: 916-556-1660

The Law Enforcement Alliance of America
7700 Leesburg Pike - Suite 421
Falls Church, VA 22043
Phone: 1-800-766-8578 or 703-847-2677
FAX: 703-556-6485

The Drug Fight:

American Council for Drug Education
6193 Executive Blvd.
Rockville, MD 20852

Communities Against Substance Abuse
(No address given.)
Phone: 1-800-580-7200
Net: http://www.drugfreeamerica.org

National Federation of Parents for Drug Free Youth
P.O. Box 722
Silver Spring, MD 20901
Phone: 301-649-7100

National Institute on Drug Abuse
P.O. Box 1909
Rockville, MD 20852

Parent Resource Institute for Drug Education
100 Edgewood Avenue, NE
Atlanta, GA 30303
Phone: 1-800-241-9746 or 404-658-2548

State Drug Abuse Authorities:

Alaska Dept. of Health and Social Services
Office of Alcoholism and Drug Abuse
Pouch H-05-F
Juneau, AK 99811
Phone: 907-586-6201

Appendix A

Alabama Dept. of Mental Health Community Programs
Division of Mental Illness and Substance Abuse
200 Interstate Park Drive
P.O. Box 3710
Montgomery, AL 36193
Phone: 205-271-9209

Arkansas Office on Alcohol and Drug Abuse Prevention
1515 West 7th Street - Suite 300
Little Rock, AR 72201
Phone: 501-371-2603

Arizona Dept. of Health Services
Office of Community Behavioral Health
701 East Jefferson Street - Suite 400A
Phoenix, AZ 85034
Phone: 602-255-1152

California Dept. of Alcohol and Drug Abuse
111 Capitol Mall - Suite 450
Sacramento, CA 95814
Phone: 916-445-0834

Colorado Dept. of Health/Alcohol and Drug Abuse Division
4210 East Avenue
Denver, CO 80220
Phone: 303-331-8201

Connecticut Alcohol and Drug Abuse Commission
999 Asylum Avenue
Hartford, CT 06105
Phone: 203-566-4145

Washington D.C. Dept. of Human Services
Office of Health Planning and Development
1875 Connecticut Avenue, NW - Suite 836
Washington, DC 20009
Phone: 202-673-7481

Delaware Bureau of Alcoholism & Drug Abuse
1901 North Dupont Highway
New Castle, DE 19720
Phone: 302-421-6101

Florida Dept. of Health and Rehabilitative Services
Alcohol and Drug Abuse Program
1317 Winewood Boulevard
Tallahassee, FL 32301
Phone: 904-488-0900

Georgia Dept. of Human Resources
Division of Mental Health and Mental Retardation
Alcohol and Drug Section
878 Peachtree Street, NE - Suite 318
Atlanta, GA 30309
Phone: 404-894-6352

Guam Dept. of Mental Health and Substance Abuse
P.O. Box 8896
Tamuning, GU 96911
Phone: 671-477-9704

Dept. of Health/Mental Health Division
Alcohol and Drug Abuse Branch
1250 Punchbowl Street
P.O. Box 3378
Honolulu, HI 96801
Phone: 808-548-4280

Dept. of Public Health
Division of Substance Abuse and Health Promotion
321 East Street
Lucas State Office Bldg. - 4th Floor
Des Moines, IA 50319
Phone: 515-281-3641

Idaho Dept. of Health and Welfare
Bureau of Substance Abuse and Social Services
450 West State
Boise, ID 83720
Phone: 208-334-5935

Illinois Dept. of Alcoholism and Substance Abuse
100 West Randolph Street - Suite 5-600
Chicago, IL 60601
Phone: 312-917-3840

Indiana Dept. of Mental Health
Division of Addiction Services
117 East Washington Street
Indianapolis, IN 46204
Phone: 317-232-7816

Kansas Alcohol and Drug Abuse Services
2700 West 6th Street (Biddle Building)
Topeka, KS 66606
Phone: 913-296-3925

Kentucky Dept. for Mental Health/Mental Retardation Services
Division of Substance Abuse
275 East Main Street
(Health Services Building - 1st Floor)
Frankfort, KY 40621
Phone: 502-564-2880

Louisiana Office of Prevention &
    Recovery from Alcohol and Drug Abuse
2744-B Wooddale Boulevard
P.O. Box 53129
Baton Rouge, LA 70892
Phone: 504-922-0730

Massachusetts Div. of Substance Abuse Services
150 Tremont Street
Boston, MA 02111
Phone: 617-727-1960

Maryland Addiction Services Administration
201 West Preston Street (Herbert O'Conor Building)
Baltimore, MD 21201
Phone: 301-225-6926

Maine Office of Alcohol & Drug Abuse Prevention
Bureau of Rehabilitation
State House - Station 11
Augusta, ME 04333
Phone: 207-289-2781

Michigan Dept. of Public Health
Office of Substance Abuse Services
3500 North Logan Street (P.O. Box 30035)
Lansing, MI 48909
Phone: 517-373-8609

Minnesota Dept. of Human Services
Chemical Dependency Program Division
444 Lafayette Road
Space Center Building - 2nd Floor
Saint Paul, MN 55155
Phone: 612-296-3991

Missouri Dept. of Mental Health
Division of Alcohol and Drug Abuse
1915 South Ridge Drive (P.O. Box 687)
Jefferson City, MO 65102
Phone: 314-751-4942

Mississippi Dept. of Mental Health
Division of Alcohol and Drug Abuse
1500 Woolfolk State Office Building
Jackson, MS 39201
Phone: 601-359-1297

Montana Dept. of Institutions
Alcohol and Drug Abuse Division
1529 11th Avenue
Helena, MT 59620
Phone: 406-444-2827

North Carolina Div. of Mental Health/Mental
　Retardation Services
Alcohol and Drug Abuse Section
325 North Salisbury Street - Room 1100
Raleigh, NC 27611
Phone: 919-733-4670

North Dakota Dept. of Human Services
Division of Alcoholism and Drug Abuse
State Capitol/Judicial Wing
Bismarck, ND 58505
Phone: 701-224-2769

Nebraska Dept. of Public Institutions
Division on Alcoholism and Drug Abuse
801 West Van Dorn Street (P.O. Box 94728)
Lincoln, NE 68509
Phone: 402-471-2851

New Hampshire Office of Alcohol and
　Drug Abuse Prevention
Hazen Drive - Health and Welfare Building
Concord, NH 03301
Phone: 602-271-4627

New Jersey Div. of Narcotics and Drug Abuse Control
129 East Hanover Street - CN 362
Trenton, NJ 08625
Phone: 609-292-5760

New Mexico Behavioral Health Services Division
Substance Abuse Bureau
725 Saint Michaels Drive (P.O. Box 968)
Santa Fe, NM 87504
Phone: 505-827-0117

Nevada Dept. of Human Resources
Bureau of Alcohol and Drug Abuse
505 East King Street
Carson City, NV 89710
Phone: 702-885-4790

New York Division of Substance Abuse Services
Executive Park South
(Box 8200)
Albany, NY 12203
Phone: 518-457-7629

Ohio Bureau of Drug Abuse
30 East Broad Street
Room 295A
Columbus, OH 43215
Phone: 614-466-7893

Oklahoma Dept. of Mental Health
Alcohol and Drug Programs
4545 North Lincoln Boulevard
Capitol Station (P.O. Box 53277)
Oklahoma City, OK 73152
Phone: 405-521-0044

Oregon Office of Alcohol and Drug Abuse Programs
301 Public Service Building
Salem, OR 97310
Phone: 503-378-2163

Pennsylvania Dept. of Health
Commonwealth and Forster Avenues
(P.O. Box 90)
Harrisburg, PA 17108
Phone: 717-787-9857

Puerto Rico Dept. of Addiction Control Services
P.O. Box B-Y - Rio Piedras Station
Rio Piedras, PR 00928
Phone: 809-764-3795

Rhode Island Dept. of Mental Health/
    Mental Retardation & Hospitals
Division of Substance Abuse
Substance Abuse Administration Building
Cranston, RI 02920
Phone: 401-464-2091

South Carolina Commission on Alcohol and Drug Abuse
3700 Forest Drive
Landmark East - Suite 300
Columbia, SC 29204
Phone: 803-734-9520

South Dakota Div. of Alcohol and Drug Abuse
523 East Capitol
Joe Foss Building - Room 125
Pierre, SD 57501
Phone: 605-773-3123

Tennessee Dept. of Mental Health/Mental Retardation
Alcohol and Drug Abuse Services
706 Church Street - Fourth Floor
Nashville, TN 37219
Phone: 615-741-1921

Texas Commission on Alcohol and Drug Abuse
1705 Guadalupe Street
Austin, TX 78701
Phone: 512-463-5510

Utah State Division of Alcoholism and Drugs
150 West North Temple (P.O. Box 45500)
Salt Lake City, UT 84145
Phone: 801-538-3939

Virginia Dept. of Mental Health/Mental Retardation
Office of Substance Abuse Services
109 Governor Street (P.O. Box 1797)
Richmond, VA 23214
Phone: 804-786-3906

Virgin Islands Div. of Mental Health,
Alcohol & Drug Dependency
P.O. Box 7309
Saint Thomas, VI 00801
Phone: 809-773-1992

Vermont Office of Alcohol and Drug Abuse Programs
103 South Main Street - State Office Building
Waterbury, VT 05676
Phone: 802-241-2170

Washington State Dept. of Social & Health Services
Bureau of Alcoholism and Substance Abuse
Office Building 44W

Olympia, WA 98504
Phone: 206-753-5866

Wisconsin Office of Alcohol and Other Drug Abuse
1 West Wilson Street (P.O. Box 7851)
Madison, WI 53707
Phone: 608-266-3442

West Virginia Dept. of Health
Division of Alcoholism and Drug Abuse
1800 Washington Street - East (Building 3 - Room 451)
Charleston, WV 25305
Phone: 304-348-2276

Wyoming Alcohol and Drug Abuse Programs
Hathaway Building - Room 354
Cheyenne, WY 82002
Phone: 307-777-7115

Government Reform (in general)

The Heritage Foundation
214 Massachusetts Avenue, NE
Washington, DC 20002

Highway Law

Mothers Against Drunk Driving
1910 "K" Street, NW
Washington, DC 20006
Phone: 202-467-6233
Net: http://www.madd.org

Juvenile Problems

Child Find of America
7 Innis Avenue (P.O. Box 277)
Phone: 914-255-1848 or 1-800-426-5678
New Paltz, NY 12561
FAX: 914-255-5706

Toughlove
P.O. Box 1069
Doyles Town, PA 18901
Phone: 1-800-333-1069

Legal Education for Citizens

Nolo Press
950 Parker Street
Berkeley, CA 94710

Phone: 510-549-1976 or 1-800-992-6656
FAX: 1-800-645-0895

Parents Television Council
Steve Allen & Shirley Jones, Co-Chairpersons
333 South Grand Avenue
Los Angeles, CA 90071

Senior Citizens' Concerns

United Seniors Association
12500 Fair Lakes Circle - Suite 125
Fairfax, VA 22033
Phone: 703-803-6747 or 1-800-887-2872

Taxation and Debt Reduction

Citizens Against Government Waste
1301 Connecticut Ave., NW - Suite 400
Washington, DC 20036   Net: http://www/cagw.org

The Concord Coalition
1019 19th Street, NW - Suite 810
Washington, DC 20036
Phone: 202-467-6222 or 1-888-333-4248
Net: http://sunsite.unc.edu/concord

It's Our Money, Not TheIRS
(Project of National Federation of Independent Business)
600 Maryland Ave., SW - Suite 700
Phone: 1-888-668-4477
Washington, DC 20024   Net: http://www.not4irs.org

National Taxpayers' Union
108 North Alfred Street
Alexandria, VA 22314
Phone: 1-800-829-4258 or 703-683-5700

Voters Education

Project Vote Smart
129 N.W. 4th Street - Suite 204
Corvallis, OR 97330
Phone: 1-800-622-7627   Net: http://www.votesmart.org

Appendix B

Federal Contact Information

Categories Listed

In the Senate and House

Agriculture
Civil Service
Constitution
Crime
Debt
Education
Environmental Issues
Ethics
Government Information
Government Management

Health Care
Immigration
Investigations
Law
Postal Service
Property Rights
Social Security
Taxes
Terrorism
Urban Problems

Federal Government Agencies

Commission on Civil Rights
Drug Enforcement Administration
Federal Communications Commission
Federal Elections Commission
Federal Reserve System
Food and Drug Administration
Environmental Protection Agency
Internal Revenue Service
Social Security Administration
U.S. Postal Service
The White House

In the Senate and House:

Agriculture

House Agriculture Committee
Longworth House Office Bldg. (Room 1301)
Independence & New Jersey Ave., SE
Washington, DC 20515
Phone: 202-225-2171
FAX: 202-225-0917
Net: http://www.house.gov/agriculture

Civil Service

Senate Appropriations Subcommittee on the
Treasury, General Government, and Civil Service
Dirksen Building (Room 190)
"C" Streets, NE
Washington, DC 20510
Phone: 202-224-7337

House Government Reform and Oversight
    Subcommittee on the Civil Service
Reyburn House Office Bldg. (Room B-371C)
Independence Ave. & S. Capitol St., SW
Phone: 202-225-6427
Washington, DC 29515
FAX: 202-225-2392

Constitution

Senate Judiciary Subcommittee on the Constitution,
    Federalism, and Property Rights
Russell Building (Room 170)
1st & "C" Streets, NE
Washington, DC 20510
Phone: 202-224-8081
FAX: 202-224-9102

House Judiciary Subcommittee on The Constitution
Ford House Office Bldg. (Room H2-362)
300 "D" Street, SW
Washington, DC 20515
Phone: 202-226-7680
FAX: 202-225-3746

Crime

Senate Judiciary Subcommittee on Youth Violence
Dirksen Building (Room 163)
1st "C" Streets, NE
Washington, DC 20510
Phone: 202-224-7572
FAX: 202-224-9102

House Judiciary Subcommittee on Crime
Cannon House Office Bldg. (Room 207)
1st & Independence Ave., SE
Phone: 202-225-3926
Washington, DC 20515
FAX: 202-225-3737

Debt

Senate Appropriations Committee
U.S. Capitol Building (Room S-128)
Washington, DC 20510
Phone: 202-224-3471

Senate Budget Committee
Dirksen Building (Room 621)
1st "C" Streets, NE
Washington, DC 20510
Phone: 202-224-0642
FAX: 202-224-4835

Senate Finance Committee
Dirksen Building (Room 219)
1st "C" Streets, NE
Washington, DC 20510
Phone: 202-224-4515
FAX: 202-224-5920

Senate Finance Subcommittee on
    Long Term Growth, Debt & Deficit Reduction
Dirksen Building (Room 219)
1st "C" Streets, NE
Washington, DC 20510
Phone: 202-224-4515
FAX: 202-224-5920

House Banking & Financial Services Committee
Rayburn House Office Bldg. (Room 2129)
Independence Ave. & S. Capitol St., SW

Washington, DC 20515
Phone: 202-225-7502
FAX: 202-226-6052
Net: http://www.house.gov/banking/

House Appropriations Committee
U.S. Capitol Building (Room H-218)
Washington, DC 20515
Phone: 202-225-2771
Net: http://www.house.gov.appropriations

House Budget Committee
Cannon House Office Bldg. (Room 309)
1st & Independence Ave., SE
Washington, DC 20515
Phone: 202-226-7270
FAX: 202-226-7174
Net: http://www.house.gov/budget/

Education

Senate Appropriations Subcommittee on
    Labor, Health & Human Services, and Education
Dirksen Building (Room184)
1st "C" Streets, NE
Washington, DC 20510
Phone: 202-224-7230
FAX: 202-228-1360

House Appropriations Subcommittee on
    Labor, Health & Human Services, and Education
Rayburn House Office Bldg. (Room 2358)
Independence Ave. & S. Capitol St., SW
Washington, DC 20515
Phone: 202-225-3508
FAX: 202-225-3509

House Education and the Workforce Committee
Rayburn House Office Bldg. (Room 2181)
Independence Ave. & S. Capitol St., SW
Washington, DC 20515
Phone: 202-225-4527
FAX: 202-225-9571
Net: http://www.house.gov/eeo/

House Education and the Workforce Subcommittee
    on Oversight and Investigations
Rayburn House Office Bldg. (Room 2181)

Independence Ave. & S. Capitol St., SW
Washington, DC 20515
Phone: 202-225-4527
FAX: 202-225-9571

Environmental Issues

Senate Environment and Public Works Subcommittee on
  Clean Air, Wetlands, Private Property, and Nuclear Safety
Dirksen Building (Room 410)
1st "C" Streets, NE
Washington, DC 20510
Phone: 202-224-6176
FAX: 202-224-5167

Ethics

Senate Select Committee on Ethics
Hart Building (Room 220)
2nd "C" Streets, NE
Washington, DC 20510
Phone: 202-224-2981
FAX: 202-224-7416

House Standards of Official Conduct (Ethics) Committee
U.S. Capitol Building (Room HT-2)
Washington, DC 20515
Phone: 202-225-7103
FAX: 202-225-7392

Government Information

Senate Judiciary Subcommittee on Technology,
  Terrorism & Government Information
Hart Building (Room 702)
2nd "C" Streets, NE
Washington, DC 20510
Phone: 202-224-4521
FAX: 202-224-9102

Government Management

Senate Appropriations Subcommittee on the Treasury,
  General Government, and Civil Service
Dirksen Building (Room 190)
1st "C" Streets, NE
Washington, DC 20510
Phone: 202-224-7337

Senate Governmental Affairs Committee
Dirksen Building (Room 340)
1st "C" Streets, NE
Washington, DC 20510
Phone: 202-224-4751
FAX: 202-224-9603

Senate Governmental Affairs Subcommittee on Oversight of Gov.
    Management, Restructuring, and the District of Columbia
Hart Building (Room 601)
2nd "C" Streets, NE
Washington, DC 20510
Phone: 202-224-3682
FAX: 202-224-9603

House Appropriations Subcommittee on the
    Treasury, Postal Service, & General Government
Rayburn House Office Bldg. (Room B-307)
Independence Ave. & S. Capitol St., SW
Washington, DC 20515
Phone: 202-225-5834
FAX: 202-225-5895

House Government Reform & Oversight Committee
Rayburn House Office Bldg. (Room 2157)
Independence Ave. & S. Capitol St., SW
Washington, DC 20515
Phone: 202-225-5074
FAX: 202-225-3974
Net: http://www.house.gov/reform/

Health Care

Senate Appropriations Subcommittee on
    Labor, Health & Human Services, and Education
Dirksen Building (Room 184)
1st "C" Streets, NE
Washington, DC 20510
Phone: 202-224-7230
FAX: 202-228-1360

Senate Appropriations Subcommittee on
    VA, HUD, & Independent Agencies
Dirksen Building (Room 127)
1st "C" Streets, NE
Washington, DC 20510
Phone: 202-224-7211

Appendix B

Senate Finance Subcommittee on Health Care
Dirksen Building (Room 219)
1st "C" Streets, NE
Washington, DC 20510
Phone: 202-224-4515
FAX: 202-224-5920

Senate Finance Subcommittee on
    Social Security and Family Policy
Dirksen Building (Room 219)
1st "C" Streets, NE
Washington, DC 20510
Phone: 202-224-4515
FAX: 202-224-5920

House Appropriations Subcommittee on
    Labor, Health & Human Services, and Education
Rayburn House Office Bldg. (Room 2358)
Washington, DC 20515
Phone: 202-225-3508
FAX: 202-225-3509

House Appropriations Subcommittee on the
    VA, HUD and Independent Agencies
U.S. Capitol Building (Room H-143)
Washington, DC 20515
Phone: 202-225-3241

Immigration

Senate Judiciary Subcommittee on Immigration
Dirksen Building (Room 323)
1st "C" Streets, NE
Washington, DC 20510
Phone: 202-224-6098
FAX: 202-224-9102

Investigations

Permanent Senate Governmental Affairs
    Subcommittee on Investigations
Hart Building (Room 432)
2nd "C" Streets, NE
Washington, DC 20510
Phone: 202-224-3721
FAX: 202-224-9603

Law

Senate Appropriations Subcommittee on
  Commerce, Justice, State, & Judiciary
U.S. Capitol Building (Room S-146A)
Washington, DC 20510
Phone: 202-224-7277

Senate Judiciary Committee
Dirksen Building (Room 224)
1st "C" Streets, NE
Washington, DC 20510
Phone: 202-224-5225
FAX: 202-224-9102

Senate Judiciary Subcommittee on
  Administrative Oversight and the Courts
Hart Building (Room 308)
2nd "C" Streets, NE
Washington, DC 20510
Phone: 202-224-6736
FAX: 202-228-1900

House Appropriations Subcommittee on
Commerce, Justice, State, and Judiciary
U.S. Capitol Building (Room H-309)
Washington, DC 20515
Phone: 202-225-3351

House Judiciary Committee
Rayburn House Office Bldg. (Room 2138)
Independence Ave. & S. Capitol St., SW
Washington, DC 20515
Phone: 202-225-3951
FAX: 202-225-7682
Net: http://www.house.gov/judiciary/

House Judiciary Subcommittee on the Constitution
Ford House Office Bldg. (Room H2-362)
300 "D" Street, SW
Washington, DC 20515
Phone: 202-226-7680
FAX: 202-225-3746

House Judiciary Subcommittee on
  Courts & Intellectual Property
Rayburn House Office Bldg. (Room B-351A)
Independence Ave. & S. Capitol St., SW

Washington, DC 20515
Phone: 202-225-5741
FAX: 202-225-3677

Postal Service

House Government Reform &
  Oversight Subcommittee on the Postal Service
Rayburn House Office Bldg. (Room B-349C)
Independence Ave. & S. Capitol St., SW
Washington, DC 20515
Phone: 202-225-3741
FAX: 202-225-2544

House Appropriations Subcommittee on the
  Treasury, Postal Service, & General Government
Rayburn House Office Bldg. (Room B-307)
Independence Ave. & S. Capitol St., SW
Washington, DC 20515
Phone: 202-225-5834
FAX: 225-5895

Property Rights

Senate Appropriations Subcommittee on the
  VA, HUD, and Independent Agencies
Dirksen Building (Room 127)
1st "C" Streets, NE
Washington, DC 20510
Phone: 202-224-7211

Senate Banking, Housing & Urban Affairs Committee
Dirksen Building (Room 534)
1st "C" Streets, NE
Washington, DC 20510
Phone: 202-224-7391
FAX: 202-224-5137

Senate Environmental & Public Works Subcommittee on
  Clean Air, Wetlands, Private Property, and
  Nuclear Safety
Dirksen Building (Room 410)
1st "C" Streets, NE
Washington, DC 20510
Phone: 202-224-6176
FAX: 202-224-5167

Senate Judiciary Subcommittee on the
   Constitution, Federalism, and Private Property
Russell Building (Room 170)
1st "C" Streets, NE
Washington, DC 20510
Phone: 202-224-8081
FAX: 202-224-9102

House Appropriations Subcommittee on the
   VA, HUD, and Independent Agencies
U.S. Capitol Building (Room H-143)
Washington, DC 20515
Phone: 202-225-3241

Social Security

Senate Finance Subcommittee on
   Social Security and Family Policy
Dirksen Building (Room 219)
1st "C" Streets, NE
Washington, DC 20510
Phone: 202-224-4515
FAX: 202-224-5920

Taxes

Senate Finance Subcommittee on
   Taxation and IRS Oversight
Dirksen Building (Room 219)
1st "C" Streets, NE
Washington, DC 20510
Phone: 202-224-4515
FAX: 202-224-5920

House Joint Committee on Taxation
Longworth House Office Bldg. (Room 1015)
Independence & New Jersey Ave., SE
Washington, DC 20515
Phone: 202-225-3621
FAX: 202-225-0832

Terrorism

Senate Judiciary Subcommittee on
   Technology, Terrorism, and Government Information
Hart Building (Room 702)
2nd "C" Streets, NE
Washington, DC 20510

Phone: 202-224-4521
FAX: 202-224-9102

Urban Problems

Senate Appropriations Subcommittee on the
 VA, HUD, and Independent Agencies
Dirksen Building (Room 127)
1st "C" Streets, NE
Washington, DC 20510
Phone: 202-224-7211

Senate Banking, Housing & Urban Affairs Committee
Dirksen Building (Room 534)
1st "C" Streets, NE
Washington, DC 30510
Phone: 202-224-7391
FAX: 202-224-5137

Federal Government Agencies:

Commission on Civil Rights
624 9th Street, NW
Washington, DC 20425
Phone: 202-376-8312
Net: http://www.usccr.gov

Drug Enforcement Administration
700 Army-Navy Drive
Arlington, VA 22202
Phone: 202-307-7363
Net: http://www.usdoj.gov/dea

Federal Communications Commission (FCC)
1919 "M" Street, NW
Washington, DC 20554
Phone: 202-418-0500
Net: http://www.fcc.gov/

Federal Elections Commission
999 "E" Street, NW
Washington, DC 20463
Phone: 1-800-424-9530
Net: http://www.fec.gov

Federal Reserve System
20th "C" Streets, NW
Washington, DC 20551

Phone: 202-452-3000
Net: http://www.bog.frb.fed.us

Food and Drug Administration
5600 Fishers Lane (Room 15A-07)
Rockville, MD 20857
Phone: 301-443-4177
Net: http://www.fda.gov

Environmental Protection Agency
401 "M" Street, SW
Washington, DC 20460
Phone: 202-260-2090
Net: http://www.epa.gov

Internal Revenue Service (IRS)
1111 Constitution Ave, NW (#1112)
Washington, DC 20224
Phone: 202-622-5000

Social Security Administration
6401 Security Blvd.
Baltimore, MD 21235
Phone: 410-965-1720

U.S. Postal Service
475 L'Enfant Plaza W., SW
Washington, DC 20260
Phone: 202-268-2000
Net: http://www.usps.gov

And, last of all,

The White House
1600 Pennsylvania Avenue, NW
Washington, DC 20500
Phone: 202-456-1414

A Final Note

This is the end of the lists of resources that can be very helpful to you. They encompass everything from private organizations to legislative and agency contacts in Washington, DC. However, as large as these lists may seem, space constraints made it necessary to include only a portion of the almost endless possible listings.

Use these lists as you need them, but be willing to go beyond them, to some of the many other contacts you will discover are out there. Most of all, don't be afraid to start your own action group when necessary.

The possibilities are only limited to your imagination and your energetic dedication.